Third edition

Published in October 2005
Alastair Sawday Publishing Co. Ltd
Yanley Lane, Long Ashton,
Bristol BS41 9LR
Tel: +44 (0)1275 464891
Fax: +44 (0)1275 464887
E-mail: info@specialplacestostay.com
Web: www.specialplacestostay.com

The Globe Pequot Press
P. O. Box 480, Guilford,
Connecticut 06437, USA
Tel: +1 203 458 4500
Fax: +1 203 458 4601
E-mail: info@globepequot.com
Web: www.globepequot.com

Design:
Caroline King

Maps & Mapping:
Maidenhead Cartographic Services Ltd

Printing:
Butler & Tanner, Frome, UK

UK Distribution:
Penguin UK, 80 Strand, London

US Distribution:
The Globe Pequot Press, Guilford, Connecticut

A catalogue record for this book is available from the British Library.

ISBN 1-901970-62-0
978-1-901970-66-1

Paper and Printing: We have sought the lowest possible ecological 'footprint' from the production of this book, using super-efficient machinery, vegetable inks and high environmental standards. Our printer is ISO 14001-registered.

ALASTAIR SAWDAY'S
SPECIAL PLACES TO STAY

FRENCH
HOLIDAY HOMES

Contents

Guide entries

Back

Index by département

Photo Souffle de Vent, entry 309

Alastair Sawday Publishing

We are the faceless toilers at the pit-face of publishing but, for us, the question of who we are and how we inter-react is important. For who we are shapes the books, the books shape your holidays, and thus are shaped the lives of people who own these 'special places'. So we are trying to be a little more than 'just a publishing company'.

New eco offices

By the end of 2005 we will have moved into our new eco offices. By introducing super-insulation, underfloor heating, a wood-pellet boiler, solar panels and a rainwater tank, we will have a working environment benign to ourselves and to the environment. Lighting will be low-energy, dark corners will be lit by sun-pipes and one building is of green oak. Carpet tiles are leased: some of recycled material, most of wool and some of natural fibres. We will sail through our environmental audit.

Environmental & ethical policies

We combine many other small gestures: company cars run on gas or recycled cooking oil; kitchen waste is composted and other waste recycled; cycling and car-sharing are encouraged; the company only buys organic or local food; we don't accept web links with companies we consider unethical; we use the ethical Triodos Bank for our deposit account.

We have used recycled paper for some books but have settled on selecting paper and printer for their low energy use. Our printer is British and ISO14001-certified and together we will reduce our environmental impact.

Thanks partially to our Green Team, we recently won a Business Commitment to the Environment Award – which has boosted our resolve to stick to our own green policies. Our flagship gesture, however, is carbon offsetting; we calculate our carbon emissions and plant trees to compensate as calculated by Future Forests. In 2006 we will support projects overseas that plant trees or reduce carbon use; our money will work better by going direct to projects.

Ethics

But why, you may ask, take these things so seriously? You are just a little publishing company, for heavens sake! Well, is there any good argument for not taking them seriously? The world, by the admission of the vast majority of scientists, is in trouble. If we do not change our ways urgently we will doom the planet and all its creatures – whether innocent or not – to a variety of possible catastrophes. To maintain the status quo is unacceptable. Business does much of the damage and should undo it, and provide new models.

Who are we?

Pressure on companies to produce Corporate Social Responsibility policies is mounting. We are trying to keep ahead of it all, yet still to be as informal and human as possible – the antithesis of 'corporate'. (We even have unofficial 'de-stress operatives' in the shape of several resident dogs.)

The books – and a dilemma

So, we have created fine books that do good work. They promote authenticity, individuality, high quality, local and organic food – far from the now-dominant corporate culture. Rural economies, pubs, small farms, villages and hamlets all benefit.

However, people use fossil fuel to get there. Should we aim to get our readers to offset their own carbon emissions, and the B&B and hotel owners too? That might have been a hopeless task a year or so ago, but less so now that the media has taken on board the enormity of the work ahead of us all.

We are slowly introducing green ideas into the books: the Fine Breakfast Scheme that highlights British and Irish B&B owners, who use local and organic food; celebrating those who make an extra effort; gently encouraging the use of public transport, cycling and walking. Next year we are publishing a book focusing on responsible travel and eco-projects around the globe.

Our Fragile Earth series

The 'hard' side of our environmental publishing is the Fragile Earth series: *The Little Earth Book*, *The Little Food Book* and *The Little Money Book*. They have been a great success. They consist of bite-sized essays, polemical and hard-hitting but well researched and methodical. They are a 'must have' for people from all walks of life – anyone who is confused and needs clarity about some of the key issues of our time.

Lastly – what is special?

The notion of 'special' is at the heart of what we do, and highly subjective. We discuss this in the Introduction. We take huge pleasure from finding people and places that do their own thing – brilliantly; places that are unusual and follow no trends; places of peace and beauty; people who are kind and interesting – and genuine.

We seem to have touched a raw nerve with thousands of readers; they obviously want to stay in special places rather than the dull corporate monstrosities that have disfigured so many of our cities and towns. Life is too short to be wasted in the wrong places.
A night in a special place can be a transforming experience.

Alastair Sawday

Acknowledgements

I don't know how she does it!

Emma manages a demanding job with massive enthusiasm and without obvious signs of stress. (Which makes me wonder what the less obvious signs might be.) She has made this book into the huge success it is, trawling France for the most interesting and 'special' places in the teeth of vast competition. The owners of these places have come to us not just because of our reputation but because Emma is such a pleasure to deal with.

Allys has provided unfailing, unflappable production support and Kate – who joined us earlier this year, fresh from university and Italian travels – has knuckled down to a complicated job with good humour and resourcefulness. She and Emma have formed a dream team.

Alastair Sawday

Series Editor Alastair Sawday

Editor Emma Carey

Assistant to editor Kate Shepherd

Editorial Director Annie Shillito

Managing Editor Jackie King

Production Manager Julia Richardson

Web & IT Russell Wilkinson, Chris Banks, Brian Kimberling

Production Paul Groom, Allys Williams, Philippa Rogers

Copy Editor Jo Boissevain

Editorial Maria Serrano, Danielle Williams

Sales & Marketing & PR Siobhan Flynn, Andreea Petre Goncalves, Sarah Bolton

Accounts Sheila Clifton, Bridget Bishop, Christine Buxton, Jenny Purdy, Sandra Hassell

Writing Jo Boissevain, Emma Carey, Viv Cripps, Gail McKenzie, Helen Pickles, Kate Shepherd

Inspections Richard & Linda Armspach, Helen Barr, Miranda Bell, Jo Bell Moore, Alyson & Colin Browne, Emma Carey, Elizabeth & Neil Carter, Jill Coyle, Meredith Dickinson, Sue Edrich, John & Jane Edwards, Valerie Foix, Georgina Gabriel, Denise Goss, Diana Harris, Clarissa Novak, Jacqueline Ollivier, Viki Rainsford, Elizabeth Yates.

And many thanks to those people who did just a few inspections.

Previous Editor Clare Hargreaves

A word from Alastair Sawday

I have to admit that any illustrated brochure about self-catering in France tends to be good looking. The architectural range from top to bottom of the country is exhilarating: stout Norman to tender Provencale, turreted Touraine to pine-clad Alpine.

But this is no brochure. It is a well-crafted tale of achievements, a survey of possibilities, a journey through the loveliest corners of a lovely country. Every page reveals a new way of living, yet another beautiful house, yet another promise of holiday contentment. These are the best of a wonderful bunch, with owners who will take more care of you than you expect. Above all, you can rest in the certainty that we have seen them all and chosen them because we like them.

Like them? We are enthusiastic about them. We are proud of them, for they carry abroad the message that, in an age of detachment, conviviality and generosity are qualities to be cherished. Those qualities are reflected in these houses: in the food that awaits you in some, the sheer scale of others, the beauty of most, the humour, the intimacy of many. The owner may pop over to ask you in for a drink or a meal. You may be swept up into the bosom of the family that owns the place, or left alone to live out your weeks in seclusion and peace. You may borrow a canoe and a bike, pop a side of beef into the owner's own fridge, pick vegetables from their garden and fruit from their orchard. They will tell you what to avoid and what to do, where to eat and where to play. I write this not as a guarantee but as a matter of personal conviction.

Let us know how much fun you have. Holidays are precious by nature, and this book undertakes to make them even more so.

Alastair Sawday

Photo Paul Groom

Introduction

WE LOOK FOR COMFORT, ORIGINALITY, AUTHENTICITY

I first stayed in a gîte on a family holiday twenty years ago. We had no firm ideas about what to expect. A French friend thumbed through the weighty Gîtes de France directory and picked a place – no photos, no booking forms, only a simple message sent by our friend and the OK relayed back to us. But it turned out to be great. We basked by the pool, scrambled down gorges, met the goats who made our cheese, explored markets and chatted for hours in franglais with the other guests.

What did it matter that we had to endure a journey in a car stuffed full of all that a family needs for two weeks: full sets of sheets, towels (beach and bath), enough clothing to survive without a washing machine. The hot water worked only if you picked the right moment – when no-one else within a 5km radius was using it.

It was a small miracle that we managed to conjure up anything other than a sandwich in our 'kitchen' (a generous title for a sink and a hot-plate). The décor was minimalist-rustic – ie. white walls and a couple of sticks of old furniture. The boiler backfired and eventually blew up, frogs moved into the pool and we co-habited with a family of friendly mice. But we loved it – and went back as soon as we could.

Over the years, gîtes gained a reputation in certain circles for being unloved buildings and boring places to stay; so much so that the word 'gîte' became almost derogatory in French. But gîtes have come of age. Over the last 15 years, their number has exploded while France has seen a corresponding fall in the number of visitors: owners have more competition and are chasing fewer visitors. It's no longer enough to fix up an outbuilding, fling in a few cast-offs and dig out a pool. Owners need to make their gîte stand out in the crowd.

Photo left Bastide des Hautes Moures, entry 346
Photo right Camont, entry 176

Some owners have taken the luxury route: fully-kitted kitchens with more mod cons than most of us have at home, heated pools, spas, maid service, chefs to whip you up sumptuous dinners; one of the places in this book even has a mini-cinema. Many give you the opportunity to stay in a special building: a water mill, a fortified castle, a converted railway station. Others offer simple treats: an organic potager from which you may help yourselves; home-baked bread delivered; a bread and croissant bag with your completed order hung on the back of your door; your own herb garden; cookery courses; writers' retreats; and delicious *table d'hôtes* meals.

What is a Special Place

We look for owners and houses that we like – and we are fiercely subjective in our choices. Those who are familiar with our Special Places series know that we look for comfort, originality, authenticity. We reject the insincere, the anonymous and the banal.

Finding the right place for you

Do read our write-ups carefully – we want to guide you to a place where you'll feel happy. If you are staying on a farm don't be surprised to hear tractors passing early in the morning, or the farmer rounding up his cattle. Many of these properties have all mod cons but an ancient building may have temperamental plumbing and be less than hermetically sealed against draughts; a remote hilltop farmhouse may have power cuts.

Use our descriptions as a taster of what is on offer and have a conversation with the owners about the finer details. Perhaps we've mentioned a pool and you want to check that it will be open at Easter; or you need to know whether the bikes will be available on your particular weekend. If you do find anything misleading in this or any of our books, please let us know. And do discuss any problem with your hosts at the time, however trivial. They are the ones who are most likely to be able to help and sort out the problem before the end of your holiday. Owners always say "if only we'd known" when we contact them on a reader's behalf after the event.

If the entry mentions other gîtes or that the owners do B&B, note that you may not be in total isolation but may be sharing the pool and garden with other guests and their families. This shouldn't spoil your holiday but, if absolute peace is vital, ask the owners how many others are likely to be around. Some of our properties have owners who live nearby; others live far away. If this matters to you, check when booking. There will usually be someone you can turn to should you lose your key!

How to use this book

Our maps

The general map of France is marked with the page numbers of the detailed maps, as are the individual entries. The entry numbers on the detailed maps show roughly where the holiday homes are and should be used in conjunction with a large-scale road map.

The address

We give only an abbreviated address for the property. Owners will supply complete addresses and detailed directions when you enquire or book.

How many does it sleep?

In some instances we give two figures, separated by a hyphen. The first figure is the number of adults the house sleeps comfortably; the second is the number of people who can actually fit in. Some owners can provide extra beds, though there may be an additional charge, and where sofabeds or mezzanine levels are provided, privacy may be compromised. If you want to bring extra people, you absolutely must ask the owner first. Some places offer special rates if you are fewer people than the number shown although generally this applies out of season only.

Photo Blacksmith's Cottage, entry 137

Bedrooms

In this book a 'double' means one double bed, a 'twin' means two single beds. A 'triple' is three single beds. 'Family rooms' include at least one double bed. Extra beds and cots for children, sometimes at extra cost, can often be provided – do ask. We also give total numbers of bathrooms and shower rooms. We don't give details about which bathrooms are 'en suite' but many are, so check with the owners if this matters. We only mention wcs if they are separate from the bath and shower rooms; these generally have their own.

Facilities

If it is important to you that your holiday home has a microwave, dishwasher, TV, CD-player, barbecue or central heating in winter, check with the owners first. Most properties will have a washing machine or shared laundry (we try to mention where they don't), and note that 'well-equipped kitchen' is open to interpretation.

Prices

Prices are in euros and/or sterling, according to the wishes of the owner. All prices are per property per week, unless we say otherwise. We give a range from the cheapest, low-season price to the highest, high-season price. Check with the owner and confirm in writing the price for the number in your party. Remember that in ski resorts, high season is February. Prices are for 2006 and may go up in 2007 so please check with the owner or on their web site if they have one. A few properties offer a reduction if you stay for more than a week but don't expect any deals during peak season. Some places require you to stay a fortnight during these months.

Winter lets

Some holiday homes can be rented all the year round, some close during the winter, while others close during the winter but open for Christmas and New Year. The winter months are often a good time to glimpse the real France; the weather in the south can be very pleasant and rates are normally extremely reasonable. In some cases, but not all, we tell you if winter lets are available, so please check with owners.

Symbols

Symbols and their explanations are listed inside the back cover. They are based on the information given to us by the owners. However, things do change: bikes may be under repair or a new pool might have been put in. Please use the symbols as a guide rather than an absolute statement of fact and double-check anything that is important to you. In particular, look out for 'B&B also' at the end of the write-up: this indicates that there may be other guests on the premises.

Practical Matters

When to go

Families with school-age children will generally take their main holiday in July and August, which is when the French will be taking theirs. For these months it is essential to book well in advance. If you can holiday outside

Photo right Maison des Cerises, entry 295
Photo left Château La Cour – Le Moulin du Pont, entry 51

those busy months, do so: it'll be slightly cooler, it'll be cheaper and you'll be less likely to get snarled up in traffic jams, especially on arrival and departure (avoid 15 August, the Assumption bank holiday, at all costs). Out of season you also have a better chance of seeing France going about its everyday business. May and June are the best months for flowers, for temperatures suitable for walking, and for visiting the Mediterranean coast. If mushrooms are your thing, September's the time, and temperatures in autumn can be ideal. The winter months, when you often get clear fine days, are well worth considering too (see Winter lets above). A word of warning, though: some restaurants in rural areas only open in July and August. Some markets too, but they tend to be the touristy and less authentic ones. Many restaurants close for the winter.

How to book

Owners will normally send you a Booking Form or *Contrat de Location* (Tenancy Contract) which must be filled in and returned with the deposit and commits both sides. The owner will then send a written confirmation and invoice, which constitutes the formal acceptance of the booking. Contracts with British owners are normally governed by British law. Remember that Ireland and the UK are one hour behind the rest of Europe and folk can be upset by enquiries coming through late in their evening. Remember – book early to avoid disappointment.

Deposits

Owners usually ask for a non-refundable deposit to secure a booking. It makes sense to take out a travel insurance policy with a clause to enable you to recover a deposit if you are forced to cancel. Your policy should also cover you for personal belongings and public liability and, possibly, for taking part in adventurous sports. Many owners charge a refundable security/damage deposit, payable either in advance or on arrival.

Payment

The balance of the rent, and usually the security deposit, is normally payable at least eight weeks before the start of the holiday. (If you book within eight weeks of the holiday, you'll be required to make full payment when you book.) A few owners take credit cards, otherwise you will need to send a euro cheque, or a sterling cheque if the owner has a British bank account.

What payment covers

Often, but not always, this covers electricity, gas and water. In some cases, the electricity meter will be read at the start and end of your stay and you will have to pay separately. In our Quick Reference indices at the back of the book, we list those places where linen is not supplied or is provided at extra cost. Even where linen is provided free of charge, towels often aren't, so check when booking. In some cases owners charge for the cost of cleaning and you will have to pay this whether or not you are willing to clean the place yourself. At other places you can either clean yourself or pay someone else to do it. In some cases the cleaning cost is deducted from the security deposit.

Changeover day

Usually this is a Saturday and where it is not we have tried to mention it under the booking details. Many owners are flexible outside the high season so, again, it is worth checking. Normally you must arrive after 4pm and be gone by 10am. Don't arrive earlier as your house may not yet be ready and you will wrong-foot your busy owners.

Consider taking...

- Electrical adaptors: virtually all sockets have two-pin plugs that run on 220/240 AC voltage.
- Electric kettles are a rarity in French-owned homes, so if you can't manage without, bring your own (with adaptor plug).
- Portable fans may be a godsend in high summer.

Photo L'Auzonnet – Hameau de Meihen, entry 300

Children

Our symbol tells you that children of all ages are welcome. If there's no symbol, it may mean there is an unfenced pool, a large boisterous dog or steep stairs. If you are convinced that your impeccably behaved child can cope, the owner may allow you to bring her – but at your own risk.

Pets

Our Pets symbol tells you which houses generally welcome them but you must check whether this includes beasts the size and type of yours, whether the owner has one too (will they be compatible?). Your hosts will expect animals to be well-behaved and obviously you must be responsible for them at all times.

Telephoning/Faxing

All telephone numbers in France have ten digits, eg. (0)5 15 25 35 45.

The initial zero is for use when telephoning from inside France only, ie. dial 05 15 25 35 45 from any private or public telephone.

- From another country to France:
- From the UK dial 00 33, omit the zero in brackets, then the rest of the number given.
- From the USA dial 011 33, omit the zero in brackets, then the full number given.
- Numbers beginning (0)6 are mobile phone numbers.
- When dialling from France to another country: dial 00 followed by the country code and then the rest of the number without the first 0.
- To ring Directory Enquires in France dial 12.

Photo Maison de Coste Perrier, entry 188

Télécartes (phone cards) are widely available in France and there are plenty of telephone boxes, even in the countryside, where you can use them. Few boxes now accept coins, and many take credit cards. Many of our holiday homes have telephones from which you can ring using a card.

Business days and hours

If you get up late and stroll to the shops at midday hoping to pick up some tasty morsels for lunch, you'll be disappointed. France closes down from midday (or sometimes 12.30pm) until around 2pm or 2.30pm for the all-important business of lunching. Some post offices have a crafty habit of closing early for lunch, so don't get caught out. Most shops and banks open from 8am or 9am on weekdays, and food shops normally stay open until around 7.30pm. Many food shops open on Sunday morning but close on Mondays.

Subscriptions

Owners pay to appear in this guide. Their fee goes towards the cost of inspections (every single entry has been inspected by a member of our team), of producing an all-colour book and maintaining a sophisticated web site. We only include places and owners that we find positively special. It is not possible for anyone to buy their way into our guides.

Internet

Our web site (www.specialplacestostay.com) has online pages for all of the places featured here and from all our other books – around 4,500 Special Places in Britain, Ireland, France, Italy, Spain, Portugal, India, Morocco, Turkey and Greece. There's a searchable database, a taster of the write-ups and colour photos. For more details see the back of the book.

Disclaimer

We make no claims to pure objectivity in judging our Special Places to Stay. They are here because we like them. Our opinions and tastes are ours alone and this book is a statement of them; we hope you will share them. We have done our utmost to get our facts right but apologise unreservedly for any mistakes that may have crept in. Sometimes, too, prices shift, usually upwards, and new buildings get put up. Feedback from you is invaluable and we always act upon comments. With your help and our own inspections we can maintain our reputation for dependability.

You should know that we don't check such things as fire alarms, swimming pool security or any other regulation with which owners of properties receiving paying guests should comply. This is the responsibility of the owners.

Photo Maison Monclar – Les Vincens, entry 227

And finally:

Do let us know how you got on in these houses, and get in touch if you stumble across others that deserve to be in our guide – we value your feedback and recommendations enormously. Any poor reports are followed up with the owners in question. Recommendations may be followed up with inspection visits. If yours leads to a place being included in a future edition, you will receive a free guide. There is a report form at the back of the book or email frenchholidayhomes@sawdays.co.uk

Bonnes vacances!

Emma Carey

General map

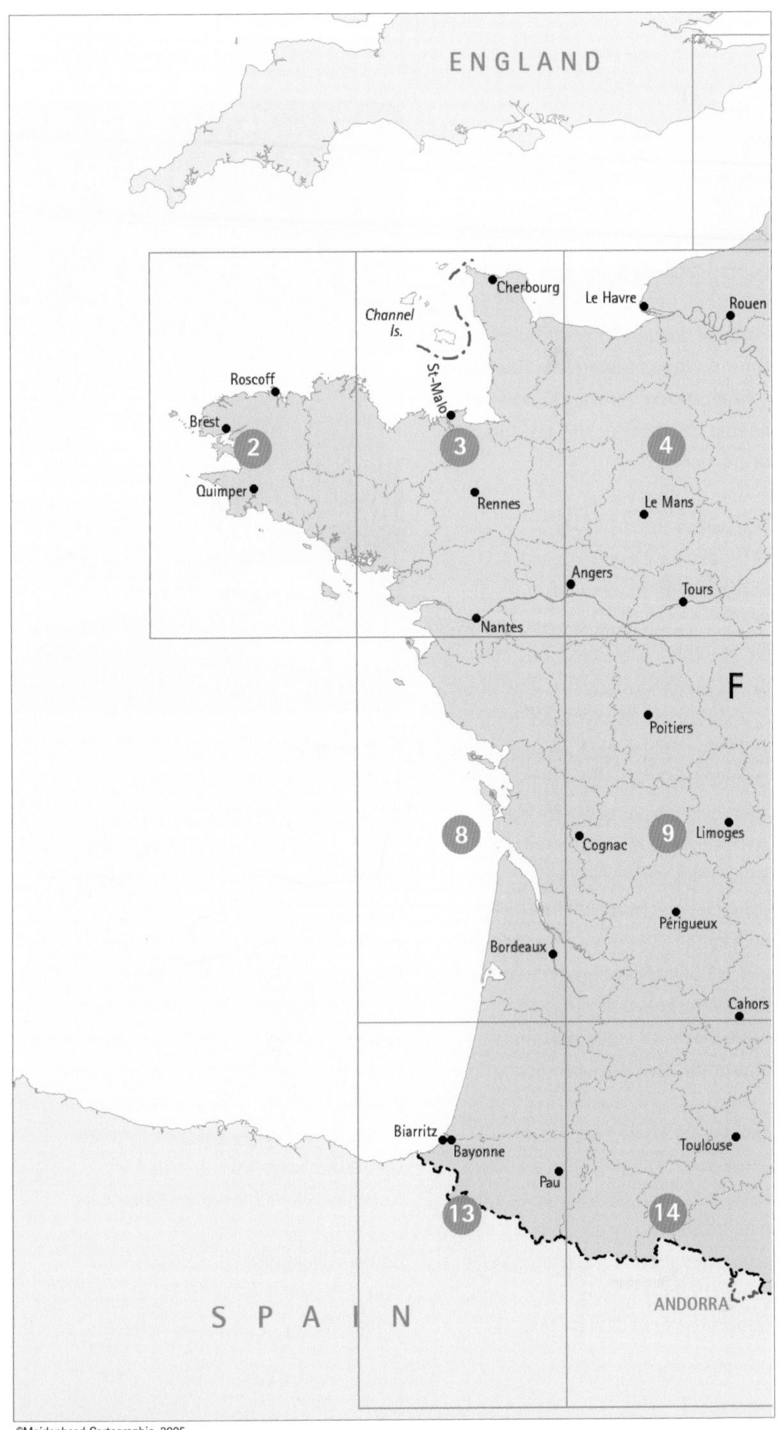
ENGLAND
Cherbourg
Le Havre
Rouen
Channel Is.
St-Malo
Roscoff
Brest
2
3
4
Quimper
Rennes
Le Mans
Angers
Tours
Nantes
F
Poitiers
8
9
Cognac
Limoges
Périgueux
Bordeaux
Cahors
Biarritz
Bayonne
Toulouse
Pau
13
14
ANDORRA
S P A I N

NETHERLANDS
BELGIUM
LUXEMBOURG
GERMANY
SWITZERLAND
ITALY
RANCE
CORSICA
Calais
Boulogne
1
Lille
Amiens
Reims
Metz
Châlons-en-Champagne
PARIS
5
6
Nancy
Strasbourg
7
Orléans
Auxerre
Mulhouse
Besançon
Annecy
10
Clermont-Ferrand
Lyon
11
12
St-Etienne
Grenoble
Valence
Millau
Avignon
16
Nice
Montpellier
Aix-en-Provence
Marseille
Toulon
15
Perpignan

Tips for Travellers

Public holidays

Be aware of public holidays; many national museums and galleries close on Tuesdays, others close on Mondays (e.g. Monet's garden in Giverny) as do many country restaurants, and opening times may be different on the following days:

Movable feasts in 2006 & 2007

Good Friday*	14 April	6 April
Easter (Pâques)	16 April	8 April
Easter Monday	17 April	9 April
Ascension (*l'Ascencion*)	25 May	17 May
Pentecost (*la Pentecôte*)	4 June	27 May
Whit Monday	5 June	28 May

*(Alsace Lorraine only)

Beware also of the mass exodus over public holiday weekends, both the first day – outward journey – and the last – return journey.

Medical & emergency procedures

If you are an EC citizen, have an E111 form with you for filling in after any medical treatment. Part of the sum will subsequently be refunded, so it is advisable to take out private insurance.

To call French emergency services dial 15: the public service called SAMU or the Casualty Department – Services des Urgences – of a hospital. The private service is called SOS MÉDECINS.

Other insurance

It is probably wise to insure the contents of your car.

Roads & driving

Current speed limits are: motorways 130 kph (80 mph), RN national trunk roads 110 kph (68 mph), other open roads 90 kph (56 mph), in towns 50 kph (30 mph). The road police are very active and can demand on-the-spot payment of fines.

One soon gets used to driving on the right but complacency leads to trouble; take special care coming out of car parks, private drives, one-lane roads and coming onto roundabouts.

Directions in towns

The French drive towards a destination and use road numbers far less than we do. Thus, to find your way à la française, know the general direction you want to go, i.e. the towns your route goes through, and when you see *Autres Directions* or *Toutes Directions* in a town, forget road numbers, just continue towards the place name you're heading for or through.

Map 1

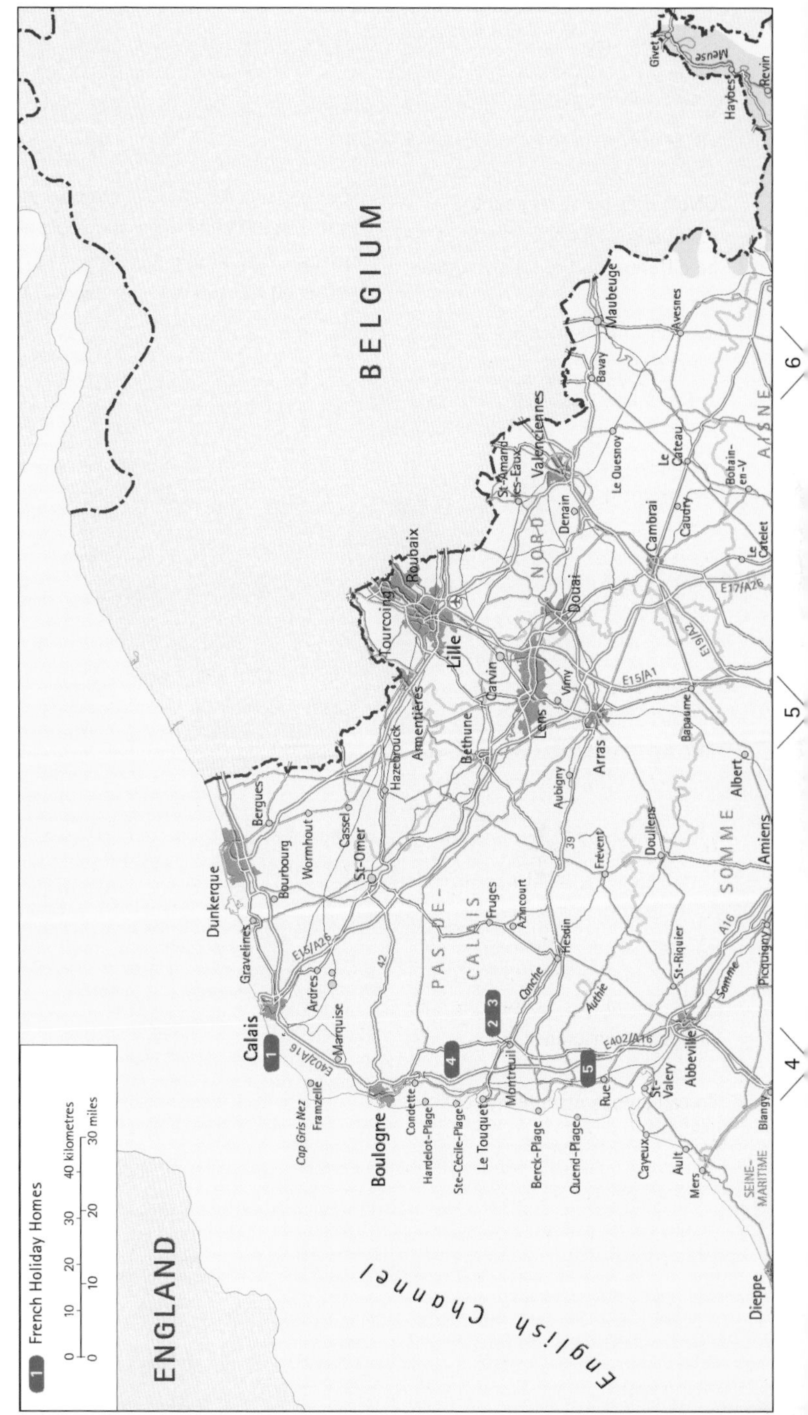
BELGIUM
ENGLAND
English Channel
French Holiday Homes
0 10 20 30 40 kilometres
0 10 20 30 miles
PAS-DE-CALAIS
NORD
SOMME
AISNE
SEINE-MARITIME
Calais
Dunkerque
Gravelines
Bourbourg
Bergues
Wormhout
Cassel
St-Omer
Hazebrouck
Armentières
Tourcoing
Roubaix
Lille
Bethune
Carvin
Lens
Vimy
Douai
Denain
St-Amand-les-Eaux
Valenciennes
Bavay
Maubeuge
Avesnes
Le Quesnoy
Cambrai
Le Cateau
Caudry
Bohain-en-V
Le Catelet
Givet
Haybes
Revin
Meuse
Arras
Aubigny
Bapaume
Albert
Amiens
Doullens
Frévent
Fruges
Azincourt
Hesdin
Ardres
Marquise
Cap Gris Nez
Framzelle
Boulogne
Condette
Hardelot-Plage
Ste-Cécile-Plage
Le Touquet
Montreuil
Berck-Plage
Quend-Plage
Rue
St-Valery
Abbeville
St-Riquier
Picquigny
Cayeux
Ault
Mers
Blangy
Dieppe
Canche
Authie
Somme
E15/A26
E402/A16
E15/A1
E17/A26
E19/A2
A16
42
39
1
2
3
4
5
6

Map 2

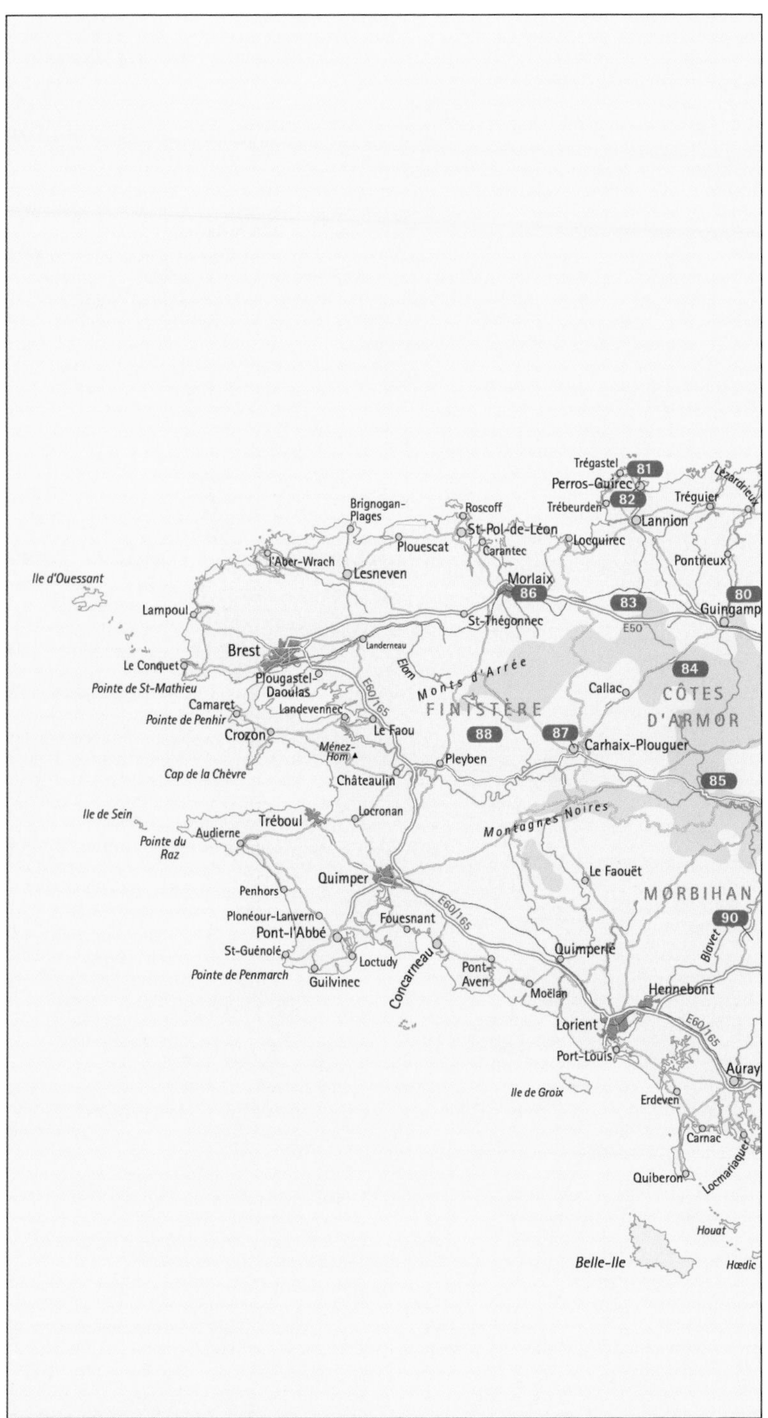

Trégastel
81
Perros-Guirec
82
Trébeurden
Tréguier
Lézardrieux
Lannion
Brignogan-Plages
Roscoff
St-Pol-de-Léon
Plouescat
Carantec
Locquirec
l'Aber-Wrach
Lesneven
Pontrieux
Ile d'Ouessant
Morlaix
86
83
80
Guingamp
Lampoul
St-Thégonnec
E50
Brest
Landerneau
Le Conquet
Elorn
84
Pointe de St-Mathieu
Plougastel-Daoulas
E60/165
Monts d'Arrée
Callac
CÔTES D'ARMOR
Camaret
Landevennec
FINISTÈRE
Pointe de Penhir
Le Faou
Crozon
88
87
Carhaix-Plouguer
Ménez-Hom
Pleyben
Cap de la Chèvre
Châteaulin
85
Ile de Sein
Locronan
Tréboul
Montagnes Noires
Audierne
Pointe du Raz
Le Faouët
Quimper
Penhors
MORBIHAN
E60/165
Plonéour-Lanvern
Fouesnant
90
Pont-l'Abbé
Blavet
St-Guénolé
Quimperlé
Loctudy
Pointe de Penmarch
Pont-Aven
Concarneau
Guilvinec
Hennebont
Moëlan
Lorient
E60/165
Port-Louis
Auray
Ile de Groix
Erdeven
Carnac
Locmariaquer
Quiberon
Houat
Belle-Ile
Hœdic

Map 3

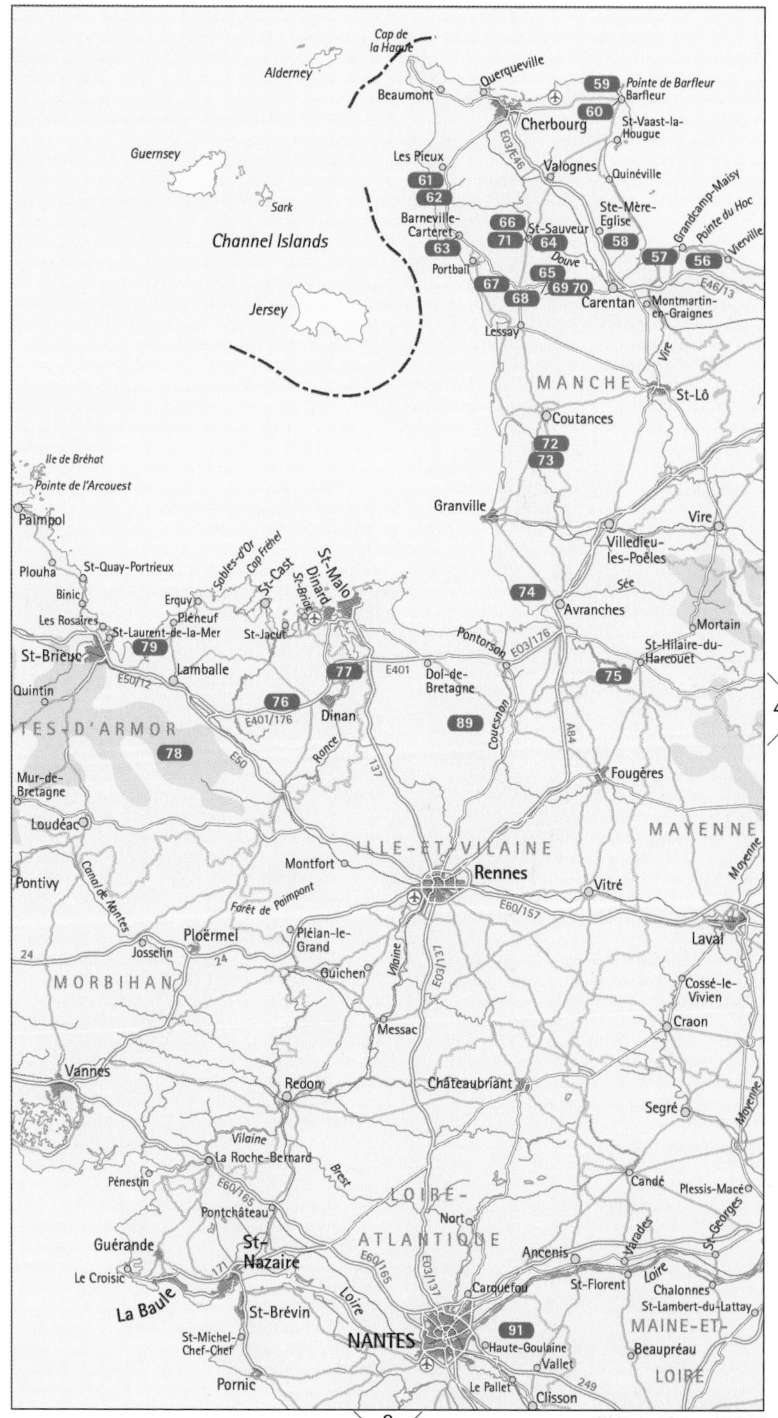
Cap de la Hague
Alderney
Guernsey
Sark
Channel Islands
Jersey
Querqueville
Beaumont
Cherbourg
Pointe de Barfleur
Barfleur
St-Vaast-la-Hougue
Les Pieux
Valognes
Quinéville
Barneville-Carteret
St-Sauveur
Ste-Mère-Eglise
Grandcamp-Maisy
Pointe du Hoc
Vierville
Portbail
Douve
Carentan
Montmartin-en-Graignes
Lessay
Vire
MANCHE
St-Lô
Coutances
Granville
Vire
Villedieu-les-Poêles
Sée
Avranches
Mortain
St-Hilaire-du-Harcouet
Pontorson
Dol-de-Bretagne
Couesnon
A84
Fougères
MAYENNE
Mayenne
Ile de Bréhat
Pointe de l'Arcouest
Paimpol
Plouha
St-Quay-Portrieux
Binic
Les Rosaires
St-Laurent-de-la-Mer
St-Brieuc
Erquy
Pléneuf
Sables-d'Or
Cap Fréhel
St-Cast
St-Jacut
St-Briac
Dinard
St-Malo
Lamballe
E401
E50/12
Quintin
E401/176
Dinan
Rance
E50
137
TES-D'ARMOR
Mur-de-Bretagne
Loudéac
Pontivy
Canal de Nantes
ILLE-ET-VILAINE
Montfort
Rennes
Vitré
Forêt de Paimpont
E60/157
Laval
Ploërmel
Josselin
Plélan-le-Grand
Vilaine
E03/137
24
MORBIHAN
Guichen
Cossé-le-Vivien
Messac
Craon
Vannes
Redon
Châteaubriant
Segré
Mayenne
Vilaine
La Roche-Bernard
Brest
Pénestin
E60/165
LOIRE-ATLANTIQUE
Candé
Plessis-Macé
Pontchâteau
Nort
St-Georges
Varades
Guérande
St-Nazaire
Ancenis
Loire
Le Croisic
171
St-Florent
Chalonnes
La Baule
Carquefou
St-Lambert-du-Lattay
St-Brévin
MAINE-ET-LOIRE
St-Michel-Chef-Chef
NANTES
Haute-Goulaine
Beaupréau
Vallet
Le Pallet
249
Pornic
Clisson
59 60 61 62 63 64 65 66 67 68 69 70 71 72 73 74 75 76 77 78 79 89 91

4

8

Map 4

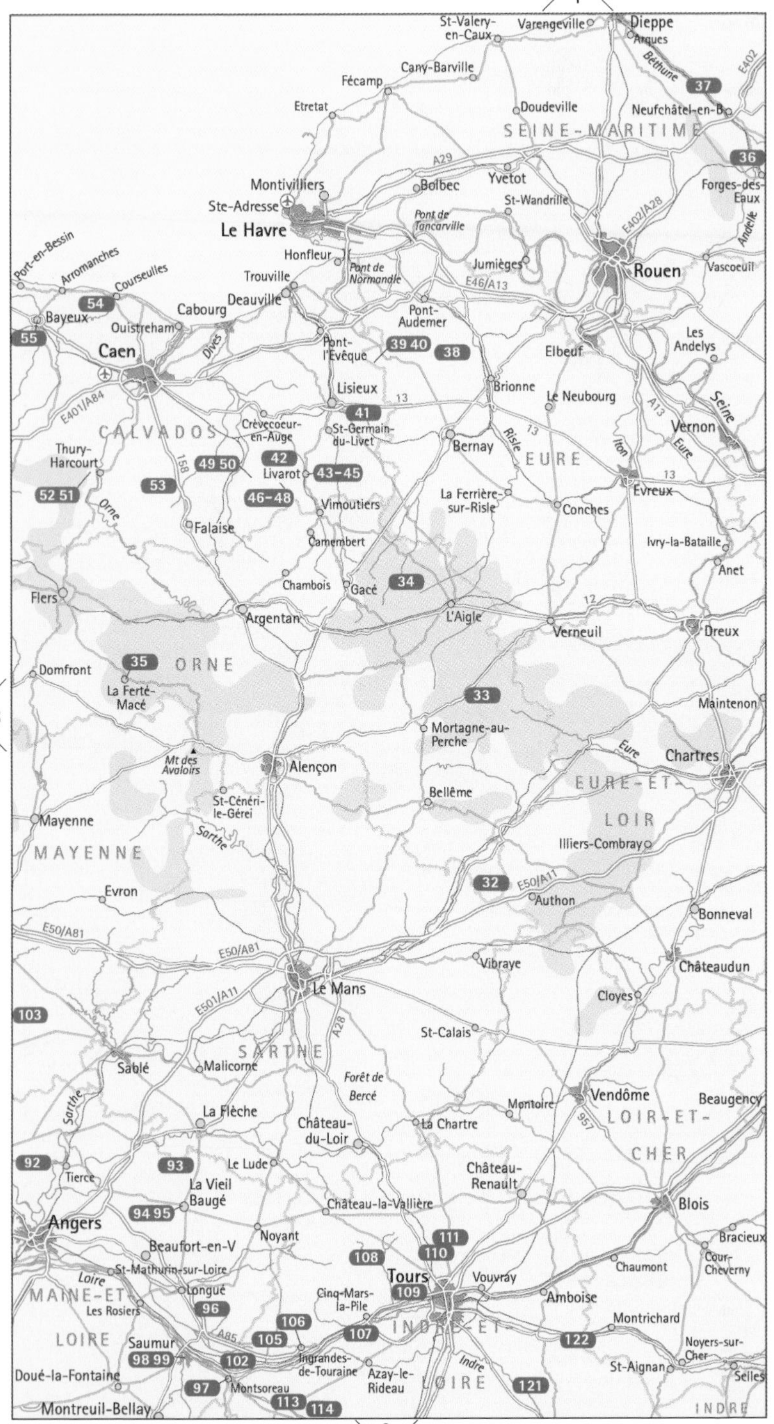
1
St-Valery-en-Caux
Varengeville
Dieppe
Arques
Béthune
37
Fécamp
Cany-Barville
Etretat
Doudeville
Neufchâtel-en-B
SEINE-MARITIME
36
A29
Montivilliers
Bolbec
Yvetot
Forges-des-Eaux
Ste-Adresse
St-Wandrille
Le Havre
Pont de Tancarville
E402/A28
Andelle
Port-en-Bessin
Arromanches
Honfleur
Pont de Normandie
Jumièges
Rouen
Vascoeuil
Courseulles
Trouville
E46/A13
54
Deauville
Cabourg
Pont-Audemer
Bayeux
Ouistreham
Les Andelys
55
Dives
Pont-l'Evêque
39 40
38
Elbeuf
Caen
Brionne
Seine
Lisieux
13
Le Neubourg
E401/A84
41
A13
Vernon
CALVADOS
Crèvecoeur-en-Auge
St-Germain-du-Livet
Risle
Iton
Eure
Thury-Harcourt
158
42
Bernay
EURE
49 50
Livarot
43-45
13
Evreux
52 51
53
46-48
La Ferrière-sur-Risle
Conches
Orne
Vimoutiers
Falaise
Camembert
Ivry-la-Bataille
Anet
Chambois
Gacé
34
Flers
12
Argentan
L'Aigle
Verneuil
Dreux
35
ORNE
Domfront
La Ferté-Macé
33
Maintenon
3
Mortagne-au-Perche
Eure
Chartres
Mt des Avaloirs
Alençon
EURE-ET-LOIR
Bellême
St-Céneri-le-Gérei
Mayenne
Sarthe
Illiers-Combray
MAYENNE
32
E50/A11
Evron
Authon
Bonneval
E50/A81
E50/A81
Châteaudun
Vibraye
E501/A11
Le Mans
Cloyes
103
A28
St-Calais
SARTHE
Sablé
Malicorne
Forêt de Bercé
Sarthe
Montoire
Vendôme
Beaugency
La Flèche
Château-du-Loir
La Chartre
957
LOIR-ET-CHER
92
93
Le Lude
Tiercé
La Vieil Baugé
Château-Renault
94 95
Blois
Angers
Château-la-Vallière
Noyant
111
Bracieux
Beaufort-en-V
110
108
Cour-Cheverny
St-Mathurin-sur-Loire
Chaumont
Loire
Tours
Vouvray
MAINE-ET-
Longué
Cinq-Mars-la-Pile
109
Amboise
Les Rosiers
96
Montrichard
106
LOIRE
A85
105
107
INDRE-ET-
122
Saumur
Ingrandes-de-Touraine
Noyers-sur-Cher
98 99
102
Indre
Azay-le-Rideau
St-Aignan
Selles
Doué-la-Fontaine
97
Montsoreau
LOIRE
121
113
114
Montreuil-Bellay
INDRE
9

Map 5

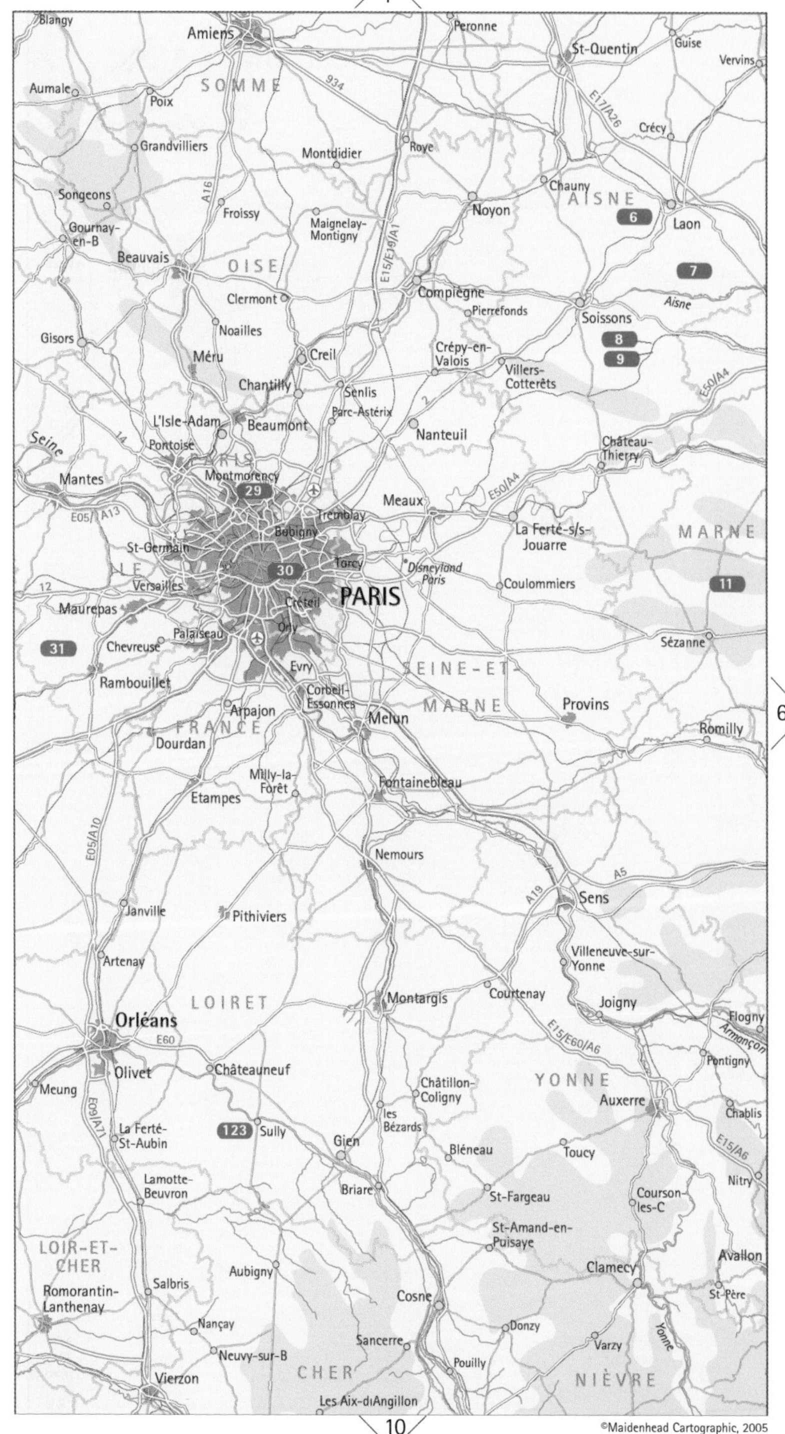
1
6
10
PARIS
Amiens
St-Quentin
Orléans
Sens
Auxerre
Melun
Fontainebleau
Meaux
Compiègne
Soissons
Laon
Beauvais
SOMME
OISE
AISNE
MARNE
SEINE-ET-MARNE
LOIRET
YONNE
CHER
NIÈVRE
LOIR-ET-CHER
©Maidenhead Cartographic, 2005

Map 6

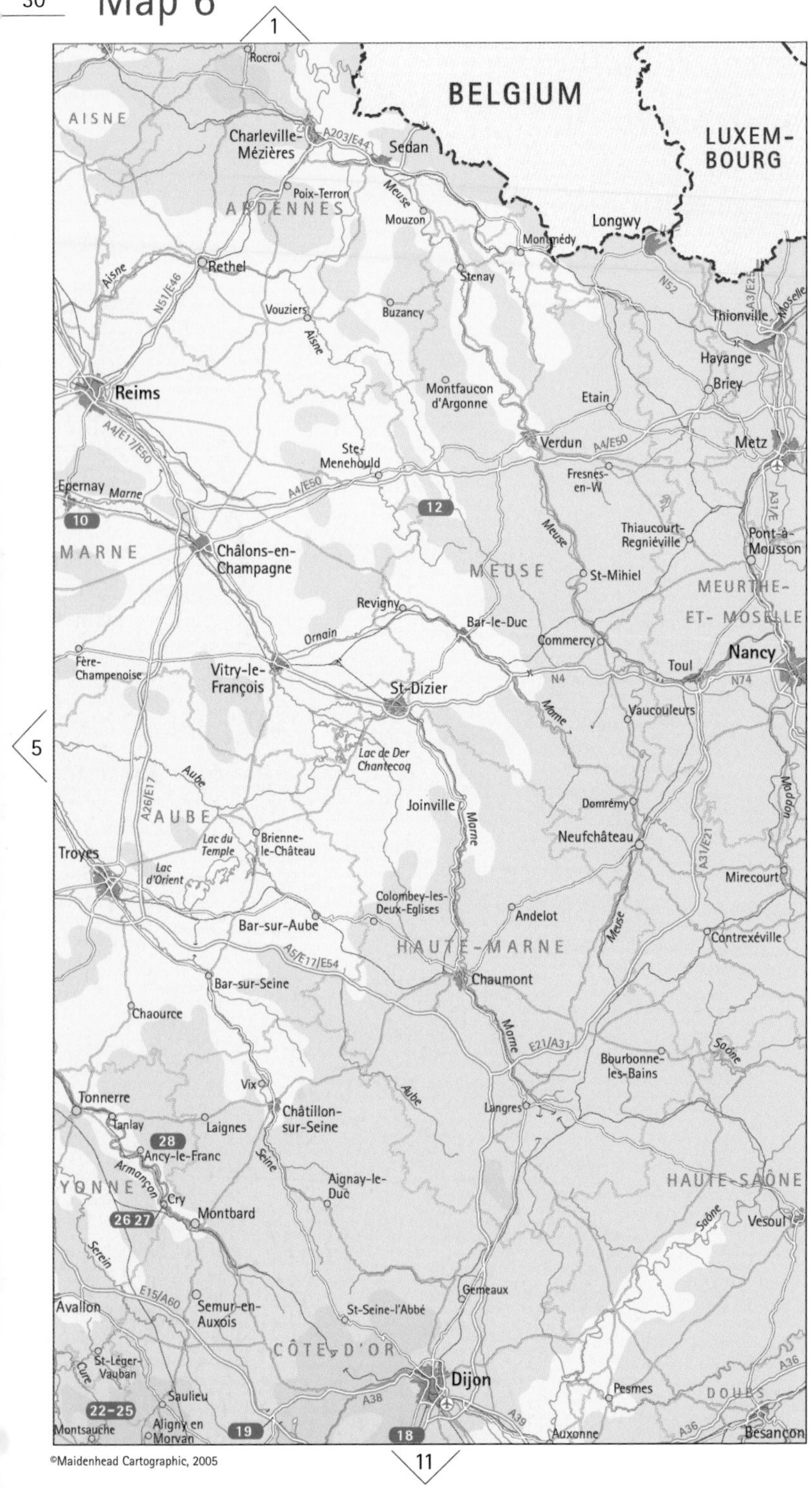

1

BELGIUM
LUXEMBOURG
AISNE
Rocroi
Charleville-Mézières
A203/E44
Sedan
Poix-Terron
ARDENNES
Meuse
Mouzon
Montmédy
Longwy
Rethel
Aisne
N51/E46
Stenay
N52
A3/E25
Moselle
Vouziers
Aisne
Buzancy
Thionville
Hayange
Briey
Reims
Montfaucon d'Argonne
Etain
A4/E17/E50
Verdun
A4/E50
Metz
Ste-Menehould
Fresnes-en-W
Epernay
Marne
A4/E50
12
A31/E
10
MARNE
Châlons-en-Champagne
Meuse
Thiaucourt-Regniéville
Pont-à-Mousson
MEUSE
St-Mihiel
MEURTHE-ET-MOSELLE
Revigny
Bar-le-Duc
Commercy
Ornain
Fère-Champenoise
Vitry-le-François
Nancy
Toul
N4
N74
St-Dizier
Marne
Vaucouleurs
5
Lac de Der Chantecoq
Aube
Joinville
Marne
Domrémy
Madon
A26/E17
AUBE
Neufchâteau
Lac du Temple
Brienne-le-Château
A31/E21
Troyes
Lac d'Orient
Mirecourt
Colombey-les-Deux-Eglises
Andelot
Bar-sur-Aube
Meuse
Contrexéville
HAUTE-MARNE
A5/E17/E54
Chaumont
Bar-sur-Seine
Chaource
Marne
E21/A31
Saône
Bourbonne-les-Bains
Vix
Aube
Tonnerre
Langres
Châtillon-sur-Seine
Tanlay
Laignes
28
Ancy-le-Franc
Seine
Armançon
YONNE
Aignay-le-Duc
HAUTE-SAÔNE
Cry
Montbard
26 27
Saône
Vesoul
Serein
E15/A60
Gemeaux
Avallon
Semur-en-Auxois
St-Seine-l'Abbé
CÔTE-D'OR
St-Léger-Vauban
Cure
A36
Dijon
Saulieu
Pesmes
DOUBS
A38
22-25
A39
A36
Montsauche
Aligny en Morvan
19
18
Auxonne
Besançon

11

Map 7

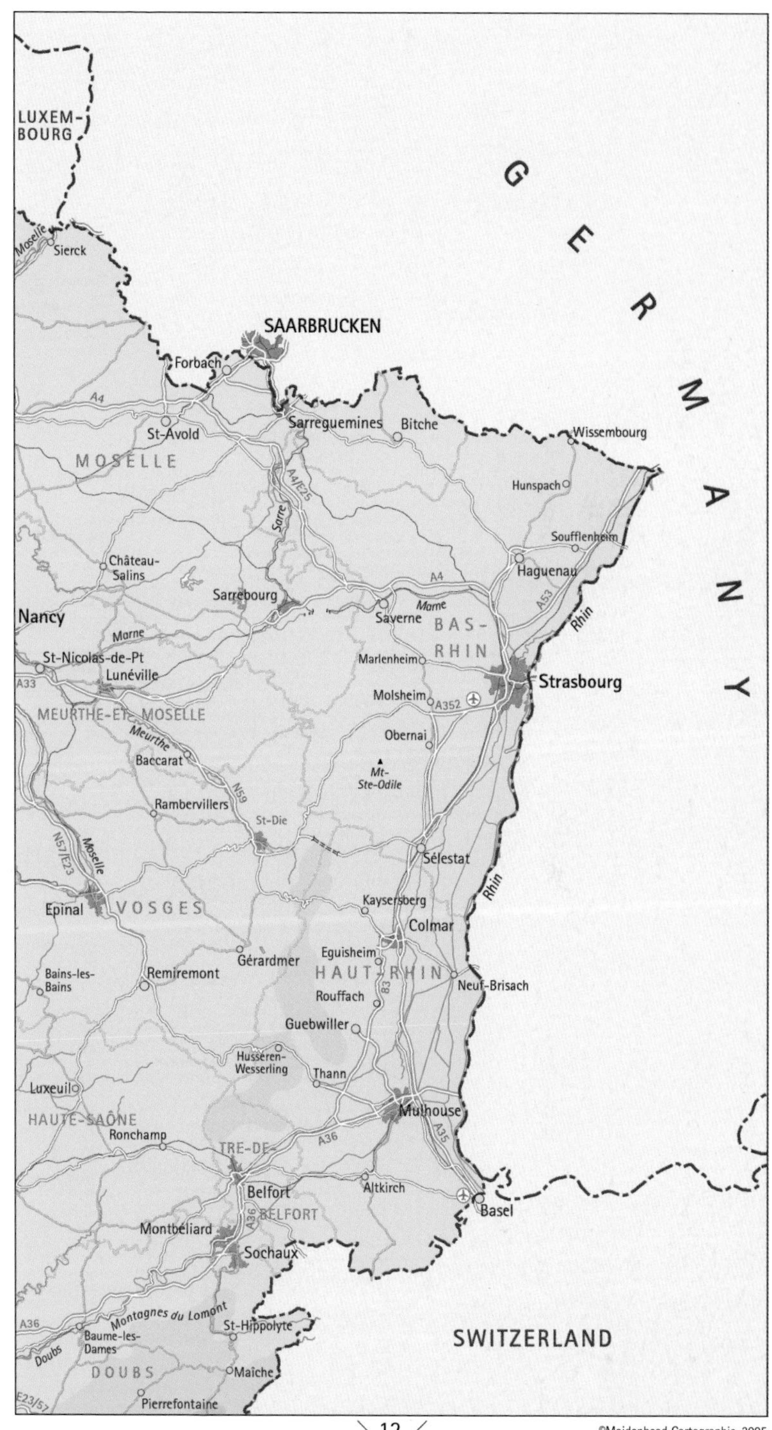
LUXEMBOURG
GERMANY
SAARBRUCKEN
Sierck
Moselle
Forbach
A4
St-Avold
Sarreguemines
Bitche
Wissembourg
MOSELLE
A4/E25
Sarre
Hunspach
Soufflenheim
Château-Salins
Haguenau
A4
A53
Rhin
Sarrebourg
Marne
Saverne
BAS-RHIN
Nancy
Marne
St-Nicolas-de-Pt
Lunéville
A33
Marlenheim
Strasbourg
Molsheim
A352
MEURTHE-ET-MOSELLE
Meurthe
Obernai
Baccarat
N59
Mt-Ste-Odile
Rambervillers
St-Die
N57/E23
Moselle
Sélestat
Rhin
Epinal
VOSGES
Kaysersberg
Colmar
Gérardmer
Eguisheim
Bains-les-Bains
Remiremont
HAUT-RHIN
Neuf-Brisach
83
Rouffach
Guebwiller
Husseren-Wesserling
Thann
Luxeuil
Mulhouse
HAUTE-SAÔNE
A35
Ronchamp
A36
TRE-DE-
Altkirch
Belfort
Basel
A36
BELFORT
Montbéliard
Sochaux
A36
Montagnes du Lomont
Baume-les-Dames
St-Hippolyte
SWITZERLAND
Doubs
DOUBS
Maîche
E23/57
Pierrefontaine
©Maidenhead Cartographic, 2005

Map 8

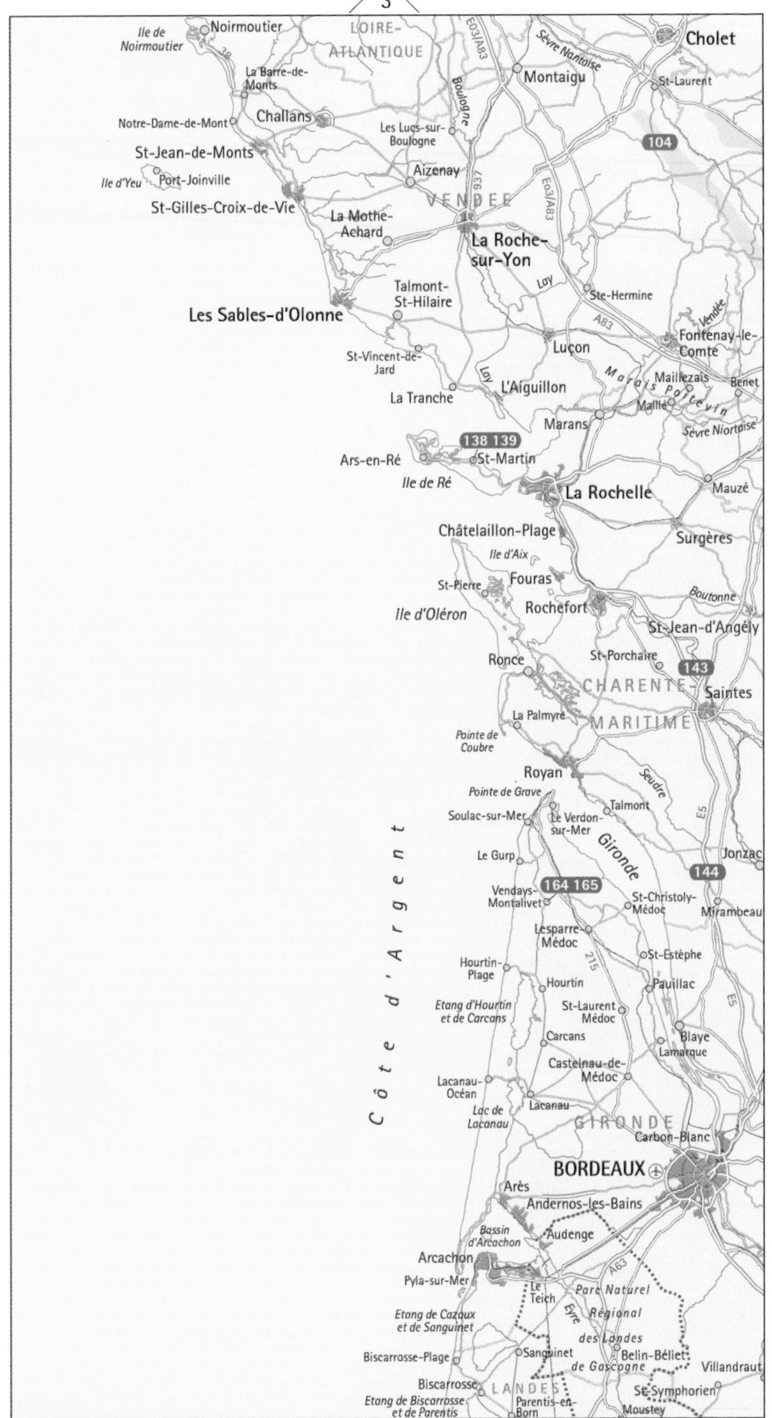
3
Ile de Noirmoutier
Noirmoutier
LOIRE-ATLANTIQUE
Cholet
Montaigu
St-Laurent
La Barre-de-Monts
Notre-Dame-de-Mont
Challans
Les Lucs-sur-Boulogne
St-Jean-de-Monts
Ile d'Yeu
Port-Joinville
Aizenay
St-Gilles-Croix-de-Vie
VENDEE
La Mothe-Achard
La Roche-sur-Yon
Talmont-St-Hilaire
Les Sables-d'Olonne
Ste-Hermine
Fontenay-le-Comte
Luçon
St-Vincent-de-Jard
L'Aiguillon
La Tranche
Maillezais
Benet
Maillé
Marans
Ars-en-Ré
St-Martin
Ile de Ré
La Rochelle
Mauzé
Châtelaillon-Plage
Surgères
Ile d'Aix
Fouras
St-Pierre
Rochefort
Ile d'Oléron
St-Jean-d'Angély
Ronce
St-Porchaire
CHARENTE-MARITIME
Saintes
La Palmyre
Pointe de Coubre
Royan
Pointe de Grave
Talmont
Soulac-sur-Mer
Le Verdon-sur-Mer
Gironde
Le Gurp
Jonzac
Vendays-Montalivet
St-Christoly-Médoc
Mirambeau
Lesparre-Médoc
St-Estèphe
Hourtin-Plage
Hourtin
Pauillac
Etang d'Hourtin et de Carcans
St-Laurent Médoc
Blaye
Carcans
Lamarque
Castelnau-de-Médoc
Lacanau-Océan
Lacanau
Lac de Lacanau
Côte d'Argent
GIRONDE
Carbon-Blanc
BORDEAUX
Arès
Andernos-les-Bains
Bassin d'Arcachon
Audenge
Arcachon
Pyla-sur-Mer
Le Teich
Parc Naturel Régional des Landes de Gascogne
Etang de Cazaux et de Sanguinet
Sanguinet
Belin-Béliet
Biscarrosse-Plage
Villandraut
Biscarrosse
LANDES
St-Symphorien
Etang de Biscarrosse et de Parentis
Parentis-en-Born
Moustey
13

Map 9

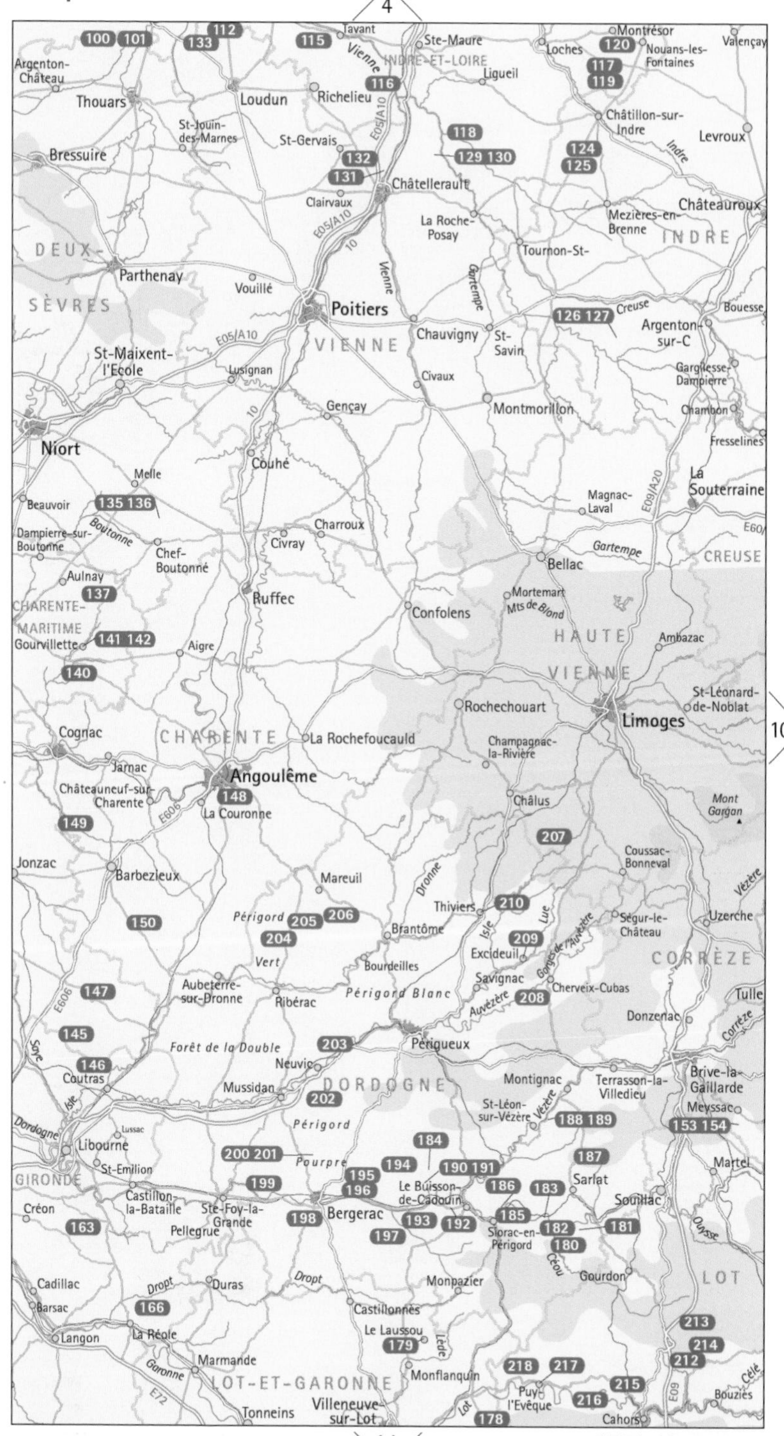
4
Thouars
Loudun
Richelieu
Bressuire
Châtellerault
Parthenay
Poitiers
Niort
Chauvigny
Montmorillon
Ruffec
Confolens
Bellac
Limoges
Angoulême
Cognac
Périgueux
Bergerac
Libourne
Sarlat
Souillac
Cahors
Brive-la-Gaillarde
Châteauroux
DEUX-SÈVRES
VIENNE
HAUTE VIENNE
CHARENTE
CHARENTE-MARITIME
DORDOGNE
CORRÈZE
LOT
LOT-ET-GARONNE
GIRONDE
INDRE
INDRE-ET-LOIRE
CREUSE
10
14

Map 10

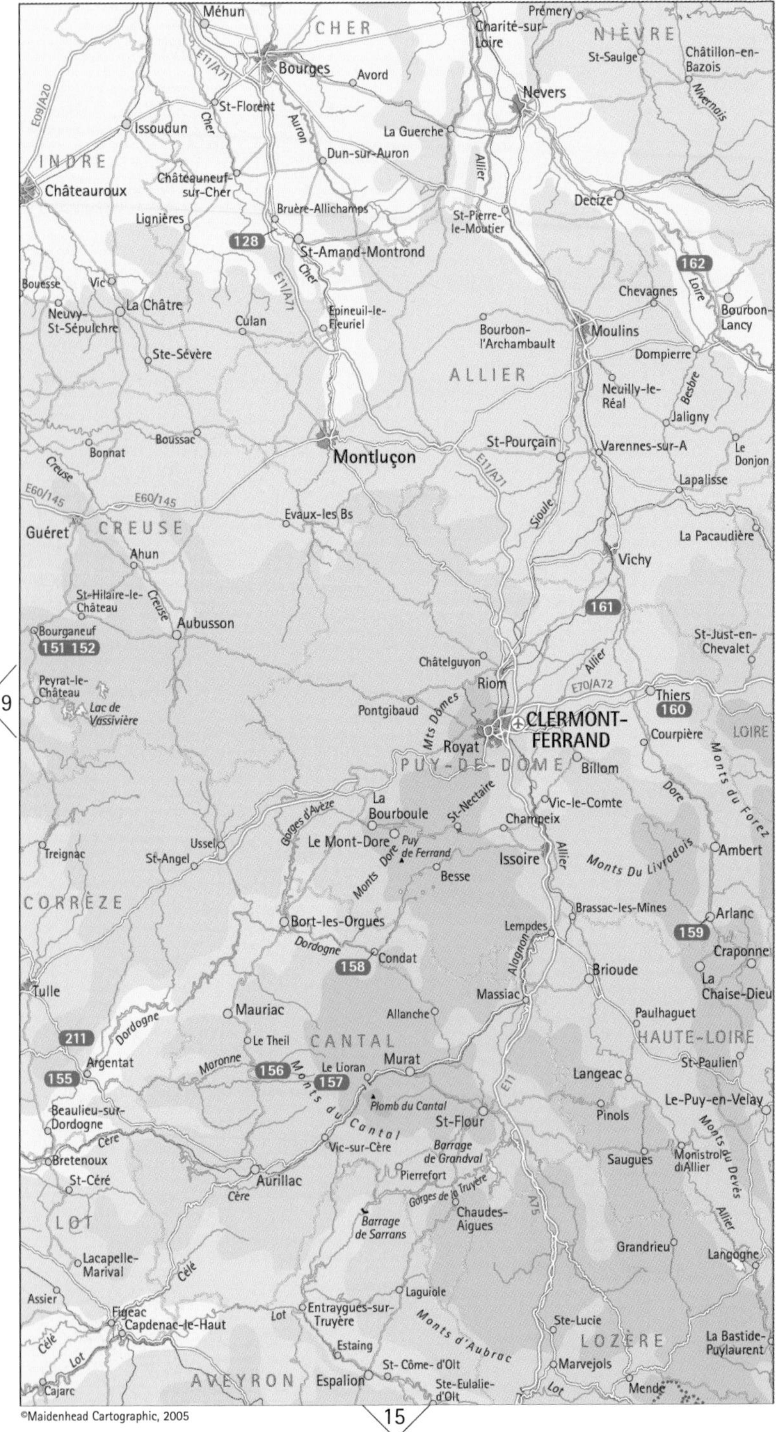

5
9
15
Méhun
CHER
Bourges
Avord
Charité-sur-Loire
Prémery
NIÈVRE
St-Saulge
Châtillon-en-Bazois
Nivernais
Nevers
E11/A71
E09/A20
St-Florent
Cher
Auron
Issoudun
La Guerche
Dun-sur-Auron
Allier
INDRE
Châteauroux
Châteauneuf-sur-Cher
Decize
Bruère-Allichamps
St-Pierre-le-Moutier
Lignières
128
St-Amand-Montrond
162
Loire
Bouesse
Vic
Chevagnes
Neuvy-St-Sépulchre
La Châtre
Culan
Epineuil-le-Fleuriel
Bourbon-l'Archambault
Moulins
Bourbon-Lancy
Dompierre
Ste-Sévère
ALLIER
Neuilly-le-Réal
Besbre
Jaligny
Boussac
Bonnat
Montluçon
St-Pourçain
Varennes-sur-A
Le Donjon
Creuse
E60/145
Lapalisse
Sioule
Evaux-les Bs
Guéret
CREUSE
La Pacaudière
Vichy
Ahun
St-Hilaire-le-Château
Aubusson
161
Bourganeuf
151 152
St-Just-en-Chevalet
Châtelguyon
Peyrat-le-Château
Lac de Vassivière
Riom
E70/A72
Thiers
160
Pontgibaud
Mts Dômes
CLERMONT-FERRAND
Royat
Courpière
LOIRE
PUY-DE-DÔME
Billom
Monts du Forez
Dore
Vic-le-Comte
La Bourboule
St-Nectaire
Champeix
Gorges d'Avèze
Le Mont-Dore
Puy de Ferrand
Ambert
Treignac
Ussel
St-Angel
Issoire
Monts Du Livradois
Besse
Monts Dore
CORRÈZE
Brassac-les-Mines
Arlanc
Bort-les-Orgues
Lempdes
159
Dordogne
Condat
158
Alagnon
Craponne
Brioude
La Chaise-Dieu
Tulle
Massiac
Mauriac
Allanche
Paulhaguet
211
Le Theil
CANTAL
HAUTE-LOIRE
Argentat
Maronne
156
Le Lioran
157
Murat
St-Paulien
155
Langeac
Monts du Cantal
Plomb du Cantal
E11
Le-Puy-en-Velay
Beaulieu-sur-Dordogne
St-Flour
Pinols
Cère
Vic-sur-Cère
Barrage de Grandval
Monts du Devès
Bretenoux
Saugues
Monistrol d'Allier
St-Céré
Aurillac
Pierrefort
Gorges de la Truyère
LOT
Chaudes-Aigues
Barrage de Sarrans
A75
Grandrieu
Langogne
Lacapelle-Marival
Célé
Laguiole
Assier
Figeac
Capdenac-le-Haut
Lot
Entraygues-sur-Truyère
Monts d'Aubrac
Ste-Lucie
LOZÈRE
La Bastide-Puylaurent
Estaing
St-Côme-d'Olt
Marvejols
AVEYRON
Espalion
Ste-Eulalie-d'Olt
Mende
Cajarc

Map 11

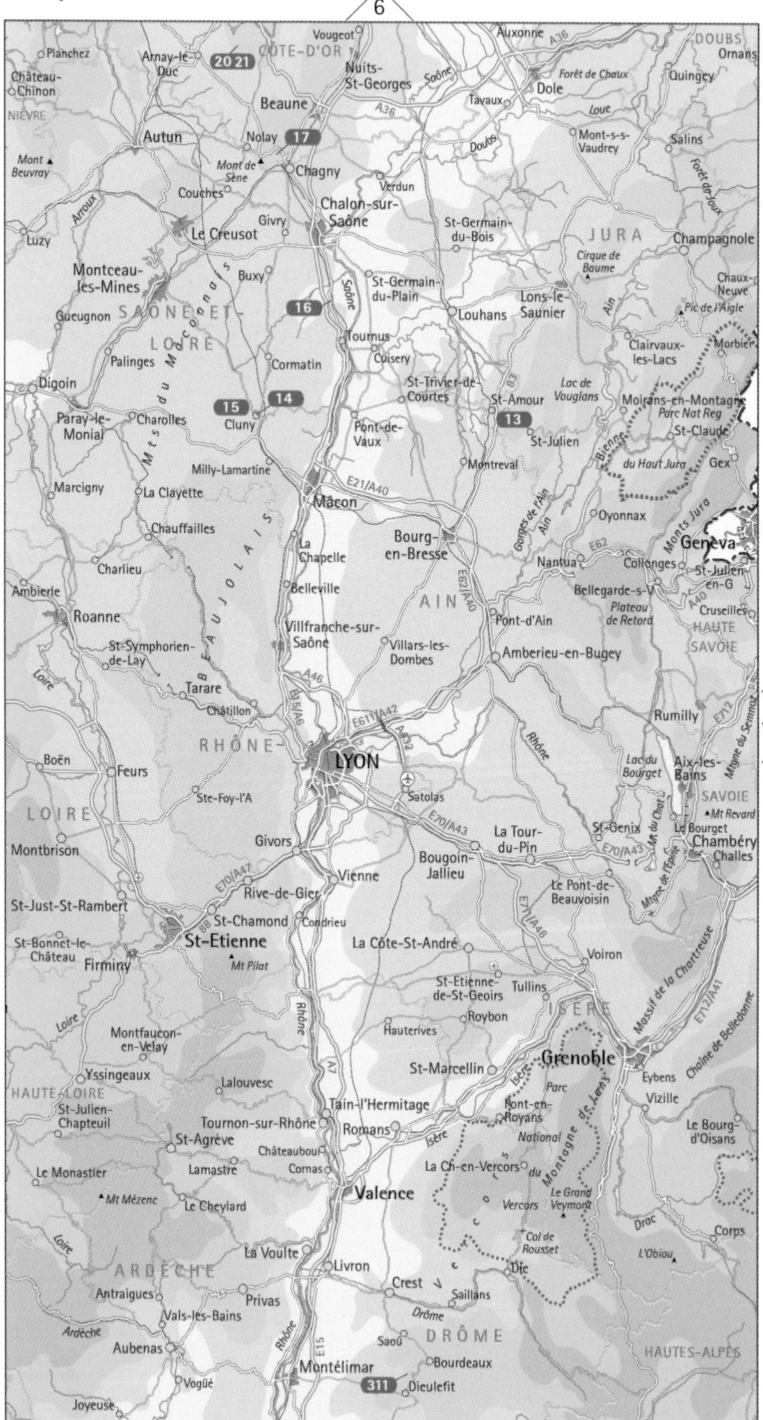

6
12
16
Vougeot
Auxonne
Planchez
Arnay-le-Duc
20 21
CÔTE-D'OR
DOUBS
Ornans
Château-Chinon
Nuits-St-Georges
Dole
Quingey
NIÈVRE
Beaune
Tavaux
Autun
Nolay
17
Mont-s-s-Vaudrey
Salins
Mont Beuvray
Mont de Sène
Chagny
Verdun
Couches
Chalon-sur-Saône
Luzy
Le Creusot
Givry
St-Germain-du-Bois
JURA
Champagnole
Montceau-les-Mines
Buxy
St-Germain-du-Plain
Cirque de Baume
Chaux-Neuve
16
Louhans
Lons-le-Saunier
Gueugnon
SAÔNE-ET-LOIRE
Tournus
Clairvaux-les-Lacs
Morbier
Palinges
Cuisery
Cormatin
Digoin
St-Trivier-de-Courtes
St-Amour
Lac de Vouglans
Moirans-en-Montagne
15
14
13
Parc Nat Reg du Haut Jura
Paray-le-Monial
Charolles
Cluny
Pont-de-Vaux
St-Julien
St-Claude
Gex
Montreval
Milly-Lamartine
Marcigny
La Clayette
Mâcon
Oyonnax
Chauffailles
Bourg-en-Bresse
Geneva
La Chapelle
Nantua
Collonges
St-Julien-en-G
Charlieu
Ambierle
Belleville
Bellegarde-s-V
AIN
Plateau de Retord
Roanne
Pont-d'Ain
Cruseilles
HAUTE SAVOIE
Villfranche-sur-Saône
Villars-les-Dombes
Amberieu-en-Bugey
St-Symphorien-de-Lay
BEAUJOLAIS
Tarare
Rumilly
Châtillon
RHÔNE
LYON
Boën
Feurs
Lac du Bourget
Aix-les-Bains
Ste-Foy-l'A
Satolas
SAVOIE
Mt Revard
LOIRE
Le Bourget
La Tour-du-Pin
St-Genix
Chambéry
Challes
Montbrison
Givors
Bougoin-Jallieu
Vienne
Rive-de-Gier
Le Pont-de-Beauvoisin
St-Just-St-Rambert
St-Chamond
Condrieu
St-Bonnet-le-Château
St-Etienne
La Côte-St-André
Voiron
Firminy
Mt Pilat
St-Etienne-de-St-Geoirs
Tullins
ISÈRE
Massif de la Chartreuse
Roybon
Montfaucon-en-Velay
Hauterives
Grenoble
Chaîne de Belledonne
St-Marcellin
Eybens
Yssingeaux
Lalouvesc
HAUTE-LOIRE
Vizille
St-Julien-Chapteuil
Tain-l'Hermitage
Pont-en-Royans
Parc National du Vercors
Montagne de Lans
Tournon-sur-Rhône
Romans
Le Bourg-d'Oisans
St-Agrève
Châteaubourg
Le Monastier
Lamastre
Cornas
La Ch-en-Vercors
Mt Mézenc
Le Cheylard
Valence
Le Grand Veymont
Col de Rousset
Corps
La Voulte
L'Obiou
ARDÈCHE
Livron
Die
Antraigues
Privas
Crest
Saillans
Vals-les-Bains
Drôme
DRÔME
Aubenas
Saou
HAUTES-ALPES
Montélimar
Bourdeaux
Vogüé
311
Dieulefit
Joyeuse

Map 12

7

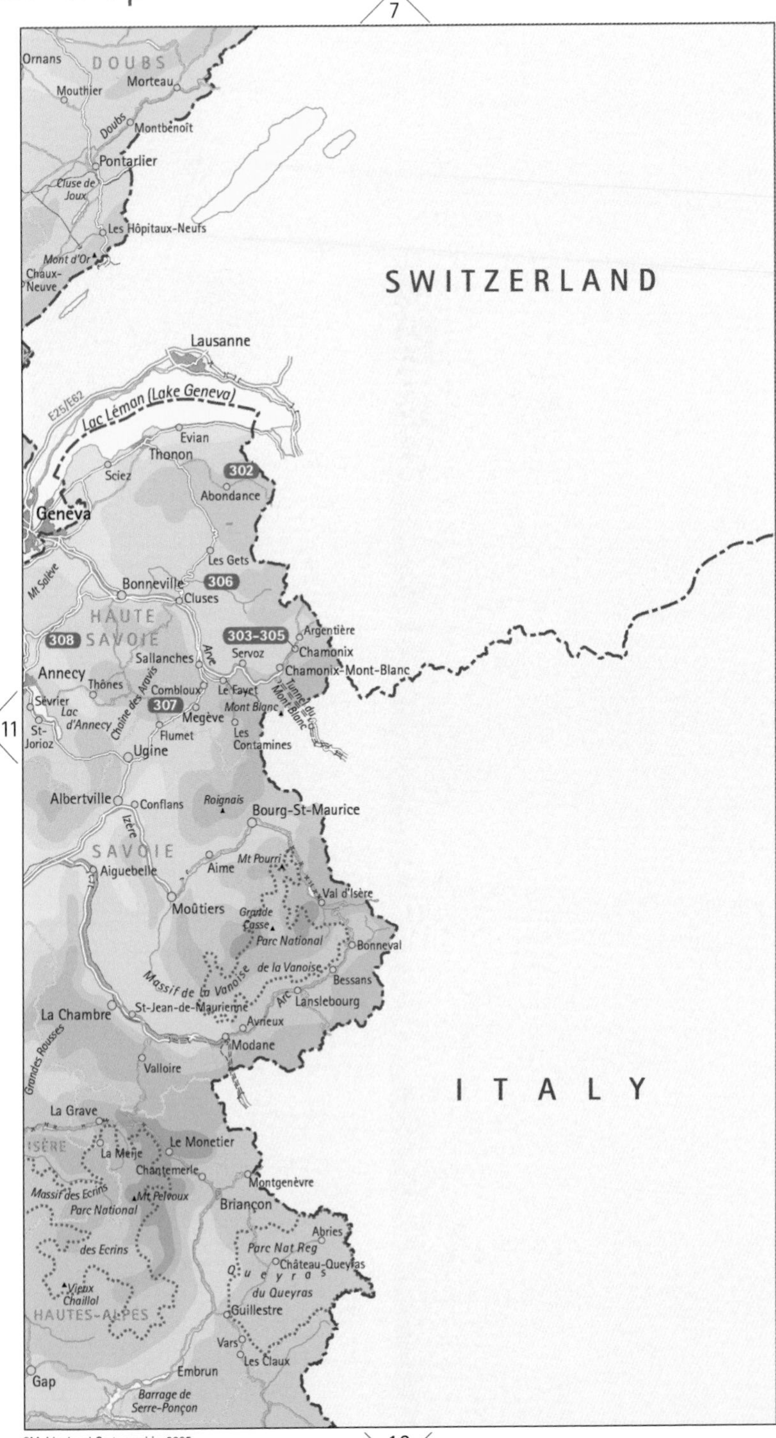

SWITZERLAND
ITALY
Ornans
DOUBS
Morteau
Mouthier
Doubs
Montbenoît
Pontarlier
Cluse de Joux
Les Hôpitaux-Neufs
Mont d'Or
Chaux-Neuve
Lausanne
E25/E62
Lac Léman (Lake Geneva)
Evian
Thonon
302
Sciez
Abondance
Geneva
Les Gets
Mt Salève
Bonneville
306
Cluses
HAUTE SAVOIE
308
303-305
Argentière
Servoz
Chamonix
Sallanches
Arve
Chamonix-Mont-Blanc
Annecy
Thônes
Combloux
Le Fayet
Tunnel du Mont Blanc
Sévrier
Lac d'Annecy
Chaîne des Aravis
307
Mont Blanc
St-Jorioz
Megève
Flumet
Les Contamines
Ugine
Albertville
Conflans
Roignais
Bourg-St-Maurice
Isère
SAVOIE
Aiguebelle
Aime
Mt Pourri
Val d'Isère
Moûtiers
Grande Casse
Parc National
Bonneval
de la Vanoise
Massif de la Vanoise
Bessans
Arc
Lanslebourg
La Chambre
St-Jean-de-Maurienne
Avrieux
Modane
Grandes Rousses
Valloire
La Grave
ISÈRE
La Meije
Le Monetier
Chantemerle
Montgenèvre
Massif des Ecrins
Mt Pelvoux
Parc National
Briançon
Abries
des Ecrins
Parc Nat Reg
Château-Queyras
Queyras
du Queyras
Vieux Chaillol
HAUTES-ALPES
Guillestre
Vars
Les Claux
Embrun
Gap
Barrage de Serre-Ponçon

11

16

Map 13

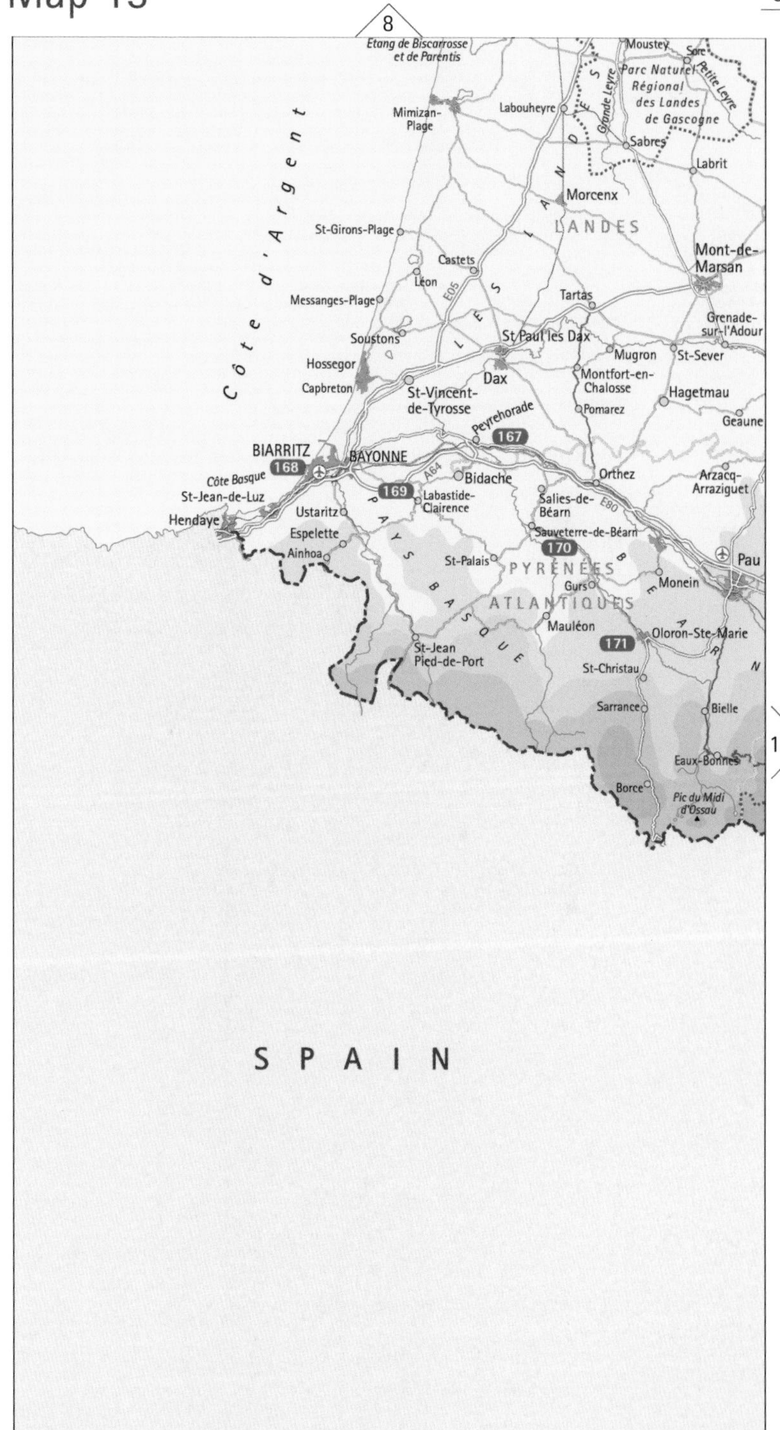
8
Etang de Biscarrosse et de Parentis
Moustey
Sore
Petite Leyre
Parc Naturel Régional des Landes de Gascogne
Mimizan-Plage
Labouheyre
Grande Leyre
Sabres
Labrit
Côte d'Argent
LES LANDES
Morcenx
LANDES
St-Girons-Plage
Castets
Léon
Mont-de-Marsan
E05
Messanges-Plage
Tartas
Grenade-sur-l'Adour
Soustons
St Paul les Dax
Mugron
St-Sever
Hossegor
Dax
Montfort-en-Chalosse
Capbreton
St-Vincent-de-Tyrosse
Hagetmau
Pomarez
Peyrehorade
Geaune
167
BIARRITZ
BAYONNE
168
Côte Basque
A64
Bidache
Orthez
Arzacq-Arraziguet
St-Jean-de-Luz
169
Labastide-Clairence
Salies-de-Béarn
E80
Hendaye
Ustaritz
PAYS BASQUE
Sauveterre-de-Béarn
Espelette
170
Ainhoa
St-Palais
PYRÉNÉES ATLANTIQUES
Pau
Gurs
Monein
BÉARN
Mauléon
Oloron-Ste-Marie
171
St-Jean Pied-de-Port
St-Christau
Sarrance
Bielle
14
Eaux-Bonnes
Borce
Pic du Midi d'Ossau
SPAIN

Map 14

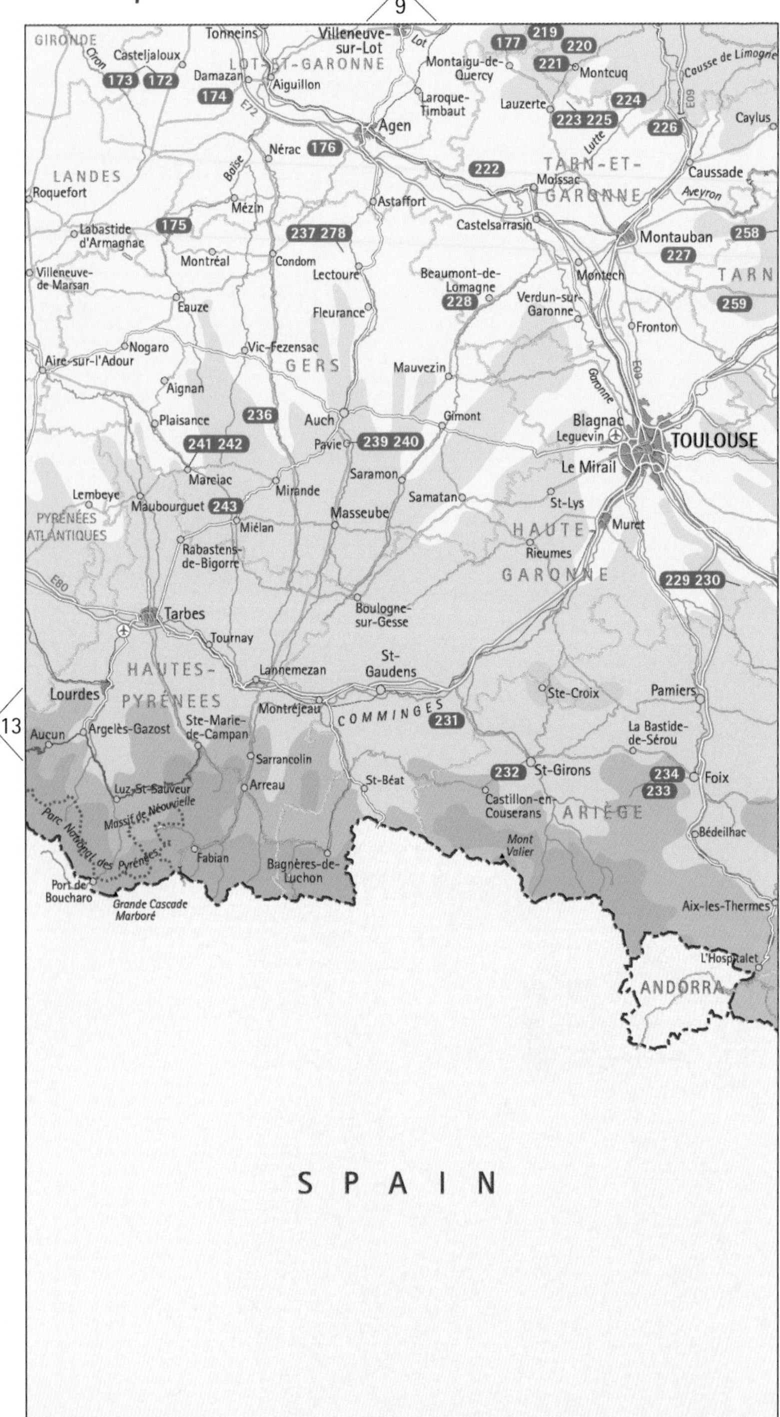
9
13
GIRONDE
Casteljaloux
173 172
Tonneins
Damazan
174
LOT-ET-GARONNE
Aiguillon
Villeneuve-sur-Lot
Lot
Montaigu-de-Quercy
177 219 220
221
Montcuq
Laroque-Timbaut
Lauzerte
224
223 225
226
Causse de Limogne
Caylus
Agen
Nérac 176
LANDES
Roquefort
Mézin
Astaffort
222
TARN-ET-GARONNE
Moissac
Caussade
Aveyron
Labastide d'Armagnac
175
237 278
Castelsarrasin
Montauban
258
227
Montréal
Condom
Lectoure
Villeneuve-de-Marsan
Beaumont-de-Lomagne
228
Montech
TARN
Verdun-sur-Garonne
259
Eauze
Fleurance
Fronton
Nogaro
Aire-sur-l'Adour
Vic-Fezensac
GERS
Mauvezin
Aignan
Plaisance
236
Auch
Gimont
Blagnac
Leguevin
TOULOUSE
241 242
Pavie
239 240
Le Mirail
Marciac
Saramon
Lembeye
Mirande
Samatan
St-Lys
PYRÉNÉES ATLANTIQUES
Maubourguet 243
Masseube
Muret
Miélan
HAUTE-GARONNE
Rieumes
Rabastens-de-Bigorre
229 230
Tarbes
Boulogne-sur-Gesse
Tournay
Lannemezan
St-Gaudens
HAUTES-PYRÉNÉES
Lourdes
Ste-Croix
Pamiers
Montréjeau
COMMINGES
231
Aucun
Argelès-Gazost
Ste-Marie-de-Campan
La Bastide-de-Sérou
Sarrancolin
Arreau
St-Béat
232
St-Girons
234
233
Foix
Luz-St-Sauveur
Massif de Néouvielle
Castillon-en-Couserans
ARIÈGE
Parc National des Pyrénées
Mont Valier
Bédeilhac
Fabian
Bagnères-de-Luchon
Port de Boucharo
Grande Cascade Marboré
Aix-les-Thermes
L'Hospitalet
ANDORRA
SPAIN

Map 15

10
16
Villefranche-de-Rouergue
Aveyron
Gorges de l'Aveyron
Rieupeyroux
Rodez
AVEYRON
Sévérac-le-Château
Causse de Sauveterre
LOZÈRE
Mt Lozère
Ste-Enimie
Ispagnac
Florac
La Malène
Causse Méjean
Parc National des Cévennes
Corniche des Cévennes
Meyrueis
Le Rozier
Causse Noir
Mont Aigoual
Millau
Hérault
GARD
Cassagnes-Begonhés
Cordes-sur-Ciel
Carmaux
Valence-d'Albigeois
Tarn
St-Affrique
Roquefort-sur-Soulzon
Causse du Larzac
Le Vigan
Ganges
Gaillac
Albi
Alban
St-Sernin-sur-R
Teillet
Réalmont
TARN
Camarès
Mas-de-Londres
St-Guilhem-le-Désert
Graulhet
Lavaur
Lacaune
Monts de Lacaune
Agout
La Salvetat-sur-Agout
Gignac
Bédarieux
Castres
Parc Naturel Régional du Haut Languedoc
Olargues
Jaur
Orb
Villeneuvette
HÉRAULT
MONTPELLIER
Puylaurens
Mazamet
St-Pons-de-Thomières
Pézenas
Montagne Noire
Pic de Nore
Mèze
Frontignan
Sète
Castelnaudary
Canal du Midi
Orbiel
Capestang
Béziers
Le Somail
Nissan-lez-Enserune
Le Cap d'Agde
Carcassonne
Valras-Plage
Aude
Lézignan-Corbières
NARBONNE
Mirepoix
AUDE
Gruissan
Limoux
A9
Alet-les-Bains
Port-la-Nouvelle
Lavelanet
Couiza
Corbières
Pic de Bugarach
Quillan
St-Paul-de-Fenouillet
Leucate-Plage
Salses
Maury
Port-Barcarès
Montaillou
Fenouillèdes
Rivesaltes
Agly
Canet-en-Roussillon
PERPIGNAN
Têt
Ille-sur-Têt
PYRÉNÉES
Prades
St Cyprien-Plage
Elne
Côte Vermeille
Pic Carlit
Villefranche-de-Conflent
Argelès-sur-Mer
ROUSSILLON
Argelès-Plage
Font-Romeu
Mont Louis
Pic du Canigou
Tech
Le Boulou
N114
Puigcerda
Prats-de-Molo
Arles
Céret
Banyuls-sur-Mer
Cerbère
SPAIN

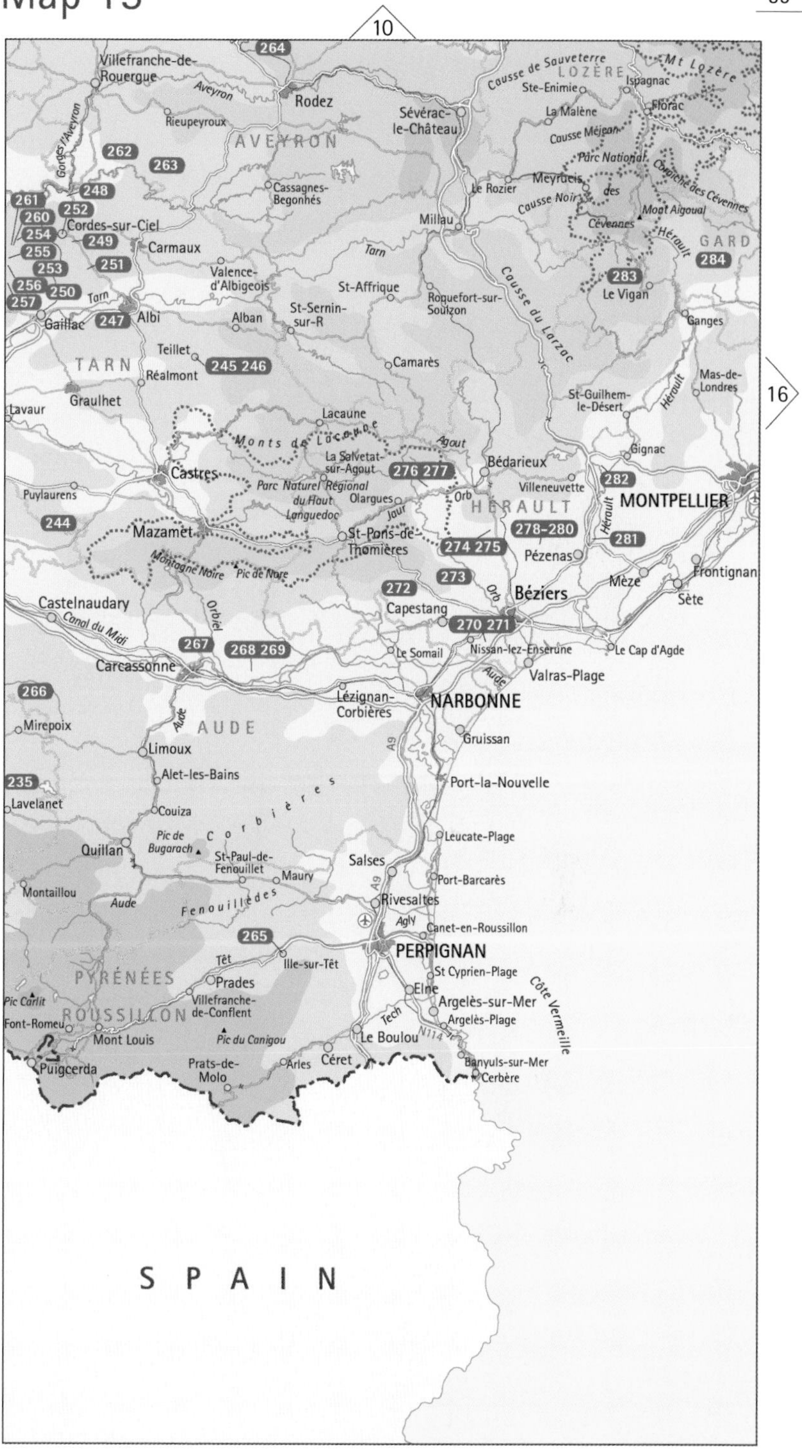

Map 16

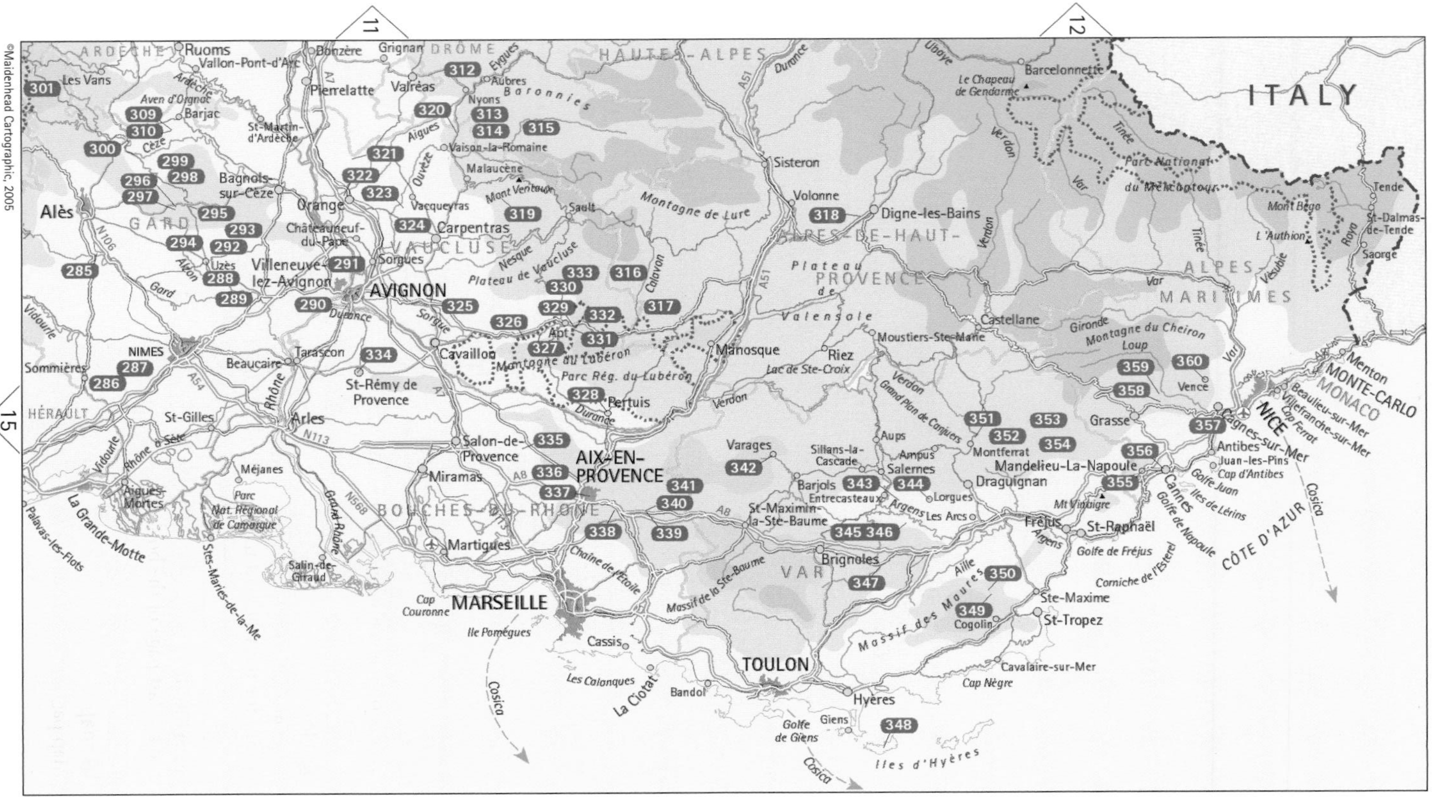

ITALY
MONTE-CARLO
MONACO
Menton
Beaulieu-sur-Mer
Villefranche-sur-Mer
Cap Ferrat
NICE
Cagnes-sur-Mer
Antibes
Juan-les-Pins
Cap d'Antibes
Golfe Juan
Iles de Lérins
Cannes
Golfe de Napoule
CÔTE D'AZUR
Cosica
Corniche de l'Esterel
St-Raphaël
Golfe de Fréjus
Fréjus
Ste-Maxime
St-Tropez
Cavalaire-sur-Mer
Cap Nègre
Cogolin
Massif des Maures
Iles d'Hyères
Hyères
Giens
Golfe de Giens
TOULON
Bandol
La Ciotat
Cassis
Les Calanques
MARSEILLE
Ile Pomègues
Cap Couronne
Martigues
Miramas
Salon-de-Provence
AIX-EN-PROVENCE
Chaîne de l'Etoile
Massif de la Ste-Baume
St-Maximin-la-Ste-Baume
Brignoles
VAR
Barjols
Varages
Entrecasteaux
Salernes
Sillans-la-Cascade
Aups
Ampus
Lorgues
Les Arcs
Draguignan
Montferrat
Mandelieu-La-Napoule
Grasse
Vence
Montagne du Cheiron
Loup
Castellane
Moustiers-Ste-Marie
Grand Plan de Canjuers
Verdon
Riez
Lac de Ste-Croix
Plateau de Valensole
Manosque
Pertuis
Durance
Parc Rég. du Lubéron
Montagne du Lubéron
Apt
Cavaillon
Plateau de Vaucluse
Sault
Mont Ventoux
Malaucène
Carpentras
Vacqueyras
AVIGNON
Sorgues
Châteauneuf-du-Pape
Orange
Villeneuve-lez-Avignon
St-Rémy de Provence
Tarascon
Beaucaire
Arles
Grand Rhône
Salin-de-Giraud
Méjanes
Parc Nat. Régional de Camargue
Stes-Maries-de-la-Me
Aigues-Mortes
La Grande-Motte
Palavas-les-Flots
NIMES
St-Gilles
Sommières
Vidourle
Alès
Les Vans
Uzès
Bagnols-sur-Cèze
St-Martin-d'Ardèche
Vallon-Pont-d'Arc
Ruoms
Barjac
Aven d'Orgnac
Pierrelatte
Bollène
Grignan
Valréas
Nyons
Vaison-la-Romaine
Baronnies
Montagne de Lure
Sisteron
Volonne
Digne-les-Bains
Barcelonnette
Le Chapeau de Gendarme
Parc National du Mercantour
Mont Bégo
Tende
St-Dalmas-de-Tende
Saorge
Roya
Tinée
Vésubie
ALPES-MARITIMES
ALPES-DE-HAUT-PROVENCE
HAUTES-ALPES
DRÔME
VAUCLUSE
BOUCHES-DU-RHÔNE
GARD
ARDÈCHE
HÉRAULT
12
11
15

How to use this book

1 region

2 abbreviated addresss
Not to be used for correspondence

3 write up
Written by us after inspection

4 italics
Mention other relevant details e.g. B&B also, children over 8 welcome.

5 sleeps
The lower number indicates how many adults can comfortably sleep here. The higher is the maximum number of people that can be accommodated.

6 rooms
We give total numbers of each type of bedroom e.g. double, triple, and total numbers of bathrooms. We give wc details only when they are separate from bathrooms.

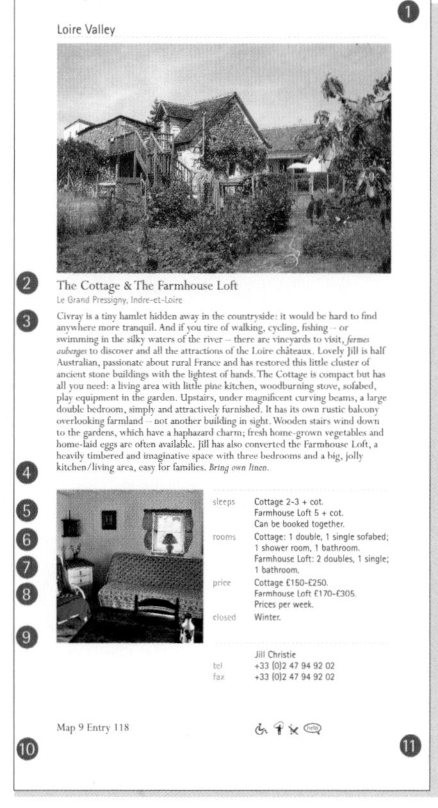

1 Loire Valley

2 The Cottage & The Farmhouse Loft
Le Grand Pressigny, Indre-et-Loire

3 Civray is a tiny hamlet hidden away in the countryside: it would be hard to find anywhere more tranquil. And if you tire of walking, cycling, fishing -- or swimming in the silky waters of the river – there are vineyards to visit, *fermes auberges* to discover and all the attractions of the Loire châteaux. Lovely Jill is half Australian, passionate about rural France and has restored this little cluster of ancient stone buildings with the lightest of hands. The Cottage is compact but has all you need: a living area with little pine kitchen, woodburning stove, sofabed, play equipment in the garden. Upstairs, under magnificent curving beams, a large double bedroom, simply and attractively furnished. It has its own rustic balcony overlooking farmland -- not another building in sight. Wooden stairs wind down to the gardens, which have a haphazard charm; fresh home-grown vegetables and home-laid eggs are often available. Jill has also converted the Farmhouse Loft, a heavily timbered and imaginative space with three bedrooms and a big, jolly kitchen/living area, easy for families.
4 *Bring own linen.*

5 sleeps Cottage 2-3 + cot.
Farmhouse Loft 5 + cot.
Can be booked together.
6 rooms Cottage: 1 double, 1 single sofabed;
1 shower room, 1 bathroom.
Farmhouse Loft: 2 doubles, 1 single;
1 bathroom.
7 price Cottage £150-£250.
8 Farmhouse Loft £170-£305.
Prices per week.
closed Winter.
9

Jill Christie
tel +33 (0)2 47 94 92 02
fax +33 (0)2 47 94 92 02

Map 9 Entry 118

10 11

7 price
The price shown is per week and the range covers low season to high season; remember high season can be winter in some areas. Some owners don't include 'extra' costs, such as heating or cleaning, in this price so please check before booking.

8 arrival
This is only given when it is not Saturday.

9 closed
If we give no details the gîte is rarely closed. When given in months, this means for the whole of the named months and the time in between.

10 symbols
see the last page of the book for an explanation.

11 map & entry numbers
Map page number; entry number.

photo corel images

the north
picardy
champagne – ardenne
lorraine
franche comté
burgundy
paris – île de france

La Petite Maison

Escalles, Pas-de-Calais

The Boutroys, retired from farming, live just over the way and speak some English; Monsieur is the local mayor and Madame manages the guests' quarters with easy, smiling professionalism. The feel is fittingly traditional for a 19th-century French village house: solid, dark wood country furniture in perfect condition, bold beams, pretty pictures, touches of floral and French-frilly. The three upstairs bedrooms are carpeted and sloping-ceilinged; beds have good mattresses, bathrooms, one ground floor, are neatly to the point. Downstairs is roomy with the kitchen/dining/sitting areas separated by a wall with a fireplace on one side and, on the other, a gas cooking range in the old open hearth. Immediate surrounds are: a gravelled front yard, with a wooden gate protecting from the road, and a big garden to the side leaning gently against the hill (plus barbecue and garden furniture). It's a three-minute walk across fields to the coast and cliffs, the village restaurant – seafood a speciality – is temptingly near, a shop and market six kilometres away. A child-friendly, good-value address. *B&B also.*

sleeps	8-10.
rooms	4: 2 doubles, 2 family rooms for 3; 2 bathrooms, 2 separate wcs.
price	€550-€630 per week.
arrival	Friday.

Jacqueline & Marc Boutroy
tel +33 (0)3 21 85 27 75
fax +33 (0)3 21 85 27 75
web lagrandmaison.chez.tiscali.fr

Le Vert Bois

Neuville sous Montreuil, Pas-de-Calais

A row of rustling poplar trees and beyond, fields to the horizon. You are deep in the Picardian countryside. The red brick and white tiled outbuilding – originally the bread oven – stands in handsome contrast to this verdant backdrop; it forms part of an 18th-century walled farm estate and there's a feeling of timeless solidity. Indeed, the owners, who live next door in the 'master house', are fifth generation farmers. Inside, honey-coloured floorboards, antique wardrobes and pale walls give the bedrooms a fresh and rustic simplicity. The downstairs shower room, like the kitchen, is neat, spotless and has all you need. In the brick and stone-walled living room there's a comfy lack of sophistication – well-scrubbed dining table, friendly old-fashioned armchairs, a fire for chillier days. The courtyard with its large central pond – walled, shallow, with ducks – is shared but you have your own space to sit out in and the owners are friendly, unassuming and unobtrusive. Visit medieval Montreuil, seaside Le Touquet or enjoy long green walks on your doorstep. There's little to disturb the peace. *B&B also.*

sleeps	2-6 + cot.
rooms	2: 1 double, 1 family room for 4; 1 bathroom, 1 separate wc.
price	€300-€400 per week.

Étienne & Véronique Bernard
tel +33 (0)3 21 06 09 41
fax +33 (0)3 21 06 09 41
email etienne.bernard6@wanadoo.fr
web gite.montreuil.online.fr

Rue du Général Potez

Montreuil sur Mer, Pas-de-Calais

Pistachio ice cream or lime sorbet? This mouthwateringly pretty town cottage looks good enough to eat. Inside everything is cute, colourful and cosy. And small. The downstairs space, with its exposed timber and brickwork, has a 'snug' of navy blue and striped chairs and sofa while, tucked behind, is the 'dining end': a floral-covered table and pale blue chairs. A slip of a kitchen, in sparkling white and blue, has all the essentials and you won't mind washing up by hand. Upstairs, a mixture of white walls, pitch pine, simple furniture and modern lighting lends a fresh cottage feel. The second double bed hides on a mezzanine level; a single bed is tucked into a corner. It is clean, tidy, inviting. In a raised, cobbled terrace of 16th- and 17th-century houses, yards from Montreuil sur Mer's town walls, you step out of the door into history. Explore the medieval streets, browse the Saturday market and, in summer, catch the *son et lumière*. Then, after a pre-prandial drink on the tiny patio, set off for one of the town's many restaurants.

sleeps	4-5.
rooms	2: 1 family room for 3, 1 double on mezzanine; 1 bathroom.
price	€350-€400 per week.

Étienne & Véronique Bernard
tel +33 (0)3 21 06 09 41
fax +33 (0)3 21 06 09 41
email etienne.bernard6@wanadoo.fr
web gite.montreuil.online.fr

Halinghen Home

Halinghen, Pas-de-Calais

This would be a first-rate holiday home for two or more families – and just across the Channel: you could be here in time for lunch. The huge garden and orchard have play space and swings; ping pong, table football, snooker and games keep everyone happy on rainy days. The big light rooms have a homely English feel with their cosy medley of furniture – it's perfect for children. From the open-plan living area, French windows spill you onto the terrace, scented with honeysuckle on summer evenings. Beds are comfortable, bathrooms are carpeted, there are spectacular country views from every window. Merelina swapped London for this gentle French village and lives in one self-contained side of the house. She is warm and helpful and will rustle up a celebration cake on request. Hardelot Plage is a 15-minute drive: its wide beaches, fringed with sand dunes and pines, have turned it into a popular sand-yachting centre. Le Touquet, too, is nearby, and there are over 100 kilometres of gorgeous sandy beaches on the Côte d'Opale.
Babysitting & hairdressing available. Flexible length of stay. B&B also.

sleeps	8-17.
rooms	4 (+ 2): 1 double with bunks & wc, 3 family rooms for 3; 2 shower rooms. (2 additional doubles on request).
price	€1,200 per week; €380 for three days in low season.
arrival	Flexible.

Merelina Ponsonby
tel +33 (0)3 21 83 04 80
email merelina@wanadoo.fr
web www.france-short-breaks.co.uk

Le Thurel

Rue, Somme

A purist's paradise. The exterior of the little pavilion, built to house a previous owner's mother, is 19th-century stately; inside, it is a minimalist's dream. This will delight all those who enjoy clutter-free living, sobriety and space. Scrubbed floorboards and perfect white walls are enriched by the odd splash of colour from ethnic rug or table cover. The huge sitting/dining room, with open fire, is a symphony of ivory, white and cream in beautiful contrast with the elegant French grey window frames, the antique dining table and chairs and the odd Flemish oil painting. There are views of the courtyard and a stunning red-brick barn to the front; behind is the large, leafy, gracious garden which you share with the Bree-Leclefs' B&B guests. There's boules, too. Bedrooms are white (of course) with fabulously luxurious linen. Glamorous and welcoming, Patrick and Claudine go out of their way to initiate you into the local lore. He is an interior architect, she is a talented gardener and cook and her suppers are open to all guests; just book. *Cleaning charge. B&B also.*

sleeps	6.
rooms	3: 1 double, 1 twin, 1 family room for 3; 1 bathroom, 1 separate wc. Extra bed available.
price	€926 per week.
closed	January.

Claudine & Patrick Van Bree-Leclef
tel +33 (0)3 22 25 04 44
fax +33 (0)3 22 25 79 69
email lethurel.relais@libertysurf.fr
web www.lethurel.com

Les Gîtes de l'Étang

Mons en Laonnois, Aisne

A fine estate set in 50 acres of wooded parkland with majestic trees, vast lawns and a delightful lake. The old coach house has been converted into two roomy gîtes, neat as new pins. Its original doors are now vast windows, the style is simple, uncluttered and stylish, light creams and honey-whites give a warm, cosy feel. So do the classic country bedrooms: padded bedheads, pretty floral bed linen and park views; bathrooms are small, neat and clean. Downstairs, the large open-plan sitting/dining room has all you'll need: sofas and armchairs, a white-tiled floor and a working fire, a compact corner kitchen, modern with all the bits. Big glass doors open to a terrace with table and chairs, separated from your neighbours by a big new fence – a fine place to eat out. The owners, courteous, welcoming and available, live in the main house close by. They lived in England – he is a retired NATO official – and speak the language well. Beyond the gates is the pretty village, holding all you need. Keep going and you'll discover Laon, its medieval quarters and remarkable oxen-guarded cathedral. *B&B also.*

sleeps 2 gîtes for 6.
rooms Gîte 1: 2 doubles, 1 twin; 2 shower rooms.
Gîte 2: 1 double, 2 twins; 2 shower rooms.
price €310-€440 each per week.

Mme P Woillez
tel +33 (0)3 23 24 18 58
fax +33 (0)3 23 24 44 52
email gitemons@aol.com
web www.gitenfrance.com

Verneuil – Gîte de Moussy

Vendresse-Beaulne, Aisne

It's deep in the country, surrounded by copses and fields – a peaceful, isolated little farmhouse. After the devastation of WWI, when all that remained of the village were the wash-house and church (a triumph for cleanliness and godliness?), this farm was the only one to be rebuilt. Play at being the farmer and his wife as you gaze on grazing cattle and acres of wheat, barley, peas and sunflowers. There are seats, swings and a barbecue in the garden; the outbuildings are used for farm equipment. Your house is bigger than it looks, with fresh, white-walled rooms and fairly minimalist furnishing; the whole place has a new and spotless feel. One end of the living room has pretty, original tiling and rustic dining furniture; the other, dark polished boards, an inviting sofa and wicker chairs. Black and white floor tiles gleam on the hall floor and the square, airy kitchen is designed to provide all you need. Upstairs are simple, pleasant bedrooms and a plain bathroom. There's a Sunday morning market nearby and a whole range of war museums, monuments and cemeteries to visit.

sleeps	6.
rooms	3: 1 double, 2 twins; 1 bathroom, 1 separate wc.
price	€230-€390 per week.

	Bruno & Blandine Cailliez
tel	+33 (0)3 23 24 41 44
fax	+33 (0)3 23 24 43 55
email	blandine.cailliez@wanadoo.fr
web	www.gitedeverneuil.fr.st

Ferme de Ressons

Mont St Martin, Aisne

Come for soothing views of smooth pastures and arable expanses; feel the simple country lives which have been played out within these old walls. There's nothing fancy about this semi-detached farmworker's cottage; it has ancient beams, woodburning stove in brick fireplace, almost secret access and quiet neighbours. Gather round the old square table in your simple but very well-equipped kitchen with its incongruously grand Henri II dresser – or join Valérie and Jean-Paul and their B&B guests for excellent dinners in the farmhouse across the gardens; just book in advance. The cottage's rooms have an eclectic mix of antique and modern pieces and colourful soft furnishings. The double bedroom is downstairs, the twins up, all are cosily carpeted and share a bathroom on the ground floor. The hilly forests of the Montagne de Reims provide unexpectedly rich walking – in sharp contrast to the flat vineyards – the beech woods at Verzy are 500 years old. And if you fancy fishing on the lake, ask Valérie about permits and rods before you arrive. The market, restaurants and shops are two miles off. *B&B also.*

sleeps	6.
rooms	3: 1 double, 2 twins; 1 bathroom.
price	€305-€380 per week.

Valérie & Jean-Paul Ferry
tel +33 (0)3 23 74 71 00
fax +33 (0)3 23 74 28 88

Le Point du Jour

Mont St Martin, Aisne

Valérie, architect and mother, has left her creative stamp on this house's attractively simple big spacious rooms. And the long, rolling vistas stretch from the edge of the garden and over the arable fields to infinity… just stride out into it all. A mile from the Ferrys' farm and B&B, the 19th-century village house exudes light, homeliness and sober good taste. The big living/dining room is generously furnished, a carved buffet holds white crockery and there are easy chairs, a piano and French windows that open onto a south-facing terrace. Upstairs, parquet floors, pretty cotton curtains, good mattresses, an ornately carved 19th-century Portuguese bed. One slopey-ceilinged twin has country-style beds, another has pine floorboards and oriental rugs; the bathroom has snowy-white tiles. Your hosts are ready with help and advice and will advise you to visit for one of the many champagne houses in Reims, a 20-minute drive, for a tasting of the bubbly stuff. Those of Mumm, Taittinger and Piper-Heidseick allow you to join (paying) tours without an appointment, including a *dégustation. B&B also.*

sleeps	6.
rooms	3: 1 double, 2 twins; 1 bathroom, 1 shower room, 2 separate wcs.
price	€350-€420 per week.

Valérie & Jean-Paul Ferry
tel +33 (0)3 23 74 71 00
fax +33 (0)3 23 74 28 88

Gîte de Cramant

Cramant, Marne

A simple little cottage in a village in Champagne. It is distinctly homely, French without the frills, a little like a doll's house – one you can live in very comfortably. The Charbonniers, who do B&B on the spot, are a delightful couple and work hard to keep everyone happy; you may even arrange to have breakfast with them if you prefer. Cosy bedrooms are upstairs and share a neat little bathroom; the double comes in yellow and blue and has a couple of beams, the twin has small beds dressed in patchwork quilts, perfect for children. Downstairs, an open-plan kitchen/living room with a tiled floor and neatly beamed ceiling – simply decorated, typically French. There's a round dining table and a decorative fireplace, too, and lots of pretty china. Outside, a postage-stamp lawn is flanked on one side by an old stone wall up which creepers clamber, and there are chairs, a café table and a barbecue, so you can eat outside. Epernay is seven kilometres away and has a fine market and lots of champagne; if you overdo it, head to Reims and its cathedral to beg forgiveness. *Babysitting available. B&B also.*

sleeps	4-5.
rooms	2: 1 double, 1 twin, 1 sofabed in sitting room; 1 bathroom.
price	€300 per week.

Éric & Sylvie Charbonnier
tel +33 (0)3 26 57 95 34
email eric-sylvie@wanadoo.fr
web www.ericsylvie.com

Auprès de l'Église

Oyes, Marne

New Zealanders Michael and Glenis first discovered Auprès de l'Église 10 years ago. Now they own it, share it with guests, do excellent *table d'hôtes* and are planning a pool. Thanks to a previous artist owner, the 19th-century house has a very special atmosphere, is full of surprises – some walls are unadorned but for the mason's scribbles! – and has been gorgeously restored. The two upstairs bedrooms and bathroom are separated by a fabulous wall of bookcases and an attic stair, the ground floor has a French country feel and harmonious colours. Kitchen, dining and living rooms merge peacefully into one airy space that overlooks Oyes church and the courtyard. Sit out here in the sun and sip the wonderful local champagne as you watch the barbecue smoulder. Quirky *brocante* abounds yet the comforts are resolutely modern. Two more rooms lead off the hall, with crisp white cotton and huge beds. Charming Sezanne is a 20-minute drive and the marshlands (now drained but an unhappy surprise for the soldiers of the First World War) are a birdwatchers' paradise. *B&B also.*

sleeps	8.
rooms	4: 2 doubles, 1 twin/double, 1 twin; 1 bathroom, 1 shower room downstairs.
price	€800-€1,500. Heating supp. €70 in winter. Prices per week.
arrival	Saturday, but flexible.

	Glenis Foster
tel	+44 (0)780 8905233
email	enquiries@aupresdeleglise.com
web	www.aupresdeleglise.com

Cottage Le Logis de Beaulieu

Beaulieu en Argonne, Meuse

Miles from the madding crowd. A hilltop village in the heart of the Meuse where time is sleepy, style is quaint, nothing untoward happens and it's 12 kilometres to the nearest supermarket. This half-timbered house with its wooden shutters and cottagey garden fits the scene… but step inside and it's surprisingly up to date. Large bedrooms are prettily decked out with draped curtains and embroidered bedspreads. Choose between brass bedstead, wooden sleigh or four-poster – with furniture to match. Two bathrooms to share, and views that stretch over countryside or enchanting village. The beamed dining/sitting room, although narrow and without a fireplace, has plenty of squashy armchairs and a handsome dresser and table: a place for posh meals. Mostly you'll gather in the well-equipped farmhouse kitchen with its sturdy oak furniture and pretty pottery made specially for the house. Useful extras include barbecue, games, telephone… and the baker's van every morning. Country walks, wartime cemeteries; this is a deep-country retreat, thoughtfully designed, astonishingly good value.

sleeps	8.
rooms	4 doubles; 1 shower room, 1 bathroom, 2 separate wcs.
price	€550-€850 per week.

Marie-José & René Eichenauer

tel	+33 (0)3 29 85 70 21
email	rene.eichenauer@wanadoo.fr
web	www.labessiere.com

Château Andelot

Andelot lès St Amour, Jura

Winding narrow roads lead higher and higher, through woods and foothills, until you reach the top... a jaw-dropping view. Conical towers, a mighty keep, thick-walled ramparts spread along a cliff top, the wooded valley falls sheer away. Pass through the monumental entrance portal and the adventure continues: the 12th-century castle is as dramatic inside as out. The bedrooms – main château or rampart buildings – are grand but beautifully uncluttered spaces for antiques, fine fabrics, cool tiles, rich rugs and lavish bedcovers. Bathrooms are as luxurious as a starry hotel. Most have million-dollar views over plunging valleys to the Jura mountains, the Swiss border – and Mont Blanc on a good day. Why rush to rise? Why, indeed. No need to make breakfast, or dinner; the château comes with staff – friendly and helpful. Eat in the vaulted dining room below the vast, beamed, tapestry-hung drawing room; retire to plump sofas, soft carpeting, old oils on the walls. Tennis court, swimming pool, formal garden and terrace, this is the place for celebrations and friends grandly reunited. Unforgettable. *B&B also.*

sleeps	12-14.
rooms	6: 4 doubles, 1 double with sofabed, 1 twin; 6 bathrooms.
price	Entire château €6,400-€6,900; part of château €3,000-€3,250. Prices per week.
closed	November-April.

Harry Lammot Belin
tel +33 (0)3 84 85 41 49
fax +33 (0)3 84 85 46 74
email info@chateauandelot.com
web www.chateauandelot.com

La Maison Tupinier

Cluny, Saône-et-Loire

A vast apartment for two or four in a vastly civilised town. Luc owns an antique shop and lives in this 16th-century judge's house. He has the first floor, you have the second, and there's a bakery on the ground floor for croissants. A spiral stone stair leads up to your stately, elegant and utterly charming quarters: lofty ceilings with decorated beams, terracotta floors, a Louis XIV fireplace, a scalloped wash basin. A large, light hall opens to the living room, stunningly elegant with pale sofabed on seagrass floor, an armoire to guard the linen, a walnut dining table under windows framed by toile de Jouy. The master bedroom has perfect proportions and is painted the colour of corn; the compact kitchen has ornate tiles and a cream central table; one bathroom has an *œil de bœuf* window and a radiator for your towels. On a lower floor a door leads onto a delightfully secluded gallery that looks onto Luc's courtyard and garden: the ideal spot for those breakfast croissants. It is surprisingly quiet in the centre of this venerable old town. *Free parking nearby. No washing machine. Central heating. B&B also.*

sleeps	2-4.
rooms	2 doubles, 1 sofabed in sitting room; 2 bathrooms.
price	€750-€850 per week. B&B €120 per night for 2.
arrival	Flexible.
closed	January-February.

	Luc du Mesnil du Buisson
tel	+33 (0)3 85 59 27 67
mobile	+33 (0)6 26 86 85 00
email	luc_dumesnil@hotmail.com
web	www.lamaisontupinier.com

Le Nid – Rouge-Gorge, Le Pinson, La Chouette, The Stables

Château, Saône-et-Loire

Another artist-owner, another dreamy place, an 18th-century Burgundian farmhouse that divides neatly into three apartments. There is an understated elegance, as if everything has been designed, but quietly so. Wander at will: here are old stone floors, limestone walls, high ceilings, colour added in small doses – a crisp sense of light and space. In the largest living room, a cream sofa, two blue armchairs, books, candles, clever lighting, a big fireplace. Two apartments have kitchenettes; Rouge-Gorge's kitchen has table and chairs to serve a multitude, and every modern thing. A broad stone stair leads from here to a hallway and delightful bedrooms. Good art hangs on the walls – sketches, old oils, watercolours – while Karen's sculpture is dotted about the grounds. The pool its loungers and lawn bathe in sunlight. Beyond, fields and woodland stretch across the hills. This part of France has been compared to Tuscany, only it's less busy, and your hosts, who do B&B in the big house next door, will cheerfully help you discover the region – and give cookery lessons in French. *B&B also.*

sleeps	RG 4. LP 2-6. LC 2-4. Main house (RG, LP & LC) sleeps 10-11 + 2 cots. Stables (separate) 5 + 2 children.
rooms	RG: 2 doubles; 2 bathrooms. LP: 1 twin, 2 sofas; 1 bath, 1 shower. LC: 1 double, 1 sofa; 1 bath. Stables: 2 doubles, 1 single, 1 twin on mezzanine; 2 baths.
price	RG €690-€795. LP €495-€645. LC €425-€535. Main house €1,500-€1,800. Stables €645-€795. Prices per week.

Marc & Karen Keiser
tel +33 (0)3 85 59 18 02
fax +33 (0)3 85 59 86 98
email info@lenid-france.com
web www.lenid-france.com

Abbaye de la Ferté

St Ambreuil, Saône-et-Loire

The Thenards have been here since the French Revolution; they not only kept their heads but their château too. It is a jaw-dropper, with ornate arched windows and a wonderfully aristocratic feel. You are in the old stables, once the mill; behind the house water spills over the weir and into the lake. You can fish here, even swim… or walk your socks off in the château's gorgeous grounds and discover the ancient abbey. The setting is impossibly pretty, with sunlight filtering through the graceful branches of tall trees and bouncing off water lilies at anchor on the lake. The gîte – attractive, uncluttered, welcoming – is a great little spot for a family stay. You have exposed beams, wooden floors, generous windows; the double bedroom, reached via an outdoor stair, has an old armoire; the long, thin triple room comes in pretty yellows with beds running against the walls on both sides. There's a kitchen for eager cooks and a terrace on which to sit and relish the results. Venture beyond the gates and you'll find horses and bikes to ride – or discover Beaune, and a glass of something special. *B&B also.*

sleeps	4-5.
rooms	2: 1 double, 1 triple; 1 shower room.
price	€331-€618 per week.

Jacques & Virginie Thenard

tel +33 (0)3 85 44 17 96

fax +33 (0)3 85 44 17 96

email thenardjacques@aol.com

web www.abbayeferte.com

La Brulardière

Santenay, Côte-d'Or

The old house in Santeray, in the family since the time of Agincourt, used to form part of a wine-growing estate. The garden at the back – which you may wander – still leads into vineyards. Your quarters, in the old vaulted cellars, are blissfully cool; your courtyard is guarded by 17th-century buttresses and a rare octagonal pigeonnier. Enter from the street into a cool, calm space. The ceiling is lofty, the paintwork cream, the floor tiles terracotta, the spot-lighting diffuse – and there's natural light from front and back. Furniture is discreet: a small sofa in green checks, a big old armoire in the corner, good prints on the walls. The bedroom is vaulted, the beds are firm, the sheets and towels changed during your stay. There's a good, modern, well-equipped kitchen too. Madame is charming, offering guests a welcome aperitif and a few words of English. All around you, vineyards stretching as far as the eye can see (those Burgundy wines will bewitch you) and lashings of history and culture. Oh, and flawless cooking at the celebrated Lameloise in the very next village.

sleeps	2.
rooms	1 double; 1 bathroom.
price	€450 per week.
arrival	Monday.
closed	15 September-15 May.

Mme Claude Reny
tel +33 (0)3 80 20 64 51
fax +33 (0)3 80 20 64 51
email jacques.reny@wanadoo.fr
web www.brulardiere.com

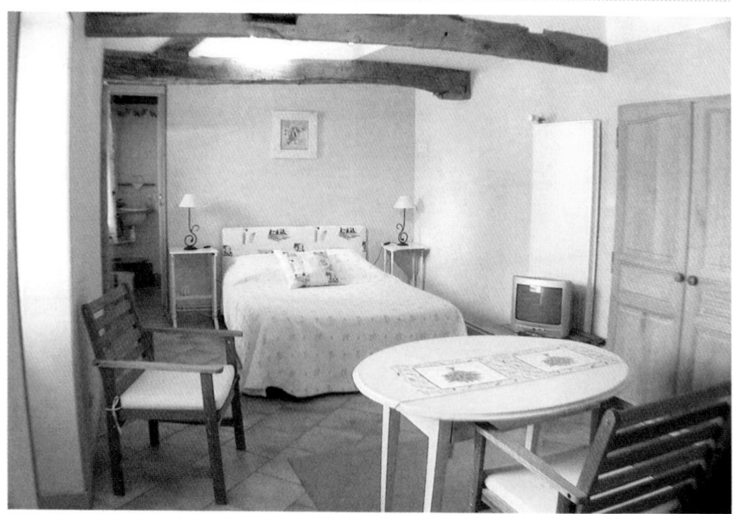

La Closerie de Gilly

Gilly lès Citeaux, Côte-d'Or

To the back of the lovely pink house with green shutters – sold off during the French Revolution, later turned into a village school – is this peaceful, country-simple studio for two. You have all the necessities but none of the frills: a light-filled room – cool terracotta underfoot, characterful beams above – a generous, all-white shower room and a cheerfully equipped kitchenette. There are a table and chairs, a big firm bed, an old wardrobe, white crockery, heated towel rails, sunflower tiles. Add a small walled barbecue garden, privacy and peace and this is bliss for two. Beyond lie the grounds, delightful with centuries-old trees and nurtured lawns, and a new heated pool, yours to share. Madame has her feet firmly on the ground and her head full of plans; she does B&B in the big house and is proud that the village lies in the very centre of the Côte d'Or – birthplace (arguably) of the best wines in the world. Ask her about the local *initiation à l'oenologie* and she will happily book you in on an illuminating tour. *B&B also.*

sleeps	2.
rooms	1 double; 1 shower room.
price	€375-€400 per week.

Sandrine & André Lanaud

tel +33 (0)3 80 62 87 74
email info@closerie-gilly.com
web www.closerie-gilly.com

Château de Créancey

Créancey, Côte-d'Or

In the grounds of a breathtakingly beautiful château, with a moat running past the kitchen door, is this noble, listed 14th-century tower. Fiona and her French husband Bruno have restored it with impeccable taste and passionate respect for the original materials and character. Arrow slits – surprisingly light-giving – are your windows; an old wooden staircase twists its crooked way upstairs; French country furniture, original *tommettes*, ochre walls and an open log fire create a mood of elegance and charm. There's a wonderful working fireplace in the living/dining room, and ancient beams in the double bedroom upstairs. The small oak-fitted kitchen, beautifully equipped with country pots and pans, leads into the château courtyard where ducks stroll. Eat on the terrace by the moat to the sound of hoopoes as you quaff those Burgundy wines – and feel free to roam. Fiona is delightful, does B&B in the château and will advise you on the region: discover the wine-tasting châteaux of the rugged Côte d'Or on foot or by bike, and Dijon, and Beaune. *Because of moat, children must be able to swim. B&B also.*

sleeps	4.
rooms	2: 1 double, 1 twin; 1 shower room.
price	€600-€720 per week.

Fiona de Wulf

tel +33 (0)3 80 90 57 50

fax +33 (0)3 80 90 57 51

email chateau@creancey.com

web www.creancey.com

Rose Cottage

Painblanc, Côte-d'Or

The best of Burgundy: vineyards, gastronomic eateries and the Morvan National Park are within easy reach. Here in tranquil Painblanc (literally, 'white bread') you get a taste of French village life – the main event of the week is the visit of the butcher's and baker's vans. Prettily draped in wisteria and roses, this 19th-century stone village house has been attractively restored by English owners Penny and Ben who live in a nearby village and will be there to settle you in. The centrepiece is the kitchen: sunny and homely, with a large wooden table to gather around for feasts in front of the woodburner. Logs are thoughtfully provided. The original hexagonal terracotta floor tiles (with cosy rugs), handsome oak beams and open fire are all intact, as are the endearingly sloping floors of the apricot and cream bedrooms. On the floor of the bathroom downstairs, the painted feet of humans and geese! Take lazy, long lunches under the enormous willow tree in the garden and orchard – scented with honeysuckle, roses and wisteria, replete with pond full of vocal frogs. Shop in pretty Bligny sur Ouche, a five-mile drive.

sleeps	6-7 + cot.
rooms	3: 1 double, 1 twin, 1 triple with cot; 1 bathroom, 1 shower room, 2 separate wcs.
price	€500-€675 per week.

Penny & Ben Martin
tel +33 (0)3 80 20 19 13
fax +33 (0)3 80 20 19 13
email benpenny.martin@club-internet.fr

Well Cottage

Painblanc, Côte-d'Or

So pretty here in early summer, with the cowslips, lady's smock and wild orchids. In autumn there are the golden colours of the woods and vines, and deer, red kite and buzzards to spot. Whenever you come, you'll love this 19th-century cottage, with its long lazy views over the garden to fields and the top of the tranquil village. Among a cluster of cottages and farm buildings on a quiet street, the deceptively large gîte has been attractively restored by English owners Penny and Ben. Oak beams, old and vast, dominate the large kitchen/living room which has attractive features such as a little stone alcove and a window seat. There's a modern terracotta tiled floor, primrose-yellow colours, a comfy sofa, a chaise longue and a woodburner (logs free of charge). An open oak staircase leads to simple carpeted bedrooms with sloping beamed ceilings and roof windows. The garden (with slide) is sun-filled from early morning to mid-evening in summer – a private space and you are not overlooked. Make time for some serious gastronomy – and for wine-tasting in the famous Côtes de Nuits vineyards.

sleeps	4-5.
rooms	2: 1 twin, 1 family room for 3; 1 shower room, 1 separate wc.
price	€380-€560 per week.

Penny & Ben Martin
tel +33 (0)3 80 20 19 13
fax +33 (0)3 80 20 19 13
email benpenny.martin@club-internet.fr

Domaine de La Chaux – Le Château

Alligny en Morvan, Nièvre

La Chaux is more village than domaine. Rent a small part of it – or the whole place for an anniversary or wedding. Madame de Chambure lives in the middle of it all, sparkles with energy and exercises a benign rule, delighting in bringing families and friends together. The peace enfolds you and the magnolias and ancient trees are beautiful in spring. The old hunting lodge or château (below) is where Madame herself once lived and its vast warren of rooms has barely changed over the years – in spite of the addition of new kitchen, modern plumbing and some elegant wrought-iron furniture. Two dining rooms, two salons, all with open fires: a warm, ample place for a large party. It has that wonderful French feel, with stippled, faux-marble walls, fine furniture from Louis XV onwards, polished parquet – a gentle elegance touched with eccentricity. Eleven bedrooms, several bathrooms and a dressing room share the top two storeys; views swoop over parkland and hills; you have all you could possibly need, from a library full of books to TV, table tennis and loungers.

sleeps	Château sleeps 15.
rooms	11: 3 doubles with wcs, 1 double, 7 singles; 3 bathrooms, 3 shower rooms, 3 separate wcs.
price	€2,200 per week.

Alice de Chambure

tel +33 (0)3 86 76 10 10
fax +33 (0)3 86 76 10 10
email giteslachaux@wanadoo.fr
web www.gites-lachaux.fr

Domaine de La Chaux – Moines & Roses

Alligny en Morvan, Nièvre

Moines is great fun, and its monk ish name is reflected in the décor – there's a refreshing, monastic simplicity. Bedrooms on the second floor, in a row of monks' cells, have two wash rooms between them – each graced with three unmonastic basins set in granite. Showers are downstairs on the ground floor, so you may suffer a bit... The two main bedrooms have wcs and basins en suite. It's a big, delightful space where you could happily retreat for a week with friends. Warm colours, solid beams, terracotta floors, three stairs; you have a library and a living room (above) with antique trestle tables and rush-seated, ladderback chairs. A carved statue of the Virgin Mary stands in one corner, two cream-coloured *fauteuils* pull up by the fire. And what a hearth – it's big enough to fit a small tree and belts out quite a heat on winter days. Across a small meadow is Roses (below) with four bedrooms (two in the attic) and another lovely fireplace. With its trestle table and wood-panelled walls it has a similarly medieval feel, but is smaller and suitable for six. The gardens are a delight. *Shared laundry.*

sleeps	Moines 13-18. Roses 6.
rooms	Moines: 3 doubles, 1 twin, 1 single, 1 family room for 3, 1 family room for 6; 2 shower rooms, 3 separate wcs. Roses: 1 double, 1 twin, 2 singles; 1 bathroom, 1 separate wc.
price	Moines €1,540. Roses €630. Prices per week.

Alice de Chambure
tel +33 (0)3 86 76 10 10
fax +33 (0)3 86 76 10 10
email giteslachaux@wanadoo.fr
web www.gites-lachaux.fr

Domaine de La Chaux – Chèvrefeuille & Glycines

Alligny en Morvan, Nièvre

These two gîtes are a step apart – Chèvrefeuille (Honeysuckle) with its farmhouse feel, and the more modern Glycines (Wisteria), custom-made for wheelchairs. Glycines' rooms are on the ground floor of the last stone cottage in a row of four (above). Chèvrefeuille has two storeys and a charming outside stone stair; its floors are new and tiled, its furniture a mix of country antique and new, its kitchen simple. Note, this is an outdoorsy place, where the grounds are more beautifully tended than the gîtes. But there's masses to do: table tennis on the estate, trout-fishing in crystal-clear creeks beyond, kayaking on the Cure. You are right in the middle of the Morvan National Park, a wonderful wild area distinguished by vast forests of beech and oak, moorland and lakes. Criss-crossed by rapids, the area is a dream for white-water enthusiasts. The walking, too, is exceptional. Take maps, go off the beaten track and look out for red and roe deer, wild boar and badgers, buzzards and woodpeckers. In the gentler, more pastoral north, there are carpets of wild flowers in spring. *Shared laundry Chèvrefeuille.*

sleeps	Chèvrefeuille 6. Glycines 6.
rooms	Chèvrefeuille: 2 doubles, 1 twin; 1 bathroom. Glycines: 2 doubles, 2 singles; 1 shower room, 1 separate wc.
price	Chèvrefeuille €630. Glycines €640. Prices per week.

Alice de Chambure
tel +33 (0)3 86 76 10 10
fax +33 (0)3 86 76 10 10
email giteslachaux@wanadoo.fr
web www.gites-lachaux.fr

Hello

Domaine de La Chaux – Iris & Clemetis

Alligny en Morvan, Nièvre

Every house in La Chaux has its own individual touch but there's one feature they share: a huge fireplace stacked with logs. So winter stays are possible as well as summer ones (the wood is provided at extra charge). Ground-floor gîtes Iris (above) and Clemetis sit opposite each other, with a good tranche of grass in between – ideal for a family and grandparents on holiday together. Clemetis's raised fireplace dominates the main bedroom (below), giving this pale-walled, red-tiled room a country feel. The living area is open plan with the kitchen in the corner (stocked with all you need, dishwasher included); the second, bigger bedroom has three beds. Iris, too, is terracotta-tiled, with russet-brown curtains and country furniture. Every house in the domaine has a barbecue and garden furniture, including loungers: summers are long and hot in the Haut Morvan. A visit to the Lac des Settons, the biggest man-made lake in Europe, will cool you down: sail, swim, waterski, windsurf or pedalo. And there's a magnificent *bateau mouche* for the less sporty. *Shared laundry.*

sleeps	Iris 2. Clematis 4-6.
rooms	Iris: 1 sofabed; 1 shower room, 1 separate wc. Clematis: 1 double, 1 family room for 4; 1 bathroom, 1 separate wc.
price	Iris €250. Clematis €555. Prices per week.

Alice de Chambure

tel	+33 (0)3 86 76 10 10
fax	+33 (0)3 86 76 10 10
email	giteslachaux@wanadoo.fr
web	www.gites-lachaux.fr

The Gate House

Cry, Yonne

Adorable, white-shuttered, independent and with a tucked-away feel, the little gate house sits in a walled garden with a gate that leads to a boat and a river – it could be trout for dinner! From the apple-treed and rose-tossed garden you step into the hall, then the large and lovely kitchen and living area. There are simple white walls, rush matting on a flagged floor, four windows full of light, good modern furniture, old country pieces, stacks of logs for the woodburner and, in winter, a just-lit fire. On the same level are the bedrooms: expect blue covers on good new beds, bright wicker furniture, boat prints on fresh white walls, garden flowers. No access to pool or park – just a romantic, cosy and comforting little house on the edge of a honeysuckled village in the heart of Burgundy: one of the best. And you should go on at least one wine tour while you are here and sample some of the area's finest burgundies and chablis; the welcome pack comes with all the info. *Ask about painting/walking/bridge courses.*

sleeps	4.
rooms	2: 1 double, 1 twin/double; 1 bathroom.
price	€240-€440 per week.

	Lady Susanna Lyell
tel	+44 (0)1582 840635
email	info@lmdc.co.uk
web	www.lamaisonduchateau.co.uk

La Maison du Château

Cry, Yonne

The charming, 18th-century manor house on the edge of the tranquil village seduces all who stay. Its English owners chanced upon it one day, fell in love with it and its 24 acres and took on the lot: chestnut avenue, grass tennis court, trout river and all. You could almost spend your entire holiday exploring the grounds; there's even a boat to row to your own small island. Large, luminous rooms have enchanting park or meadow views and captivating art on ochre walls. Floors are pale stone with slate inlay or oak parquet, curtains are linen and white, there's a gracious hall with an elegant staircase and a kitchen with two ovens and china for 30. One bathroom has a stone fireplace and an antique washstand, beds are beautifully dressed, sofas are merry with throws. Two en suite bedrooms are in the barn – a grand piano, a long period table, colourful rugs on a planked floor: as generously embracing as all the rest. Stone stairs take you down to the enclosed pool with teak loungers, barbecue and fridge. The house comes with a wonderful cook and staff (optional). *Ask about painting/walking/bridge courses.*

sleeps	17 + children's beds & cots.
rooms	9: 6 twin/doubles, 2 doubles, 1 single; 7 bathrooms.
price	£1,650-£5,500 per week. Short stay availability out of season.

Lady Susanna Lyell
tel +44 (0)1582 840635
email info@lmdc.co.uk
web www.lamaisonduchateau.co.uk

La Poterne

Stigny, Yonne

Old stone steps lead up to a farmhouse door. Step inside and this renovated cottage opens, tardis-like, into an adorable little gîte, all exposed stone walls, low beamed ceilings and polished floors. Furnished with rustic simplicity, the sitting room welcomes you with a bottle of wine, a large sofa (extra bed if pushed) and vast fireplace with logs for cool nights – and opens onto a sheltered, sweet-smelling garden with lawn and barbecue. The bedrooms are timeless spaces of plain white walls and stripped wood floors. Quirkily, the bathroom is downstairs (the cottage is built into a slope) next to the low-beamed kitchen – not big but fine for holiday cooking – dominated by the original bread oven. The dining room is a delight; half-underground, a window peeping over the garden, it demands flickering candles. Beyond, châteaux, chablis vineyards, medieval Vézelay, canoeing and cycling. The Calderwoods, friendly Australians, live next door. They offer home grown organic vegetables and invite you to join in authentic village life.

sleeps	4
rooms	2: 1 double, 1 twin; 1 shower room, 1 separate wc.
price	€425-€505 per week.

Karen Calderwood
tel +33 (0)3 86 75 03 36
email karen.calderwood@wanadoo.fr
web perso.wanadoo.fr/lapoterne/

Montparnasse district

Paris

Behind Montparnasse, beneath the chestnut tree that spreads over the cobbled alley, you will find what looks like a garden shed. Enter: the shed turns into a smart dark grass-papered hall, beyond it a blue-plush, white-walled double-height indoor 'garden' full of happy plants and northern light from the sloping glass roof, and generous living space for two. It is the nicest, most unexpected Parisian hideaway imaginable, totally sheltered from road noise, highly original and delighting in a tiny, pretty kitchen. Up a steep staircase, the bedroom looks into the living room: three cottage windows light its beige, green and brown quietness. The owner's oriental origins show discreetly through in Chinese prints and vases, in her taste for rich dark colours and unobtrusive class. After the bedroom comes the study – big glass writing table, single divan and... deep-freeze; then the laundry – useful washer/dryer – and the splendid black and white bathroom that gives onto a leafy courtyard straight from a provincial backwater. A secret cocoon, restaurants galore, the whole of Paris to hand.

sleeps	2-3.
rooms	1 double, 1 sofabed; 1 bathroom, 1 separate wc.
price	€750 per week; €2,950 per month.

Alice de Chambure
tel +33 (0)3 86 76 10 10
+33 (0)1 43 22 46 37
fax +33 (0)3 86 76 10 10
email alicedechambure@wanadoo.fr

Montparnasse district

Paris

No, that little white-faced blue-shuttered terrace house in a stunningly quiet cobbled alley is not a country village dream, it's a most delectable place that can be yours for a good, long summer stay in the centre of sophisticated Left Bank Paris. The hall, which also leads to another flat upstairs, welcomes you with shelves of books. To the left, a good square bedroom with a pleasingly eclectic mix of warm fabrics, honeycomb tiles, old chest and contemporary paintings. The new white and pine bathroom has space, all mod cons and good cupboards. To the right is the pretty, wood-ceilinged and very well-equipped kitchen/diner. Beyond lies the richly French sitting room – modern art alongside antiques, an alcove stuffed with music and books – and the inestimable privilege of the little patio with its table, chairs and plants. The second big bedroom is at the back with its smart bathroom. Public transport abounds, so do shops, restaurants and cafés. This is an ideal way to mix peace and quiet in a Parisian home with sightseeing and shopping, night life... or academic research. *B&B only October-June.*

sleeps	4.
rooms	2 doubles; 2 bathrooms.
price	€1,000 per week.
arrival	Flexible.
closed	October-June.

Janine Euvrard
tel +33 (0)1 43 27 19 43
fax +33 (0)1 43 27 19 43
email euvrard@club-internet.fr

Domaine des Basses Masures

Poigny la Forêt, Yvelines

There are riding stables nearby, so you can saddle up and go deep into the Rambouillet forest; it encircles this peaceful hamlet. Madame, who is friendly and informal, takes care of several fine horses. They graze in the field behind the house – do introduce yourself. The house is an old stables: long, low and stone-fronted, built in 1725 and covered in Virginia creeper and ancient wisteria. Madame lives in one end and does B&B; the gîte is at the other end. It is a homely little place with a cottagey feel. Whitewashed bedrooms are up in the eaves, carpeted and cosy, with sky-light windows and the odd beam. New beds are dressed in crisp cotton and fat pillows. The sitting room downstairs has a cheerful blue sofa that opens to a bed, a big oriental rug, modern wicker armchairs, an open fireplace and white-painted beams. There are views to the back of the surrounding fields. The kitchen, more functional than aesthetic, has a round dining table and is very well equipped; it leads into the garden, with outdoor furniture. Versailles is only 20 minutes, Paris 45 and there's excellent walking from the door. *B&B also.*

sleeps	4-6.
rooms	2 doubles, 1 sofabed; 2 bathrooms.
price	€750 per week.

Mme Walburg de Vernisy
tel +33 (0)1 34 84 73 44
fax +33 (0)1 34 84 73 44
email domainebassesmasures@wanadoo.fr
web www.domaine-des-basses-masures.com

photo corel images

normandy brittany

La Grande Rosaye

Ceton, Orne

Could this be the country house that has everything? From grand piano to indoor swimming pool, superb 18th-century fireplaces to plain modern kitchen, this former cider farm is magnificent. Restored with old materials from virtual ruin by its totally committed owners, it has space, taste, country style and oodles of atmosphere. Antoine, a charming intellectual, found himself learning several new trades in the process (lime plaster, Versailles parquet flooring, roof carpentry …). Nothing is overdone, there's not a scrap of clutter, just the soft yellow stone melding finely with innumerable timbers, easy print fabrics and some massive antiques. The big, well-lit kitchen/diner is brilliant beneath its massive tree-trunk beams: simple tables on re-laid ancient floor tiles, handmade units, more space. There are seriously good armchairs, art ancient and modern, the latest technology, and that fabulous pool among its jungly plants. Bedrooms are reminiscent of older simpler times: Jouy prints, old framed pictures, lovely chests of drawers – and excellent new bathrooms. Remarkable value. *B&B also.*

sleeps 10 + 4 children.
rooms 5 doubles; 5 bathrooms. (2 children's rooms optional).
price €880-€1,880 per week.

Antoine Meley
tel +33 (0)2 37 29 76 79
fax +33 (0)1 34 84 74 38
email lagranderosaye@wanadoo.fr
web lechateaudepoigny.com

L'Onglée

L'Hôme Chamondot, Orne

The converted 19th-century barn stands next to the Normandy farmhouse where Alan and Jackie live. Rural France wraps itself around you with open fields to the front, woodland behind, red squirrel, deer and buzzard nearby – follow the paths out from the house and you may meet them. The cottage has been renovated from top to toe. There's a beamed ceiling, thick stone walls and a woodburner in the fireplace. The feel is light and airy, relaxed and user-friendly with all the bits you need for comfort, from TV and CD player to dishwasher; books, videos, games and jigsaws, too. Outside are a good wooden table and chairs, parasol, barbecue and the raised pool. The pool is shared with B&B guests but your secluded garden is private. You will find your beds made when you arrive in the pretty bedrooms and if you don't feel like cooking, join the people in the farmhouse for sociable dinners on the terrace. Jackie and Alan keep lots of rare-breed chickens so eggs – rare ones – may be available. You get a boules pitch, table tennis and even a field for football here, and there's golf at Bellême. *B&B also.*

sleeps	6.
rooms	3: 1 double, 2 twins; 2 shower rooms.
price	£245-£515 per week.

Alan & Jackie Ainsworth

tel	+33 (0)2 33 73 81 46
fax	+33 (0)2 33 73 81 46
email	jackieainsworth@hotmail.com
web	www.chamondot.com

La Poterie

St Evroult Notre Dame Du Bois, Orne

In the grounds is a dairy where camembert was once made. It evidently did rather well, for the owner made enough money to build himself this big, late-19th-century house. It stands by the road, backing onto open countryside. Don't worry if the exterior looks a trifle forbidding: inside all is airy and impressive. The long, inviting sitting room has windows on three sides and an abundance of books, videos and games; the immense oak table in the green-and-white dining room seats 14. Cooking for that number shouldn't be too daunting, given the superbly designed kitchen and a dresser packed with local organic produce – paté, honey, jam, cider (plus price lists and honesty box). White bedrooms have their original parquet floors, at least two windows and beds made up with pretty white linen. Down in the vast cellar is an enticing selection of bicycles and tricycles, doll's prams, garden toys, a paddling pool… Sue and Dan have worked hard to make this a great place for families. The dairy is now a games room with a pool table, and there's a lake in the village (1km) – good for fishing and swimming.

sleeps	14.
rooms	7: 5 doubles, 2 twins; 1 bathroom, 1 shower room, 1 separate wc.
price	£900-£1,500 per week.

Sue & Dan Gascoyne

tel	+44 (0)1206 790828
fax	+44 (0)1206 790828
email	info@lapoterie.co.uk
web	www.lapoterie.co.uk

La Brochardière – Four Gîtes

La Ferté Macé, Orne

Aimed at families with small children and sporty teenagers, four new gîtes – think plain, inexpensive and well equipped. Sharing two farm outbuildings and a courtyard, they belong to the same people who run the delightful auberge down the road, Auberge de la Source, with its fabulous lake and huge sports complex. The Gîte d'Etape has pristine white walls and new pine beds in hostel style, a refrectory table, a neat kitchen; Cour is more characterful – beams in the kitchen, rush-seated chairs, its own outdoor space. All feel spotless and new. The action is a mile away, and it's a nice walk to get there. You'll find windsurfing and a sailing school, riding, a climbing wall, archery, fishing and 'swing-golf' – easy to learn, apparently. Young children have a play area, pony rides, mini-golf and pedal boats. If you want real nature, the forest is nearby and you should see huge stags without too much searching. For dining there's the auberge; the restaurant is designed to make the most of the lake view and the food is simple, centring on fresh farm produce and steaks cooked over a wood fire. *Auberge also.*

sleeps	Gîte d'Etape 6-12. Cour 5. Du Tisserand 4. Rez de Jardin 2.
rooms	Gîte d'Etape: 3 quadruples; 2 bathrooms. Cour: 1 double, 1 twin, 1 single; 1 bathroom. Du Tisserand: 1 double, 1 twin; 1 bathroom. Rez de Jardin: 1 double; 1 shower.
price	€204-€340 per week.

Serge & Christine Volclair
tel +33 (0)2 33 37 28 23
fax +33 (0)2 33 38 78 83
email auberge.lasource@wanadoo.fr
web perso.wanadoo.fr/auberge.lasource/

Le Gaillon

Haussez, Seine-Maritime

Two hours from Calais, in deep countryside, a solid little farmhouse just right for a family or close friends. Red terracotta tiles run throughout the ground floor; there's a sitting room with fine oak ceiling beams, old-fashioned easy chairs, a brick fireplace (logs for winter), piles of videos, books and board games. In the dining room, a refectory table for eight, a patterned rug, a huge mirror; in the light, well-equipped kitchen, a table for six and a further fireplace. The master bedroom is also on this floor, with its feather-filled duvet and pretty patchwork quilt, and so is the one large shower room that the household shares. Then upstairs to a long, large, uncluttered sleeping space under the eaves – white, open, airy, all beautiful gnarled timbers and endless views. Stow away most of the party up here and they'll be happy. Fencing keeps the frisky cows framed in their buttercup meadow, leaving you the run of the pleasing garden. As dusk falls, you can sit, chat and barbecue as the poplars rustle and the fairylights twinkle like fireflies. Good value, gorgeous views.

sleeps	6-9 + cot.
rooms	3: 2 doubles, 1 triple, 1 sofabed on mezzanine; 1 shower room, 2 separate wcs.
price	£250-£650 per week.

	Aysen Slack
tel	+44 (0)1435 866688
email	info@legaillon.com
web	www.legaillon.com

Château Le Bourg

Bures en Bray, Seine-Maritime

The 1860's *petit château* has tall windows, a grand position in the middle of the village and was once owned by the mayor of Dieppe. You get the top floor to yourself and with it the best views – of the village, church and surrounding low hills. The interior comes in comfortable, homely-château style: high slanting ceilings (you are up in the eaves), colourful stylish fabrics, vibrant quilts, polished wooden floors. The odd timber runs from floor to ceiling and there are skylights and dormer windows. The master suite is big, the twin room smaller, one room has a mural and the beds are excellent. A spacious sitting room has sunny yellow walls, comfy sofas and much colour. Léonora, a retired lawyer from Hereford, is an excellent cook and you are welcome to join her for sumptuous dinners – 'bistro' or 'gastronomique'. Relax in the dining room decorated in the grand style: old oils, period wallpaper, candelabra on a mahogany table. And there is a garden to share, with barbecue and trees for your children to climb. Beyond, cows mow the meadows and the market town of Neufchatel is close. *B&B also.*

sleeps	6 + 1 child.
rooms	4: 1 twin/double, 2 twins, 1 child's room; 1 bathroom, 2 shower rooms.
price	€750 per week.

Léonora Macleod
tel +33 (0)2 35 94 09 35
email leonora.macleod@wanadoo.fr

La Vallée Blonde

St Georges du Vièvre, Eure

You might expect Hansel and Gretel to step out of this fairytale, half-timbered cottage, deep in the Normandy woods. The only passers-by are the cows in the neighbouring fields, the only sounds that of the owl, cuckoo and woodpecker. Peace is yours as you eat out in the grassy glade under the geraniums; walks start from your tiny sky-blue front door. The house, once a bakehouse, has been simply furnished by its English owners; they have kept the wooden beams, brick and stone skirting and oak floor boards, and added local country furniture, interesting bric-à-brac and a kitchen with mini oven, hob and fridge. There's a traditional Godin woodburner – with logs – in the sitting/dining room, and a bedroom in the rafters up a steep stair. Rouen and Honfleur are less than a hour away, the magical Abbaye de Bec Hellouin much nearer; be sure to visit the Château de Launay with its breathtaking Renaissance dovecot. There are shops in St Georges du Vièvre and a restaurant/bar in the nearby village; eat and be merry, then roll down the hill and up to bed. *No washing machine. Bring own linen.*

sleeps	2.
rooms	1 double; 1 shower room downstairs.
price	£195-£325 per week.
closed	December-February.

Jennifer Murray

tel +44 (0)1273 888033

fax +44 (0)1273 245855

email jenmurray@20powis.fsnet.co.uk

web www.normandy-cottage.co.uk

Clos Vorin – La Maison Bleue & La Petite Maison Verte

Triqueville, Eure

The painted, timbered doll's-house cottages are so pretty, the apple trees which surround them so lush, you have to pinch yourself to believe they're real. Even when you've crept inside, the fairytale continues: white plaster and painted beams, a simple kitchenette screened off by vertical timbers, fluttering voile… a piano in one, a Provençal-patterned wall in another. Furniture is a good mix of old and new, expensive and budget – Bleue has a wonderful baroque-style antique bed and an old trunk for a coffee table. Both are intimate, simple, delightful. Outside, a cobbled terrace safe for children, a barbecue, perhaps a hammock slung between nearby trees. This magical farm group (four gîtes plus the owners' house) is the creation of Eddy and Delphine, who have two small children and put on weekly drinks for all. In 20 minutes you can be in Honfleur – picturesque architecture, sea front, seafood restaurants, autumn shrimp festival. Trouville and Deauville – bathing beaches, casinos and period villas – are not much further.
No washing machines.

sleeps	Bleue 2-4. Petite Verte: 2.
rooms	Bleue: 1 double, 1 sofabed in living room; 1 shower room. Petite Verte: 1 double; 1 shower room.
price	Bleue: €290-€400. Petite Verte: €250-€350. Prices per week.

Eddy & Delphine Cayeux
tel +33 (0)2 32 56 53 15
fax +33 (0)2 32 56 53 15
email gite.closvorin@wanadoo.fr
web www.leclosvorin.com

Clos Vorin – La Maison Verte & La Grange

Triqueville, Eure

Amid rustling poplar trees, fields of corn and cattle-grazed meadows is this charming ensemble of four timbered farm buildings, clustered round the owners' house, surrounded by greenness and space. The Grange, with its decent-sized swoop of lawn in front and ample outdoor eating space, is the most sheltered of the gîtes; all have their own patch of private lawn, pretty garden furniture and screening shrubs. Indoors, Verte has a generous serving of ground-floor rooms, kitchen opening to dining room to living room to library, and steps down to a conservatory at the end; then up to a lovely large open-plan sleeping area sandwiched between two doubles. Grange is as gorgeous, its double room on the mezzanine overlooking the living room below (cream tiles, dark timbers, white wrought-iron seats stylishly cushioned), and leading – no doors – into the family room, palely, elegantly informal, with oatmeal carpeting and roof timbers painted pastel blue. The shower room is downstairs; the 'conservatory' is a stunningly converted farm treadmill. Normandy at its enchanting best.

sleeps	Verte 8. Grange 6.
rooms	Verte: 2 doubles, 1 family room for 4; 1 shower room, 1 separate wc. Grange: 1 double, 1 family room; 1 shower room, 1 separate wc.
price	Verte: €680-€900, €500 for four, €400 for two. Grange: €472-€690, €450 for four, €350 for two. Prices per week.

Eddy & Delphine Cayeux
tel +33 (0)2 32 56 53 15
fax +33 (0)2 32 56 53 15
email gite.closvorin@wanadoo.fr
web www.leclosvorin.com

La Baronnière

Cordebugle, Calvados

A 200-year-old barn in the grounds of a manor house; nine lush acres and a forest to silence the outside world. The barn once stood elsewhere; the Fleurys dismantled it piece by piece, then reassembled it 20 paces from the lake. It is a stunning timber and brick building, renovated with boundless verve and sublime style. Pristine white walls soak up Normandy light, exposed beams and sand-blasted timbers stand out like ribs. Uncluttered bedrooms have garden views, trim carpets, contemporary wooden beds, maybe a hi-fi; you lack nothing. The Fleurys run painting and cookery courses and you can gorge on a four-course feast at the manor house if you don't wish to cook. They'll do your shopping for you, too, before you arrive; just ask. Visit Monet's garden at Giverny or the tractor-pulling championships in Beenay in June! Or stay put and watch the koi carp in the lake. Later you will fall asleep to the sound of water: the stream that feeds the lake tumbles over a sluice gate close by. Too much camembert and calvados is inevitable – why resist? *B&B also.*

sleeps 6-8.

rooms 3: 2 doubles, 1 twin; 1 bathroom, 1 shower room, 1 separate wc. Extra double and shower room available with separate entrance.

price €500-€750 for three bedrooms; €750-€1,000 for four. Prices per week.

Christine Gilliatt-Fleury
tel +33 (0)2 32 46 41 74
fax +33 (0)2 32 44 26 09
email labaronniere@wanadoo.fr
web www.labaronniere.connectfree.co.uk

Les Petits Matins Bleus

Ste Marguerite de Viette, Calvados

This little red-and-black brick cottage with a romantic name was once a distillery where cider bubbled into calvados in an alembic on the fire. Now French windows lead to a neat, brick-paved terrace complete with pergola, climbing roses and vines. Pictures and ornaments, magazines and books, TV and hi-fi give the living room a homely yet uncluttered air. There's an old stone fireplace, a sofa, cane armchairs with cushions and a built-in cupboard with glasses for champagne and bowls for nibbles. The kitchen has piles of plates, plenty of pots and pans, good kitchen knives; even dishwasher tablets are provided. One bedroom is on the ground floor, made up with pretty blue-and white-checked sheets; a second bedroom is under the roof, thrillingly reached by wooden loft ladder – rickety but safe! Anne's welcome to her guests may include fresh flowers, wine, home-backed apple tart or fresh herbs. She also plans to put on themed weekends in the future. A place to relish. *Children over seven welcome. B&B also.*

sleeps	4-5.
rooms	2: 1 double, 1 twin/double with extra single available; 1 shower room.
price	€290-€430 per week.

Anne Bourbeau

tel +33 (0)2 31 20 62 88

email matinsbleus14@wanadoo.fr

web www.petitsmatinsbleus.com

La Boursaie – Le Pressoir

Livarot, Calvados

You can almost smell the intoxicating aroma of fermenting apples as you dine in the groove where the great granite wheel of the old cider press turned. Apples have made this superb cluster of half-timbered buildings tick since medieval times, and English owner Peter and his German wife Anja have done a remarkable and original job restoring them. The interiors of what are now five holiday cottages are decorated with 'ciderabilia' that Peter has bought over the years, and ancient cider barrels, wheelbarrows and apple baskets have been used in ingenious ways around the grounds. The whole of the ground floor is living space. The open-plan, terracotta-floored sitting, dining and kitchen area has the hugest beams, pink velvet armchairs, and butter churns for side tables. Up a ladder stair to cosy bedrooms (the master bedroom overlooks the press). Other guests are around but with 65 acres there's room to roam. Watch the buzzards from your private patch of garden, soak up valley views, join the apple harvest in autumn. The Davieses are happy to put up wedding parties, and can host dinners. *B&B also.*

sleeps	7.
rooms	4: 2 doubles, 1 twin, 1 single; 1 bathroom, 1 shower room, 1 separate wc.
price	€690-€1,290 per week.
arrival	Saturday July-August, flexible low season.

	Anja & Peter Davies
tel	+33 (0)2 31 63 14 20
fax	+33 (0)2 31 63 14 20
email	laboursaie@wanadoo.fr
web	www.laboursaie.com

La Boursaie – La Grange

Livarot, Calvados

You'll spot deer in the early mornings, and foxes, badgers and the occasional wild boar roam the magical woods. The hamlet takes its name from *bource*, the old Norman word for source. Drink in the ancient beauty of this cider farm under the shade of the 300-year-old walnut tree, which towers and protects like a friendly giant. Anja and Peter will bring walnuts, apples and pears to your cottage, and you can buy their home-produced cider and calvados. La Grange, with its stupendous views over the courtyard, duck pond and valley beyond, was formerly the hayloft, and has been converted into a delightful split-level, first-floor living area. Ceilings slope and glorious old beams have been skilfully used to divide the space, blending atmospherically with old and new furniture and seagrass floors. Peter has his painting studio below – his work is on display in several of the cottages – and there's a dining room where the couple entertain guests to a weekly feast: Norman cooking at its best. They also hold art and cookery courses in spring and autumn. *B&B also.*

sleeps	4.
rooms	2 twins; 1 shower room, 1 bathroom.
price	€590-€980 per week.
arrival	Saturday July-August, flexible low season.

Anja & Peter Davies

tel +33 (0)2 31 63 14 20

fax +33 (0)2 31 63 14 20

email laboursaie@wanadoo.fr

web www.laboursaie.com

La Boursaie – Le Trou Normand

Livarot, Calvados

Even the ducks and chickens live in a half-timbered cottage. No modern building disrupts the black and white beauty of this tranquil farmstead, clustered around a large grassy courtyard, set in a fold between rolling hills. Couples will love this most private of cottages where once calvados was distilled; now you may relax by the fire in winter tasting a glass of home-produced cider. It is a delicious nest for two: cream walls, tiled floors and pink toile de Jouy on the sofa downstairs; low cruck beams and minute windows in the bedroom up; views that sail over orchards of apple, cherry and pear. With a restaurant in the old cowshed and a play area for kids: a small community to join if you wish; or enjoy your own well-furnished piece of garden. If you love walking, the Tour du Pays d'Auge footpath runs almost from the door; there's riding on the beach at Deauville – a half-hour drive – and Camembert is not far either. The cheese's creator, Marie Harel, whose promotion campaign included sending free samples to Napoleon, is commemorated in the next-door village of Vimoutiers. *See previous page.*

sleeps	2.
rooms	1 double; 1 shower room.
price	€390-€490 per week.
arrival	Flexible.

Anja & Peter Davies

tel	+33 (0)2 31 63 14 20
fax	+33 (0)2 31 63 14 20
email	laboursaie@wanadoo.fr
web	www.laboursaie.com

Le Domaine des Sources – Le Pressoir

Montviette, Calvados

Margaret and Philippe have pulled out all the stops at Le Pressoir, their latest project at Domaine des Sources. It stands right at the top of the sloping garden and has been given the *grand luxe* treatment. Margaret's feeling for colour and texture is apparent throughout. The big salon, lit by several windows, is a study in pinks, ochres, coffees and creams. There are leather sofas and armchairs, a large open fireplace (logs provided), masses of books, games and magazines. From the snazzily equipped and furnished kitchen/dining room a door leads to a covered, open-sided veranda and brick-paved terrace. From the salon, stairs lead up to the first floor and wall-to-wall oak parquet. The main bedroom has wonderful, elevated views over the valley and a stunning, teak-floored bathroom, and there are two good shower rooms, too, one up, one down. The other bedrooms are charming, all sloping ceilings, exposed beams and interesting features; the twin room even has its own small balcony with table and chairs and you can, of course, enjoy all the collective delights laid on by your hosts. *See next page.*

sleeps	6.
rooms	3: 2 doubles, 1 twin; 1 bathroom, 2 shower rooms.
price	€650-€850 per week.

Margaret Love & Philippe Kalk
tel +33 (0)2 31 20 35 35
fax +33 (0)2 31 20 36 35
email dessources@aol.com
web www.le-domaine-des-sources.com

Le Domaine des Sources – Les Pommiers

Montviette, Calvados

The half-timbered building that Les Pommiers shares with La Grange was moved lock, stock and barrel from Orbec and rebuilt here. Like its twin, it feels good the moment you step inside: so much thought and care have gone into making it comfortable. The living room is yellow, with an ornamental antique-pine fireplace; the kitchen has a cottagey flavour. Pale yellow stairs lead to the bedroom where a treadle sewing machine serves as an occasional table and a glass door connects with outdoor stairs down to the garden. On the south side is a brick-paved terrace – perfect for that evening glass of calvados. All your needs are anticipated: there are excellent laundry facilities in a converted farm building (even soap powder is provided) and you're welcome to wander at will round the 50-acre estate. Margaret also offers language courses and 'franglais' dinner parties. Another nice touch is the bread service: hang your bread bag with an order slip on the outside gate at night and the local baker will deliver your baguettes and croissants in time for breakfast. *See previous page.*

sleeps	2.
rooms	1 double; 1 shower room & separate wc.
price	€400-€500 per week.

Margaret Love & Philippe Kalk

tel	+33 (0)2 31 20 35 35
fax	+33 (0)2 31 20 36 35
email	dessources@aol.com
web	www.le-domaine-des-sources.com

Le Domaine des Sources – La Grange

Montviette, Calvados

Like a hamlet in a fairy tale – a group of half-timbered buildings surrounded by orchards. There's something magical about the welcome basket awaiting you, too… All this plenty is provided by Margaret and Philippe, generous and good company. She is Scottish and a part-time air hostess, he's a retired gendarme; between them they have turned the buildings on this 18th-century former cider farm into delightful gîtes. All are immaculately decorated and Margaret has obviously enjoyed choosing pieces of old furniture, bric-a-brac and fabrics to create a stylish, cosy mood. La Grange is open plan and painted in sunny colours, its shelves overflowing with books and maps. The kitchen corner has all you could possibly need – and more – and you can breakfast in the morning sun on the terrace. Up a wide, primrose staircase is your pretty bedroom (with space for a cot or a child's folding bed) and a good bathroom with a sunflower theme. From the bedroom a door leads to an outside wooden staircase with views down the gentle, very pretty valley.

sleeps	2.
rooms	1 double; 1 bathroom & separate wc.
price	€400-€500 per week.

Margaret Love & Philippe Kalk
tel +33 (0)2 31 20 35 35
fax +33 (0)2 31 20 36 35
email dessources@aol.com
web www.le-domaine-des-sources.com

La Ferme de l'Oudon – Les Tulipes

Berville l'Oudon, Calvados

This stone farmhouse has a dovecote and is partly 15th century. Although the days of farming have long gone, free-range hens survive, as do the ducks who sail upon their pond with highfaluting grace. Monsieur and Madame have horses; guests can bring theirs. They are hands-on owners, do B&B in the main house, will provide picnic baskets on request and are extremely welcoming. Madame is learning English with the local Chamber of Commerce while Monsieur runs a kitchen-and-bathroom design company. His work is on view in the old dairy, now Les Tulipes – a light, bright, sunny, one-bedroom gîte sited at the far end of the courtyard. It is a well-nigh perfect ground-floor conversion that has been carried out with great flair and a consummate eye for detail. In the open-plan living area find colourwashed walls, an L-shaped sofabed, warm colours, wicker chairs and a brilliant corner kitchen. You have your own enclosed garden with table tennis, barbecue, furniture and darts, there's a potager where you can pick herbs and salads, and bicycles to rent. *B&B also.*

sleeps	4-6.
rooms	2 doubles, 2 sofabeds; 2 bathrooms.
price	€700-€890 per week.
closed	3-23 January.

Patrick & Dany Vesque

tel	+33 (0)2 31 20 77 96
fax	+33 (0)2 31 20 67 13
email	contact@fermedeloudon.com
web	www.fermedeloudon.com

La Ferme de l'Oudon – Le Pressoir

Berville l'Oudon, Calvados

Another enchanting farm building at Oudon, another fine restoration. This was the old cider press, its ground floor now a vast, light living space, comfortable and contemporary. You have red leather sofas, beautiful floor-to-ceiling curtains and a brand-new woodburning stove. A well-equipped kitchen leads to a private garden; there's a big sunny bedroom and a paved terrace; even the outdoor tables and chairs are ultra-stylish. Walls are white plaster or creamy exposed stone, floors are pale-tiled, there are old beams and joists and new windows to pull in the light. Ascend the new staircase with tiled treads to a mezzanine with sofa and three skylit bedrooms under the eaves, one large, all delightful. Bathrooms shine. The friendly Vesques give you a bottle of cider, homemade jam and farm eggs on arrival, and everything is included: linen, electricity, logs. Twice a week there's *table d'hôtes* – a chance to meet the B&B and other guests over a civilised meal. The orchards, rich pastures and half-timbered manor houses of the Pays d'Auge are yours to discover. Superb. *B&B also.*

sleeps	6-8.
rooms	3: 2 family rooms for 3, 1 twin; 2 bathrooms.
price	€700-€890 per week.
closed	3-23 January.

Patrick & Dany Vesque
tel +33 (0)2 31 20 77 96
fax +33 (0)2 31 20 67 13
email contact@fermedeloudon.com
web www.fermedeloudon.com

Château La Cour – Le Moulin du Pont

Culey le Patry, Calvados

Nothing but the sound of rushing water and rustling trees. Despite its mature gardens and its graceful good looks, this house was built on the site of a mill in the 1970s. Everything is designed to capitalise on the setting. Water flows under the house (it's on stilts), a rose-clad Monet-style bridge crosses the mill race, gardens stretch along the river bank, windows drink in the views. Bedrooms reflect the hand of a designer: suede-clad walls and French sleigh bed in one; darkly romantic wallpaper and an alcove bath in another. The star bedroom has French windows to the garden and a sunken marble bath. The open-plan dining and living room want for nothing – fireplace (logs provided), comfy sofas, elegant dining table, soft lamps, soft rugs and a fleet of windows leading to a marble terrace: perfect for suppers overlooking the floodlit garden. Cooking is no hardship in a kitchen where only the best will do. Everything has been thought of, from binoculars for birdwatching to tumble-dryer to stocked larder. Close to the charms of the Normandy coast – if you can tear yourself away.

sleeps	6.
rooms	3 doubles; 3 bathrooms.
price	£1,000-£1,600 per week.
arrival	Flexible but minimum stay 3 nights.

Lesley & David Craven
tel +33 (0)2 31 79 19 37
fax +33 (0)2 31 79 19 37
email lesleycraven@chateaulacour.com
web www.chateaulacour.com

Château La Cour – Le Jardin

Culey le Patry, Calvados

Up a stone staircase, through a small door and into an unexpected world of grand windows, oak-panelled doors and elegant rooms. Lesley and David, who have wisely chosen to settle in France, are the friendly lord and lady of this 13th-century château in deep countryside, with views stretching over the Suisse Normande. Your apartment, a private and discreet three-room suite, is light, spacious and gracious – from the parquet corridor with floor-to-ceiling windows to the oak-panelled doors and the richly coloured curtains falling in folds to the floor. If you think the bedroom is swish – king-size bed, stacks of cushions – just wait until you see the bathroom; gleaming white with brushed chrome, its roll-top bath has space enough to perch a G&T. The living area – a soft, roomy space of sofas, hi-tech lights and natural linen with a dining table by the window to feed your daydreams, too – has a futuristic, corner kitchen, a showpiece of stainless steel and gadgets. Flowers, welcome groceries, binoculars for birds, hosts who love to spoil… Sawday *grand cru*.

sleeps	2.
rooms	1 double; 1 bathroom.
price	£500 per week.
arrival	Flexible but minimum stay 3 nights.

Lesley & David Craven

tel +33 (0)2 31 79 19 37
fax +33 (0)2 31 79 19 37
email lesleycraven@chateaulacour.com
web www.chateaulacour.com

Manoir de Laize – Le Pressoir & La Grange

Fontaine Le Pin, Calvados

Apples used to be pressed for cider and calvados in the grandiose, medieval *pressoir*. Across the lawns, pretty with blossoming apple trees in the spring, is the 15th-century manor farmhouse where the owners live. Horses graze in the meadows, dogs and cats doze in the barns, and David and Emily are the friendliest, most thoughtful of hosts. Inside the Pressoir, much country charm: ceiling beams, tiled floors, soft colours, the odd antique and plenty of space. The lovely light living area is open plan, with a well equipped kitchen in the corner; French windows lead down a step to a walled suntrap patio with barbecue. Upstairs: new beds dressed in crisp white linen, a bathroom filled with soft towels. Books, toys, games – and central heating for winter cosiness. More open-plan living in the adjoining La Grange, new carpeting and harmonious colours. The place is brilliant for families: a superb games room, a fenced pool, a stream to dam. Soak up the setting, stock up at the weekly market in Falaise, cycle or canoe the gorge of the Orne, pick wild flowers in spring. *Babysitting available.*

sleeps	Pressoir 7 + cot. Grange 6.
rooms	Pressoir: 2 twins, 1 family room for 3; 1 bathroom. Grange: 3: 1 double, 2 twins; 1 bathroom, 1 shower room.
price	Each gîte £300-£625 per week.
arrival	Saturday or Tuesday.

David & Emily Lloyd
tel +33 (0)2 31 20 93 74
email emlloy@aol.com

Le Clos St Bernard – Les Camélias & Les Fuchsias

Reviers, Calvados

The very first farmhouse built in this Normandy village – well placed for countryside and coast – has been transformed into two gîtes and sits in the walled courtyard opposite the owner's house. Les Camélias, on the ground floor, has a living/kitchen room with exposed stone and beams, cane armchairs, floral drapes, a sofabed and dining table. There's an array of equipment in the kitchen, including raclette machine and electric mixer. An open-tread stair leads to carpeted blue and white bedrooms; the double has the original stone sink with spout, now a display unit, and a fitted pine wardrobe; the twin has English-style pillows. A corner of lawn in the courtyard has been set aside for this gîte, complete with loungers, parasol, table, chairs and barbecue. Visitors can drive in to unload, then park safely outside; gates are securely locked at night. Les Fuchsias, on the first floor, is reached via a stone stair. It has a charmingly beamed kitchen/sitting room with pretty tiles and curtains and a white tiled floor; again, it is very well-equipped, even sporting a fondue set! *Electricity not included. B&B also.*

sleeps	Camélias 5. Fuchsias 2-4.
rooms	Camélias: 1 double, 1 twin, 1 single; 1 shower room. Fuchsias: 1 twin, 1 double sofabed; 1 bathroom.
price	Camélias €270-€400. Fuchsias €250-€360. Prices per week.

Nicole Vandon

tel +33 (0)2 31 37 87 82
fax +33 (0)2 31 37 87 82
email nicole@leclosbernard.com
web www.leclosbernard.com

Manoir des Doyens

Bayeux, Calvados

If military history is your thing, this 17th-century stone farmhouse is for you. Bayeux, with its tapestry, cathedral and military cemetery, is within walking distance, the Normandy landing beaches are a short drive away, and Lt-Colonel Chilcott, a military historian, will take you on a private battlefield tour if you are keen. He and his gentle wife moved here from the Isle of Wight and run a B&B in the main house (once the property of the Deans of Bayeux, according to the Lt-Colonel). But even if military history isn't your bag, you'll appreciate the peace and space of this farm with its grassy courtyard, animals and ancient stone pond. The wing where you lodge also has its own walled garden (complete with swings, sandpit, slide) and you may use the barbecue. The kitchen and living room are plain but functional and furnishings basic and somewhat worn, but up the steep narrow stair things get better: pretty antiques and a woodburning stove mingle with modern furniture in the gabled bedrooms and it is absolutely perfect for a family with children. Good value. *B&B also.*

sleeps	2-7.
rooms	2: 1 family room for 3, connected to 1 twin, sofabed downstairs; 1 bathroom, 1 separate wc.
price	€225-€320 per week.

Lt-Col & Mrs Chilcott
tel +33 (0)2 31 22 39 09
fax +33 (0)2 31 21 97 84
email m-jp.chilcott@tiscali.fr

La Commune

Cricqueville en Bessin, Calvados

A very nice little two-person gite has been created from the former bakehouse that stood in the gardens of the owners' house. They are exceptionally welcoming, going so far as to include a packet of hand-made bonbons in their welcome pack. Even better, Monsieur has a 12-metre sailing boat and will happily take you out to view the landing beaches from the sea, or prepare a barbecue for you on the island of St Marcouf. La Commune is well named – there's an easy feel. The sitting area was the former bakehouse, an old stone manger and pretty floor tiles are intact, as is the original fireplace, with logs provided. It is not designer-decorated, preferring a low-key, easy-going style: a round dining table and four chairs, a sofa, a sideboard for the crockery. Up the open stairs to the mezzanine bedroom, full of light from big roof windows; down to the shower. The setting is verdant, a magnificent and ancient pear tree provides your own garden with shade and the travelling baker passes by each morning at about 10.30, so late breakfasts are obligatory.

sleeps	2.
rooms	1 double; 1 shower room.
price	€320-€430 per week.

Chantal Henkart
tel +33 (0)2 31 22 66 82
email c.henkart@wanadoo.fr

Manoir de la Rivière

Géfosse Fontenay, Calvados

Isolated at the end of the manor's walled garden, this little gem is the ultimate lovers' retreat. Built into the high walls around the old manor, it was once the watchtower for the fortified farm and was probably also used by customs officers controlling the smuggling along this coast. All you'll spy today are the Leharivels' 80-odd dairy cows munching the lush pastures of the Cotentin peninsula. Arrive in winter and Isabelle will have lit a fire for you in the woodburner; come in summer and you have a sun-drenched terrace to lounge on. Pale stone walls and pretty toile de Jouy create a mood of light and calm for the bedroom, with its corner shower cubicle. A steep staircase leads down to the tiny beamed living room, just big enough to squeeze in a sofa, a drop-leaf table and a corner kitchenette. The beach is a stroll away; restaurants and shops are a short drive. And you can visit the D-day landing beaches, including Pointe du Hoc on Omaha Beach where you'll still see German bunkers and shellholes in the cliffs.
Second gîte in manor house. B&B also.

sleeps	2.
rooms	1 double; 1 shower room, 1 separate wc.
price	€280-€380 per week.

Gérard & Isabelle Leharivel

tel	+33 (0)2 31 22 64 45
fax	+33 (0)2 31 22 01 18
email	manoirdelariviere@wanadoo.fr
web	www.chez.com/manoirdelariviere

Le Manoir

Écoquenéauville, Manche

Step into the garden and swoon to the scent of roses. Over 50 different species, in a blistering array of colours, cover one of the walls. Twins Graham and Barry – photographers with a passion for gardening and bags of artistic flair – can name each one. The former bakehouse cottage is hidden in the grounds of their 16th-century manor house. With a walled garden and vine-covered terrace to the front and lawns and patio to the back, you catch the sun all day. Inside, it's big for two, snug for four; exposed beams, plastered walls and sunny Provençal colours add a welcoming rusticity. The living room has an open fireplace while the kitchen – the former bread oven – has a good selection of cooking equipment and willow-pattern china. One glass too many and you may forget to duck as you enter the low-beamed bedroom: it's pretty, with floor level windows overlooking the garden. Days out exploring the landing beaches and fishing ports or birdwatching on the marshlands can be eased under the ultra-smart bathroom's hydromassage shower. Or just wallow in the scented peace of the garden.

sleeps	4.
rooms	2 doubles; 1 bathroom.
price	€490-€630 per week.

Graham & Barry Wallis
tel +33 (0)2 33 95 09 05
fax +33 (0)2 33 95 09 05
email grahamwallis2000@yahoo.com

La Fèvrerie No 1

Ste Geneviève, Manche

The creeper-clad 16th-century house was a farm labourer's cottage; the other half is also rented out (see opposite), and each has its own private garden, divided by a high hedge. The owners are a delight: she charming, bubbly and elegant, he full of kindness; together they've grown vegetables on their farm near the sea for as long as they can remember. They're now retired and run an idyllic B&B 50 yards down the lane. Madame's passion is interior decoration, and it shows: ancient-beamed rooms are furnished with solid, comfortable sofas and chairs, beautiful country antiques, plain or checked curtains. The kitchen is both practical and pretty, and a wooden, open-tread stair leads from the large open-plan living room to charming bedrooms above. The tiny fishing village of Barfleur is just across the fields, and the landing beaches a short drive to the south. In summer you can pop over to the nearby island of Tatihou for atmospheric concerts. Don't forget to taste the local oysters. *Supplement for cleaning at end of stay. B&B also.*

sleeps	4-5.
rooms	2: 1 twin, 1 triple; 1 bathroom.
price	€285-€480 per week.

Marie-France & Maurice Caillet
tel +33 (0)2 33 54 33 53
fax +33 (0)2 33 22 12 50

La Fèvrerie No 2

Ste Geneviève, Manche

The old stone cottage is buffered from the rugged rocky Normandy coast by a swathe of dreamy fields where Monsieur Caillet's racehorses graze. The owners are a sparkling and cultivated couple who have given up vegetable farming and full-time stud farming to run a successful B&B, although Monsieur still breeds a few horses every year. Inside the large living room, a magnificent stone fireplace with woodburner, exposed stone walls, some impressive beams, comfortable seating and French windows with yellow curtains that open to a small patio for dining out. A delicious retreat, whose pretty carpeted bedrooms have dark antique furniture, charming French wallpapers and tranquil views over surrounding fields. Explore the Cotentin peninsula on foot, visit the weekly markets at Barfleur and St Pierre Église, or stroll along the bay in attractive St-Vaast-la-Hougue where Edward III landed on his way to Crécy. There are some excellent seafood restaurants in little Barfleur, a two-mile drive, and in Saint-Vaast. And all that Franco-English history. *Supplement for cleaning at end of stay. B&B also.*

sleeps	4-5.
rooms	2: 1 twin, 1 family room; 1 shower room, 1 separate wc.
price	€300-€480 per week.

Marie-France & Maurice Caillet
tel +33 (0)2 33 54 33 53
fax +33 (0)2 33 22 12 50

Le Château – La Maison

Le Rozel, Manche

Spend a week here and there will still be nooks, crannies and secret courtyards to discover. Turrets and towers, high walls and crenellations give the 15th-century château – fortified against the English, among others – a regal grandeur as well as a fairytale mystery. In woeful disrepair when bought by the Grandchamps 25 years ago, its restoration is their life's mission. The gîte, in the 18th-century stables and grooms' quarters, helps fund the process. Tucked into a corner of the courtyard, a lobby opens into an open-plan living area which welcomes with sunny yellow walls, a collection of English china, plenty of chairs, antiques, and a modern kitchen. Stone steps lead to two large bedrooms each with grand double doors. Rugs on parquet floors, pictures, tapestries, soft lamps, more antiques give a gracious feel. Bathrooms are roomy and smart with marble tiles and teak floors. Children can play make-believe in the huge garden enclosed by the ancient defensive walls; mature trees give shade for grown-ups to doze over a book. The Grandchamps have a passion for their home which is infectious. *B&B also.*

sleeps	4-5.
rooms	2: 1 double, 1 family room for 3; 2 bathrooms.
price	€540 per week.

Josiane & Jean-Claude Grandchamp

tel +33 (0)2 33 52 95 08

fax +33 (0)2 33 02 00 35

Les Sources

Surtainville, Manche

A maze of narrow lanes between high banks and hedges bring you at last to Les Sources. Hydrangeas and old-fashioned roses surround the early 19th-century *longère*, newly restored and thoughtfully equipped by Roger and Sandra. They used to own an award-winning restaurant-hotel in Wales and understand perfectly what makes a good holiday home. They'll also cook dinner one evening – just ask. The rooms are beamed and attractively furnished, the big granite fireplace in the sitting room is just the place to curl up by with a book. Open-tread stairs lead up to a landing bedroom (the bathroom is on the ground floor), its single bed and child's crib screened by a heavy curtain. One of the other bedrooms, up a couple of steps, has a big roof window onto the garden. It's a lovely place – nearly an acre of lawns, trees and shrubs, with a stream on one side. There's a herb garden, too, and an orchard full of cherry trees, plums and apples. All around are fields and the sea is less than two miles, with deserted sandy beaches and a view of Jersey. *Babysitting available. French cookery courses.*

sleeps	4-6 + cot.
rooms	3: 1 double, 1 family room, 1 single on landing; 1 bathroom downstairs, separate wc.
price	£250-£550 per week.

Roger & Sandra Bates
tel +33 (0)2 33 52 12 89
email rogersandrabates@wanadoo.fr
web www.lessourcesgite.com

La Ferme des Grèves – Jersey, Alderney, Guernsey

Barneville-Carteret, Manche

Stroll into Barneville to buy market-fresh lobsters, oysters and mussels. The farmhouse cheeses look good, too, and a bottle of calvados wouldn't go amiss. Spend a happy afternoon at the nearby beach – sandy and safe – or cycle to the pretty port of Portbail. Forty minutes from Cherbourg, this is a plumb-perfect position. James and Pascale (he's English, she's French) have a hotel-catering background and a sympathetic eye for restoring buildings. They have converted the dairy and stable block – across the courtyard from their farmhouse – into three gîtes, keeping the original shutters and the handsome façades of brick and charcoal-grey stone. All have an open-plan ground floor kept light and simple with pale floor tiles, stone or white plaster walls, rustic tables and bright sofabeds (no charge for extra bodies!). Kitchens are modern and well thought-through while bedrooms are cottagey with low windows, colourful bedspreads and wooden floors. The cottages are close but have private gardens and share the field down to the river estuary. James will even cook for you.

sleeps	Jersey 4-6. Alderney 2. Guernsey 4-5.
rooms	Jersey 2: 1 double, 1 twin; 1 bath. Alderney: 1 family room for 3; 1 bath. Guernsey 2: 1 double, 1 twin; 1 bath.
price	Jersey €535-€610. Alderney €400-€548. Guernsey €535-€610. Prices per week. €70 for two, €90 for four, per night (low season only).
arrival	Saturday in high season.

James & Pascale Boekee

tel +33 (0)2 33 93 16 48

email james.boekee@wanadoo.fr

web www.ahouseinnormandy.co.uk

La Brumannerie

Rauville La Place, Manche

Before you can say 'bonjour' you will be chatting over a drink with Barry and Shaheen, your helpful but never intrusive hosts. An Irish insurance broker turned garden designer and his Indian wife, they have thrown themselves into village life and live with their young daughter in the farmhouse opposite. Your converted stabling is a good, workable family gîte with the charm of original features – beams, joists, sloping ceilings. The open-plan ground floor has a well-equipped kitchen, comfy chairs, dining table and attractive sideboard; the long landing, with its creamy walls, lofty rafters, parquet floor and armchairs is a quiet spot to rest with a book. Children's bedrooms are simple and bright while the master room has a king-size bed, attractive open-stone walls and fresh colours. The shower room is spotless. Parents relax around the garden and terrace, kids let off steam in the nearby field, teenagers play basketball in the barn. No TV. Heaven. Beaches are 25 minutes, and there are castles, walks and birdwatching. Shaheen will produce a tempting Indian meal when you feel like being spoiled.

sleeps	4-6.
rooms	3: 1 double, 1 single with fold-out bed, 1 room with bunks; 1 bathroom.
price	€350-€575 per week.

Barry & Shaheen Battersby

tel	+33 (0)2 33 21 38 76
email	barryjp55@hotmail.com
web	www.battersbygites.com

Le Bas du Parc – The House

St Sauveur le Vicomte, Manche

Off the old courtyard, next to the Cottage (see opposite), looking onto shared gardens, this farmhouse sleeps 11. The two houses together would be perfect for big families, and the whole place is child-friendly: high chairs, cots, babysitting, English TV and the coast 20 minutes away (bring the buckets and spades). You have a tile-floored parlour with ceiling-to-floor curtains, sofa and chairs, a charming dining room/kitchen wonderfully equipped, easy chairs round the fireplace and a utility room (dishwasher, washing machine, freezer). Up the wooden staircase to three sunny bedrooms on the first floor: a beautiful antique carved bed, an oak armoire, white linen, fat pillows. More bedrooms in the attic, cosy for kids. Bathrooms are spotless and white. You'll be snug in winter, with logs crackling in the old fireplace downstairs and central heating throughout. Kathleen lives in a cottage next door, has done for years and is there whenever you need her. Birds, squirrels, flowers, peace – a wonderful place. *Highchair. Babysitting available. Bring your own linen.*

sleeps 9-11.
rooms 5: 2 doubles, 1 twin, 1 single, 1 quadruple; 2 bathrooms, 1 shower room.
price £400-£780 per week.

Kathleen Byles
tel +33 (0)2 33 41 39 22
email lebasduparc@hotmail.com
web www.lebasduparc.com

Le Bas du Parc – The Cottage

St Sauveur le Vicomte, Manche

You leave a country lane, follow a track through the woods, cross a bridge and when the road runs out... Le Bas du Parc awaits, in deepest Normandy. It's stylish, too: Kathleen has given her 18th-century barn a 21st-century makeover. Old stone walls are festooned with hollyhocks and roses while inside the odd wall has come down to give it all an open-plan feel. You have pale wooden beams, rugs on tiled floors, white walls, old pine doors. China plates and good prints adorn the walls, and the fabrics – curtains, bedspreads, tablecloths and upholstery – are the work of Kathleen's exceptionally gifted hands: gently floral curtains here, a bedcover in toile de Jouy there. The quaint, country-style sitting room has a video and TV, the modern kitchen a dishwasher, and there are heaters for winter. Upstairs: three simple but pretty bedrooms overlook the garden or the courtyard; one has a wisteria mural. French windows open to a patio and the garden runs into a field where paths have been mown through the long grass – perfect for dens. *Highchair. Babysitting available. Bring your own linen.*

sleeps	5-7 + cot.
rooms	3: 1 double, 1 twin, 1 single with bunk; 1 bathroom, 1 separate wc downstairs.
price	£200-£490 per week.

Kathleen Byles

tel	+33 (0)2 33 41 39 22
email	lebasduparc@hotmail.com
web	www.lebasduparc.com

La Bergerie

St Rémy des Landes, Manche

After a day on the dunes, cook your dinner, Norman-style, in the great inglenook fireplace, then enjoy it with a flask of local cider. All is wooden inside this ancient farmhouse, from the gorgeous panelling round the hearth to the inviting oak settle and heavy ceiling beams. The high-quality, very personal furnishings make this feel like a much-loved home rather than a holiday let – probably because it *is* a home much of the year. Even though the Lea family won't be here when you are, they'll make you feel welcome on arrival by leaving you food and drinks. Enjoy serene views over the house's eight acres of fields from the huge, south-facing master bedroom; children will be in heaven in the carpeted, primrose-coloured dorm. There's a games room if it's wet; if not, head for nearby Portbail to swim, sail or ride. If you're not persuaded to cook (despite the lovely Paul Bocuse range in the well-equipped kitchen), try the mussels in the town's many restaurants. Ideal for two families holidaying together – beaches and sailing are no distance at all – and temptingly close to England.

sleeps	8-12 + cot.
rooms	4: 3 doubles, 1 twin with bunks & sofabed; 2 shower rooms, 1 bathroom.
price	£350-£675 per week.

Oriana Lea
tel +44 (0)1963 359234
fax +44 (0)1963 351433
email oj.lea@btinternet.com

La Ferme de l'Église – Chèvrefeuille, Stable Cottage, Jasmin

St Nicolas de Pierrepont, Manche

Take your pick: the pig barn, the milking parlour or the cider store. All are simple and comfortable with white walls, tiled floors and splashes of colour. Deep in the Parc du Marais, the farmstead is tucked behind the village church. Chèvrefeuille and Jasmin are attached to the house; Stable Cottage is separate with an enclosed garden. Décor is a happy, homely mishmash of varnished pine and new fabric, and spotless. Stable Cottage is the grandest, with a carpeted, beamed sitting room and a stone fireplace; Jasmin is the smallest – and most adorable – as befits a cider store. One Chèvrefeuille bedroom is wheelchair-friendly; all are a good size, with comfy beds, decent wardrobes and garden views. Bath and shower rooms are small and sparkling, kitchens rustic and well-equipped, and a pot of homemade marmalade welcomes all. There's a vegetable patch tended organically by owners Richard and Jay, and speckled eggs from their chickens (yours to buy). Swings, bikes, ping-pong and gardens; cats, goats, chickens and ducks; free binoculars for walks that start from the door. *B&B also.*

sleeps	Chèvrefeuille 6. Stable 6. Jasmin 4.
rooms	Chèvrefeuille: 2 doubles, 1 twin; 2 showers, 1 separate wc. Stable: 2 doubles, 1 twin; 1 bath, 1 shower, 1 separate wc. Jasmin: 1 double, 1 twin; 1 shower, 1 separate wc.
price	Chèvrefeuille & Stable €290-€530. Jasmin €240-€390. Prices per week.

Richard & Jay Clay
tel +33 (0)2 33 45 53 40
fax +33 (0)2 33 45 53 40
email theclays@wanadoo.fr
web www.normandie-cottages.com

La Merise

Gerville la Forêt, Manche

Another impossibly pretty cottage, with rambling pink roses by the front door. The house basks on the sunny side of Mont Castre, an island of stone in a sea of green. You are in a national park: marshland, coastal dunes and woods burst with all sorts of birds; wild flowers flourish. Back at the ranch John and Valerie, two ex-pat Aussies who do B&B, have brought a colourful organic garden to life; you have your own piece of it, with barbecue, for outdoor dining. Your semi-detached gîte is encased within 300-year-old walls: simple, homely, ideal for two and very good value. The front door opens to a sunny kitchen/living room, small but cosy, and a dear little mezzanine bedroom, reached via an Everest stair. There are bicycles to borrow and old railway lines to cycle along. In summer, grab the boogie boards and head for the beach. There's a local market for each day of the week, or you can try the fisherman's cooperatives for oysters, mussels, lobster, crab. Lessay with its abbey is well worth a visit; its September festival, the oldest country fair in Europe, has been going for over 900 years. *B&B also.*

sleeps	2-3.
rooms	1 double; 1 shower room. Extra single bed available.
price	€215-€270 per week.

Valerie & John Armstrong
tel +33 (0)2 33 45 63 86
email the.armstrong@free.fr

La Campanule

Gerville la Forêt, Manche

The croissants brought fresh to your door are worth rousing yourself for. On a quiet, winding road this old farmworker's cottage has been smartly revived. Still in its infancy, its fresh face can only improve with age; inside, all is spanking new. It's a thoughtful renovation, with underfloor heating downstairs to keep you as warm as toast in winter. The soberly elegant sitting room has a lime-rendered fireplace and French floral sofas, soft yellow tones fill the space, and the dining room, sandwiched between the all-mod-cons kitchen and the sitting room, seats eight. A hardwood staircase leads you up to a star-gazing double bed, the twin room has a rustic planked floor, the triple would be perfect for kids. Australian owners Valerie and John, artist and historian, are as friendly as can be, offer you a welcome drink, introduce you to your new home and fill you in on the local history. Green fingers have tackled the large garden – all swirling paths and lawn. You are on an official cycle and walking route, so two free bikes come in handy. Mont St Michel and Bayeux are nearby. *B&B also.*

sleeps	6-7.
rooms	3:1 double, 1 triple, 1 single; 1 bathroom, 1 separate wc.
price	€395-€575 per week.

Valerie & John Armstrong
tel +33 (0)2 33 45 63 86
email the.armstrong@free.fr

Les Pommiers

Gerville la Forêt, Manche

The local farmer, who is also the mayor, makes calvados from the apples that fall in the orchard. You are in the middle of nowhere: a narrow lane skirts the forest and leads across open farmland to this 200-year-old stone barn. It was converted by Don, Gilly's husband, an English builder who sits on the Comité de Fêtes. Local artisans helped him out and their fine handiwork is evident in the tiled floors, exposed beams and ceiling joists. The feel is warmly rustic with all the comforts you'd hope for: a big family kitchen, a woodburner, a balcony in the first-floor sitting room with views over the orchard. Bedrooms are excellent. The downstairs family room – bunks and two singles – is huge, lovely and sunny; upstairs, yellow walls, more exposed timbers and a pretty stained-glass window in the large double. Outside, a 500-year-old oak casts generous shade while paths lead out into the forest; if you're lucky you'll see buzzards resting on the fence posts. In April and May the lane teams with foxglove and orchids flourish in summer. There are long sandy beaches close by, too. Perfect for young families.

sleeps	6-10 + 2 cots.
rooms	3: 2 doubles, 1 family room with bunks & 2 singles; 2 bathrooms, 1 shower room, 1 separate wc.
price	€375-€740 (£250-£495).

Gilly Turner & Anne Corden

tel +33 (0)2 33 21 35 95
+44 (0)1730 829277

email gacorden@btopenworld.com

Le Mesnil Gonfroy

Hambye, Manche

Loads of bedrooms and bathrooms, masses of character and a garden you can lose the kids in. Find honey-coloured heaven in this old Normandy farmhouse with its acre of well-tended, fenced garden, apple orchard and heated pool (extra fee). The house is almost two in one: one front door, two ground floors – on one side, a pretty room adapted for wheelchair users, nicely private, on the other, kitchen, dining room and sitting room. Bedrooms are upstairs – traditional, friendly, with solid sober furniture and the odd surprise: a massive mirror, a stunning French dresser, a tiny stained-glass window. The largest, with its ancient cross-beam and single beds, was tailor-made for midnight feasts! One bathroom, with 'wooden' boards, has a nautical air. Blue and white tiles brighten the kitchen, deep sofas and wood-burner warm the sitting room, French windows fling open to a south-facing terrace and the breakfast room is charmingly rustic. Amble down to the pool on the lower lawn, with its glorious views of forested hills. Table tennis and boules here, sandy beaches a 20-minute drive.

sleeps	12-13 + cot.
rooms	6: 2 doubles, 3 twins, 1 triple; 3 bathrooms, 1 shower room.
price	£575-£1,600 per week.

Brian & Sue Smart
tel +44 (0)1747 812 019
fax +44 (0)1747 811066
email hambye@hartgrovefarm.co.uk
web www.normandyfarmhouses.co.uk

Hello

La Germainière

Guéhébert, Manche

Find bucolic bliss at this grand old farmhouse, hidden behind high hedgerows. Past orchards and fields of munching cows, down a private half-mile drive, the 300-year-old grey stone façade comes into view. This is a house that feels solid, loved and lived in – three floors of robust stone walls, characterful beams, tiled floors and a huge Normandy fireplace. The big modern kitchen – beech units and all the equipment – leads into a dining room with massive table and dresser. In the warm, low-beamed lounge, cocoon yourself before the fire on the occasional rainy day in velvet and leather sofas. Bedrooms are big, carpeted, personal: a 1920s' poster here, silk flowers there, the odd friendly antique. The twin room is a vision in shocking pink, there are yellows and golds in the master room and calming lavender and blue elsewhere. Note, no space for wardrobes in the two rooms at the very top. Outside, a shaded vine veranda for leisurely meals, lawn and a hidden orchard to keep the children happy and, for those venturing further, five old bikes for free. A peaceful place full of comfort and charm.

sleeps	12.
rooms	6: 2 doubles, 4 twins; 1 bathroom, 2 shower rooms.
price	£395-£1,050.

Brian & Sue Smart

tel +44 (0)1747 812 019

fax +44 (0)1747 811066

email lagermainiere@hartgrovefarm.co.uk

web www.normandyfarmhouses.co.uk

Hotel la Ramade – Gîte Country Garden

Marcey les Grèves, Manche

In a courtyard behind the hotel run by kind Véronique stands a little one-storey granite house originally built for *grand-mère*, a comfortable resting place for two or four, and even a baby (cots are available). From a wooden-slatted, pot-dotted patio you enter a tiled living room furnished with black leather convertible sofa, two recliners, a dining table and wrought-iron shelving filled with knick-knacks and radio. Wall heaters give year-round warmth. The kitchen – white, brand new and well-equipped – has a door to the grounds: full of mature trees that give privacy from the road, they are yours to share. And if you're a reluctant cook, there's a crêperie you can walk to, or restaurants in Avranches. You can also eat at the hotel. Véronique serves delicious food: *salade aux gésiers* in the spring, perhaps, followed by *navarin de veau* and early strawberries – be sure to book ahead. With such privacy and grounds this would be a good place for young children, if you feel like squeezing them in. You are 100 yards from the river and a short drive from Mont St Michel and the sea. *Hotel also.*

sleeps	2-4 + cot.
rooms	1 double, 1 sofabed in living room; 1 bathroom.
price	€260-€410 per week.

Véronique Morvan
tel +33 (0)2 33 58 27 40
fax +33 (0)2 33 58 29 30
email vmorvan@wanadoo.fr
web www.laramade.fr

La Cahudière – Marguerite, Coquelicot & Bleuet

St Martin de Landelles, Manche

The lane runs out at La Cahudière: expect peace and quiet in the rolling folds of deep country. A family venture, this 100-year-old stone farmhouse with hay barn has been neatly converted into three gîtes. Window boxes brim with colour, butterflies come for the peach trees, you may gather the fruit. There are white walls and new pine, shuttered windows, pastel fabrics and tiled floors. Stone fireplaces and woodburners give winter warmth, thick walls keep you cool in summer. Pretty bedrooms are spotless and come with check curtains, cane furniture, good beds. There are big double rooms for adults and bunk rooms for children. Sit out infront and watch the cattle graze; spot deer, even badgers, in the woods. There's badminton in one of the fields, tennis and fishing nearby and a video library for the horizontally inclined. Children have masses of space to run around in safely and there's a private patio for each gîte. The village, a mile away, has good little shops and a restaurant for lunch. Mont St Michel is within striking distance; Cancale, a pretty coastal town, is known for its oysters. *Shared laundry.*

sleeps: Marguerite 4-6.
Coquelicot 4-7.
Bleuet 8-11.

rooms: Marguerite: 1 double, 1 twin, 1 sofa; 1 bath.
Coquelicot: 1 double, 1 single with bunks, 1 sofa; 1 bath.
Bleuet: 2 doubles, 1 single with bunks, 1 room with bunks, 1 twin on mezzanine; 1 bath, 1 shower.

price: £185-£695 per week.

Margaret Atherton
tel: +33 (0)2 33 49 30 45
mobile: +44 (0)79 7381 7338
email: enquiries@lacahudiere.co.uk
web: www.lacahudiere.co.uk

Launay Arot – Sabine, Hélène, Pascale, Germaine, Marguerite

La Landec, Côtes-d'Armor

A peaceful cluster of gîtes in beautiful countryside near Dinan, St Malo and lovely beaches – perfect for families or holiday chums. Blue paintwork decorates each granite cottage – quintessentially French – of which three are converted farm cottages and two, the former stables, attached to the house where your English hosts live. The Thains are the kindest people, proud of their new enterprise and generous to guests: there's wood for open fires, fresh linen weekly, barbecues, cots, high chairs and stairgates, a welcome pack of goodies and a great information pack. Rooms are a good size, nothing feels poky, walls are whitewashed, electricity is included. Bedrooms, some at mezzanine level – ever popular with children! – are simply furnished with pale fabrics and new beds, modern kitchens hold all you need, sitting rooms are homely (real fires) and washing machines shared. There's not much that isn't within a half-hour drive, the countryside is open and pretty and there's a really special restaurant at Plélan le Petit (3km). All this, boules, swings and two acres of gardens to roam.

sleeps	2 gîtes for 4; 3 gîtes for 6.
rooms	Sabine, Hélène: 1 double, 1 twin; 1 bathroom. Pascale, Germaine, Marguerite: 1 double, 2 twins; 2 bathrooms.
price	€250-€580 per week.
arrival	Wednesdays & Saturdays.

Sue & Nick Thain

tel +33 (0)2 96 84 54 44

email nick@bretoncottages.com

web www.bretoncottages.com

La Channais

Plouër sur Rance, Côtes-d'Armor

No frills but plain comfort in this 18th-century terraced cottage in a quiet back lane 500 yards from the river Rance. Guests are asked to mow the badminton court and clean the house before they go but this seems fair exchange for the use of four new bikes and an eight-foot dinghy on the river. Inside, a fully equipped IKEA kitchen sits on a grey, slate floor. There's ample seating in the cosy sitting room, an old Breton armoire, two oak ship's timbers in the ceiling, and a granite wall at the foot of the steep, stone spiral stair. A spliced and knotted rope handrail – 'Turkshead' for those in the know – hauls you up to the landing and the pretty iron balcony on the front of the house. Plain bedrooms – blue and white for the double room, red and white for the bunk beds – overlook woods and gardens. And it's a garden for living as well as playing in, being part terraced and part large lawn enclosed by hydrangeas and shrubs. There's teak furniture and a barbecue, plentiful instructions and advice for visitors and logs for your fire. Plouër is up the road for shops, supermarket, two restaurants and several sports.

sleeps	5-7.
rooms	3: 1 double, 1 twin, 1 room with bunks & single; 1 bathroom.
price	£200-£450 per week.

Neil & Pamela Millward

tel +44 (0)1803 782981

fax +44 (0)1803 782391

email pamela@nmillward.eclipse.co.uk

Ville Lieu de Fer – Manor House, Garden House, Artist's Studio

Le Gouray, Côtes-d'Armor

Luxurious is the living in these three houses round the garden courtyard. They have all been beautifully restored, even the barbecues are top-of-the-range. In the Manor House (below): a vast 50-foot living room with warm yellow walls, French windows, open fire and table for 12, and a super all-singing, all-dancing kitchen. Fine oak stairs lead to grand bedrooms: beds are king-size, the singles are 'Breton' (larger than usual) and there's fine French wallpaper. In the conservatory-living room of the Garden House: an African theme, pale washes, lots of light. The communal laundry has washing machines, driers and ironing boards. The coach-house games room is stocked with table tennis, darts, even plugs for Gameboys. The Studio, a loft apartment with a sunny balcony, is above. The pool, encircled by lawns and loungers, can be heated to 30 degrees. It's a gorgeous setting, the village has both bakery and bar, and medieval Lamballe, a 15-minute drive, has the rest. *July-August both houses and studio must be rented together. 'Manor' and 'Garden' are connected by a central hall for combined rental.*

sleeps	Manor 4-6. Garden 4. Studio 2.
rooms	Manor: 1 double, 1 twin, 1 twin on mezzanine; 1 bath, 1 shower, 1 separate wc. Garden: 1 double, 1 twin; 1 bath; 1 shower. Studio: 1 double; 1 shower.
price	Manor £600. Garden £400. Studio £200. Manor & Garden July-Aug: £2,400. Prices per week.

Mike & Gaile Richardson
tel +33 (0)2 96 34 95 30
fax +33 (0)2 96 34 95 30
email richardson.michael@wanadoo.fr

Château de Bonabry

Hillion, Côtes-d'Armor

This little gem used to house the archives of the château (built by the Vicomte's ancestors in 1373): the family discovered piles of musty parchment documents when they restored it a few years ago. With the sea at the end of the drive, your own rose- and shrub-filled walled garden to spill out into in the summer, and two lively, loveable hosts who do B&B in the château, this is a wonderful place for a small family to stay. Furnishings are simple but adequate. Downstairs rooms have stone vaulted ceilings, crimson-washed walls and age-old terracotta floors, a new sofa, a stripey *fauteuil*. The kitchen is fitted white, with a round table and yellow chairs. In the twin, a stripped pine floor and pink toile de Jouy; more beams and lovely yellow fabric-clad walls in the double – an enthusastic redecoration by the Vicomtesse. If they aren't out riding, your hosts will be on hand to help if you need them, and the Vicomte may bring offerings from his personal vegetable garden. Your 'English' garden is furnished with parasol, barbecue and plastic loungers – a pretty spot in which to unwind. *Bring own linen. B&B also.*

sleeps	4.
rooms	2: 1 double, 1 twin; 1 shower room.
price	€400-€1,000 per week.

Vicomte & Vicomtesse du Fou de Kerdaniel

tel +33 (0)2 96 32 21 06
fax +33 (0)2 96 32 21 06
email bonabry@wanadoo.fr
web bonabry.fr.st

Manoir Le Cosquer

Pommerit Le Vicomte, Côtes-d'Armor

A lake with its own small island, a rose garden, lawns, a copse... The seven-hectare grounds of this old granite manor are full of enticements. You can fish or boat and there's a play area for children. The house, going back in part to the 15th century, is reached via a tree-lined drive; the baker's is a stroll. Two wings have been converted for guests and divide easily for two parties holidaying together: there are two separate entrances and two staircases, one 15th century. Some bedrooms are in the oldest part of the house, others are more modern, and furniture is a fine mix of old and new. The high-ceilinged attic room sleeps five or six: children love it. A glorious Breton fireplace dominates one end of the vast, tile-floored sitting room. No dining room, but the lofty, raftered, slightly dated kitchen has a generous table. At the back, a terrace for sunsets and drinks. Alison and Mauro are friendly and hardworking, with two daughters of their own; enthusiastic about their new venture, they have created a fitness room and can organise a cook if you don't fancy cooking. *B&B when not rented.*

sleeps	12-18.
rooms	6: 2 doubles, 1 twin, 1 room with 2 singles & bunks, 1 family rooms for 3, 1 family room for 5; 2 baths, 4 showers.
price	€2,500-€3,800 per week.

Alison Sinclair & Mauro Leccacorvi

tel	+33 (0)2 96 21 74 12
fax	+33 (0)2 96 21 74 12
email	lecosquer@tiscali.fr
web	www.lecosquer.com

Ti-Koad

Perros-Guirec, Côtes-d'Armor

The charming Coquendeaus built this high-tech little house five years ago, on the far side of their pretty, sloping, shrub-filled garden with views to the sea. Walls, steps, decking: your home is warmly woody, as is your summer house for fishing nets and bikes. The ground floor is coolly tiled, white-beamed and open plan, there's a fresh, modern feel and the attention to detail is impressive – from the welcome pack with Breton cider to the electric blinds. Up an open-tread spiral stair are two ship-shape bedrooms with a nautical air; open the windows and you can sniff the sea. Nicely painted floors, high rafters, excellent beds and a small dressing room between the rooms; *tout simple*. Downstairs is the bathroom, gorgeous with twin zinc basins, matching driftwood mirrors and big shower, and there's a laundry in the basement. The house is beautifully planned, has a wood-burner for cosy winter nights and is perfect for a civilised holiday by the sea. Visit the gannets on Les Sept Iles, hire a boat from the yacht club and enjoy the seafood – your hosts have all the info. *Heating included in winter. B&B also.*

sleeps	4 + cot.
rooms	2: 1 double, 1 twin + cot; 1 shower room.
price	€595-€870. €476 for 2 low season. Prices per week.

M & Mme Coquendeau
tel +33 (0)2 96 91 15 61
+33 (0)2 96 23 08 90
fax +33 (0)2 96 23 08 90
email coquendeaucy@wanadoo.fr

41 rue de la Petite Corniche

Perros Guirec, Côtes-d'Armor

The ever-changing light of the great bay shimmers in through all your French windows. Sit in your armchair and gaze as the boats go by, or walk to the beautiful sands and waters of Trestriguel beach – it's 10 minutes away. (The village is close too.) Marie-Clo does B&B in the big house; attentive and generous, she has decorated your teensy white cottage in soft blues and lemons, enlivened by her patchworks and embroideries. On a single floor you have an open-plan sitting and dining room with a diminutive (but well-equipped) kitchen behind, and more radiant views from the little bedroom. Furniture is fresh and new and in keeping with the house; the bed is pine, the dining room chairs blue with painted birds. Outside, your own patch of garden with small terrace, barbecue and lawn. Set out for walks along the pink granite coast, make the most of the seafood restaurants and be sure not to miss the Sept Iles archipelago – the most magnificent seabird colony in France. *Cot & highchair available. Use of washing machine in main house. B&B also.*

sleeps	2-4 + cot.
rooms	1 double, 1 sofabed in sitting room; 1 shower room.
price	€450-€500 per week.
closed	December-January.

Marie-Clo Biarnès
tel +33 (0)2 96 23 28 08
email marieclo.biarnes@wanadoo.fr
web perso.wanadoo.fr/corniche/

L'Ancien Presbytère

Trégrom, Côtes-d'Armor

The scent of climbing roses and honeysuckle greets you as you arrive at this stunning 17th-century grey stone presbytery: Madame's passion is gardening, as you'll see from her colourful borders. You even have a large walled orchard all to yourselves. The house is a wing of the main house where B&B guests lodge but you have complete privacy. Interior decoration is homely and personal – all Madame's handiwork – with plenty of painted wood in smoky hues. There's a small kitchen with blue-painted cupboards, waxed terracotta floor and sunny, yellow, wallpapered walls. Bedrooms, on the first and attic floors, are in old-fashioned pastels with matching floral curtains and bedspreads, unusual canework beds and antique painted wardrobes. Views are peaceful and of the garden. Buy your morning croissants at the organic baker's behind the house; for fruits, vegetables and cheeses there are local weekly markets. Charming Madame knows the area "like her pocket" and has itineraries for your deeper discovery of secret delights, as well as beaches and châteaux to visit. *B&B also.*

sleeps	4.
rooms	2 twins; 2 bathrooms.
price	€600 per week.
arrival	Saturday or Sunday.
closed	October-April.

Nicole de Morchoven

tel +33 (0)2 96 47 94 15

fax +33 (0)2 96 47 94 15

email nicole.de-morchoven@wanadoo.fr

web tregrom.monsite.wanadoo.fr

Hello

La Maison de Bruyère

St Servais, Côtes-d'Armor

Never mind the thrice-daily church bells and the frogs in June, this is a tranquil place and the views over the village to the forest are lovely. The austerity of the Breton-stone exterior belies the warmth within. To the left of the brown and yellow tiled hall: a sunny family kitchen, well-equipped, with good high ceiling and original 1930s sink; to the right: a decent-sized sitting room with three-piece suite, books, CDs, videos, silk flowers, period lights and woodburner; and a large bathroom with a blue bath. Up the stairs are plain oak floors and ceilings, robust furniture and flowered fabrics, soft duvets and feather pillows, a green-tiled shower; it is Breton through and through. There's space and light aplenty, and a large enclosed garden outside with big paddling pool, badminton and boules. The owners live in England but the friendly neighbours are there should you need them. Then there's the village, sweet, peaceful, traditional – bar, shop, church, more boules – a short walk downhill. Beyond, the Gorge de Corong, the forest of Dualt and all of the glorious north coast.

sleeps	6 + 1 child & cot.
rooms	4: 2 doubles, 1 twin, 1 single for child; 1 bathroom, 1 shower room.
price	£395-£495 per week.
closed	October-March.

Andrew & Heather Taylor
tel +44 (0)1204 847035
fax +44 (0)1204 841113
email heather.taylor@btinternet.com

Toul Bleïz – Kerpoence

Laniscat, Côtes-d'Armor

Pretend you're playing doll's houses! This is an entrancing place, a one-up, one-down cottage in a quiet street in the village of Laniscat. And it doesn't feel the least bit cramped; every inch of space has been used to simple, stylish effect. Ceramic tiles cover the open-plan ground floor, a Moroccan rug and bright armchairs add colour; diminutive windows are hung with cream cotton tatting done by Julie's great aunt; a tiny, perfect kitchen is tucked under the stairs. Bedroom and bathroom are up in the beamed roof space where Julie's paintings decorate the walls and the low bed, flanked by niche lights, is covered with gingham. Admire Jez's expert carpentry on the bath panelling (but don't expect to lie full stretch in the bath: it's three-quarter size). You'll like Julie and Jez. They're ex-teachers and live five minutes away. If you want to avoid going in search of restaurants in nearby Gouarec, you may book a vegetarian meal with them. This is a terrific place for a couple – though not if you're at all creaky. Listen to the church bells and enjoy the lavender in the garden.

sleeps	2.
rooms	1 double; 1 bathroom.
price	€230-€380 (£150-£250) per week; €58 (£38) per night.
arrival	Sunday.

Julie & Jez Rooke

tel	+33 (0)2 96 36 98 34
email	jezrooke@hotmail.com
web	www.phoneinsick.co.uk

Coat Amour

Morlaix, Finistère

Surrounded by 12 lush acres of ancient oak, lime trees, sequoia, Japanese maple and orchard, you could be on a country estate. But no: the centre of Morlaix, with its bustling port and medieval streets, is five minutes, the one clue the distant traffic hum. This converted stable block of a 19th-century manor house – on one level and wheelchair-friendly – is your introduction to country-style living; the soft, sober colours, the space and the light lend a low-key luxury. In the beamed, open-plan living area are Persian rugs on tiled floors, cream leather sofas, antique pine, a polished dining table and a winter fire. A bar separates the new and well-equipped kitchen. Bedrooms are airy and sunny and have good quality curtains and bedspreads. Large windows overlook the grounds; one room has French windows onto a terrace. Bathrooms are traditional, one designed for disabled guests. Explore Morlaix, the fishing ports and the beaches, or pick a shady spot to read, dip into the pool (shared with B&B guests) and enjoy an evening stroll in a green paradise. *B&B also.*

sleeps	4-7.
rooms	6: 1 double, 1 twin, 1 room with bunks & single; 1 shower room, 1 bathroom, separate wc.
price	€600-€1,200 per week.
arrival	Friday.

	Stafford & Jenny Taylor
tel	+33 (0)2 98 88 57 02
email	stafford.taylor@wanadoo.fr
web	www.gites-morlaix.com

Le Manoir de Prevasy

Carhaix Plouguer, Finistère

You don't only get this stunningly renovated 16th-century manor but all that encircles it: large barns and stables, high walls and a chapel. It is exceptional in every way – original stone-flagged floors, a 16th-century oak staircase (it creaks delightfully), huge fireplaces, high ceilings, big beams. There's a sitting room carpeted with seagrass and rugs, an armoire for china, and blinds, not curtains, to show off ancient stone. In the cottage next door, a lovers' nest: you lie in bed under a painted blue sky, angels watching over you. Modern comforts include the fabulously equipped kitchen (with Smeg oven), powerful showers, central heating, an oak-framed conservatory. Off the lovely courtyard in yet another old building live the owners, happy to help and advise. A perfect place for families, with table tennis, badminton, boules and a decked, fenced pool. Through the old stone arch watch the cows from the nearby dairy farm wander up the lane – the only passing traffic. Carhaix Plouguer is two kilometres away so walk in or cycle – or follow your nose along the canal tow path. Magnificent.

sleeps	8-12.
rooms	5: 2 doubles, 1 twin, 1 family room for 4; 4 bathrooms, 1 shower room. 1 double in separate cottage; 1 shower room.
price	£600-£1,700 per week.
closed	January-March.

Peter & Clarissa Novak

tel +33 (0)2 98 93 24 36

fax +33 (0)2 98 93 24 36

email novak.prevasy@wanadoo.fr

Guillec Vihan

Collorec, Finistère

In a wooded valley deep in the Breton countryside is a cluster of farm buildings, a lazy river winding through the fields below. It's all part of Robbie and Fiona's 50-hectare organic arable farm: a lively, sociable place to bring the family! Their own children and grandchildren are often around, plus nine cats, one dog and an assortment of horses. Close by is another gîte and the Rainbirds' own house – there's always something going on. The cottage, recently restored, has traditional stone doorways and oak window frames. Fiona has an eye for a dramatic effect, coupled with an interest in the past. In the kitchen/dining room, rush-seated chairs pull up around an oil-clothed table; upstairs, the dormer-windowed bedrooms are star-spangled. The ground-floor double, ideal for the less mobile, has a huge canopied bed, an old armoire and a hand-painted mural. On one side of the cottage is a gravelled terrace, on the other a big lawn; everywhere, climbing roses and clematis – Fiona loves her garden. One of Robbie's passions is tractors (you'll hear the odd rumble), another is restoring old cars.

sleeps	6.
rooms	3: 1 double, 2 twins; 2 bathrooms.
price	€325-€665 per week.

Robbie & Fiona Rainbird

tel	+33 (0)2 98 73 93 60
fax	+33 (0)2 98 73 93 60
email	info@rainbird-gites.com
web	www.rainbird-gites.com

Le Bois Coudrais – Bakery, Granary, Mills One & Two

Cuguen, Ille-et-Vilaine

Claire and Philippe manage the impossible, an away-from-it-all atmosphere where there's masses to do. A campsite, pool, play areas, bicycles, café/bar, animals to feed – all this among private patios and shady trees. Beyond, woodland walks and countryside. The four gîtes – converted farm outbuildings, three linked, one detached – are prettily grouped around the pool: close enough for the children to make friends but distant enough for privacy. Cosy, characterful and homely, with beams, exposed stonework and granite fireplaces, the open-plan living areas have simple furniture, earthy coloured rugs on tiled floors, open fires or woodburning stoves and compact kitchens suitable for holiday meals. Whitewashed walls, laminate floors (soon to be in all) and pretty fabrics make the most of the small, slopey-ceiling bedrooms. The simple shower rooms are are being updated. The Yberts are energetic, enterprising people and will steer you towards the nearby zoo, aquarium, castles, markets and, of course, Emerald Coast beaches. This place is about having fun, making friends and relaxing out of doors.

sleeps	Bakery, Mill Two & Granary 4 each. Mill One 4-5.
rooms	Bakery, Mill Two, Granary: 1 double, 1 twin; 1 shower. Mill One: 1 double, 1 triple; 1 shower.
price	€205-€684 (£140-£475) per week.
arrival	Saturday, but flexible.

Claire & Philippe Ybert

tel	+33 (0)2 99 73 27 45
fax	+33 (0)2 99 73 13 08
email	cpybert@wanadoo.fr
web	www.vacancebretagne.com

Le Rhun – Four Gîtes

Pluméliau, Morbihan

Your children will tumble out of the car and head for the sandpit, swings and small pool, or volleyball, basketball and boules. For grown-ups, there are shady hammocks and a sauna. Family-friendly, easy-going, this lovely German couple have done a high-class renovation job on their cluster of Breton outbuildings – and with two B&B rooms as well as four gîtes, the farmstead becomes a lively place in the holidays. Rooms are simply furnished, colours light and fresh, kitchens modern and well-equipped and everyone gets a terrace and a garden. The ground floors are open-plan; the cooking areas are tucked into a corner or quite separate. You have tiled floors, white walls and beamed ceilings, perhaps an old armoire, a stone table or a drawing by Jurgen's cousin to add an individual touch. Bedrooms feel Scandinavian – pale, uncluttered spaces with shots of colour from curtain or headboard; bathrooms are clean and functional. Cows graze next door, the little lake attracts birds and there are five acres to explore. Beyond: beaches, the castle at Pontivy and canoeing on the river Blavet. *B&B also.*

sleeps	4 gîtes: 1 for 2; 1 for 6; 2 for 4.
rooms	Gîtes One & Two: 2 doubles; 1 shower room. Gîte Three: 1 double; 1 shower room downstairs. Gîte Four: 3 doubles; 1 bathroom.
price	€237-€530 per week.
closed	October-April.

Eva & Jürgen Lincke

tel +33 (0)2 97 51 83 48
fax +33 (0)2 97 51 83 48
email eva.lincke@wanadoo.fr
web www.lerhun.de

photo corel images

western loire
the loire valley

Le Relais de la Rinière

Le Landreau, Loire-Atlantique

You're surrounded by vines: this is Muscadet country and the clay soils of the area produce some particularly ambitious wines. Indulge in some private tastings in the huge garden – a cocktail of wisteria, lawns and colourful surprises (with some excellent play equipment for children). Or pop off to one of the nearby *caves*. You'll enjoy your delightful hosts Françoise and Louis, who run a B&B in the imposing coaching inn next door – your cottage is one of the outhouses. He used to be a baker, she's a keen jam-maker, and they moved here from Normandy bringing some lovely antiques with them. A fine old dresser/armoire holds pretty crockery in a light and sunny living area with a well-equipped kitchen, there's an old oak table for family gatherings, a sofa with a bright throw. Colour schemes are adventurous: ochre-sponged walls downstairs, and, in a bedroom for children, low beams painted blue. The downstairs bedroom has the old bread oven. Discover historic Nantes, with its splendid 18th-century houses and its château, or visit the slick wine museum at Le Pallet. There's great cycling, too. *B&B also.*

sleeps	4.
rooms	2: 1 double, 1 twin; 1 shower room.
price	€220-€450 per week.

Françoise & Louis Lebarillier

tel	+33 (0)2 40 06 41 44
fax	+33 (0)2 51 13 10 52
email	riniere@netcourrier.com
web	www.riniere.com

Le Fruitier des Briottières

Champigné, Maine-et-Loire

Wind your way through the forested park of the Château des Briottières to the cool-stone, 18th-century Fruitier where orange and lemon trees once flourished: windows stretch its length and breadth. Savour the earthy aroma of the oak beams and terracotta floors as you lay out your fruits and vegetables – just purchased from the weekly market in Champigné, perhaps – on the original sorting table. Ripe-red throws brighten beds and armchairs, rich Persian rugs protect floors and the Age of Decadence springs from every corner; owners François and Hedwige have beautified the orangery with Louis XIV furniture from the château. Bedrooms span two floors, one with a balcony, another sharing its amazing rounded windows with the room below. Borrow bikes from the hotel and cycle off to other châteaux, enjoy a game of tennis in the grounds, take a leisurely swim in the pool; even a babysitter can be arranged. If you prefer to sit quietly away from the handful of hotel guests, you have a private garden opening off the kitchen from where you may gaze on your beautiful home. *Hotel also.*

sleeps	12-16.
rooms	6: 2 double, 4 twins; 4 bathrooms.
price	€3,500-€7,750 per week.

François & Hedwige de Valbray

tel +33 (0)2 41 42 00 02

fax +33 (0)2 41 42 01 55

email briottieres@wanadoo.fr

web www.fruitier-briottieres.com

La Besnardière

Fougeré, Maine-et-Loire

Wandering chickens, fresh eggs for breakfast, ducks on the pond, a few goats and a donkey: a lovely sense of being 'down on the farm'. It's close to Baugé, yet acres of woodland – a carpet of flowers in the spring – poplar trees and fields are all that can be seen. Delightful Joyce has turned the farmhouse into a two-room B&B and the stabling into a gîte – a bright, sunny space of exposed beams, roof timbers and terracotta floor tiles. Roof windows flood the upper rooms with light, bedrooms are jolly affairs with colourful bedspreads and rugs, simple wooden furniture and modern lamps, and shower rooms are neat and spotless. Relax in the sitting room or pick the sunny spot on the landing with its little seats. There's a holiday mood in the kitchen – a quirky room of mismatched china, scrubbed wooden table and the original hayrack. It's not flash but there's all you need. Or let Joyce cook a vegetarian meal – organic produce from her garden – and eat under the stars. Loire châteaux, local markets, swimming in the lake at La Flèche; a super place for families. *Aromatherapy treatments available. B&B also.*

sleeps	4-6.
rooms	2: 1 double, 1 quadruple; 3 shower rooms.
price	€450-€500 per week.
closed	January-February.

Joyce Rimell
tel +33 (0)2 41 90 15 20
fax +33 (0)2 41 90 15 20
email rimell.joyce@wanadoo.fr
web www.holidays-loire.com

Les Bouchets

Le Vieil Baugé, Maine-et-Loire

The best of both worlds: deep in the countryside – a gentle Loire landscape of copses and fields, orchards and vines – yet two miles from town. Baugé has shops, restaurants, a twice-weekly market, tennis and a pool – perfect. Madame is proud of her home and her rooms, welcomes you with a drink and a full basket of goodies and recommends you join her *table d'hôtes* at least once. It would be a pity not to: she and Monsieur were restaurateurs in Angers and now hold cookery courses on certain weekends. Your farmhouse (once their own holiday home) is next to the Bignons' and your garden is safe for the children to play in; at the end of a no-through road, the rolling countryside spreads in every direction. Inside feels generous, roomy, tidy and in tip-top condition, the house's history most evident in the kitchen's large open *four au pain.* Gleaming reproduction furniture mixes with the odd antique, the 'cons' are 'mod' but the feel is traditional and bedrooms sit cosily under the eaves. The bathroom may be a touch dated but, like all the rest, it is spacious and spotless. *B&B also.*

sleeps	6-7 + cot.
rooms	3: 1 double, 1 twin, 1 family room for 3; 1 bathroom.
price	€370-€430 per week.

Michel & Géraldine Bignon

tel +33 (0)2 41 82 34 48
email bignonm@wanadoo.fr
web www.lesbouchets.fr

La Chalopinière

Le Vieil Baugé, Maine-et-Loire

Michael and Jill live the country life. There are three horses, two children, a couple of cats and a guinea pig. Views stretch out over open country and in the courtyard garden a towering willow weeps: on summer nights you can eat beneath its generous canopy; Jill has been known to bring out the candelabra. A very friendly place, where you are met with a cup of tea and a slice of homemade cake, and copious quanties of wine if it's after 6pm! Your apartment – a neat and cosy renovated grain store – has its entrance up a steep outside stair. Inside are parquet floors, exposed beams and fresh white walls and, in the huge area of the kitchen/living/dining room all rolled into one, a woodburner and ceilings among the rafters. Bedrooms have light yellow walls, chests of drawers, good wardrobes and plenty of books. Jill does B&B in the main house and will happily give help and advice. The market town of Baugé has restaurants and shops while long walks start from the front door. Or head for the pretty forest of Chandelais. *B&B also.*

sleeps	4.
rooms	2: 1 double, 1 twin; 1 bathroom.
price	€475-€500 per week.
closed	1 week in February, 1 week in July.

Michael & Jill Coyle
tel +33 (0)2 41 89 04 38
fax +33 (0)2 41 89 04 38
email rigbycoyle@aol.com

Château de Salvert – La Brosse & Le Pressoir

Neuillé, Maine-et-Loire

Quel château! It's a neo-gothic masterpiece, and your little houses lie deep within its parkland. Handsome, comfortable and a delight to spend time in, both were restored by the indefatigable Monsieur, with deft combinations of old and new. La Brosse is a 14th-century farmhouse, modest but dignified, all stone walls and great oak beams upstairs and down. Old the bedsteads may be, on floors of wood or *tomettes*, but the mattresses are new and the rugs are seagrass. Unexpectedly luxurious is the mood. Bathrooms are very 21st-century, some tiled imaginatively with old terracotta, all with old beams and tiny windows, kitchens are big, authentic and well-equipped, furniture is classically French. The swimming pool is a four-minute stroll through the grounds, and you also have a private, enclosed garden (but can join forces with your neighbours in Le Pressoir should you wish). Monsieur is jovial and welcoming, his wife equally friendly and impressively energetic. This is a fine address, in an area is impossibly rich in culture, starting with France's largest Romanesque church in nearby Canault.

sleeps	La Brosse 6. Le Pressoir 8.
rooms	La Brosse: 3 doubles; 2 bathrooms. Le Pressoir: 2 doubles, 1 single, 1 triple; 1 bathroom, 1 shower room.
price	La Brosse €1,250. Le Pressoir €1,500. Prices per week.

Monica Le Pelletier de Glatigny

tel +33 (0)2 41 52 55 89
fax +33 (0)2 41 52 56 14
email info@salvert.com
web www.chateau-de-salvert.fr

Haute Rue

Montsoreau, Maine-et-Loire

Up a steep, narrow street and above a smart antique shop is a rare gem. Hélène is an interior designer, Yannick deals in antiques and this flat (across the courtyard from their house) is the perfect canvas for their talents. From inside you catch your first glimpse of the Loire; from the enchanting terraces, hewn from the hillside, even better views. Winding paths and stone steps draw you up past vegetable and herb gardens to a swimming pool at the very top; seats and benches, in sun and shade, allow you to dream. Inside, under the rafters, is a cool blue living area with a nautical theme; curl up in a cushioned armchair and gaze down on town and river. The kitchen end has a long bar with a solid, wooden worktop; the smallish bedroom, its shower en suite, is illuminated by a skylight and exquisitely dressed in soft blues and greys. From this peaceful hideaway it's walking or cycling distance to a good crêperie and several posh restaurants in town. Pretty Montsoreau also has its own château, a farmer's market and a monthly flea-market along the embankment.

sleeps	2-3.
rooms	1 double, 1 sofabed in sitting room; 1 shower room.
price	€800-€1,000 per week.

Hélène & Yannick Lafourcade
tel +33 (0)2 41 50 72 12
email lafourcade.y@wanadoo.fr

Manoir du Buisson Perron – Main House

Saumur, Maine-et-Loire

A crunchy drive sweeps through gates to a perfectly-proportioned, creamy façade. Despite its elegance, this 18th-century manor does not intimidate; it's the Tarrades' family home. (They move between house and cottage according to the let.) Rooms are big, friendly and lightly furnished with antiques (Arnauld is an antique dealer). Step through the door and you're swept into the kitchen/dining room: beams, polished tile floor, big dressers, a range in the fireplace and a candelabra over the table. There are plenty of places to relax: a light-filled salon of comfy chairs and paintings, magnificently beamed billiard room, snug study. No-one will feel outdone in the bedroom stakes; choose a Venetian bed, a four-poster or a Louis XVI-style room with exposed stone walls. Children will love their sunny room with toys, books and funny pictures. Modern bathrooms are slipped into beautifully timbered rooms. With utility rooms, twice-weekly cleaning, pool, patio, huge garden and helpful, cultured hosts nearby this is a terrific place for family or friends' gatherings. *See opposite.*

sleeps	8-10.
rooms	4: 3 doubles, 1 suite; 4 bathrooms, 1 shower room.
price	€2,400-€3,800 per week.

Arnauld & Annick Tarrade

tel	+33 (0)2 41 51 00 52
mobile	+33 (0)6 08 77 49 34
email	arnauld-tarrade@wanadoo.fr
web	www.saumurfrance.com

Manoir du Buisson Perron – La Petite Maison

Saumur, Maine-et-Loire

A cosy retreat in the bountiful grounds of a manor house – you have the best of all worlds here. Spread over the ground floor of an 18th-century stone cottage, your rooms overlook gardens or rich farmland and combine a simple elegance with traditional charm. The beamed sitting room – with a sofabed for an extra couple – opens into a sunny dining room lightly furnished with antiques. A well-equipped American style kitchen is tucked into the corner while French windows open onto a pretty patio. The bedroom is small but stylishly arranged in olive and burgundy with painted furniture and soft lighting. There's a good-sized bathroom – pretty touches of flowers and perfume bottles – although sofabed guests must cross the bedroom to reach it. Wander where you will; behind the gracious manor is a pool and large garden with bosky corners for snoozing. The owners, an artistic, interesting and helpful couple, are happy to chat over a drink or respect your privacy. You are wonderfully well-placed for vineyards and castles in the Loire and restaurants in Saumur – rejoice!

sleeps	2-4.
rooms	1 double, 1 sofabed in living room; 1 bathroom; 1 separate wc.
price	€450-€600 per week.

	Arnauld & Annick Tarrade
tel	+33 (0)2 41 51 00 52
mobile	+33 (0)6 08 77 49 34
email	arnauld-tarrade@wanadoo.fr
web	www.saumurfrance.com

La Maison Aubelle – Tour, Gaudrez & Jardin

Montreuil Bellay, Maine-et-Loire

A 16th-century nobleman's house in an old country town. It stands in secluded gardens flanked by high stone walls, renovated by craftsmen and thoughtfully equipped by Peter and Sally. The original apartments are Tour, Jardin and Gaudrez. Tour – in the tower, as you'd expect – is one flight up a spiralling stone stair; it has a beamed living room/kitchen below with trim red sofas and wraparound views. The garden apartment, with terrace, is as neat as a new pin; white-walled Gaudrez has a 16th-century window, discovered during restoration. The feel is airy, relaxing, comfortable; crisp linen, central heating and daily cleaning are included and the quality is superb. There's a terrace and games room for all and an appropriately large pool. If you can't face cooking, let the Smiths do it for you: they whisk up delicious meals five times a week, cheerfully served in the dining room in winter, on the terrace in summer. Peter and Sally are also on hand to advise, translate or leave you in peace. They run French courses, too.
Children over 12 welcome. Shared laundry. *See next page.*

sleeps	Tour & Gaudrez 4. Jardin 2.
rooms	Tour: 2 doubles; 2 shower rooms. Gaudrez: 2 doubles; 2 shower rooms. Jardin: 1 double; 1 bathroom, 1 separate wc.
price	Tour & Gaudrez €900-€1,050 each. Jardin €800-€925. Prices per week. Apartments rented separately or together. Minimum 3 nights.

Peter & Sally Smith

tel	+33 (0)2 41 52 36 39
fax	+33 (0)2 41 50 94 83
email	maison.aubelle@aubelle.com
web	www.aubelle.com

Hello

La Maison Aubelle – Coach House & Stable

Montreuil Bellay, Maine-et-Loire

No sooner had the Smiths finished one renovation than they turned their hands to the old stable and coach house. And with aplomb: the impeccable exterior is matched by equally excellent interiors. Walls are whitewashed or exposed stone, some ceilings slant, there are lovely old beams and attractive new windows. In the old stable (below), the original hayrack graces the sitting room. You'll find the odd country chest, good sofas, heating beneath terracotta floors (winter warmth is guaranteed). In summer, play chess in the garden, dine on the terrace, meet fellow guests round the pool. There's daily cleaning, the fitted kitchens are packed with mod cons and linen is provided; all you need do is turn up. Venture beyond the walls to discover the last remaining walled town in the region; the three-minute stroll to the château is rewarded by gorgeous watery views of the Thouet. Stretch out a little further and explore Fontevraud Abbey: Eleanor of Aquitaine and Richard the Lion Heart are buried here. *Properties interconnect for same-party bookings. Children over 12 welcome. Shared laundry.*

sleeps	Coach house 4. Stable 2.
rooms	Coach house: 2 doubles; 2 shower rooms. Stable: 1 double; 1 bathroom, 1 separate wc.
price	Coach house €1,000-€1,150. Stable €900-€1,050. Prices per week. Minimum 3 nights.

Peter & Sally Smith

tel	+33 (0)2 41 52 36 39
fax	+33 (0)2 41 50 94 83
email	maison.aubelle@aubelle.com
web	www.aubelle.com

Le Manoir de Champfreau

Varennes sur Loire, Maine-et-Loire

In spite of imposing dimensions, there's a soft luminosity to this ancient place. It's a 15th-century fortified farmhouse – a place of huge character and style. History oozes from every crevice: family portraits and tapestries hang from thick limestone walls, solid antique furniture and coats-of-arms recall grand inhabitants. The kitchen, with its black tiles, pewter plates, dishwasher and every modern aid, is a dream; there are even 200 recipe books and Bruce, who has cooked professionally, is generous with advice – should you need it. (He and Steven live next door and are delightful yet discreet.) Bedrooms are smallish and sumptuous… a four-poster with velvet plum drapes, an antique claw-footed bath; the living room is baronial but cosy – deep sofas before a blazing fire, CDs, books and flowers; central heating, too. Views are of the three walled acres and the courtyard topiary. You are brilliantly placed for visiting some of the finest châteaux of the Loire, there's a fish pond and a brand new pool, bikes to borrow and cookery courses. A heavenly place. *Children over 14 welcome.*

sleeps	6.
rooms	3 doubles; 2 bathrooms.
price	€1,200-€1,700 per week.

Steven Guderian & Bruce Riedner

tel	+33 (0)2 41 38 40 41
email	stevenguderian@aol.com
web	www.saumurfrancemanor.com

Le Four de Villeprouvé

Ruille Froid Fonds, Mayenne

Oodles of history and a cranny-filled cottage full of stories and character. It used to be the grain store for the monks who lived in the 15th-century priory nearby, now it's a farm and B&B run by the delightful Christophe and Christine. Alongside raising cattle and children and caring for guests, they've miraculously found time to lavish care and attention on this exquisite stone house: she sewed the colourful drapes for the antique four-poster, he fashioned a new stair within an old frame. Original features have been kept – stone walls, roof timbers, bread oven – and aged artefacts added – a travelling chest, an old miller's ladder, a Corsican settle in which the hens used to lay their eggs. The sitting room and kitchen are cosy with a medieval feel; the equipment is bang up to date; the bathrooms are small. Enjoy a barbecue in the small fenced garden as the children swing, or book in for Christine's wholesome *table d'hôtes* if the B&B is not full. Ducks paddle in the enchanting pond, cows graze the grass, apples become cider and your hosts are generous and charming. *B&B also.*

sleeps	4-8.
rooms	4: 1 double, 1 double on mezzanine, 1 family room for 4; 2 bathrooms, 2 separate wcs.
price	€239-€367 (£150-£230) per week.

	Christine Davenel
tel	+33 (0)2 43 07 71 62
fax	+33 (0)2 43 07 71 62
email	christ.davenel@wanadoo.fr
web	perso.wanadoo.fr/villeprouve/gite

Map

Château de la Flocellière – The Keep & The Pavilion

La Flocellière, Vendée

The Vicomtesse has exacting standards and everything is just so. Her dominion is vast and she oversees every detail, from the grounds' topiary to the maids' attire. Everything is done to please, all is opulence and beauty and beeswax infuses every room. There are chambres d'hotes in the château and two gîtes in the grounds – a four-storey Keep and a two-storey Pavilion. Impossible to choose between the two, the one sturdy 11th century, the other modelled in the days of Louis XIII. Both are architecturally pleasing, both beautifully equipped, both exceedingly grand. The Renaissance fireplace in the Keep's salon is monumental and roars with logs in winter, the ceiling is splendidly painted and domed. The Pavillion, equally refined, has a gracious, immaculate and 'refurbished' feel. This is living at its most sedate – children are welcome providing they don't run and food is no-go in the swimming pool area: "a terrace, not a beach." You also have your own secluded garden with barbecue. Weddings and receptions happen most weekends but the rest of the time peace reigns. Historic, magnificent, hospitable. *Hotel also.*

sleeps	Keep 8-9. Pavilion 8.
rooms	Keep: 4 twins/doubles + sofabed, 2 baths, 1 shower, 1 separate wc. Pavilion: 4 twins/doubles, 1 bath, 1 shower, 3 separate wcs.
price	Keep €1,800. Pavilion €1,350. Prices per week.

Vicomte & Vicomtesse Vignial

tel +33 (0)2 51 57 22 03

fax +33 (0)2 51 57 75 21

email flocelliere.chateau@wanadoo.fr

web www.flocellierecastle.com

5 rue des Averries

Bourgueil, Indre-et-Loire

This elegant sweep of 19th-century stone started life as a *longère* (a long, low outhouse) and the dormer window in the small bedroom was the entrance to the hayloft. Michel, an interior designer and erstwhile antiques dealer, has a wonderful eye and has brought an uncluttered grace to the interior. In the sitting room, shiny stone walls are adorned with the odd oil painting, the terracotta-tiled floor is warmed by a bright rug and the beams have been scrubbed clean – neat, simple and easy on the eye. Low, slopey-ceilinged bedrooms are under the eaves; smallish, simple, delightful. One has a pretty 18th-century-style bed. You'll find antique bedside tables, good prints on the walls and fine linen. The largest room in lilac and green has a door that opens onto an outside stone staircase to sweep you down into the garden. Here are shade-giving trees, an unobtrusive pool and sunbeds. Doors from the perfectly equipped kitchen open onto the terrace with wrought-iron tables and chairs. The house stands in a residential neighbourhood in a small market town, but it is private nonetheless.

sleeps	6.
rooms	3 doubles; 1 bathroom, 1 shower room, 2 separate wcs.
price	€900-€1,400 per week.

Michel Rondeau

tel +33 (0)2 41 51 47 95

fax +33 (0)2 41 51 74 86

email m.rondeau@wanadoo.fr

Le Clos Saint André

Ingrandes de Touraine, Indre-et-Loire

A converted barn, a long, low stone building, typical of the region. The Pinçons have renovated with some style, keeping exposed stone walls and adding terracotta-tiled floors. The sitting room is huge, open to the rafters, flooded with light and swimming in space. Staircases at either end lead to bedrooms. The master suite is the pick of the bunch, with a low-slung bed that lies under a beamed roof and an antique dressing table in one corner. Elsewhere: good fabrics, patchwork quilts on children's beds, a traditional stone fireplace, wicker armchairs, cushioned sofas, an antique dresser and a small forest of flourishing greenery. The kitchen is immaculate and a delight to use, though on lazy days you may choose to spurn the allure of the eye-level oven and let Michèle rustle up something sublime. The Pinçons, kind and easy-going, live in the old wine-grower's house opposite where they do B&B; you share the pool. Here time is measured in vintages, not hours; you are surrounded by vineyards and Saumur, with its château, is close by. *B&B also.*

sleeps	8-10.
rooms	4: 2 doubles, 1 twin, 1 family room for 4; 2 bathrooms, 1 shower room, 3 separate wcs.
price	€700-€1,300 per week.

Michèle & Michel Pinçon

tel	+33 (0)2 47 96 90 81
fax	+33 (0)2 47 96 90 81
email	mmpincon@club-internet.fr
web	www.clos-saint-andre.fr

La Petite Giraudière

Villandry, Indre-et-Loire

An exceptional find, a luxurious working farm where you can enjoy the cheese that the owners produce. Béatrice has a herd of 40 goats and will show you round the milking parlour and the dairy. The place was inhabited by nuns until 1790, then it became a tithe farm to the château next door (magnificent Villandry). The gîte is exhilarating, a 17th-century house conversion with a terracotta-tiled roof and old stone walls. A weeping willow dips its branches into a duck pond behind; an entirely private roof terrace catches the sun at the top. In between lies dreamland. There are exposed stone walls, big beds and rich toile de Jouy fabrics. One bedroom is in a gallery above another – you climb a spiral staircase to get to it – and another has a chest of drawers that turns into a writing desk if you press the right button. The whole place swims in light, and there's a garden in which to seek silence. Wonderful Béatrice speaks fluent English and Spanish; her Italian isn't bad either. Her way is to provide the best of everything, which she does. There's a farm shop and a restaurant, too – prepare to indulge.

sleeps	4-6.
rooms	3: 2 doubles, 1 twin on mezzanine; 1 bathroom, 1 separate wc.
price	€885-€1,020 per week.

	Béatrice de Montferrier
tel	+33 (0)2 47 50 08 60
fax	+33 (0)2 47 50 06 60
email	beatrice.de-montferrier@wanadoo.fr
web	www.letapegourmande.com

Château de l'Hérissaudière

Pernay, Indre-et-Loire

Your pleasant quarters are in the long, low *longère*, once the tack room for the château horses (and the château was Diane de Poitiers' hunting lodge). It's a one-storey building, one-room deep, airy and light. You have the bedrooms on your right and the living area on your left: a blue sofabed before a small open fire (helped by central heating on chilly days), blue curtains, a tablecloth on a round table. Walls are white, beams dark and low, a rug adds warmth to tiles, country furniture adds personality. The kitchen, separated by a breakfast bar, is new and well-designed with matching blue and white crockery. The double bedroom is a good size, with a large painted wardrobe (blue, of course): crisp and cool; the twin is a lot smaller. Outside, the best of both worlds: the privacy of your own walled and fenced garden, with barbecue and games, and the lovely grounds, with tennis court to hire (the pool is for B&B guests only; a good public pool lies 10km away). A peaceful place for a family to stay – and a well-priced restaurant in nearby Semblançay, recommended by Madame. *B&B also.*

sleeps	4-6 + 1 child.
rooms	2: 1 double + child bed, 1 twin, 1 sofabed in sitting room; 2 shower rooms, 1 separate wc.
price	€500-€800 per week.

Claudine Detilleux

tel	+33 (0)2 47 55 95 28
fax	+33 (0)2 47 55 97 45
email	lherissaudiere@aol.com
web	www.herissaudiere.com

La Cornillière

Tours, Indre-et-Loire

What once rambled is now trim and clipped and ever so neat. Monsieur, an antique dealer and interior designer, is originally from the Charente. He studied art in Tours 40 years ago, met Madame and that was that. In the grounds of their elegant house, this dear little 18th-century cottage has been decorated with restraint, in a traditional and pleasing style. Luckily for Madame, Monsieur is also a passionate gardener and happily digs and delves, bringing peace and a little serenity to the outside as well. Inside, all is as neat, charming and relaxing as your hosts. The furniture is country antique, the walls are plain, the tiles are polished old and spotless. The sitting room is small, with an open fireplace, a sofa and armchairs, an un-rugged, tiled floor. There is antique crockery in the kitchen/dining room, antique garden furniture and deckchairs in the garden. Beyond the stone walls of the grounds are gardens, festivals, markets, the Loire valley with its vineyards, châteaux and the elegant city of Tours, with its opera house and gourmet restaurants. Auberges for simpler dining lie nearby.

sleeps 5.
rooms 3: 1 double, 1 twin, 1 single; 2 shower rooms, 2 separate wcs.
price €540-€770 per week.

Catherine Espinassou
tel +33 (0)2 47 51 12 69
email catherine@lacornilliere.com.fr
web www.lacornilliere.com.fr

Château du Plessis – The Cottage

St Antoine du Rocher, Indre-et-Loire

Some cottage! It's huge. Step into the big old-fashioned kitchen full of mod cons and central heating for winter. Next door, a dining room, quintessentially French – its walls yellow and red striped, its furniture dark wooden, its floor parquet. There's a big homely sitting room with a tiled floor and seating that includes a comfortable leather sofa. Then up to the bedrooms and yet more space: a bedknobs-and-broomsticks brass bed, a Henry II wardrobe dressed up in Louis XVI style, traditionally carpeted floors, a big, light, lovely bathroom in cream and blue. Outside is a private garden full of flowers and 12 acres beyond for the children to explore. There's a well defined play area with wooden climbing frame shared with the owners' young sons, and other areas designed for more violent sports such as football. For the grown-ups: a 1930s grass tennis court (expect the odd strange bounce) and a delicious pool with teak loungers. Loire châteaux, riding and boating are nearby; two good restaurants are a ten minute drive. A fun, friendly place. *See opposite.*

sleeps	6.
rooms	3: 2 doubles, 1 twin; 1 bathroom, 1 separate wc.
price	€750-€1,275 (£500-£850) per week.

Elizabeth & Gil Barrios
tel +33 (0)2 47 56 50 69
fax +33 (0)2 47 56 50 69
email elizabeth@chateauduplessis.com
web www.chateauduplessis.com

Château du Plessis – The Lodge

St Antoine du Rocher, Indre-et-Loire

Sweep through parkland, step out of the car, fall in love with the setting. The Lodge is attached to one end of the turreted 1750 château, once home to the playwright Eugene O'Neill. A later, less romantic use of the château was as a horticultural boarding school; such is the size of the place. Now it is all being revived by Elizabeth and Gil (she from Kent, he from Paris) who live in their own well-defined quarters but are very much there for you if you need them. You enter directly into a large living room with cool tiled floors, big solid windows and woodburner in the fireplace (backed up by electric radiators for winter). An old-fashioned burgundy leather sofa and chairs for comfort, a dresser equipped with all the crockery, a big sober table and chairs, a practical kitchen next door. Two of the bedrooms are on this floor: patterned carpets, an Empire wardrobe, a dressing table, a sparkling new bathroom; then up to a twin, a large, low, beamy double and a corner bath big enough to fit a few toddlers. Outside is a lovely private garden – and all the park to share. *B&B also.*

sleeps	6 + 2 children.
rooms	4: 2 doubles, 1 twin, 1 children's twin; 3 bathrooms.
price	€900-€1,650 (£600-£1,100) per week.

Elizabeth & Gil Barrios

tel +33 (0)2 47 56 50 69

fax +33 (0)2 47 56 50 69

email elizabeth@chateauduplessis.com

web www.chateauduplessis.com

La Blanchière – Cottage & Studio

Couziers, Indre-et-Loire

Slip into the pages of *Alice in Wonderland* in this one-up, one-down tufastone cottage. Built above caves, it gazes across rolling farmland and forests, not another house in sight. Karen, an enthusiastic American with a house on the property, rescues the unloved and has restored the cottage using traditional materials. Step into the open-plan living space from the garden – a sweet mix of lavender, fruit trees and vines. Terracotta tiles shine, light floods in through windows, a small but perfectly formed kitchen is tucked into the corner. Furniture has been gleaned from local brocantes – a pretty painted cupboard, an iron bed piled with cushions. Wooden stairs lead to a romantic bedroom with a cathedral-beamed roof, rugs on heated floors and fluttering muslin. A claw-foot bath stands to the side of the room with views over the valley; the loo is behind a low wall. Explore Loire châteaux, Chinon and Saumur, or step straight out onto a trail through Fontevraud forest to the Abbey. Return to your garden gazebo and raise a glass to the sunset.
Can be rented with studio/conservatory for two.

sleeps	2 (4 with studio).
rooms	Cottage: 1 double; 1 bathroom. Studio: 1 twin/double; 1 shower room.
price	Cottage €550-€750; with studio €650-€850. Prices per week.

Karen Normandy
tel +33 (0)5 49 98 37 08
email knormandy@aol.com
web www.lablanchiere.com

Le Pigeonnier

Chinon, Indre-et-Loire

No artificial pool here but swim in a watery world where fish jump, coypu and the occasional beaver nest and kingfishers, terns and herons fish. There are three gîtes in all. Reached through lush water meadows, Le Pigeonnier is attached to the main house, with views up and downstream. Only the frogs disturb the perfect peace of the garden and riverside 'terrace' with barbecue. Inside it's a clean, comfortable space for up to five. The main bedroom, up steep, wooden, open-tread stairs, is in the pigeon loft itself, complete with nesting holes. Across the landing, the second bedroom has a lovely garden view. The bathroom is small, its bath tucked behind a beam. The ground floor is open plan, with a step up from the kitchen/dining area to the pleasant three-piece-suited sitting section. An excellent spot for châteaux lovers, cyclists, gourmets, twitchers, or those wishing to mess about in boats – a punt, rowing boat and small sailing boat are all available. And you can swim in the river, but watch the sandbanks.

sleeps	4-5.
rooms	2: 1 double, 1 twin, 1 sofabed; 1 bathroom.
price	€295-€525 per week.
closed	End October-March.

Gordon Baker
tel +44 (0)1440 702627
fax +44 (0)1440 708790
email bookings@pigeonnier.co.uk
web www.pigeonnier.co.uk

The Well House

Anché, Indre-et-Loire

This 18th-century worker's cottage has a garden to beguile you. It faces south to soak up sun, has wild roses rambling on its stone walls and is bordered by an orchard… cypress trees and lavender, geraniums in pots and a carpet of colour in between. A fig tree grows against the wall and there's a covered terrace where you sit on cushioned stone benches. A great sense of peace envelops this pretty hillside village. David, who teaches in Alexandria, fell in love with the house when he was a student. He scraped the money together to buy, then spent his summers renovating. He also bought the 17th-century farmhouse next door and lives there for three months a year. The interior is a delightful mix of French and English. There's an open fireplace in the beamed sitting room, a big carved wardrobe in one of the bedrooms and a light and airy kitchen with French windows that open onto the terrace. Bedrooms are ample, with fine furniture and garden views. One looks onto the orchard; you can glimpse the church tower beyond. There are vineyards and châteaux nearby and a swimming hole in the river.

sleeps	4-6.
rooms	2: 1 double, 1 triple, extra bed on landing; 1 bathroom.
price	£400-£480 per week.
closed	November-April.

David Thomas
tel +33 (0)2 41 51 47 95
email m.rondeau@wanadoo.fr

Hameau de la Saucraie

Lémeré, Indre-et-Loire

Three houses snuggle round a sun-trapping courtyard. The property was probably a winery while part of the gîte once housed a pig sty and chicken loft. Karl and Carol live in one of the houses for half the year, otherwise in Florida. They have renovated with flair, imagination and determination, are lively and fun and love being part of local life. Carol trawls the flea markets for pretty things: an oak table, wicker chairs, an old panelled door stained grey-blue for a bedstead... all bear witness to a good eye. You are in a long, low, tiled barn of rough-cut stone walls, a place with much rustic comfort. Expect a natural 'raw' look with original stonework and beamed ceilings, excellent bathrooms, a charming kitchen. The ground-floor bedroom has pine, soft-pink candlewick and ceilings rising to part of the old chicken loft. The main bedroom is big and lovely. French windows lead onto a terrace, courtyard lime trees offer shade, there's badminton in the field and a garden you can share. All around lie gentle country and vineyards with glimpses of the nearby château and the church steeple of the church.

sleeps	4-6 + 1 child.
rooms	2: 1 double with child bed, 1 twin, 1 sofabed in sitting room; 2 shower rooms.
price	€650-€700 per week.
closed	Mid-October-mid June.

Carol & Karl Lindquist
tel +33 (0)2 47 95 79 52
email islandfeverckl@aol.com

La Coquetière

Ports sur Vienne, Indre-et-Loire

A staircase of old railway sleepers, and rescued stones and beams. Christophe has restored this farm building from salvaged materials to create a historically authentic house. The airy, open-plan living area, with grand fireplace for chillier nights, is traditionally beamed and terracotta-tiled, furnished with country antiques and Claudine's paintings (she's a talented amateur). A small but well-equipped kitchen is to one side plus a useful utility room. No tantrums over choosing the bedrooms: all are equally stylish. One has a lofty cathedral-style ceiling, two have platform-raised beds behind beautiful curtains, and there's a pretty children's room; all overlook the Vienne valley or the garden. The family's 16th-century manor house is next door with three acres of deer-filled woodland, water, and scented and medieval gardens to explore. You also have your own private terrace and pool. The owners are delightful, happy to tell you about walks, bike trails, rides (stables nearby), weekly markets and the summer cheese festival. And it's a lovely walk through the woods to the village restaurant.

sleeps	8-10.
rooms	4: 3 doubles, 1 quadruple; 1 bathroom, 2 shower rooms, 2 separate wcs.
price	€500-€1,500 per week.

Christophe Leroux & Claudine Leprince

tel	+33 (0)2 47 65 15 88
email	leprince2leroux@aol.com
web	www.lacoquetiere.com

La Maison Rose

Loché sur Indrois, Indre-et-Loire

Slip through the blue door in the wall and you could be in *The Secret Garden*. With its gorgeous pink roses and creeper-clad stone walls, the private courtyard garden in which this 18th-century farm cottage stands is magical; sit out among the lavender bushes and absorb the peace of the pretty village on the poplar-lined banks of the Indrois. Inside is no less bewitching, the bohemian furnishings and old oak beams exuding warmth and well-being. James, the English owner, teaches art and design (and runs courses here for adults and children) and the white walls are hung with his colourful paintings. Bedrooms are traditional with arty touches; the twin, on the landing, leads into one double. Artists will celebrate the limpid Touraine light, children will enjoy the covered ping-pong shared by hosts and guests, everyone will love Loches, its medieval citadel and blue slate roofs, and the walks along the river valley. On their well-established cookery weekends you're met at Tours, taken to the wonderful market at Loches, then back to cook and eat together. *Shared pool for those on courses only.*

sleeps	6.
rooms	3: 2 doubles, 1 twin; 1 bathroom, 1 shower room.
price	€422-€677 (£295-£495) per week.
arrival	Saturday, but flexible.

Flora & James Cockburn
tel +44 (0)1732 357022
+33 (0)2 47 92 61 79 (school holidays)
email mrsfscockburn@aol.com
web www.lamaisonrose.com

The Cottage & The Farmhouse Loft

Le Grand Pressigny, Indre-et-Loire

Civray is a tiny hamlet hidden away in the countryside: it would be hard to find anywhere more tranquil. And if you tire of walking, cycling, fishing – or swimming in the silky waters of the river – there are vineyards to visit, *fermes auberges* to discover and all the attractions of the Loire châteaux. Lovely Jill is half Australian, passionate about rural France and has restored this little cluster of ancient stone buildings with the lightest of hands. The Cottage is compact but has all you need: a living area with little pine kitchen, woodburning stove, sofabed, play equipment in the garden. Upstairs, under magnificent curving beams, a large double bedroom, simply and attractively furnished. It has its own rustic balcony overlooking farmland – not another building in sight. Wooden stairs wind down to the gardens, which have a haphazard charm; fresh home-grown vegetables and home-laid eggs are often available. Jill has also converted the Farmhouse Loft, a heavily timbered and imaginative space with three bedrooms and a big, jolly kitchen/living area, easy for families. *Bring own linen.*

sleeps	Cottage 2-3 + cot. Farmhouse Loft 5 + cot. Can be booked together.
rooms	Cottage: 1 double, 1 single sofabed; 1 shower room, 1 bathroom. Farmhouse Loft: 2 doubles, 1 single; 1 bathroom.
price	Cottage £150-£250. Farmhouse Loft £170-£305. Prices per week.
closed	Winter.

Jill Christie

tel +33 (0)2 47 94 92 02

fax +33 (0)2 47 94 92 02

Hello

La Basse Lande

Loché sur Indrois, Indre-et-Loire

Another lovely old farmstead in the gentle Touraine, where you can walk and cycle for miles. The house sleeps ten, with an extra room in an attractive building outside. And there are plenty of corners in the garden in which to find solitude and shade. Downstairs are two double bedrooms furnished in neat country style, with good French wardrobes and peaceful views, and a light and tranquil living room that opens to the garden. Floors are fine old terracotta, subtle lighting reveals the beauty of the 200-year-old beams and the fireplace guards a woodburner – logs provided. Upstairs are three big bedrooms that lead one into the other (plus a small snooker table) – fun for children. The partly open garden has fruit trees and grass and a big level space that's just asking for a good old English game of rounders. The pretty village, a short drive, sits in the valley of the Indrois, with a 12th-century church and one baker… not to be confused with medieval Loches, famous for its culture, its citadel and its squares that burst into life when the cheese makers, wine producers and market gardeners come to town.

sleeps	11.
rooms	6: 5 doubles, 1 single; 2 shower rooms.
price	€630-€1,120 per week.
arrival	Saturday but flexible.

Sally Markowski
tel +44 (0)208 998 6851
email sallymarkowska@aol.com
web www.holiday-gite-france.co.uk

La Challerie – La Dépendance

Villeloin-Coulangé, Indre-et-Loire

Floor-to-ceiling windows in the main bedroom and a full Touraine view: the restoration is excellent, the setting a balm. In two grassed acres with orchards, close to unrestored farm buildings full of charm, the 15th-century *Dépendance* has an irresistible appeal for those who love 'la belle France'. Its spacious two storeys have been charmingly furnished with country antiques and the best of brand new: warm red sofas in the salon, beechwood table and chairs in the dining room, a fine oak bed upstairs. The walls are pale exposed stone or fresh white plaster, ceiling beams are painted, the kitchen is delightful and there's new oak for the stairs. L-shaped bedrooms, a woodburner (logs provided) and original floor tiles add character. You have a terrace for barbecues under the stars, the orchard's peaches, plums and pears to pluck and a goat-cheese producer down the road. Stroll into 11th-century Montrésor for delectable bread and patisseries, visit Loches for its twice-weekly market. There's a lake at Chemillé, a pool here (shared with the owners), and concerts, châteaux and wines to discover.

sleeps	4-6.
rooms	2: 1 double, 1 triple, 1 sofabed on mezzanine; 2 shower rooms, 1 separate wc.
price	€350-€700 per week.

Henry & Sue Dixon

tel +44 (0)1824 790254

fax +44 (0)1824 790030

email sue@allthedixons.com

Moulin de la Follaine

Azay sur Indre, Indre-et-Loire

A tranquil place that feels as old as the hills. The mill workers who worked opposite lived in this house; ask Danie to show you the old Azay flour sacks. Your charming young hosts run a B&B in the medieval millhouse but gîte guests have their own patio, barbecue and cottage garden (colourful flowers, immaculate lawn) so there's privacy and peace. The dining/sitting room is pleasingly decorated with a mix of modern and antique country pieces, the stone fireplace is stacked with logs for low season stays. Bedrooms are similarly uncluttered, white walls sport friezes and the kitchen has every mod con. All is spotless, everything matches – Danie is a stickler for detail – and baguettes are delivered for breakfast. There's masses to do right here, from cycling to ping-pong to fishing (tackle supplied) and gardens to enjoy, their trickling waterways and the lake dotted with ornamental ducks. Don't miss the weekly markets in Azay and Loches and, when you've had enough of cooking, there's an auberge to walk to that specialises in regional dishes. *Unsuitable for young children: unguarded water. B&B also.*

sleeps	4-6.
rooms	2 family rooms for 3; 1 bathroom, 1 separate wc.
price	€380-€600 per week.

	Danie Lignelet
tel	+33 (0)2 47 92 57 91
fax	+33 (0)2 47 92 57 91
email	moulindelafollaine@wanadoo.fr
web	www.moulindefollaine.com

Les Petites Ouldes

Francueil, Indre-et-Loire

Through impressive wrought-iron gates, up a drive flanked by vines, enter a world of timeless and graceful elegance. The house has been restored over three decades by equally gracious Valerie, who has transformed the ground-floor stable block into the most enticing place to stay. Expect lofty light rooms, orangery-style French windows, terracotta floors, charming furniture; a sunny kitchen, a sitting room in serene French greys and a bedroom simply but elegantly furnished: Valerie gives you crisp cotton, fresh flowers, orchard views. She also leaves a light meal and a bottle of crisp Sauvignon in your fridge for your arrival – so welcoming – and will happily cook you a gourmet dinner if required, using as much organic produce from the garden as possible. A delightful walled terrace is all yours, the pool, elegant in its Italianate garden, is available by arrangement, and the village, with shops, is a walk away. You are also within cycling distance of the Loire's glittering prize, the Château de Chenonceau.

sleeps	2.
rooms	1 double; 1 bathroom.
price	€700-€750 per week.
arrival	Wednesday.

	Valerie Faccini
tel	+33 (0)2 47 23 95 07
fax	+33 (0)2 47 23 95 07 (on request)
email	faccini@freesurf.fr
web	lespetitesouldes.free.fr

La Taille Rouge

Viglain, Loiret

One misty morning you may catch a glimpse of a doe and fawn deep in the woods. La Taille Rouge's 120 tranquil acres are heaven to explore and the house, with its steep, tiled roof and silver-brown beams, is lovely, too. A long, pretty living room, full of books and country antiques, takes up much of the ground floor. Big comfortable sofas and chairs are grouped around the stone fireplace at one end; at the other, a fine old table with wrought-iron chairs. On both sides are windows looking out to the woods or the heated pool. The ultra well-equipped kitchen has a veranda – a pleasant place to breakfast – and a laundry room. Upstairs are four charmingly individual bedrooms, each with an old, carved door and a gorgeous bathroom. They're furnished with a few choice antiques and extra-wide double beds which can also be twins. Out in the summer house are many bicycles – early risers can be dispatched two miles to the village bakery for fresh breakfast rolls.

sleeps 8-9.
rooms 4 twins/doubles, 1 single on landing; 1 bathroom, 2 shower rooms.
price €975-€1,630 per week.

Thierry & Nicole Hiltzer
tel +33 (0)3 25 41 83 52
fax +33 (0)3 25 41 91 33
email taille.rouge@laposte.net
web www.la-taille-rouge.fr

La Brosse

Cléré du Bois, Indre

The white stone cottage was the next door monastery's bread oven. Now it's a remarkable retreat, restored single-handedly by a remarkable owner. Generous Isabelle has two large dogs, lots of hens and a zest for living; when she moved into her medieval cloisters three years ago, she barely knew the tumbledown, bramble-smothered cottage existed. Now it is an adorable bolt hole for two, ingeniously re-designed to maximise the space. The ceiling is white, the rafters exposed, the mezzanine window is triangular and there's a loft ladder uniting the two floors. The bedroom is cheerfully carpeted and has a low, pattern-sprigged bed, and the bathroom and kitchen are a decent size. The setting is bucolic; you overlook a large pond mercifully free of mosquitoes, surrounded by trees with farmland beyond, and have your own little terrace with a pergola. There's an amazing wildlife park two miles from the house – listen for the wolves! – a good, cheap restaurant in the village and glorious old Loches with its market a 20-minute drive. At the end of a long lane, seclusion and peace – a singular writer's retreat.

sleeps	2-3.
rooms	1 double, 1 sofabed in living room; 1 bathroom.
price	€360.

Isabelle de Billy

tel +33 (0)2 54 38 79 28
fax +33 (0)2 54 38 79 28
email idebilly@hotmail.com

La Chemolière

Cléré du Bois, Indre

Tomatoes, peppers, peas, strawberries, melons are yours for the asking, from the family's vegetable plot. Organic, too. Your warm and friendly hosts have done a fine restoration on these old farm buildings just outside the little village (one shop, one café-bar). Relax in the shade of an ancient pear tree, repair for a barbecue to your vine-clad pergola warmed by a woodburner on cool nights. Inside, the huge, stone-floored living/dining area is a timbered delight, its thick walls keeping you warm in winter, cool in summer, its aged character married with modern comforts: a floral three-piece suite, a woodburning stove, books, games and videos aplenty. The kitchen, with limed units, country tiles and olive trim, has every conceivable appliance to tempt one to cook, the dining area is rustically stone-walled. Up the old oak stair to two en suite bedrooms under the eaves; roof windows open to the sky and there's space for a coffee table and a French sofa. With the B&B guests you share a raised plunge pool, lawns for outside games and 25 peaceful acres of pasture and wood. *B&B also.*

sleeps	4.
rooms	2: 1 double, 1 twin/double; 1 bathroom, 2 shower rooms.
price	£195-£525 per week.

Nick & Bev Bull
tel +33 (0)2 54 38 86 32
email la_chemoliere@yahoo.co.uk
web lachemoliere.com

Le Grand Ajoux – Lavande

Chalais, Indre

One family comes here every year to watch the dragonflies hatch on the estate's two lakes. On the edge of the Brenne National Park – famous for its thousand lakes – and in 53 hectares of private parkland, the place is a paradise for birdwatchers and nature lovers. Lavande is one of two stables (see opposite) which have been converted in a country-rustic style by the owner – sometimes absent – who lives in the old manor house next door. At opposite ends of a lavender-fringed pool each cottage has a secluded patio pretty with Mediterranean plants. Inside, cheerful blue chairs and soft furnishings contrast sympathetically with the old stone walls, ceiling beams and lovely terracotta floors, with old and new pieces of furniture sitting happily side by side. The galley kitchen is well-equipped; the bedroom's French windows open to the main courtyard and views of the paddocks where horses and donkeys graze. There are plenty of walks from the door – the countryside is truly magnificent – and Georges Sand fans can drive to the Vallée Noire, where she lived, and visit the museum at La Châtre.

sleeps	2-4.
rooms	2: 1 double, 1 sofabed in living room; 1 shower room.
price	€275-€535 per week.

Aude de la Jonquière-Aymé
tel +33 (0)2 54 37 72 92
fax +33 (0)2 54 37 56 60
email audeayme@wanadoo.fr
web grandajoux.tripod.com

Le Grand Ajoux – Amande

Chalais, Indre

Great swathes of park and woodland are yours to roam – if you're lucky, you'll spot a couple of deer or a wild boar. Alternatively, fish in the private lake (bring your own rod), or simply unwind by the rose- and lavender-bordered pool – it's a few steps from your pretty blue bedroom door. Charmingly cosy, this tiny 300-year-old converted stable has been imaginatively restored while keeping original stone walls and tiled floors. The beamed bedroom – green checked bedspread, big old wardrobe – sits cosily next to the rustic, pretty sitting room with its two armchairs, check curtains and small stone fireplace. Outside, your secluded west-facing patio overlooks fields of horses, donkeys and a tree-lined pond: bucolic. There's the Abbey of Saint Savin with its 13th-century frescoes of the hermit Saint Savinus to visit, the Loire châteaux are a 90-minute drive, there are wines to taste, if you're an *aficionado*: try Vouvray and Chinon from Touraine... At the end of the day you'll want to rush back to blissful seclusion and let the owls hoot you to sleep.

sleeps	2.
rooms	1 double; 1 shower room, 1 separate wc.
price	€245-€535 per week.

Aude de la Jonquière-Aymé

tel +33 (0)2 54 37 72 92
fax +33 (0)2 54 37 56 60
email audeayme@wanadoo.fr
web grandajoux.tripod.com

Les Genêts

Nozières, Cher

Compact, stylish and tranquil: this charming stone farm cottage looks like something out of *Alice in Wonderland*. Roses decorate the pale stone front, a great vine drapes over the pergola and in the fields all around Charolais cows gently munch. The house is far larger than it looks from the outside: rooms are light and airy, and are furnished simply but with French flair. Marie-Claude, the charming, dynamic, elegant owner who lives in the farmhouse – and runs B&B – a kilometre away, has thought through every detail, from moon and star cut-outs in the bedroom shutters to tartan bows on the picture hooks. Downstairs, tiled floors and whitewashed walls give a homely, country feel. The sitting room has inviting sofas with tartan throws and you can still see the old bread oven in the dining room fireplace. The two bedrooms have pine floorboards, antique beds and pretty fabrics. The kitchen leads into the grassy garden and you can eat on the patio in the front. There's good cycling all around and a Saturday market in Saint Amand. A real gem. *B&B also.*

sleeps	4-7.
rooms	2: 1 family room for 3, 1 family room for 4; 1 shower room downstairs, 1 separate wc.
price	€300-€365 per week.

Marie-Claude Dussert
tel +33 (0)2 48 96 47 45
fax +33 (0)2 48 96 07 71

photo corel images

poitou – charentes
limousin
auvergne

La Grande Métairie – The Cottage

Leugny, Vienne

The stuff of dreams! Rose was bewitched by La Grande Métairie which she thought looked like an Arthur Rackham illustration. Fourteen years on, this ancient farm cottage with views over the Creuse valley has kept its enchantment. The stone farm buildings with their unusually angled roofs surround a courtyard shaded by fruit trees; under one stands a life-size effigy of your opera-singer host Richard. This fun and cultured couple do B&B next door and are often around to help if needed. The inside of the cottage will cast its spell over you too: friendly old armchairs round a woodburner in the cool kitchen/living room, wonderful gnarled beams. Upstairs there are ancient iron bedsteads (with modern mattresses!) and thoroughly beamed ceilings. Have a game of tennis on the private court, dine out on your terrace in the large dreamy garden, slip into the shared, enclosed pool, landscaped with shrubs and 200 rose bushes beyond. The well-named Rose runs rose-pruning days in season and makes splendid jams. *Can be let with adjoining studio: see opposite. Babysitting available. B&B also.*

sleeps	4-5.
rooms	3: 1 double, 1 twin, 1 single on landing; 1 bathroom.
price	€540-€930 (£360-£620) per week.

Richard & Rose Angas
tel +44 (0)20 8743 1745
+33 (0)5 49 85 97 02
email angas@freeuk.com
web www.lagrande-metairie.com

La Grande Métairie – The Studio

Leugny, Vienne

There's wood everywhere in this jewel-among-the-rafters in the old farm stables. Stripped age-worn beams carry the sloping ceilings and there are hefty old boards on the floor. A large iron-framed double bed is screened from the living area and kitchen corner by pretty Indian-print curtains; similar fabrics cover a sofabed. You look onto the grassy courtyard on one side and onto the Creuse valley on the other – wonderful. A tennis court and a lovely, enclosed pool are shared with the owners and the B&B guests but you get privacy too: stone steps lead up to your front door and down to a private terrace and patch of garden. Come to enjoy the company – out of season – of your interesting hosts, Rose and Richard, and to discover this unspoiled area of France. Once you've explored the farmstead's three acres of gardens and woodland there are châteaux to visit, restaurants and wines to sample and pleasant walks and cycle rides. A baker delivers daily; you can buy fresh eggs and honey from the local farm. *Can be let with adjoining cottage: see opposite. Babysitting available. B&B also.*

sleeps	2-3.
rooms	1 double, 1 single sofabed; 1 shower room.
price	€360-€600 (£240-£400) per week.

Richard & Rose Angas
tel +44 (0)20 8743 1745
+33 (0)5 49 85 97 02
email angas@freeuk.com
web www.lagrande-metairie.com

Château de la Gatinalière – La Maison du Jardin

Antran, Vienne

A tree-lined avenue leads to a sophora tree and a lake of shimmering lavender. To the side of the château your cottage peeps out between well-ordered lime trees and surveys the gorgeous scene. Hidden behind, a private, informal garden bursts with colour and fruit (pick and pluck as you will), perfectly positioned for the evening sun. Stylish but simple, the Maison's rooms are large, liveable spaces. The sitting/dining room, with windows on three sides, has plenty of sofas, a polished oak table and a large fireplace; to one side, the well-equipped kitchen overlooks the garden. Bedrooms spoil for choice. Downstairs is elegant with seagrass flooring, whitewashed walls, deep claw-foot bath and French windows to the courtyard. Upstairs (steepish staircase) is a cathedral-beamed loft with masses of windows, a curtained-off bedroom and a little salon in which to pen a first novel. There are two other gîtes and B&B in the château but, with all that parkland, there's space for everyone. Come for stylish country living close to the Loire châteaux and Romanesque Poitou, and good walking and cycling. *B&B also.*

sleeps	4-5.
rooms	2 doubles, sofabed in sitting room; 1 bathroom, 1 shower room.
price	€800-€2,000 per week.

Bernard de la Touche

tel	+33 (0)5 49 21 15 02
fax	+33 (0)5 49 85 39 65
email	gatinaliere@chateauxcountry.com

Château de la Motte

Usseau, Vienne

Stark against the skyline is a pearly grey, turreted, medieval castle, dominating the village as if plucked from a fairytale. And there, sheltering in the lee of its walls, is your farmhouse home. Its views stretch serenely over Usseau and down a long, soft valley – stunning. Wisely, the interior does not try to compete – a rustic elegance with simple but attractive furniture set against polished parquet, dark-red, beautifully worn quarry tiles and exposed stone walls. There are two good-sized bedrooms in fresh colours – more views – and a cosy room under the eaves that peeps over the garden. The Bardins' paintings are everywhere and there's a butterfly stencil in the shining bathroom. The light-filled sitting/dining room has doors to the garden – you may barbecue from the old bread oven – and a brand-new kitchen. This is easy living: close to the Loire, restaurants in Châtellerault, a pool shared with the castle's B&B guests. The Bardins are sixtysomethings full of energy – creating a monastic garden, running art courses, intelligently filling you in about the area. Great hospitality. *B&B also.*

sleeps	6-7.
rooms	3: 2 doubles, 1 triple; 1 bathroom, 1 shower room, 1 separate wc.
price	€450-€600 per week.
arrival	Saturday but flexible.

Jean-Marie & Marie-Andrée Bardin

tel	+33 (0)5 49 85 88 25
fax	+33 (0)5 49 85 88 25
email	chateau.delamotte@wanadoo.fr
web	www.chateau-de-la-motte.net

Hello

Les Vignes de la Cure – Cottage & Studio

Morton, Vienne

A welcoming drink and a basket of home-grown fruit and vegetables – wine and cheese, too: this is a relaxed and homely place. David and Diane retired here, starting a new life renovating their farmhouse and your little stone cottage. In the grounds of a former vineyard, on the edge of a peaceful village, it has a comfortable, easy charm. There's a woodburning stove – and a vast pair of forge bellows – a colourful sofa, wicker armchairs and a large pine dining table in the beamed living room. The pretty green and white kitchen is good enough for rustling up a gourmet meal in. Bedrooms are tucked away in the roof space; cool and fresh with stained wood floors, exposed stone walls and garden views. Children have a grassy play area while you have a shady terrace. Or pick your spot in the Jones's large garden. They're keen environmentalists so flowers seed naturally and it's a haven for wild birds. Saumur, Fontevraud, the Loire châteaux, cave dwellings, an ususual zoo... all are nearby, and this is good biking country, so do borrow one. There's also the Studio flat for extra guests.

sleeps	Cottage 4. Studio 2.
rooms	Cottage: 1 double, 1 twin; 1 shower room, 1 separate wc. Studio: 1 twin; 1 shower room.
price	Cottage: €350-€595. Studio: €245-€350. Prices per week.
arrival	Saturday but flexible.

David & Diane Jones

tel +33 (0)5 49 22 62 45

fax +33 (0)5 49 22 62 45

email jones.david@tiscali.fr

La Maison-Nette

Personne Ne, Vienne

'Set thine house in order, for thou shalt die': the Second Book of Kings was ahead of the professionals who tell us how to de-clutter our homes. But the twee, ordered perfection of the house is almost unbearable. How can anyone so successfully reduce their needs and clutter? The rest of us tiptoe through the minefields of our lives in a succession of vain attempts to make sense of our possessions and available space. We usually fail; the explosions, marital and familial, resonate through our days. Here is an ideal, not romantic but simply practical. *Reductio ad absurdum*, perhaps, but it works for these owners. The colours are pure 'dolly', the furniture pure plastic, but at least you know what you are getting and there is nothing surplus – though the cooker, absurdly, takes up much of the space. The owners have taken a cynical view of global warming, noting that we are likely to experience hotter summers. So guests will spend much of their time outside, and ignore the diminutive house. Perhaps unwisely: bring wellies, tent and brolly for the inevitable wet days.

sleeps	Maximum two tiny, tidy guests.
rooms	One multi-purpose 'space', though not much of it.
price	Proportional to dimensions and décor: only bright, plastic coinage accepted.

email la_maison-nette@propriétéspropres.fr
web www.homes-on-the-rangé.fr

Rue de la Cour – Les Écuries

Mandegault, Deux Sèvres

Enjoy a glass of chilled pineau de Charentes, the wickedly delicious aperitif, under the wisteria-clad pergola of these sweet stone stables. Alison and Francis, the delightful, artistic owners, have put their combined talents to wonderful use in this rustic, charming, ground-floor cottage. As in the old bakery next door (see opposite), natural colours and fabrics predominate and rooms keep their honey-coloured open-stone walls and oak beams. Spotless bedrooms are small and simple yet elegant, with scrubbed wooden floorboards and iron or polished wooden beds. Pick herbs from your garden and sprinkle them over the fresh organic vegetables the Hudsons supply; they also serve a delicious four-course dinner. Your garden is secluded and pretty, with fig trees, lawn and teak loungers, and can interconnect with the one next door if two families rent the cottages together. There's a large paddling pool for children to share and bikes to hire. Chef Boutonne, the nearest town, has a fairytale château, fascinating ancient *lavoirs* (washhouses) and a Saturday market: don't miss the Charentais melons.

sleeps	4.
rooms	2: 1 double, 1 twin; 1 shower room.
price	€305-€530 per week.

Francis & Alison Hudson

tel +33 (0)5 49 29 65 31

email mandegault@aol.com

web www.ruralretreats.org

Rue de la Cour – Le Four de Boulanger

Mandegault, Deux Sèvres

With its sunflower fields, honey stone walls and carthorses, the tiny village of Mandegault reminds us of how rural France used to be. Life slows to a tranquil trot, a pace which English owners Alison and Francis have been delighted to adopt at their 18th-century farmstead. Hens and ducks potter in the courtyard (children may collect the eggs at feeding time), a family of black sheep grazes their garden and wisteria strews the pergola of yours (which is private and charming). The couple have been equally respectful of local styles in their conversion of the bakery and stables. Here, in the bakery, the original vaulted stone bread oven and authentic diamond-shaped *œil de bœuf* windows have been kept, while beautiful natural fabrics, oak beams and walls of creamy stone create a mood of soothing elegance. There's pretty red stencilling on the floorboards in the main bedroom, and curtains give a dash of colour to the splendid, carved, cream-coloured bed and wardrobe. The owners are lovely and do an excellent *table d'hôtes*, and there's a shared games area with a small raised pool. Great for families.

sleeps	4-6.
rooms	2: 1 double, 1 twin, 1 sofabed in living room; 1 bathroom downstairs.
price	€335-€600 per week.

Francis & Alison Hudson
tel +33 (0)5 49 29 65 31
email mandegault@aol.com
web www.ruralretreats.org

Blacksmith's Cottage

Romazières, Charente-Maritime

Another pretty stone cottage, once the village blacksmith's house. His forge is next door and Elspeth and Graham have breathed new life into its old stones. The dapper exterior hides a snug interior and the full architectural works: beamed ceilings, stone walls, smart wooden floors – the latter courtesy of an artisan carpenter who excelled himself. The style is clutter-free, authentic and easy on the eye. The downstairs bedroom has French windows that open onto the garden where a walnut tree looms; the kitchen/sitting/dining room has plastered walls, stone-flagged floors and a wooden staircase that spirals up to the other rooms, one of which has a low ceiling and is for small children only. The kitchen holds all you need. A pretty walled garden offers lawn, parasols, a barbecue and shade-giving trees. There is also a wild vegetable and fruit garden from which you are free to harvest whatever is in season; the nearest shops are at Néré, three miles away. The shared pool is beautifully private in its walled and gated garden between the cottage and the owners' house. *Extra room for two available close by.*

sleeps	4 + 2 children.
rooms	3: 1 double, 1 twin with wc downstairs, 1 children's room; 1 bathroom.
price	£315-£425 per week.

Graham D'Albert & Elspeth Charlton

tel +33 (0)5 46 33 60 88

fax +33 (0)5 46 33 60 88

Fisherman's Cottage

St Martin de Ré, Charente-Maritime

Leave the summer throng behind you, wind through the creamy, cobbled backstreets of St Martin and discover your peaceful fisherman's cottage. Step in from the street and straight into the beamy sitting room snug with open fire, comfy sofas and the owner's collection of ceramics. The sitting room blends into the peppermint kitchen and then into a small but perfectly-formed garden. It may be teensy but everything is here: walls for privacy, tumbling plants… dine on the terrace, sprawl on the rug-sized lawn, gaze on the buttresses of the medieval abbey that rise majestically above. The twin upstairs comes with portholes that look on to the stairway; the double has a brass bed, a sloping pine ceiling and a picture window overlooking the garden, the terracotta roofs and the abbey, illuminated at night. If you don't feel like cooking, stroll down into fashionable St Martin, pick a harbourside retaurant and watch the bobbing boats. Lovely white sand beaches are a short walk or bike ride away. *Plently of places to hire bikes nearby.*

sleeps	4.
rooms	2: 1 double, 1 twin; 1 bathroom.
price	£345-£465 per week.

Graham D'Albert & Elspeth Charlton
tel +33 (0)5 46 33 60 88
fax +33 (0)5 46 33 60 88

Maison Cothonneau

St Martin de Ré, Charente-Maritime

Swap four wheels for two on the peaceful Ile de Ré. The island is criss-crossed with cycle paths and wrapped in 30km of white beaches. Your cottage is in a quiet backstreet – stunningly stylish but beautifully relaxed. Eat out in the sunny, flagged, high-walled courtyard dotted with potted palms and outdoor shower for washing down sandy children. Downstairs is one large and lovely living space: chunky beams, terracotta tiles, a gentle palette of whites and greys. The smart kitchen can be screened off, an armoire holds your crockery, a cupboard hides the telly, a Louis XVI fireplace keeps you cosy on chilly evenings. Up the white-painted, 17th-century staircase are three bedrooms pretty with pistachio paintwork, seagrass flooring and flowery throws. The third bedroom is suitably shipshape with a lantern for bedtime reading, cabin-style cupboard doors and a top bunk with a sliding ladder. The bathroom has sparkling new tiles, a 1920s basin, a vintage showerhead. Pop down the road and tuck into local oysters from the chic-ly bustling harbourside, watch the boats arrive with the daily catch.

sleeps	5-6.
rooms	3: 1 double, 1 twin/double, 1 room with bunks; 1 bathroom, 1 separate wc.
price	€850-€1,850 per week.

mobile	+33 (0)6 10 28 09 14
email	infos@maison-cothonneau.com
web	www.maison-cothonneau.com

Le Clos du Plantis – Le Goulet

Sonnac, Charente-Maritime

Le Clos du Plantis is wrapped in two private acres. Beyond its walls the hamlet of Le Goulet basks in undiscovered country… this is a charming pocket of France, full of Romanesque delights. And here, a warm, inviting place to stay, with delightful hosts who do B&B in the main house. Meet the other guests round the large pool; and fish, in season, in the trout stream that runs through. You will feel nicely private in your stone-walled barn, beautifully renovated in Charentais style. Smartly painted shuttered windows come in sage green, one ceiling is beamed, walls are colour-washed plaster or stone. The interior is simply furnished with a hotchpotch of pieces; white cotton throws on old sofas, pretty white curtains. Bedrooms have pale carpets, rough plaster walls, voile curtains – a neat contemporary feel. The kitchen has all (new) mod cons, French windows open onto a terrace, and your own garden (watch young children as the gate does not shut) has country views. There's boules and table tennis and Madame is an enthusiastic gardener who grows organic veg. A lush and lazy paradise. *B&B also.*

sleeps	4-6.
rooms	2: 1 double, 1 twin, 1 sofabed in sitting room; 1 bathroom, 1 separate wc.
price	€320-€1,090 per week.

Frédérique Thill-Toussaint
tel +33 (0)5 46 25 07 91
fax +33 (0)5 46 25 07 91
email auplantis@wanadoo.fr
web www.auplantis.com

Manoir Souhait – Le Verger

Gourvillette, Charente-Maritime

You can still see the stone oven in the dining room in which the former inhabitants cooked their pigeons. The birds, a delicacy reserved for the gentry, were reared in the pigeonnier just outside the gates. In the tiny village of Gourvillette, the house stands in the grounds of the 19th-century manoir which is also rented out by British owners Liz and Will (see opposite page). Camaraderie between the two houses is encouraged, guests at both are invited to an aperitif on the day they arrive, and you'll get to know each other by the fenced, terraced and heated pool – great for families, it has a section for children. There's snooker, badminton and table tennis, too. The interior is light and clean and the furniture mostly modern pine, with ancient roof beams to add character. Le Verger used to house farmworkers who made cognac, and in the pretty town of the same name (a 20-minute drive) you can tour the distilleries of Rémy Martin, Hennessy and Courvoisier. Try the area's other tipple too, pineau de Charentes, a sweet aperitif. Bikes can be hired locally and there are lovely rides and walks. *B&B also.*

sleeps	4-5.
rooms	2: 1 family room for 3, 1 twin; 1 bathroom.
price	€490-€1,050 (£350-£750) per week.

Will & Liz Weeks

tel	+33 (0)5 46 26 18 41
fax	+33 (0)5 46 24 64 68
email	weeks@manoirsouhait.com
web	www.manoirsouhait.com

Manoir Souhait – Le Manoir

Gourvillette, Charente-Maritime

The name means 'wish': why not make one to come here. The majestic arched Charentais porchway promises something grand and you won't be disappointed by this stunning 19th-century manor house in an enclosed garden, its old washhouse and pigeonnier intact. Liz and Will, the friendly British owners who do B&B next door, have researched the manor's origins meticulously and can show you the coat of arms of the Merveilleux family who built the house in 1620. There's a homely kitchen with a terracotta-tiled floor and a massive table; in summer you move onto the patio for lunch and dinner; fresh bread can be delivered daily. An amazing period staircase takes you to bedrooms that combine good traditional furnishings with modern comforts. This is ideal walking and cycling terrain, the coast and La Rochelle are only an hour's drive, and you can visit the distilleries in nearby Cognac. Or stay here and relax on one of several lovely terraces by the heated pool (fenced and with a section for children), shared with guests from the neighbouring cottage. For large family gatherings it's perfect. *B&B also.*

sleeps	12 + cot.
rooms	6: 3 doubles, 3 twins; 2 bathrooms, 1 shower room.
price	€1,190-€3,080 (£850-£2,200) per week.

Will & Liz Weeks
tel +33 (0)5 46 26 18 41
fax +33 (0)5 46 24 64 68
email weeks@manoirsouhait.com
web www.manoirsouhait.com

Château Mouillepied – La Maison du Vivier

Port d'Envaux, Charente-Maritime

Big French windows overlook the lily-strewn fishpond which gives the house its name. It was once the château's summer house and stands at the edge of the gardens: a graceful, 18th-century cottage, built of creamy stone and covered with vines. Inside, all is airy and open plan, with unobtrusive, modern furniture and a cool, understated feel. The whole of the first floor one big family room where whitewashed walls, exposed beams and a new pine floor give an effect of freshness and simplicity. The single bed is hidden behind by heavy linen curtains. The big sunny living room has an open fireplace and a well-equipped kitchen area. (Martine and Pierre are lovely and will, on request, deliver croissants to your door.) You have your own, unfenced garden *and* the beautiful grounds, which hold a fine dovecote and various intriguing outhouses, including one with huge decorated *lessiveuses*, the 18th-century precursor of the washing machine. All this in pretty countryside close to the Charente; stroll the banks, pick up a fishing licence from the local bakery. *B&B also.*

sleeps	2-3.
rooms	1 family room for 3; 1 bathroom, 1 separate wc.
price	€270-€485 per week.

Pierre & Martine Clément

tel +33 (0)5 46 90 49 88

fax +33 (0)5 46 90 36 91

email chateau-mouillepied@voila.fr

web www.chateaumouillepied.com

Le Moulin des Agrilles

Lorignac, Charente-Maritime

A gracious, friendly house, outside and in, and a marvellous place for a family party or group of friends. Built in the 17th century as a *maison de maître*, it has seven acres of land, semi-wild in places, and views on all sides. (From one point you can see as far as the Gironde estuary.) The pretty, formal front faces the garden and there's a real feeling of seclusion. Even the lovely pool lies discreetly away behind some trees. Josette and Rodney have done wonders indoors, too, creating a fresh, pretty elegance. The pale yellow country kitchen with its Charentaise fireplace and huge farmhouse table is splendidly equipped. There are two very attractive sitting rooms, one designed for the adults of the party, the other has TV, music and games for all ages. From the tiled hall, a graceful stone staircase curves its way up to the first and second floors, where bedrooms are big and delightful. Josette and Rodney do all they can to make things easy for you; they'll send you a grocery list so you can pre-order supplies, and Josette can sometimes be prevailed upon to cook. *B&B also.*

sleeps	15 + cot.
rooms	8: 4 doubles, 3 twins, 1 single; 5 bathrooms, 1 separate wc.
price	€2,050-€3,500 (£1,600-£3,000) per week.

	Josette Cooke
tel	+33 (0)5 46 48 17 09
email	josettecooke@aol.com
web	www.lesagrilles.co.uk

Moreau – The Farmhouse

Cercoux, Charente-Maritime

Understated elegance and homeliness are skilfully combined in this 18th-century farmhouse; its mood of tranquillity and sophistication beguiles and soothes. Plain yet luxurious, it is decorated throughout with antiques; no surprise to learn that the English owner Marian, is an antiques dealer. The house used to be a wealthy farm where the aperitif pineau was made; the chestnut beamed ceilings and stone fireplace have been superbly preserved. The spectacular kitchen – the old distillery – has a huge vaulted ceiling, a woodburning range and dazzling white walls and floors to set off a sensational display of navy and white china. Enjoy the dreamy views over the fields from the big carpeted bedroom with fabulous antique bed and huge beams. Outside, a private garden with a raised pool. Stock up in Cercoux, or shop at the twice-weekly market at pretty Coutras, a 20-minute drive. Nearby medieval Montguyon holds a folklore festival in July and August; there's also a lake for swimming and a beach area with a little café. Marian is delightful, available yet unobtrusive. Readers are full of praise.

sleeps	6-7.
rooms	2: 2 family rooms for 3, 1 daybed in sitting room; 1 bathroom, 1 shower room.
price	£300-£490 per week.
closed	November-March. Winter lets by arrangement.

Marian Sanders

tel	+33 (0)5 46 04 01 66
fax	+33 (0)5 46 04 01 66
email	marianatmoreau@hotmail.com
web	www.holidayatmoreau.com

Moreau – Le Pressoir

Cercoux, Charente-Maritime

Like the house next door, this fine 18th-century Charentais house is a treasure chest of fascinating antiques and artefacts, all chosen and carefully composed by Marian. The front doors were once French windows from a local château, there's a pitch-pine armoire from a priest's house in Bordeaux and, in the kitchen/dining room, brass chandeliers from Nantes. Marian's great skill, however, is that she's kept furnishings as simple as possible so as to let this lovely stone building speak for itself. Rooms are large, airy and stylish, with pure white walls and original terracotta tiled floors. French windows lead from the kitchen to a big walled terrace, perfect for sunny breakfasts, and a big, private garden with a raised pool beyond. The cool and spacious downstairs double bedrooms are in the old pressoir where grapes were pressed to make pineau de Charentes, the aperitif for which the area is famous. Colours are muted beiges and pinks, beds are handsome brass and views are of the garden. Worth every penny. *Owners organise trips to antique markets in low season.*

sleeps	7.
rooms	3: 2 doubles, 1 triple; 1 bathroom, 2 shower rooms.
price	£400-£590 per week.
closed	November-March. Winter lets by arrangement.

	Marian Sanders
tel	+33 (0)5 46 04 01 66
fax	+33 (0)5 46 04 01 66
email	marianatmoreau@hotmail.com
web	www.holidayatmoreau.com

Les Galards

Montlieu la Garde, Charente-Maritime

The wonderful 17th-century *maison de maître* has never left the family and it fell to Monsieur Menanteau to renovate and revive. The attached one-storey building is your gîte. The kitchen is wonderful – the hub of the house with an original sink carved from stone, three black cooking pots hung on whitewashed walls and the finest of mod cons. There's central heating, too. French doors open to a terrace with barbecue and a young garden with trees, swings and sandbox. Soft yellow bedrooms are equally minimalist and pleasing. Expect high beams, terracotta or stripped floors, an ancient stone fireplace, a Louis Philippe chest of drawers, a delightful small-pebble floor. Bathrooms are excellent: yellow-tiled, beamed, spotless. The salon has upright antique wooden settles, an exquisite grandfather clock and simple chandelier – and there's delicious, local cognac in the cupboards for you to buy. Outside are unbroken views of rolling countryside, a private wood and a small lake where you can swim, fish or get pedalo-fit. For things watery, try Lac Baron; and Chepniers, two miles up the road for a perfect meal. *B&B also.*

sleeps	8 + cot.
rooms	4: 2 doubles, 2 twins, 1 bathroom; 2 shower rooms, 2 separate wcs.
price	€445-€690 per week.

Pascal Menanteau

tel	+33 (0)5 46 04 53 62
fax	+33 (0)5 46 04 32 33
email	menanteau.pascal@free.fr
web	www.lesgalards.com

Tailliveaux

Villebois Lavalette, Charente

A big, generous-hearted old place that will restore your faith in the old-fashioned concept of 'gite'. It is a barn of mighty beams, where you can totter dreamily from the vast old bed to the balcony, past the leather trunk and dining table, to gaze luxuriously upon the countryside. You live above the old barn – now a garage if you need it – in the *grenier*, an open-plan apartment for two. The living space is a generously proportioned room, with a modern kitchen and bathroom to one side. You have your own courtyard garden and covered eating area, and can make full use of the mature gardens of the main house – read, doze, paint, sleep. The swimming pool is in a very private and quiet place, so you may dream there too. These English owners will bend over backwards for you, meeting you at the station as a favour or ferrying you to airports. Be reclusive or ask for support: relaxation therapy, Alexander technique, guided visits – and there's terrific food at madly low prices. The apartment, with balcony, faces south, so you may be reluctant to leave this place of bucolic, easy bliss. *B&B also.*

sleeps	2.
rooms	1 double; 1 bathroom.
price	£250 per week.
arrival	Flexible.
closed	June-September.

Deborah Cranston
tel +33 (0)5 45 25 24 62
email deborah.cranston@wanadoo.fr

Les Deux Marronniers – House & Barn

St Palais du Né, Charente

One *marronnier* greets you at the entrance, a second shades the peaceful courtyard. This used to be a farmhouse and then a school. Nowadays the Thomas's family home stretches the length of one side of the courtyard; the two gîtes make up a second. Inside, the feel is elegantly cool: smart modern sofas, wrought-iron tables, shades of off-white. Both gîtes have open fires and central heating for winter and their own small terrace for eating out when it's warm. Bedrooms are creamy and beamy with pretty toile de Jouy or crisp checks; views are bucolic. Crunch across the courtyard, through a stone archway to the lovely shared pool hidden behind high walls, with canvas parasols and a terracotta-roofed lean-to for shade. Leighan shares produce from the potager during bumper months; Michael can sort out a fishing permit for just down the river, arrange a visit to a pineau producer or organise a trip out on a neighbour's pony and trap; the two teenage daughters are happy to babysit. A spring-fed lake with pedalos and restaurant is a 20-minute drive. Perfect.

sleeps	Barn 6. House 3-4.
rooms	Barn: 1 double, 2 twins; 1 shower room, 1 bathroom. House: 1 double, 1 room with bunks; 1 bathroom.
price	Barn £450-£850. House £250-£650. Prices per week.

Michael & Leighan Thomas
tel +33 (0)5 45 78 47 25
fax +33 (0)5 45 78 47 06
email info@charente-gites.net
web www.charente-gites.net

Buffetaud

Passirac, Charente

Remote and peaceful – a hamlet of two houses! This 18th-century scrubbed-stone farmhouse has a fenced pool, a big garden and is encircled by farmland. Inside, a large hall bisects the house. Terracotta runs throughout the ground floor, graced by the odd Persian rug, while space has been created by removing the double doors from dining and sitting rooms. White walls soak up light. Bedrooms are excellent and the downstairs doubles are huge; one has a lovely fireplace, the other, double doors to the terrace. Both are uncluttered, light and airy, and furnished with the odd antique. Upstairs rooms have exposed beams; compact bathrooms come with shining white tiles and plush towels. The feel is not grand but handsome and homely, with stone fireplaces, comfy sofas and armchairs, lots of space. The kitchen has new appliances and absolutely all you need; in summer you can eat on the terrace by the pool. There's also a good restaurant nearby. A great place for one huge family or three small ones. Don't miss the Charente, one of France's best kept secrets, or the town of Cognac, within striking distance.

sleeps	10.
rooms	6: 2 doubles, 4 singles; 2 bathrooms, 2 shower rooms, 2 separate wcs.
price	€450-€1,200 per week.
arrival	Saturday, but flexible.

Florence Descoqs

tel +33 (0)1 39 53 50 02

email albert.descoqs@wanadoo.fr

web perso.wanadoo.fr/gitebuffetaud

L'Abbaye du Palais – Moines

Bourganeuf, Creuse

Another graceful restoration by Dutch owners in rural France. Embraced by five hectares of forest, meadow and orchard, a Cistercian abbey, chapel, outbuildings and ruins. Your delightful hosts have three children and a background in hotel management; they have poured hearts and talents into this special place. They live in the 12th-century abbey, do luxury B&B and have converted the old abbey bakery into a gîte for six. A tangle of greenery envelops this generous, two-storey cottage, with its terracotta floors, stone walls, cream drapes, antiques and open fire. The bread oven – still intact – is medieval, the kitchen brand new. A U-shaped bar separates it from the dining area, there are French windows to a west-facing patio with wooden loungers and barbecue, serenity and light. Children love the whole place: they have an attic above the stables full of games, a treehouse, swings, farm animals, tractor rides, from time to time, with the owners' children, and early meals for early bed. Martijn is a passionate cook and produces three-course dinners: a treat for gîte guests as well as B&B-ers. *B&B also.*

sleeps	6.
rooms	3: 1 double, 2 twins; 1 bathroom.
price	€600-€900 per week.

Martijn & Saskia Zandvliet-Breteler

tel	+33 (0)5 55 64 02 64
fax	+33 (0)5 55 64 02 63
email	info@abbayedupalais.com
web	www.abbayedupalais.com

L'Abbaye du Palais – Templiers & Pèlerins

Bourganeuf, Creuse

Attached to Moines (previous entry), the old stable block, a low-slung building with an ancient-stoned terrace and a relaid roof. One-storey Pèlerins is a new house built near the main gates away from the rest and custom-made for wheelchairs; both have open-plan kitchens, country furniture, an open fire or woodburning stove and plenty of space. Terraces come with wooden loungers and barbecues. The whole domaine (abbey, outbuildings, treehouse) has been beautifully renovated by the Dutch owners who, with offspring of their own, are family-friendly *par excellence*. Not only is there a play area and games room but also, in their house, a library, billiards and a piano tuned to play. These several private acres lie in a richly forested wood, chestnuts and lakes, bordered by the river Thavrion; no wonder they call it Little Canada. Fish, canoe, ride and swim – or visit the spectacular Gorges du Thavrion. Saskia collects baguettes for your breakfast and prepares picnic baskets; Martijn promises wonderful dinners – just book in advance. *Ask about cookery courses. B&B also.*

sleeps	Templiers 6. Pèlerins 4-5.
rooms	Templiers: 1 double, 2 twins; 1 bathroom. Pèlerins: 1 double, 1 family room for 3; 1 bathroom.
price	€550-€800 per week.

Martijn & Saskia Zandvliet-Breteler

tel +33 (0)5 55 64 02 64

fax +33 (0)5 55 64 02 63

email info@abbayedupalais.com

web www.abbayedupalais.com

Fleuret – Main House

Curemonte, Corrèze

The setting of this solid stone 17th-century farmhouse is breathtaking: views of hills and woodland fill every window. This is a sensitive restoration by the architect owner, who lives with wife Gilly and their family in the other half of the building. Walls are thick and space plentiful. The kitchen/dining room is immense with warm wooden flooring, a woodburner in the ancient hearth, an antique table for family feasts; the sitting room has colourwashed walls, some exposed stone, comfortable sofas – wholly delightful. One double room is downstairs, the other four are in the attic with gabled ceilings, white walls, no clutter. There are books, games, a video library and Tim's photographs on the walls (ask about his courses on landscape photography). On the same site are a separate barn and a cottage – all share farmyard, games room and pool. So, plenty of comings and goings, but peace and privacy too. Medieval, hilltop Curemont, its turrets peeping across the valley, has a market that opens in summer, and there are masses of castles and caves to discover. *Further house for 4 with private pool, 8km from Beaulieu.*

sleeps	9-10.
rooms	5: 2 doubles, 1 twin, 1 triple, 1 single; 1 bathroom, 2 shower rooms.
price	€1,190-€1,950 per week.

Tim & Gilly Mannakee

tel	+33 (0)5 55 84 06 47
fax	+33 (0)5 55 84 05 73
email	info@fleuretholidays.com
web	www.fleuretholidays.com

Fleuret – The Cottage

Curemonte, Corrèze

The old bread oven adds a rustic note to the big characterful kitchen, its brick surround charred by the ages. It was discovered and restored by Tim and Gilly, who have revived the red sandstone farm cottage with imagination and sensitivity. Stonework and ancient beams have been properly preserved and terracotta floors and pine cupboards added; cookery books, strings of garlic and board games add a personal touch. Attic bedrooms are simple and cosily carpeted, with small dormer windows to pretty views. French doors lead from the sitting room, charming with cherry-pink sofas and stove, to an outdoor barbecue area where you can dine and gaze on fields, woods and never-ending hills. Outside you find a big, walled-off pool, shared with your delightful British hosts next door, and an amazing barn with a vast oak floor that you may use whenever you like: table tennis, billiards, dancing, grand piano; it can also be hired for weddings. A wonderful home for a family in search of peace and space. *With Main House (opposite) sleeps 14.*

sleeps	4.
rooms	2: 1 double, 1 twin; 1 bathroom.
price	€550-€990 per week.

Tim & Gilly Mannakee
tel +33 (0)5 55 84 06 47
fax +33 (0)5 55 84 05 73
email info@fleuretholidays.com
web www.fleuretholidays.com

La Farge

Monceaux sur Dordogne, Corrèze

As ideal a hideaway today as it was for refugees during the war, this large Correzian barn overlooks the pastures of the plateau above the Dordogne. The English owners Helen and Keith also do B&B across the lane, have a wealth of local knowledge and give guests a big welcome; their charming neighbours may stop for a chat, too. Hens potter about the lane, the beautiful Limousin cows occasionally pass by. Inside, there's a fresh feel to the big, terracotta-floored living room, amply furnished with chunky chairs in flowery covers and usefully stocked with books, games and CDs. The kitchen is equally well-equipped. There's a large white bathroom and a cool, blue bedroom with new pine beds, blue-painted furniture and round blue rug. Big blue pots of geraniums surround the barn in summer and 'Le Parc', as it is known by the locals – a large, enclosed area of lawns and trees, with good garden furniture and a barbecue – is all yours. There's a shared pool for summer and *table d'hôtes* to join for dinner (book ahead). A perfect spot for those seeking quintessential rural France. *B&B also.*

sleeps	2.
rooms	1 twin; 1 bathroom.
price	€195-€295 per week + £30 with pool.

Helen & Keith Archibald
tel +33 (0)5 55 28 54 52
email archi-at-lafarge@wanadoo.fr
web www.chezarchi.com

Longevialle

St Paul de Salers, Cantal

Pack the hiking boots. Bang in the heart of the dramatic Parc des Volcans d'Auvergne, this newly converted barn will delight walkers and anyone who wants a glimpse of an area of rural France which has changed little in centuries. Nearby medieval (if touristy) Salers with its cobbled streets, gateways and turreted mansions made of dark Auvergnat volcanic rock is another treat. Don't miss the weekly market where farmers sell delicious Cantal and other cheeses for which the area's lush pastures are famous. Although in the hamlet, the house feels totally private and has south-facing views over a pleasant garden for al fresco dining. The downstairs is open plan, with new pine floors and panelled walls which give a roomy, airy feel. The kitchen has one of the original stone walls and the (absent) French owner thoughtfully leaves a selection of recipes for you. Spotless pine-clad bedrooms, one a mezzanine, have fabulous views. Walk from the door onto the GR400 Tour du Cantal footpath which takes in Puy Violent and Puy Mary. And there's cross-country skiing in winter.

sleeps	6-8.
rooms	3 twins, 1 sofabed in living room; 2 shower rooms, 1 separate wc.
price	€300-€585 per week.
closed	November-March.

Marie-Geneviève Bauchant

tel +33 (0)2 47 29 50 70
fax +33 (0)2 47 99 50 70
email mg.bauchant@wanadoo.fr
web membres.lycos.fr/longevialle

Raymond

Aurillac, Cantal

Walk out of this traditional Auvergnat house with its steely slate roofs into stupendous countryside. You can hear a gurgling stream from your bed and all around are breathtaking views of the cone-shaped *puys*. The 200-year-old house used to be two cottages. One half retains the living room where once the family lived, ate and slept: it still has the original wooden beams, long table and inglenook fireplace where you can toast your toes and wind down after a day in the mountains. The other half, a ruin when the Haines found it, has a more modern feel and extra windows add aririness and light. Bedrooms are a blend too: ancient, crannied and characterful or well-lit modern; one leads to a terrace. Visit local cheesemakers to sample Cantal, shower under the waterfall in the river, visit the market in Aurillac. You can buy fresh milk, yogurt and goat's cheese from the farmer next door and a travelling shop comes to the house three times a week – listen for his horn. There are guided mountain walks and adventure sports all summer long, and mushroom-picking in the autumn. Marvellous.

sleeps	6.
rooms	3: 2 doubles, 1 twin/double; 2 shower rooms, 1 separate wc.
price	€300-€500 per week.
closed	December-Easter

Ann & Stephen Haine

tel	+44 (0)20 7267 8936
fax	+44 (0)20 7813 5573
email	annhaine@blueyonder.co.uk
web	www.auvergne-cottage.com

Sweet Little House

Condat, Cantal

Tiny, south-facing and built into the rock, this stone house is described by its owners as "doll's-house pretty". Di and her farmer husband Peter moved here from Devon in search of solitude; they live nearby and hope you'll drop in for a glass of wine and a chat. The little house was built a century ago for the haymaker and its slate roof (steeply sloped to fend off snow) is typical of the Auvergne. Materials are basic – there's lots of pale pine – but Di has given it style through careful choice of furniture and furnishings. A set of antique copper pans decorates the compact but beautifully equipped kitchen; in the bedrooms upstairs are a fine wrought-iron bed and country antiques. Rooms are uncluttered and immaculately clean, creating a feeling of light and space. The living room has parquet floors and a Godin woodburner; the walls are decorated with with the tools used by the original haymaker. There's a tiny patio where you can eat out; your gardens are the narcissi-filled meadows, your backdrop, the mountains of the national park. Birdwatchers and walkers will be in heaven. *Two further houses for four.*

sleeps	4.
rooms	2: 1 double, 1 twin; 1 bathroom, 1 separate wc.
price	£265-£530 per week.

Di Scott

tel +33 (0)4 71 78 63 57

fax +33 (0)4 71 78 50 33

email di.scott@wanadoo.fr

web www.auvergnehols.co.uk

Château de Coisse – Gîte & Studio

Arlanc, Puy-de-Dôme

After years in tourism and adventure sports, this dynamic couple met a greater challenge: to transform a muster of rambling ruins (dated 1100s to 1700s: carvings, towers, remnants of former rustic grandeur) where the local lord reigned. The river Dore (for picnics) and 'toy' railway run at the bottom, long fields stretch to distant hills, birds flock, cats and dogs thrive. With their own high barn door and fine great hallway, the two gîtes are independent in blue, white and pine with superior fittings, kitchen equipment and bedding. The big first-floor flat is fully child-friendly (stair gates, cots, high chair). A vast plateau of a living room, pine-floored, beamed and light, leads out to a private patio-terrace and up to three bedrooms, one blue, one green, one peach, under the sloping roof: simple and pretty, with practical hanging racks and sock baskets. Within immensely thick walls, the small ground-floor flat is cosy and just as well done. Fiona leaves a super welcome quiche. She and Graham are fascinating about their project-of-a-liftetime but you can be as close or distant as you please.

sleeps	Gîte 6-8 + 2 cots. Studio 2-4 + cot.
rooms	Gîte: 1 double, 2 twins, 1 sofabed in living room; 1 shower room, 1 separate wc. Studio: 1 twin/double, 1 sofabed in living room; 1 bathroom.
price	€400-€600. Studio €200-€300. Prices per week.

Fiona & Graham Sheldon

tel	+33 (0)4 73 95 00 45
email	fiandgra@chateaudecoisse.com
web	www.chateaudecoisse.com

Château de Vaulx – Old Dairy & Coachyard

Ste Agathe, Puy-de-Dôme

Discover the undiscovered, the wooded hills and enchanted valley of Vaulx, the silence of nature, the rugged history, and go exploring. Your hosts, anchored to their château "for 800 years", offer unpretentious, family-furnished converted farm buildings and the run of the garden. The old dairy once housed the landlord's food growers; now a small holiday house, it has its own fenced garden for lounging and barbecues, a cosy living room with big stone fireplace and good old armchairs, three small, simple bedrooms in pastels and light florals, a pine-ceilinged kitchen to seat you all. In the upstairs/downstairs coachyard gîte there's lots of space, a long porch with brick barbecue instead of a private garden, a dramatically high living room (an ancestor had his 'theatre' here) with kitchen attached, country antiques and soft old fabrics. The two-room family suite (double with en suite bathroom, twin next door) is nearby, the palely feminine single upstairs, the darkly masculine double downstairs in the old saddlery with another bathroom. Loving dogs and donkeys, an ever-running spring – marvellous. *B&B also.*

sleeps	Old Dairy 6. Coachyard 7.
rooms	Old Dairy: 2 doubles, 1 twin: 1 shower room, separate wc. Coachyard: 1 family suite for 4, 1 double, 1 single; 1 shower room, 1 bathroom.
price	€390 per week.

Guy & Régine Dumas de Vaulx
tel +33 (0)4 73 51 50 55
fax +33 (0)4 73 51 50 55
web www.auvergne.maison-hotes.com

Château de Maulmont – Les Pavillons

St Priest Bramefant, Puy-de-Dôme

In the old potager below the château, beneath a steep, skinny wood, two neat little houses, clean as new pins, stand beside a third (they are just out of the picture on the right.) The cool, blue middle one and the red end one are yours for the asking. The decoration and fittings are high quality and the bathrooms have excellent taps and pretty tiles. Kitchens, pale grey or pinky-beige, may be better equipped than your own, and open widely onto a north terrace. Living rooms, one blue and cream, the other ochre and orange, are full of light, furnished for six and lead to a south terrace where wooden furniture invites you to linger long over the lovely view. The hedges are growing fast and the neighbours will soon be invisible – your garden is your own soft grassy space. There shouldn't be much traffic on the small road when you get back from your explorations – riding, walking, golf practice in the château grounds – and if you're too tired to cook, indulge in the château chef's Michelin-starred cuisine: an exceptional treat. *Hotel also. Two more château gîtes sleeping 6 & 12, 6km.*

sleeps	2 houses for 4-6.
rooms	2 houses each with 1 double, 1 twin, 1 sofabed in sitting room; 1 bathroom.
price	€900-€1,170 per week. €150-€195 per night.
arrival	Saturday or Wednesday.
closed	January-4 February.

Mary & Théo Bosman
tel +33 (0)4 70 59 03 45
fax +33 (0)4 70 59 03 45
email info@chateau-maulmont.com
web www.chateau-maulmont.com

Domaine du Bourg – La Grande Grue & La Somme

Gannay sur Loire, Allier

With verve and organisational skills, Peter and Trudi care for four children and various pets as well as up to 60 happy holidaymakers on their three acres of grass. Besides the two gîtes, there are a number of B&B rooms and ten well-spread camping spaces; add the pool, swings, volleyball, boules and *table d'hôtes* for all and you have one lively place, brilliant for families. On their work-laden old floors, both gîtes are furnished with brocante finds of tremendous character and little fragility; in La Grue you have a high-efficiency Danish wood burner, a decent open kitchen, a well-fitted shower room, beautiful exposed beams and dining tables that feel like old friends. Set slightly apart, with an air of cosy intimacy and its own private piece of garden, La Somme has a nice little double room beside the shower room and a steep low attic space for the young (twin beds on one side, a 120cm bed on the other). On the first floor of the great old barn, this larger gîte has space and light, a smaller double and twin beds on the mezzanine. Dutch families love it here and it is all huge fun. *B&B also.*

sleeps	La Grande Grue 6-7. La Somme 6-8.
rooms	La Grande Grue: 2 doubles, 1 twin with campbed; 1 bath. Somme: 1 double, 1 twin, 1 family room with double & bunks; 1 shower, 1 separate wc.
price	La Grande Grue €100-€460. Somme €120-€560. Prices per week.

Trudi & Peter de Lange

tel +33 (0)4 70 43 49 01

fax +33 (0)4 70 43 43 01

email info@domainedubourg.com

web www.domainedubourg.com

photo corel images

aquitaine

La Grange de Bellefontaine

Bellefond, Gironde

This is claret country and those who like their wine 'red and French' will be in heaven. The immaculately renovated 17th-century barn opposite the *mairie* was once part of Madame's family farm; views uphill take in the village and its ancient church, those down stretch across field, orchard and vineyard. The spotless interior is a mix of uncluttered contemporary and classical French. A floating, light-wood staircase slinks up the wall, French windows in the salon rise to the top of the house and most walls are cream-washed rough plaster – simple and striking. Furniture is painted in light pastel colours, much by Madame, a talented artist. Floors are pale-tiled, underfloor-heated and graced with the odd rug, the open-plan kitchen/dining room is wonderfully light and brilliantly equipped. Bedrooms are exceptional: painted brass beds, sloping ceilings, delicate fabrics, elegant swags. There's a balcony, a terrace for evening drinks and a small secluded garden. The village dates from the 11th century, St Émilion is four miles away, Bordeaux is close. *Children over eight welcome. B&B also.*

sleeps	6.
rooms	3 doubles; 1 bathroom, 2 shower rooms.
price	€1,100-€1,400 per week.

France Prat

tel	+33 (0)5 57 47 13 74
email	france.prat@wanadoo.fr
web	www.gites-bellefontaine.fr.st

Pey au Bruc

Venday Montalivet, Gironde

Despite the elegance and the antiques, this is the warmest, most child-friendly of places. An 18th-century stone farmhouse, it has the unmistakeable air of a house that is lived in and enjoyed. Jane describes it as 'shabby-chic' but there's not a lot shabby! Everywhere has been subtly and thoughtfully restored without in any way being precious. The big, delightful bedrooms have comfortable antique French beds – Napoleonic *lits d'enfants* for the little ones – and the nursery room is packed with toys, games and dressing-up costumes. Children will also love discovering the house's secret places, reached by unexpected ladders and low doors. They have their own sitting room, too, just off the (fabulous) kitchen, so adults can keep a watchful eye. The main sitting room is gracefully proportioned, with warm stone walls and an open log fire. Out in the big garden, set in woods and very private, is a lovely stone-edged swimming pool and an organic potager which guests are welcome to use. You'll be greeted by Jane and her daughter who do B&B when the house is not let. *B&B also.*

sleeps	10-11 + 5 children + cots.
rooms	6: 3 doubles, 1 double with child's bed, 1 family room for 3, 1 children's room for 4; 5 bathrooms.
price	€2,000-€3,000 per week.

	Jane Butler
tel	+33 (0)5 56 41 73 44
	+33 (0)5 56 41 27 04
fax	+33 (0)5 56 41 73 44
email	jane.butler@wanadoo.fr

Hello

The Beachhouse

Venday Montalivet, Gironde

It matters not a jot if the children trail sand into the house or bounce beach balls in the bedroom. This pretty 1930s wooden seaside house, five minutes from the beach, is just perfect for a family. It's painted green and white and is wholly simple yet very inviting. Jane has bleached the floorboards and painted the smallish bedrooms attractive shades of blue and green. The furniture is 1930s – including the beds, with their firm new mattresses and dazzling white covers – and there are two small galley kitchens. The sitting room isn't huge either; no matter, you'll be spending every spare moment in the cane rocker on the gorgeous covered veranda. This stretches the length of the house and is decorated with floats from old fishing nets; a great place for lunch. The house has its own little garden and is on a small estate that springs to life in the summer, so expect some noise. There are miles of Atlantic beaches, no shortage of bars and restaurants and a huge daily market in Montalivet. And the fabulous wines of Médoc are just a short drive away. Charming.

sleeps	10-11 + 3 children. Can easily be divided into 2 apartments for 4 & 8.
rooms	6: 4 doubles, 1 family room for 3, 1 children's room for 3; 3 bathrooms.
price	€1,200-€1,800 for whole house, €580 per week for four, €1,160 for eight. Prices per week.
closed	15 November-15 March.

Jane Butler

tel	+33 (0)5 56 41 73 44
	+33 (0)5 56 41 27 04
fax	+33 (0)5 56 41 73 44
email	jane.butler@wanadoo.fr

Manoir du Gaboria – St Émilion, Médoc, Entre-Deux-Mers

Ste Gemme, Gironde

Willy has his own vineyard, produces a good drop, and visits can be arranged. He and Mieke run cookery courses, too. They are a delightful couple – warm, human and keen to promote the quiet, rambling country that surrounds you and which teems with bastides, vineyards, medieval villages, walking paths, cycling tracks, and fast-flowing rivers. They do B&B – their 18th-century manor house is immaculate – and have three gîtes, but the gardens and lawns are so extensive and the mood so relaxed that no one seems to mind and peace and quiet prevail. There are low stone walls, wandering roses, a well in the courtyard and a sense of rightful permanence. You are high on the hill – views stretch over fields and vineyards (the competition's) and you can gaze out from the smart terrace round the pool. All gîtes have a private terrace, too. Expect a contemporary style, white walls, coir matting, pretty views and lots of space. Furniture is simple, clean and neat. You might have a high-ceilinged room in yellow, a vast kitchen/living room or an old original terracotta-tiled floor. Wonderful. *B&B also.*

sleeps	St Émilion 6. Médoc 4-5. Entre-Deux-Mers 2.
rooms	St Émilion 3: 2 doubles, 1 twin; 2 baths. Médoc 2: 1 double, 1 triple; 1 bath. Entre-Deux-Mers: 1 double; 1 bath.
price	St Émilion €525-€1050. Médoc €375-€750. Entre-Deux-Mers €420-€650. Prices per week.

	Mieke & Willy Borremans
tel	+33 (0)5 56 71 99 57
fax	+33 (0)5 56 71 99 58
email	manoir@gaboria.com
web	www.gaboria.com

Les Quatre Vents – Le Clos I & II

Cauneille, Landes

Swiss-born Denise and Arnold did B&B, happily, for years; now they care for their gîte guests and their few donkeys and sheep in these secluded 20 acres, a hill-top hideaway with magnificent views. They live 100 yards away and are there when you need them, full of advice and happy for you to share their pool. Clos I and Clos II fill two floors of a chalet-style house: one on the ground floor, with French windows to the terrace, the other above, reached via an outside stair. They are not the last word in contemporary chic but are comfortable, carpeted and newly equipped: pine on the walls, patterned duvets on the beds, the odd wool rug and framed poster. Kitchen/sitting rooms are open plan and your terraces are well furnished. Sally forth to discover this off-the-beaten-track part of Gascony, dubbed 'the new Dordogne'. The wooded hills are glorious, golf courses abound, Biarritz isn't far, nor Dax, surrounded by a Romanesque wall, famous for its waters that steam at a steady 64 degrees. Worth visiting not just for its restorative mud baths but also its bustling Saturday market. *Children over 12 welcome.*

sleeps	2 apartments for 4-6.
rooms	Each apartment: 1 double, 1 twin, 1 sofabed in sitting room; 1 bathroom.
price	€500 each per week.

Denise & Arnold Brun
tel +33 (0)5 58 73 25 57
fax +33 (0)5 58 73 70 60
email arnold.brun@wanadoo.fr

Résidence Lilinita

Biarritz, Pyrénées-Atlantiques

Watch the rolling waves of the Atlantic from five French windows. Perched on the cliffs above Biarritz's Côte des Basques, this luxury turret was built by a Polish countess in search of vistas to paint; the views are staggering, the sunsets superb. And if you tire of watching the surfers, gaze at the distant peaks of the Spanish Pyrenees. Don't be deceived by the apartment's turn-of-the-century exterior – at the top of two flights of stairs a cool, modern interior awaits. The state-of-the-art kitchen opens into a large dining/living room with polished floors and generous sofas; a futuristic central staircase leads to bedrooms with immaculate white bedcovers and lovely antiques. There are books, videos, music, internet, oodles of towels. You're brilliantly placed to taste the delights of the resort, made fashionable by Victorian ladies in search of winter sun. Boutiques and restaurants are a five-minute walk, as is the Casino Municipal, restored to its 1930s grandeur. *No children under 15. Rates for two, or for longer stays, on request. Min. three nights.*

sleeps	4.
rooms	2 twins/doubles; 1 bathroom, 1 shower room.
price	€1,575-€1,995 per week.
arrival	Flexible.

Sue & Bill Barr

tel +33 (0)5 59 34 34 14
fax +33 (0)5 59 34 35 44
email barr.bill@online.fr
web www.summerflat.com

Hello

Les Collines Iduki – Apartments

La Bastide Clairence, Pyrénées-Atlantiques

A surprisingly attractive holiday complex (there are 22 gîtes in all, in a choice of two styles) that overlooks one of the prettiest bastide villages of France. A dreamy river sweeps round at the foot of the hill, 100-year-old oak trees and fields surround you. The 'village' was designed in Basque style by the architect who built Les Halles in Bayonne and it fits its landscape perfectly. Whitewashed apartments have private terraces with teak furniture and parasols, brightly painted shutters and pretty interiors. Small bedrooms are dressed in colourful modern and ethnic fabrics, in checks and stripes, bathrooms are white, kitchens contain all you need. Sitting rooms have stencilled walls, tiled floors, old wooden furniture nicely painted. All is comfortable and gently stylish. There's a shared pool, a play area and a games room: this is a sociable place, brilliant for families. The Haramboures run the restaurant by the river and meet you on arrival. The village is a four-minute walk; come in the last week of July for the fête and three days of carousing in the square. *Shared laundry.*

sleeps	22 apartments in total. Type A 2-4. Type B 4-6.
rooms	Apartment A: 1 double, 1 sofabed in lounge; 1 bathroom. Apartment B: 1 double, 1 twin, 1 sofabed in lounge; 1 shower room, 1 bathroom.
price	Apartment A €305-€900. Apartment B €379-€1,145. Prices per week.

Marie-Joelle Haramboure

tel +33 (0)5 59 70 20 81
fax +33 (0)5 59 70 20 25
email iduki@iduki.net
web www.iduki.net

Chemin Pruet

Viellenave de Navarrenx, Pyrénées-Atlantiques

Volga the pony will whinny for sugar lumps, Henri will give the children a tractor ride, Sylvie will invite you for a drink. This is a friendly farm which the Lacamoire family have worked for over a century. Your gîte is a typical Bearnaise barn with steeply pitched roof, stone and plaster walls and large arched entrance. It's been little altered other than to add glass doors in the archway. Step into an open-plan living area, simple but comfortable with traditional Bearnaise furniture and farm bowls and cowbells adding rustic touches. A kitchen tucks into one end – small, but with all you need and brand new. You'll probably eat on the terrace with its dreamy views of fields, forests and distant villages. Bedrooms, including one perfect for wheelchairs, are simply furnished – wooden or tiled floors, pale walls, cheerful duvet covers and Sylvie's nature photographs to add warmth. The bathrooms are spanking new and roomy. (Sofa and z-beds for extra guests.) Woodland walks from the door, hiking in the Pyrenees, the spa at Salies de Bearn, Bearnaise and Basque towns to explore. Great value.

sleeps	5-6.
rooms	3: 1 double, 1 twin, 1 single, 1 sofabed in living room; 1 bath, 1 shower.
price	€480 per week; €200 for 3 nights.

Sylvie & Henri Lacamoire
tel +33 (0)5 59 66 53 48
email lacamoire@club-internet.fr

Château d'Agnos – Agnos 1, 2 & 3

Agnos, Pyrénées-Atlantiques

The hallmarks of stately style are here in abundance: a huge stone archway, iron gates, a fountain in the rose garden. The château paddles with one toe in the village, the other in open country, and on clear days the view across the fields stretches reaches the Pyrenees. The gîtes themselves are simple – good value, not overly plush – and will suit those in search of a simple base from which to explore. The single-storey wing was once a dormitory for the nuns who lived here when the château was a convent; bedrooms are lightly furnished – white walls, wicker chairs, pine beds, colourful linen – and windows open to a communal terrace that runs along the front and flanks the garden. Each open-plan kitchen/sitting/dining room comes with sofas and armchairs, garden chairs round the dining table and a few books. There are trim carpets, good plain bathrooms and all is spotlessly clean. Heather and Desmond do B&B and are not short of ideas for an active holiday: white-water rafting, mountain fishing, paragliding, horse riding, hiking, cycling, skiing – and hot-air balloon flights from the château. *B&B also.*

sleeps — Agnos 1: 6.
Agnos 2 & 3: 4 each.

rooms — Agnos 1: 2 doubles, 1 twin; 1 bathroom.
Agnos 2 & 3: each 1 double, 1 twin; 1 bathroom.

price — Agnos 1 £350-£500.
Agnos 2 & 3 £250-£400 each.
Prices per week.

closed — Occasionally.

Heather & Desmond Nears-Crouch
tel +33 (0)5 59 36 12 52
fax +33 (0)5 59 36 13 69
email chateaudagnos@wanadoo.fr

Manoir Coutenson

Grezet Cavagnan, Lot-et-Garonne

The electronically controlled gates and the sweeping gravel drive, floodlit at night, announce grandness and luxury. And the 18th-century manoir does not disappoint: a large heated pool in a part-walled garden, French antiques, deep verandas, a cellar stocked with 250 bottles – and a stone tower that's a perfect little nest for two. This and the neighbouring farmhouse were discovered a few years ago by Louisa, who's French, and husband Christopher, who once ran an architectural salvage business. Both are perfectionists and it shows. Downstairs rooms have terracotta floors and twisted-oak-beamed ceilings; a fireplace stands at each end of the sitting room; the oak-fitted kitchen is large and lovely. Plates on the walls and artfully arranged pots of dried flowers make the Manoir feel like home. Carpeted bedrooms are reached via two separate staircases leading to landings so comfortably furnished you'll want to go no further: one has a polished floor and an antique desk and chair. Dine on the generous, shaded patio by the swimming pool or play pool or table tennis in the games room.

sleeps	16.
rooms	8: 6 doubles, 2 twins; 8 bathrooms.
price	€1,585-€2,390 (£995-£1,500) for up to 7 people. €2,390-€4,261 (£1,500-£2,895) for up to 16. Prices per week.
closed	Long winter lets available.

Christopher & Louisa Taylor
tel +33 (0)5 53 20 88 03
fax +33 (0)5 53 83 61 79
email taylor.christophe@wanadoo.fr
web www.frenchmanoirs.net

Manoir Desiderata

Grezet Cavagnan, Lot-et-Garonne

Sip a gin and tonic by the floodlit pool as the sun sets over distant woods and hills: Desiderata, comfortable and immaculately restored, demands that you unwind. Its owners have spared no effort in adapting this 300-year-old building to contemporary tastes and needs: period features mixed with good sofas and furniture, an excellently equipped kitchen, walk-in showers. Most rooms lead off the vast dining and activity room (darts, exercise machine, refectory table); a long, wooden balustraded walkway runs above leading to four of the bedrooms; the other three bedrooms are downstairs. From the large tower room, so pretty in its sandy open-stone walls and florally-dressed antique bed, there are peaceful views of woods and the 12th-century church. Visit the bastide town of Casteljaloux, on the edge of the pine forest of Les Landes, and its luxury thermal baths; the more energetic might prefer to hang-glide or fly. With table tennis, billiards, a big garden and a most attractive (and safe) pool area this is a super place for families to stay. The attention to detail is remarkable.

sleeps	14.
rooms	7: 4 doubles, 3 twins; 1 bathroom, 7 shower rooms.
price	€1,585-€2,390 (£995-£1,500) for up to 5 people. €2,390-€3,744 (£1,250-£2,595) for up to 14. Prices per week.
closed	Long winter lets available.

Christopher & Louisa Taylor

tel	+33 (0)5 53 20 88 03
fax	+33 (0)5 53 83 61 79
email	taylor.christophe@wanadoo.fr
web	www.frenchmanoirs.net

Manoir Serenita

Fargues sur Ourbise, Lot-et-Garonne

In a huge clearing in a wood, at the end of a drive planted with young poplars and willows, stylishly floodlit at night, another restoration from the indefatigable Taylors. Up the steps and into a huge sitting room, its tiled floor and open fireplace standing in immaculate contrast to its aged oak beams. Antique stained-glass doors lead off one side to a TV room, off another to a dining room that seats 18 with no trouble at all. The kitchen is oak-fitted, the French windows open to the pool, the gardens stretch beyond and the vast games room trumpets darts, exercise machines and snooker; everything is on a grand and generous scale. Upstairs are old armoires and period beds, tapestry-style curtains with matching cushions, pictures and plates on ochre walls, sisal-wool carpets and fine rugs, brand new mattresses and top of the range linen. Bathrooms have blue or green tiles, gleaming fittings and old oak doors. Thanks to ten acres of gardens and field – fenced to keep out the deer – children may roam to their hearts' content while you lounge on the long, deep patio with a barbecue for star-lit nights.

sleeps	18.
rooms	9: 5 doubles, 4 twins; 2 bathrooms, 5 shower rooms.
price	£1,995-£3,350 per week.

Christopher & Louisa Taylor

tel	+33 (0)5 53 20 88 03
fax	+33 (0)5 53 83 61 79
email	taylor.christophe@wanadoo.fr
web	www.frenchmanoirs.net

La Gare de Sos

Ste Maure de Peyriac, Lot-et-Garonne

Once your wake-up call would have been the hoot of the 6.27 from Sos to Nérac, and the platforms, so peaceful now, would have bustled. This railway station, which finally ground to a halt in 1970, has been delightfully converted by its English owner David, who gave up a City career in London for life at the end of the line. He lives in the village and is happy to make meals on occasion, even to act as tour guide. The former waiting-room and parcels office are your living and dining room, where 1900s advertising posters, a 1924 timetable and some of the original clocks adorn the walls. The old wooden benches on which passengers waited have been swapped for jolly red sofas, good terracotta tiles have replaced workaday boards, and there's a woodburner, piano and books. It's a happy place. The ticket office makes a superb kitchen and pantry; the original oak staircase leads up to bedrooms in the former station master's apartment. For children: a fabulous attic, with four beds, an outdoor pool, and a model railway, of course. Unmissable. *B&B when house not let.*

sleeps	8-10.
rooms	4: 2 doubles, 1 twin, 1 quadruple; 1 bathroom, 1 shower room.
price	£385-£1,450 per week.

	David Heath
tel	+33 (0)5 53 97 09 93
fax	+33 (0)5 53 97 09 93
email	adavidheath@aol.com
web	www.garedesos.com

Camont

Ste Colombe en Bruilhois, Lot-et-Garonne

Lazy afternoons, barges drifting on the canal, a shepherd moving his flock. The pace of life doesn't get much slower than this, or the sense of peace much better. Wander through the pergola, past herb garden and potager, along the canal to a shady, spring-fed pond. Or gaze at these views from your three-storied stone and brick pigeonnier. Rooms have a timeless tranquillity. The two bedrooms – one above the other, linked by steepish stairs – have polished floorboards, antique mirrors, rustic furniture, overhead fans, shades of blue and green. One room has a curtained cast-iron bath; the other, with walk-in shower, wakes to the morning sun. Lovingly polished tiles, antiques, books, paintings and an open fire fill the small sitting room. The kitchen is a serious affair with working hearth, oak beams and eight-burner stove, the walls hung with utensils and country crockery. Kate, the warm and friendly owner who lives in the nearby houseboat, gives cookery courses here. Boat, cycle (bikes and kayak available), visit village fairs and markets... then back to supper on the terrace. *B&B also.*

sleeps	4.
rooms	2 doubles; 2 bathrooms.
price	€1,250 per week.

Kate Hill

tel	+33 (0)5 53 47 56 29
mobile	+33 (0)6 75 41 79 54
email	camont47@wanadoo.fr
web	www.camont.com

Château de Rodié

Courbiac de Tournon, Lot-et-Garonne

It's more fortress than château, complete with canon holes, long-drops and tower... do wander. The story of how Pippa and Paul have breathed new life into these old stones is inspiring: Paul had a serious accident, they bought the 13th-century ruin and its 135 acres (now a nature reserve) and began the triumphant restoration. Your quarters are in the old bakery and stables, across the arched, flowered courtyard from where the owners live. The old smokery is one of the bathrooms; the kitchen, delightfully modern, has two of the old bread ovens. A beautiful stone stair made by Paul leads to antique beds under the eaves; rich rugs sit on tiled floors; there's underfloor heating. Walls are white or pointed stone, windows are small and low. Paul and Pippa farm sheep and run a B&B: Pippa cooks her guests sumptuous organic dinners using much of their own produce: you may join them, by arrangement. There's a terrace off your living room, your own back garden, a shared pool, swings for the children, wild countryside. A deeply authentic place with special hosts. *B&B also.*

sleeps	7-9.
rooms	3: 2 twins, 1 triple, 2 single beds on request; 3 bathrooms.
price	€585-€1,160 per week.

Paul & Pippa Hecquet

tel	+33 (0)5 53 40 89 24
fax	+33 (0)5 53 40 89 25
email	chateau.rodie@wanadoo.fr
web	www.chateauderodie.com

La Gabertie

Thézac, Lot-et-Garonne

Monsieur Faffa is as charming as his name suggests. This rabbit warren of stone cottages perches on the plateau that runs above the vineyard-chequered valley, and has outrageously beautiful sunset views from the long, tiled veranda. It is wonderfully old and informal, though the interior has been recently – and beautifully – decked out. Bedrooms hide up worn stone steps and the whole place is far bigger inside than you would think – you may still be unearthing rooms at the end of your stay. Children are well catered for with table football, billiards, ping-pong, board games and a pool, yet there are myriad hidden corners and a large scrub garden into which the more sedate may retreat. The decoration is unfussy – stone walls, clean stretches of wooden flooring, dark wooden shutters, an antique armoire – and offers cool respite from the summer heat. Geared towards large groups, the kitchen has a vast cooker, an industrial-sized fridge and cooking pots reminiscent of school canteens. Open-air dinners for 28 are wild fun – especially after a day's canoeing on the river Lot. *Gîte for 6-10 also available.*

sleeps 20-28.
rooms 10: 3 doubles, 5 twins, 1 quadruple, 1 annexe with 4 sets of bunks; 1 bathroom, 5 shower rooms, 7 separate wcs.
price €950-€4,450 per week.

Jean-Claude Faffa
tel +33 (0)5 53 40 74 36
fax +33 (0)5 53 40 23 20
email faffa@wanadoo.fr
web www.agades.com/faffa

Manoir de Soubeyrac

Le Laussou, Lot-et-Garonne

Up the tiny winding road to the *gardien's* house, hiding behind its gates in a garden of trees. It sits across the lane from the manor where Monsieur Rocca does sumptuous B&B. Pale old stones and sun-bleached tiles; inside, a surprising mix of humble and grand. Monsieur has thought it all through with great care: the lavender-blue paintwork, the lush fabrics, the bedroom fans. Exposed brickwork and terracotta floors are a plain foil for lavish taste in the ground-floor bedroom, replete with its apricot-satin-swagged bed. Up the steepish stair to the cottagey triple, where beds line up in a row – a light room under the eaves with valley views – perfect for children. The living/dining room is inviting, too: a clothed table with painted country chairs, patterned rugs, a good sofa, an antique mirror. The little kitchen has an old dresser and bags of charm; the bathroom cossets with aromatic oils. Outside, one of those amazing infinity pools that looks as if it spills over the edge of the hill – all yours. Dine at the manor: you'll eat well; or pick a restaurant in hilltop Monflanquin. *B&B also.*

sleeps	4-5.
rooms	2: 1 double, 1 triple; 1 bathroom.
price	€250-€1,143 per week.
arrival	Saturday June-August.

Claude Rocca

tel +33 (0)5 53 36 51 34

fax +33 (0)5 53 36 35 20

web www.manoir-soubeyrac.com

Lavande

Cénac et St Julien, Dordogne

Brigitte and Christophe spotted this 18th-century farmhouse and its wooded acres while on holiday. It was love at first sight – a *coup de cœur*; several busy years on they run an enchanting B&B and have converted the stone stables into two self-catering cottages. Lavande, with its serene views over wooded hills, is the larger and, despite the proximity of the other buildings, is peaceful and private. The inside has been thoroughly restored and, despite the old beams and exposed walls, has a newish feel. In the living room: sumptuous black leather armchairs and a sofa on an immaculately polished wooden floor; in the dining room: an antique trestle table and chairs. The pièce de résistance, however, is the beamed white and blue bedroom which looks like a piece of Delft china. Gourmets will make a beeline for the restaurant L'Esplanade in Domme – you can glimpse the splendid hilltop town from here. You share the delightful park – and saltwater pool – with other guests; if you like good home cooking, you may share meals, too. Do buy Brigitte's delicious homemade pâtés for your picnic baguettes. *B&B also.*

sleeps	6.
rooms	3: 2 doubles, 1 attic twin; 1 bathroom, 1 shower room, 1 separate wc.
price	€579-€1,143 per week.
closed	November-March.

Brigitte & Christophe Demassougne
tel +33 (0)5 53 29 91 97
fax +33 (0)5 53 29 91 97
email contact@la-gueriniere-dordogne.com
web www.la-gueriniere-dordogne.com

Le Petit Tilleul

Domme, Dordogne

The Dordogne laps 150 yards from the door (great for summer swims) and busy, beautiful Domme is up the hill. Here you have privacy and peace. The compact stone cottage was built around 1650 as a hay barn, which later became the baker's house. Friendly owners Mary and Alan live down the lane: they do B&B and Mary holds painting classes from May to September (booked in advance). She was an art teacher and Alan taught woodwork and design; see his handiwork in this simple, successful conversion. Old beams and stone walls are all intact and there's a woodburner in the beautiful stone fireplace in the living room. The well-lit kitchen has white formica worktops and French windows onto the terrace and garden. Bedrooms are simple, with wooden shutters and open hanging space. The double has views of the Domme and fields, the twin is furnished in pine. Your problem will be to decide what to do first: there's fishing and canoeing on the spot, the GR64A footpath runs past the door, there's a riding school four miles away, and medieval Sarlat is a delight. *B&B also.*

sleeps	4.
rooms	2: 1 double, 1 twin; 1 shower room.
price	€375-€675 per week.
closed	November-March.

Alan & Mary Johnson
tel +33 (0)5 53 29 39 96
fax +33 (0)5 53 29 39 96
email montillou@hotmail.com
web www.montillou.com

Château Marcousin

St Germain de Belvès, Dordogne

Handsome rust-red shutters, black and white tiled entrance, wrought-iron chairs scattered on the terrace – this is a country château of understated, very French good taste. Nothing too fussy, too ostentatious. It's been in Veronique's family for generations and exudes a contented, well-loved air. Ceilings are lofty, floors are polished parquet, colours are soft, open fireplaces, good antiques and paintings add warmth. There's acres of space: a huge drawing room littered with sofas and with French windows to the garden, a red-walled library, an elegantly rustic dining room and a cooks' dream of a kitchen – huge range, marble sink, an armoire of crocks and every imaginable gadget. Bedrooms are *Country Living* cool with pale colours, country antiques and soft drapes floating at large windows. Bathrooms are equally stylish, one with a claw-foot bath, another with a walk-in shower. Take breakfast on the terrace with views over wooded valleys, visit Sarlat, browse local markets, laze around the pool (close but discreetly tucked away) or take a very long stroll through your 56 hectare estate.

sleeps	12.
rooms	6: 4 doubles, 2 twins; 2 bathrooms, 1 shower room, 3 separate wcs.
price	€2,500-€4,000 per week.

Véronique Bordes

tel	+33 (0)5 53 28 29 10
mobile	+33 (0)6 16 24 07 35
fax	+44 (0)870 1205860
email	chateaumarcousin@wanadoo.fr

La Treille Haute – The Barn

Castelnaud - La Chapelle, Dordogne

The setting smacks of a fairytale and five of the Perigord's most spectacular châteaux, clinging to the craggy cliffs of the Dordogne, are a short drive from your converted stone barn. You can even see the floodlit Château de Beynac, awesome and grand, from the comfort of the bed. English owner Felicity lives in the house at right angles to the barn; metre-thick walls between the two buildings ensure total privacy and you have your own sweet garden with amazing views. Furnishings are modest, the bathroom is downstairs, the kitchenette fits a hob and a microwave/oven, and exposed stone walls and vaulted bedroom beams speak of the days when the building sheltered pilgrims visiting the Knights Templar. The enchanting village has a shop with fresh produce and an excellent charcuterie. Treat yourself to some of the local specialities and picnic in the fields and wooded hills, or explore the steep, fascinating, honey-stone villages of this understandably popular area. *Babies & children over four welcome: garden unsuitable for toddlers. B&B also.*

sleeps	2-3 + cot.
rooms	1 double with sofabed; 1 bathroom.
price	€250-€520 per week. Extra twin with separate entrance, €40 per night.
arrival	Saturday, flexible in winter.

Felicity Martindale
tel +33 (0)5 53 29 95 65
fax +33 (0)5 53 29 95 65
email martindale@free.fr
web martindale.free.fr

La Font Trémolasse – La Grange

Ste Alvère, Dordogne

Once you'd have heard the ruminating of cows in this house. As its name suggests, this was a barn and a cowshed; the old chestnut cow stalls divide the kitchen and living room still, the headholes forming perfect hatches. This peaceful hideaway for two is the ground floor of a wing of a vast 19th-century Périgord farmhouse, inhabited by delightful British owners Victoria and Julius and their family. He's a landscape gardener and will supply herbs if you need them; she once cooked professionally and will lay on dinner (using much of their own produce) if you book. You get a sunny modern kitchen with hardwood work surfaces and terracotta floor, and a nicely old-fashioned, English-cosy, warm-in-winter living room. The bedroom, with cheerful red curtains and good armoire, has tranquil views of the garden – accessed via steps – and fields of the estate – yours to roam. Eat out on your own south-facing terrace, swim, fish or sail (dinghy provided) in the lake, or set off and visit the fascinating prehistoric caves of the area. Sainte Alvère, the nearest village, is famous for its truffles.

sleeps	2.
rooms	1 twin/double; 1 bathroom.
price	€350-€458 (£195-£300) per week.
arrival	Saturday but flexible.

Victoria White
tel +33 (0)5 53 23 94 33
fax +33 (0)5 53 23 94 87
email vjwhite@club-internet.fr

Hello

La Grande Marque – Cottage & Studio

Marnac St Cyprien, Dordogne

The views are liberating from this hilltop haven overlooking the Dordogne. Twelve acres of private parkland surround you, dotted with walnut groves and fruit trees. Jenny and Michael are friendly hosts and have poured energy into their enterprise: four gîtes, chambres d'hôtes, tennis, gym, sauna, play area, restaurant and pool. There's a roomy stone cottage on three floors with a big old fireplace, a vine-draped pergola and divine views from the kitchen sink; a studio with a tiny kitchen, an open-plan living area on the mezzanine and a quiet, shady garden. (*En plus*: two cheerful, light and airy homes in the barn where they once dried tobacco, their terraces side by side – ideal for young families together.) Furniture is a mix of styles, beds are extremely comfortable and floors are wooden or blue-carpeted. There are music systems and TVs, books, videos and games aplenty; all bar the studio have long valley views. There's something to keep everyone happy here, even cookery classes with ex-hotelier Jenny, a talented cook. If your children are eight or over they, too, may learn to chop, season and stir. *B&B also.*

sleeps	Cottage 7-8. Studio 2-5.
rooms	Cottage: 2 doubles, 1 room with bunks, 1 twin; 1 bath, 1 shower, 2 separate wcs. Studio: 1 twin/double, 1 sofabed & single in living room; 1 shower.
price	Cottage €480-€1,600. Studio €320-€720. Prices per week.

Jennifer Cockcroft

tel	+33 (0)5 53 31 61 63
email	grandemarque@perigord.com
web	www.lgmfrance.com

Château de Cazenac – La Maison

Coux et Bigaroque, Dordogne

A divine 16th-century Périgord farmhouse, the sort of place you expect to see in a magazine. Windows frame sublime views of valley and forest while beautiful rooms mix contemporary minimalism, classical design and a kaleidoscope of colour. Vast bedrooms are lime-rendered and terracotta-floored, and have vaulted ceilings and exposed beams; (the one on the ground floor has an original fireplace). Bathrooms have a Moroccan touch. In open-plan sitting/dining room sliding glass doors open to a terrace and, beyond, the pool; the kitchen is top-notch. You'll find pretty dressers, rugs to soften tiled floors, the odd chandelier. There's a vine-shaded terrace under which you can barbecue, a delightful garden in which to fall asleep to the sounds of the valley. The house stands high on a steep hill whence dreamy views over the river... you're in the middle of nowhere, beyond the call of the outside world. Perfect for all things Dordogne: the château trail, prehistoric rock art, medieval cities, fishing, golf, canoeing, good food. Or stay and discover the 27 hectares of private château grounds. *B&B also.*

sleeps	6-8.
rooms	3: 2 doubles, 1 twin, 2 extra beds available; 3 shower rooms, 3 separate wcs.
price	€1,800-€2,500 per week.

Philippe & Armelle Constant

tel	+33 (0)5 53 31 69 31
fax	+33 (0)5 53 28 91 43
email	info@cazenac.fr
web	www.cazenac.fr

Beaux Rêves

St Crépin Carlucet, Dordogne

Only the honey-coloured stone walls and one window are original but you'd never guess it: this 18th-century barn has been so perfectly restored. Three years ago it was in ruins; now it stands, complete with pigeonnier, under a demure grey roof. Opposite is the main house where Éric and Helen live. She's English, he's French and they juggle B&B with running a five-hectare estate and bringing up two young children. They've given enormous thought, care and money to this new project. The ground floor is one vast room, with tawny floor, stone walls and a wood-burning stove at its very centre. A few steps lead up to the kitchen, arresting in its faultless simplicity and superbly equipped. Lounging on a white leather sofa in the sitting area, enjoy the dazzling view of St Anne's church, spectacularly floodlit at night. Upstairs are three big, white bedrooms, each with vivid rugs, interesting pictures, a fine antique. Bathrooms too are big, bright and excellent. You have the gardens to explore, your own private fenced pool, and a Michelin-starred restaurant a stroll away. *B&B also.*

sleeps	6-8.
rooms	3: 2 doubles, 1 family room for 4; 2 shower rooms, 1 bathroom.
price	€950-€1,950 per week.

Éric & Helen Edgar
tel +33 (0)5 53 31 22 60
email lescharmes@carlucet.com
web www.carlucet.com

Le Manoir de Coste Perrier

Valojoulx, Dordogne

Imagine this – a rambling stone manoir with a freckled roof and a tower, set on a broad green hilltop. It stands in a 26-hectare estate surrounded by forested hills as far as the eye can see – a magical spot. Inscriptions on the fireplace reveal that a judge lived here during the time of the French Revolution, but the old stone walls are much older than that – and were crumbling fast when Marc Babic, a Burgundian engineer, came to the rescue. Now the medieval manoir, immaculately restored, gives an impression of assured, relaxed stylishness. Its sitting/dining room is a deliciously lofty retreat on hot summer days, there's a small, sunny annexe just off it and a wonderful stone spiral staircase leading to the terrace. Exposed stone walls, terracotta tiles and a cavernous old oven give the fabulous kitchen a welcoming feel. The main bedroom has an elegant four-poster bed and a jacuzzi; on the second floor is a vast and appealing room set under golden rafters. Outside: a massive pool and a small one for tinies, a fitness room and a new play area. *See opposite.*

sleeps	10 + cots.
rooms	Le Manoir: 5 doubles; 5 bathrooms.
price	€3,770-€6,150 per week. July-August rental of all three houses by one party only.

Marc Babic
mobile +33 (0)6 81 93 78 06
fax +33 (0)5 53 51 40 94
email marc.babic@wanadoo.fr
web www.periloc.com

Le Manoir de Coste Perrier – Les Marquises

Valojoulx, Dordogne

From big plate-glass windows, a breathtaking panorama. The owner has converted not only the manoir but these two outbuilding wings: each is as high spec as the other. Pale beams and creamy stones remain while an exterior spiral wooden stair and tall radiators add a contemporary feel. Bedrooms (two reached via the spiral stair) are themed: Indian and Portuguese in Gauche, African in Droite. Furniture feels oriental, bedheads are silky, throws velvety, colours exotic; no knick-knacks, no clutter, a simple, clean feel. Bath and shower rooms have rustic tiles, sitting rooms have chunky oak chairs and big squishy sofas, lovely light dining rooms have bench seating and refrectory tables, kitchens are smartly new. It would be ideal for a free-range family who like a bit of style but not too much formality, and there are vast amounts of space outside for children to safely roam. Lots to keep other ages happy: it's a six-mile hike to the Lascaux Caves, a short drive to the market at Montignac, and there are truffle courses for foodies planned for 2006. *See opposite.*

sleeps	Marquise Gauche 6. Marquise Droite 8.
rooms	Gauche: 3 doubles; 3 bathrooms. Droite: 4 doubles; 4 bathrooms.
price	Gauche €3,370-€6,180. Droite €3,370-€6,180. Prices per week. July-August rental of all three houses by one party only.

Marc Babic

mobile	+33 (0)6 81 93 78 06
fax	+33 (0)5 53 51 40 94
email	marc.babic@wanadoo.fr
web	www.periloc.com

Domaine des Blanches Colombes – Monet & Renoir

Grand Castang, Dordogne

The doves are still here: only their cooing ruffles the calm – and the hum of a tractor. The Domaine is a 17th-century manor in a hilltop hamlet, built of golden stone, encircled by high walls. It belongs to Clare and Steven, a delightful, friendly, enthusiastic couple. Steven organises rock concerts in Poland, Clare runs cookery evenings and B&B. Two of their cottages stand side by side in the west wing but still manage to feel private. Renoir is creeper-covered, Monet (above) has an array of hanging baskets. They are engaging, comfortable, homely: wooden or tiled floors, open-plan living rooms, blue and white crockery, gay gingham. The furnishings are a mix of old-fashioned and funky modern and the kitchens are brilliantly equipped. If you don't feel like cooking or going out one evening, Clare and Steven will rustle up boeuf bourguignon and fresh fruit pavlova (for example), deliver it to your table, then clear up afterwards. They can arrange for bread and croissants to be delivered each morning, too. With a games room and pool, it's ideal for families. *Babysitting available. B&B also.* *See opposite.*

sleeps	Monet: 4. Renoir: 6.
rooms	Monet: 1 double, 1 twin; 2 bathrooms. Renoir: 1 double, 2 twins; 1 bathroom, 1 shower room.
price	Monet €395-€1,200. Renoir €595-€1,400. Prices per week.

Clare Todd
tel +33 (0)5 53 57 30 38
email clare.todd@quality-gites.co.uk
web www.quality-gites.com

Domaine des Blanches Colombes – Degas & Matisse

Grand Castang, Dordogne

Just over the road are Clare and Steven's other two gîtes, converted from an old village house. They're relaxing, friendly, comfortable places to stay, each with its own terrace and brand new kitchen. Degas (above) is diminutive and cosy with a painted double bed and views over rooftops to the rolling hills; its little yellow and terracotta bathroom is downstairs. Matisse is larger and full of character, with a wooden staircase that winds up to two attractive, big bedrooms (below). Both cottages share the delights of the Domaine. The fabulous L-shaped pool shelters in the angle of two barns and is surrounded by trees and shrubs. One barn has been converted into a games room. If the pool table, darts and table tennis don't keep the young happy, every cottage has a DVD player (you can hire titles from Steven's vast collection) and there are board games available – just ask. Six miles off is Lalinde, a pretty village with a spectacular Thursday market. Bergerac is close by, and there are the caves of Lascaux. *Babysitting available. Two apartments for two next to river in Mauzac also available. B&B also.* *See opposite.*

sleeps	Degas 2. Matisse 4.
rooms	Degas: 1 double; 1 bathroom. Matisse: 1 double, 1 twin; 1 bathroom.
price	Degas €300-€475. Matisse €395-€1,100. Prices per week.

Clare Todd
tel +33 (0)5 53 57 30 38
email clare.todd@quality-gites.co.uk
web www.quality-gites.com

Domaine des Farguettes – Manoir & Grange

Le Buisson de Cadouin, Dordogne

With Françoise and Claude as hosts, you'll soon discover which concerts and plays are on! She is a songwriter and an accomplished potter; he used to direct a theatre company. They're a friendly, lively couple and Le Manoir (the first of their two houses, of which you have a private wing) reflects their interests: a baby grand graces the salon and there are books, pots, paintings and puppets everywhere. Pleasantly traditional bedrooms have carpets, antiques and big windows that make the most of the spectacular, all-round, hilltop views. About 50 metres lower down is La Grange, steep-roofed and bright. Its exposed beams and vaulted ceilings are a reminder of its more modest origins, while wooden floors, bright colours and big glass doors give it a modern, informal feel. Both house and barn were built in 1664 by artisans whose signatures and date are set in stone. The swimming pool is shared and there are plenty of good walks round the 15-hectare estate. You can also enrol on a cookery course: the *chef de cuisine* will accompany you to the wonderful market at Sarlat to choose the menu. *B&B also.*

sleeps	Manoir 11-13. Grange 10. Must be rented together high season.
rooms	Manoir: 3 doubles, 1 family room for 3, 1 twin, 1 single with pullout bed; 5 bathrooms. Grange: 4 doubles, 1 twin; 5 bathrooms.
price	Whole house 3,500,€5,700 per week. Low season La Grange €1,500 for 8.

Françoise & Claude de Torrenté
tel +33 (0)5 53 23 48 23
fax +33 (0)5 53 23 48 23
email clagazel@wanadoo.fr
web www.farguettes.fr

Domaine de Leygue

Bourniquel, Dordogne

This is a pretty pocket of France, peaceful and pleasing on the eye: five acres of grounds insulate you from all but wildlife. And here are four little cottages: two near the courtyard and the house where the owners live, two (more modern) beyond a pretty grove of walnut trees. All are utterly private and ideal for couples. There are even two pools; as the sun loungers stay by the cottages, you'll get plenty of private swims. And more: an excellent tennis court, boules, even bikes for those who wish to pedal round paradise. Peter and Geraldine have thought of everything. Leygue was once a small farm and two of the gîtes are conversions, two newly built; all have stone walls and a private terrace. Bedrooms are on the ground floor – except in Tower Cottage, whose views stretch over woods and farmland. All is spotless, light, immaculate – checked sofas in one, new cherrywood in another, chestnut beams, good linen, Villeroy & Boche china. There's central heating for cool days, fans for warm nights and no TV to spoil the peace. The Dordogne, its river, markets, vineyards and prehistoric caves beckon.

sleeps	4 cottages for 2.
rooms	3 cottages with 1 double; 1 shower room. 1 cottage with 1 double; 1 bathroom.
price	£470-£660 each per week.
closed	October-May.

Peter & Geraldine Jones

tel +33 (0)5 53 73 83 12

fax +33 (0)5 53 73 83 20

email geraldinejones@shieling.biz

web www.shieling.biz/leygue

Les Bigayres

Liorac sur Louyre, Dordogne

You won't forget the bedrooms of this elegant converted pigeonnier: one has old gnarled beams that grow like trees through the tall pointed ceiling, another has an amazing *Princess and the Pea* bed with the highest mattress ever. Teenagers will go for the third – a sunny bunk bedroom with its own poolside entrance. In 30 acres of grounds belonging to a lovely 17th-century manor, and with its own private drive and terrace, this beautifully furnished cottage is quite a find. You share the pool with the French owners but they use it infrequently so you are likely to have it all to yourself. The open-plan kitchen, sitting and dining area is pure, light and roomy, with white or exposed stone walls, grey-green beams supported by unusual stone columns and prettily-patterned red and green curtains. Fine, hexagonally-laid tiles run through the ground floor, there are wooden boards upstairs. Wallow in luxurious sofas by the stone fireplace, stroll out of the French doors to the lawn with its long wooded views. You have everything you need, from dishwasher to barbecue, and charming Bergerac is no distance at all.

sleeps	6-8.
rooms	4: 2 doubles, 1 room with bunks, 1 sofabed; 1 bathroom, 1 separate wc.
price	€800-€1,700 per week.
closed	November-February.

Jane Hanslip

tel	+44 (0)7768 747610
fax	+44 (0)20 7221 6909
email	jhanslip@aol.com
web	www.dordognerental.com

Bourdil Blanc

St Sauveur de Bergerac, Dordogne

All this could be yours: a fine 18th-century manor with a long, tree-lined avenue, views down to the lake and a super big pool. When you've finished lazing in the huge grounds or being sporty around tennis or croquet balls, retreat to the sitting room, with its lovely old wooden floors, open fire, comfortable sofas. The dining room seats 14 on upholstered chairs – magnificent with William-Morris-type fabrics, mirrored fireplace and polished floors. Upstairs, a long, light passage leads to the roomy bedrooms, every one en suite, and a loft dormitory for eight – brilliant for kids. The sunny kitchen and the bathrooms are more functional than fabulous, and there's central heating so you're as warm as toast in winter. The Wing is less grand than the main house but has an open fire, tiled floors, warm kilim rugs, some good antiques and a fitted kitchen; the Pigeonnier is charming, with fine furnishings, stunning stone fireplace and private walled garden. So much space indoors and out, and stacks to do in the area. *Cooking & babysitting. Riding & wine-tasting. Rent House & Wing together in July & August.*

sleeps	House 14-18. Wing 2. Pigeonnier 4.
rooms	House: 3 doubles, 3 twins, 1 quadruple, 2 sofas, 8 baths. Wing: 1 double, 2 sofas, 1 bath. Pigeonnier: 1 double, 1 twin, 1 bath.
price	House €1,400-€2,900. Wing & Pigeonnier €800 each. July-August: House & Wing €6,000 (with Pigeonnier €6,800). Prices per week.

Jane Hanslip

tel +44 (0)7768 747610

fax +44 (0)20 7221 6909

email jhanslip@aol.com

web www.dordognerental.com

La Martigne

Lamonzie Montastruc, Dordogne

This glorious stone *chartreuse* could be nowhere else but France. Utterly French, it's a pleasing mix of simple yet luxurious, unadorned yet ornate. Splendidly isolated, with magnificent views of the Périgord Noir, the house has been beautifully restored by its French owners who have lived here for generations. They occasionally use the grounds but otherwise the cascading terraced lawns, the private park and the pool are all yours. The house is furnished with dark antiques and pretty fabrics to harmonise with the simple bare stone, the soft painted walls and the aqua-blue-painted doors with their porcelain handles. The two living rooms have polished wooden floors, comfy sofas and elegant blue and white upholstered Regency chairs; next door is a formal dining room with rich red wallpaper and attractive rugs. There are several open fireplaces, one in one of the bedrooms which, huge and light, open onto the south-facing terrace with the loveliest views. The kitchen is as well fitted out as you'd expect, bathrooms are super. *Security deposit of £400 payable when booking.*

sleeps	8-9.
rooms	4: 1 double, 2 twins, 1 family room for 3; 1 bathroom, 2 shower rooms, 2 separate wcs.
price	€1,400-€2,500 per week.

Jane Hanslip

tel +44 (0)7768 747610

fax +44 (0)20 7221 6909

email jhanslip@aol.com

web www.dordognerental.com

Château de Monsac

Monsac, Dordogne

It looks and is ancient, begun in the 1300s as one of a string of defences on the English-Guyenne border, in spite of an unpropitious site (it shelters in a hollow). The vestiges of the moat remain, a coat of arms spans the front door and the views rise to the lovely village of Monsac. The Delibies and their two daughters are there should you need them and will invite you over for a welcoming drink. The garden is large, there's a safe saltwater pool, an area with swings and sand for children, a driving range for golfers and your own covered patio for balmy days and nights. Inside, a modern galley kitchen and a vast dining room with a big stone fireplace, cream tiles heated underfoot and country antiques. Bedrooms, two interconnecting, are reached via a monumental stone stair – watch little ones! – and range from big to vast. Heavy beams, stone walls, red and white checked four-posters, ingeniously curtained-off showers, sofas and good quality wicker chairs, BBC on the TV... Beyond this room, pool and darts under a big vaulted ceiling; outside, a pigeonnier with a sauna and twin beds. Historic.

sleeps	8.
rooms	4 doubles; 4 bathrooms.
price	€995-€1,990 per week.
closed	November-March.

Frédéric & Fabienne Delibie
tel +33 (0)5 53 27 59 04
fax +33 (0)5 53 27 59 03
email monsac@club-internet.fr
web www.chateau-en-perigord.com

Le Roudier – Le Chai, La Garenne, La Ferme, Le Nid

Razac d' Eymet , Dordogne

The gites at Le Roudier lie in a pretty rolling countryside of sunflowers and corn, with five acres of bird-rich woodland in which to roam. Converted from old farm buildings with letting in mind they are clean, comfortable and perfect for families. There's even satellite TV… not that you'll be spending many days indoors. What makes this place special is the vast terraced pool that drops away to the meadows. In the old bakehouse is a summer kitchen and games room with table tennis, plus a paddling pool, slides, swings and mountain bikes. The smaller gîtes have patios on which you may barbecue; the larger have shady, vine-strewn terraces that face the pool but are fenced and secure. Inside, the usual terracotta floors and open-plan kitchen/diners, spotless and excellently equipped. In La Garenne and La Ferme, steepish staircases lead to extra bedrooms sky-lit under the eaves. The whole enterprise is run by the Smiths, an English/Irish couple with a young child who do all they can to make you happy. Rabbits in the meadows, three golf courses within striking distance, canoes at Eymet, vineyards all around. *B&B also.*

sleeps	Garenne 7-8. Ferme 8. Chai 4. Nid 2.
rooms	Garenne: 1 double, 1 twin, 1 triple, 1 single on landing; 1 bath, 1 shower. Ferme: 1 double, 3 twins; 1 bath, 1 shower. Chai: 1 double, 1 twin; 1 bath. Nid: 1 double; 1 shower.
price	Garenne & Ferme €760-€1,750 each. Chai €530-€1,165. Nid €395-€775. Prices per week.
arrival	Friday.

Paul & Dearbhla Smith

tel	+33 (0)5 53 24 54 96
email	leroudier@wanadoo.fr
web	www.leroudier.com

Le Moulin de Jarrige

St Méard de Gurçon, Dordogne

The road from here goes blissfully nowhere. Woodland and fields stretch as far as the eye can see; within minutes you'll be packing a picnic and out of the farmhouse door. There are bikes to borrow, a children's den in the barn, badminton and boules; the more slothful may prefer gazing over the countryside from the pool. This 200-year-old farmhouse is about simple pleasures. Colours are mellow, rooms uncluttered and natural features retained – exposed stone walls, beamed ceilings, open fireplaces. The large kitchen, with its Shaker-style fittings and big farmhouse table, is a cook's joy; it opens into a comfy sitting room invitingly strewn with cushions and throws. There's also a light-filled study where you can curl up with a book. Bedrooms spread over the ground floor on gently split levels – creamy-cool spaces of simple painted furniture, wooden floors and brightly checked bedcovers. Plenty of bathrooms, too, all white, bright and super-duper. Although remote, you're not isolated; local shops are two miles, tennis, canoeing and riding are nearby and you're surrounded by vineyards. *B&B also.*

sleeps	8.
rooms	4: 2 doubles, 2 twins; 2 shower rooms, 2 bathrooms.
price	£800-£1,800 per week.

Keith & Maureen Fenton
tel +44 (0)777 8170431
+33 (0)5 53 82 27 40
email keithfenton25@hotmail.com
web www.jarrige.co.uk

Domaine de Foncaudière – Gros Dondon & Ange Gardien

Maurens, Dordogne

Hard to believe you're minutes from Bergerac town. A winding driveway takes you through woodland and suddenly, in a clearing, voilà! – the manoir, built 250 years ago on the foundations of a medieval castle. Beyond: the tiny estate hamlet – a scattering of extraordinarily pretty cottages which Marcel and his partner have restored with tender care. Each honey-coloured building has oak beams, stone and timbered walls, wood or terracotta floors. Each is charmingly furnished – antiques and new sofas, perfect kitchens and bathrooms. One-storey Gros Dondon (above) was the baker's house (the great stone ovens are still in place); Ange Gardien (below) the caretaker's. Both have their own gardens with lawns, fruit trees (figs, walnuts, cherries), barbecues, rustic furniture. Age-old paths criss-cross the meadows; the pool is down a sloping hill; views are wonderful. The estate covers 100 acres and takes its name from a hot spring. Farmers used to bring their animals to drink here when everywhere else was frozen. The sense of peace and history is profound. *Shared laundry. B&B also.* *See opposite.*

sleeps	Gros Dondon 3-4. Ange Gardien 6.
rooms	Gros Dondon: 1 double, 1 room with bunks; 1 bathroom. Ange Gardien: 1 double, 2 twins; 1 bathroom.
price	€1,100-€2,000 per week.

Marcel Wils

tel	+33 (0)5 53 61 13 90
fax	+33 (0)5 53 61 03 24
email	info@foncaudiere.com
web	www.foncaudiere.com

Domaine de Foncaudière – Fraise Soûle & Parfum de Rose

Maurens, Dordogne

Two more delightful cottages on the domaine; they share one roof but are otherwise independent. Fraise Soûle, with its large kitchen/dining room and separate sitting room, has three fine bedrooms; Parfum de Rose has two and is next to ancient stalls which once housed the estate's farm animals. (Is there an irony in the name?). Both cottages have been restored, then furnished with care. The jolly kitchens are a pleasure to cook in, the shower rooms gorgeous, the beds well-sprung. Apart from the pool there's a barn full of games to gladden children's hearts, a period library in the château, bikes for hire so you can pedal beyond. You could spend a whole week just exploring these 40 hectares; Marcel gives you a map – seek out La Cave, where a medieval priest went into hiding during the Wars of Religion. There's a pond, too, inhabited by a 100-year-old carp, and a beech walk, even a medieval potager. You can buy organically grown herbs and vegetables from the estate and your lovely hosts are happy to advise on markets, wine-tastings and regional specialities. Magical. *Shared laundry. B&B also.*

sleeps	Fraise Soûle 6. Parfum de Rose 4.
rooms	Fraise Soûle: 2 doubles, 1 twin; 1 shower room. Parfum de Rose: 1 double, 1 twin; 1 shower room.
price	€800-€2,000 per week.

Marcel Wils

tel +33 (0)5 53 61 13 90
fax +33 (0)5 53 61 03 24
email info@foncaudiere.com
web www.foncaudiere.com

Les Jonies

St Séverin d'Estissac, Dordogne

In a little valley – part meadow, part woodland – is the tiny, secluded and delightful hamlet of Les Jonies. The talented couple who own it and its 55 acres have focused their creativity on the country house with the perigord tower – all yours. The stairs and woodwork are superbly crafted and the big, mellow-stone rooms are an arresting mix of periods and styles. The airy, immaculate living space stretches up to the rafters, has a fabulous open kitchen and five comfortable sofas. The shower rooms, too, are ultra-chic (no baths). Although gorgeous and stylish, this is a child-conscious, family-friendly place: there are bikes, ping-pong, badminton, hammock... and the gardens and wide-terraced pool are fenced in. The house faces south, its lavender-fringed steps leading to a lawn, its vine-draped terrace next to a herb garden – a fragrant spot for barbecues. Cross the road and wander down a grassy track to two lakes full of carp. A little further on, its tiny balcony overlooking the water, is a captivating Fisherman's cabin; basic but charming, it sleeps two and you can fish to your heart's content. Heaven.

sleeps	Farmhouse 10-12. Cabin 2.
rooms	Farmhouse 5: 3 doubles, 1 twin, 1 family room for 4; 4 shower rooms. Cabin: 1 twin; 1 shower room.
price	Farmhouse £8,50-£1,750. Cabin from £250-£400. Prices per week.

Rosalie Docwra
tel +33 (0)5 53 81 26 03
email rjdocwra@wanadoo.fr
web lesjonies.com

Château de Bruneval

St Astier, Dordogne

The picturesque four-square château, once owned by a Chanel model, now belongs to a listed-building restoration specialist from Glasgow who has transfigured the place with the help of one plumber. It sleeps ten in overwhelming comfort – and if you bring extra kids or a nanny they can stay for free. Perfectionism reigns. The influences are French 19th-century, Scottish Victorian and, in two bathrooms, Art Deco, though bathrooms in the towers have been given a contemporary touch: claw-foot baths, shield-shape windows, cream swags. In the grown-ups' rooms, four-posters, half-testers and wood panelling are de rigeur and dark reds and petrol-blues prevail, though the Venetian room is washed gold and blue. In the children's rooms, décor is lime green and dark blue, with the odd giant spider dangling above the bed (generally appreciated). The gorgeous kitchen is beech, steel and creamy open stone, the salon has notably grand gilt mirrors, the grounds are a hectare and the pool embraces a stone-fountain fish. Magnifique! *Cookery courses planned.*

sleeps	12-13.
rooms	7: 5 doubles, 1 twin, 1 triple; 7 bathrooms.
price	£3,600-£5,950 per week. Couple available to shop, cook & clean: €160 per day.

Douglas Loan

tel	+33 (0)5 53 04 92 16
fax	+33 (0)5 53 04 92 16
email	info@chateau-de-bruneval.com
web	chateau-de-bruneval.com

La Geyrie- Gîte Maison

Verteillac, Dordogne

La Maison is attached to the Dunns' house and across the yard is Le Pigeonnier. The goats are organically raised, there are solar panels to heat water and Louise has allowed dry stone walling students to practice on her walls – many are tumbledown. This is a working farm: the sheepdog roams, the cats doze, there are hens in the yard and a clutch of Jack Russells. Farmstead and countryside have a marvellously ancient feel, Louise is busy but committed and everyone may happily muck in. Inside are the usual limewash walls and terracotta floors, chairs are straight-backed, the sofa is small and a 1930s dresser houses the crockery – plain but genuine. Bedrooms and bathroom upstairs feed into each other; the bedroom at the front is a lovely size and dominated by an old open fire, the bedroom at the back is big enough to fit in a double bed, two singles and bunks. Mattresses are new, cotton sheets are coloured, the bathroom is for everyone and the small kitchen has an unexpected dishwasher! This is an outdoorsy place and free-range families will be happy. *Service wash available.*

sleeps	4-8.
rooms	2: 1 double, 1 quadruple + bunks; 1 bathroom.
price	£230-£370 per week.

Louise & Peter Dunn

tel +33 (0)5 53 91 15 15

fax +33 (0)5 53 90 37 19

email peter.dunn@wanadoo.fr

web perso.wanadoo.fr/gites.at.la.geyrie

La Geyrie – Le Pigeonnier

Verteillac, Dordogne

A pair of nesting owls sometimes takes up residence in the tower of this charming 15th-century pigeonnier. You might spot short-toed eagles and roe deer in the woods, too. Furnishings are basic and well-used – an upright pale green sofa, a set of pine shelves with yellow crockery, a corner kitchen with a new gas cooker. You may not be steeped in *le grande luxe*, but the simple pleasures of a farm and a small tribe of animals should more than compensate. Your little pigeonnier is pleasantly cool, with tiled floors downstairs, floorboards up and everywhere, heavenly old rafters. Bedrooms (one downstairs) have rugs scattered on floorboards, 1940s furniture, a fine armoire, pastoral views. The almost-as-big shower room reveals its pigeon holes and a rustically paved floor. Borrow the bikes or bring your own: the nearest shops, market and restaurant are a mile away in La Tour Blanche. Down the road, the wonderful Limousin-Périgord National Park; in the Limodore reserve nearby, rare orchids. Louise knows the area and has all the guides. *Service wash available.*

sleeps	2 + 2 children.
rooms	1 double, 2 singles; 1 shower room.
price	£195-£305 per week.

Louise & Peter Dunn

tel	+33 (0)5 53 91 15 15
fax	+33 (0)5 53 90 37 19
email	peter.dunn@wanadoo.fr
web	perso.wanadoo.fr/gites.at.la.geyrie

Hello

Jovelle – The Dependency

Leguillac de Cercles, Dordogne

White walls, pale oak floors, a rolling loft space, peace – city chic in the country. The 19th-century house, on the site of a monastery, has been rigorously renovated by the owners (who live across the courtyard in the main house) to create a modern space alongside original features. The open-plan living area sweeps across the ground floor; quarry tiles, a grand fireplace, antique furnishings, underfloor heating. The shiny-smart kitchen – convivially at one end – is a cook's delight. Bedrooms are bright, uncluttered spaces of oak boards and sand-blasted beams. Bring well-behaved friends and you also get the use of the vast attic apartment in the main house: two bedrooms, sloping beamed ceilings, antique furniture and claw-foot baths, and a soaring loft space scattered with rugs and comfy sofas. There's a smallish garden, a terrace for alfresco meals, a pool with a shower, and you are well-placed for exploring the Dordogne, the vineyards of St Emilion and pretty riverside Brantôme. Too tired to rustle up a meal? A Leith-trained cook is to hand – just say when.

sleeps	4 (8 with main house).
rooms	2: 1 twin, 1 double; 2 bathrooms (2 doubles, 2 bathrooms available in main house).
price	£700-£950 per week.
closed	Christmas.

John & Sally Ridley-Day

tel	+33 (0)5 53 56 51 19
fax	+33 (0)5 53 56 52 53
email	sallyridleyday@hotmail.com

Hello

Les Taloches – La Châtaigne

Tourtoirac, Dordogne

You're faced with a dilemma here, in 18 lovely hectares of woodland and meadows: which house to choose? Set either side of a courtyard, one is the old farmhouse, the other its barn. Both are spacious and extremely comfortable, both have their own private gardens and fenced pools. La Châtaigne is beautifully proportioned and full of character with creaky old staircases, twisted beams and bright white walls. The attractive sitting/dining room has a warm stone fireplace at either end and russet floor tiles; the kitchen is super, modern and well-equipped, with a breakfast area overlooking the pool. A double bedroom on the ground floor opens on to the terrace; two more (a double with a small, bunk-bedded room off) are on the first floor while up in the attic is a vast and delightful family suite – but mind your head in the bathroom! Set well away from both houses are a communal play area and a covered barn with table tennis. There's also an outdoor summer kitchen – a brilliant touch – where Jo will cook meals for guests from time to time. *See following page.*

sleeps 10-14.
rooms 5: 2 doubles, 1 twin, 1 room with bunks, 1 family suite for 4; 4 bathrooms, separate WC.
price £650-£1,600 per week.

J Sturges
tel +33 (0)5 53 50 20 26
fax +33 (0)5 53 50 60 94
email jsturges@wanadoo.fr
web www.les-taloches.com

Les Taloches – La Grange

Tourtoirac, Dordogne

Another big, comfortable place to stay in the same grounds as its neighbour La Châtaigne. The airy living space, reaching up to the rafters, has great glass doors across the entrances at either end – a legacy from its past as a drive-through barn. Today a courtyard lies to one side and a large shared pool to the other. In the main room is a magnificent fireplace, a long monastery table that could seat two dozen; down a few steps is the kitchen. Also on the ground floor, hidden behind the fireplace, is a large bedroom with its own wisteria-clad patio and a rather grand four-poster. A second sitting area on the mezzanine, filled with a lustrous light, houses the television, DVD and a tempting library of books. Upstairs, beds and walls are patterned or floral, there are two small and dramatically beamed twins and a discreet double, with a private entrance and a balcony terrace. Peaceful, tranquil, secluded, Les Taloches is a lazy walk from the pretty riverside village of Tourtoirac – take a drink in the café/bar, pick up your croissants. The Château of Hautefort and its gardens are near, too.

sleeps	8.
rooms	4: 2 doubles, 2 twins; 2 bathrooms.
price	£560-£1,400 per week.

J Sturges

tel	+33 (0)5 53 50 20 26
fax	+33 (0)5 53 50 60 94
email	jsturges@wanadoo.fr
web	www.les-taloches.com

Domaine d'Essendiéras

St Médard d'Excideuil, Dordogne

You could walk for three hours and still not reach the estate's border – the domaine spreads for thousands of acres. This is a super place for busy families: a play area in the woods with a tree hut and platform, mountain bikes for teenagers, a 'beach' for tinies, fishing on one lake, swimming and pedaloeing on another. B&B in the château, camp in the orchards, self-cater in the chalets – or in the white, shuttered, 1819 farmhouse. It has recently been renovated from top to toe, so all is new and everything works – beautifully. Downstairs, an L-shaped living area with black leather furniture, a refectory table and a corner kitchen, marvellously equipped; up an open-tread stair to carpeted floors and big comfortable beds. There are spectacular apple-orchard views – though not from your garden – and space for everyone. Hardworking Mrs Bakker juggles the running of it all with a young family, jumping in the jeep several times a day to check everyone's happy. You can rent a jeep, too, and take yourselves off for an hour or a day. *B&B also. Sauna available.*

sleeps	6-8.
rooms	3: 1 double, 2 triples; 1 bath/shower room, 1 bathroom & separate wc downstairs.
price	€225-€2,195 per week.

Ellen & Jeroen Bakker

tel +33 (0)5 53 52 81 51
fax +33 (0)5 53 52 89 22
email info@essendieras.fr
web www.essendieras.fr

La Brugère

Nantheuil de Thiviers, Dordogne

A treasure trove of surprises lies behind the sober facade of this 19th-century house, once a hunting lodge. Tapestries and curtains glow in the dining room off a wood-panelled entrance hall, the drawing room is elegant in cream and gold, and has stone fireplace, sofas and antiques. Vast French windows open onto two sides of the terrace. There's a panelled library with TV and a fabulous kitchen: two fridges, a large oven, silver cutlery for the dining room, stainless steal for the terrace. Two of the double rooms have four-posters with luscious curtains, chandeliers and polished wooden floors; the master bedroom is reached by its own staircase and the trompe l'œil in its bathroom is fantastic. The twin room has antique sleigh beds. The decoration and comfort is lavish, even breathtaking, right down to the parasols round the pool and the delicious towels. Yet the house feels like a home and children will love it; there's badminton and table tennis and three acres of parkland to explore – and swimming and fishing in the river Isle. The owners' daughter lives nearby, full of friendly advice. A magnificent place.

sleeps	12.
rooms	6: 5 doubles, 1 twin; 5 bathrooms.
price	£1,200-£2,600 per week.

Lisa Grist

tel	+44 (0)1992 632612
fax	+44 (0)1992 630038
email	pgrist@tractionseabert.com
web	www.labrugere.com

Le Balet du Val – Gîte

Bertric Burée, Dordogne

Rustle up lunch in the summer kitchen of the *balet*, the covered terrace that gives the place its name. The gîte for four, on the ground floor of the farmhouse, faces south-west. Thick walls keep you cool in summer; shutters shade you from the sun. It is not huge or luxurious but the conversion has been perfectly done. Floors are newly tiled, beams are chunky, plain walls are adorned with Marie's fresh paintings. The whole place is finely proportioned with a contemporary feel. Furnishings are minimalist: a plant here, a white rug there, muslin curtains. You have two rooms, each with two single beds and built-in cupboard space; a kitchen with hob, microwave, fridge; an ultra-modern shower room. You share barbecue, garden and delicious, bamboo-fringed pool with Éric, Marie and daughter Joséphine – but you're private here, with your own large terrace and sweeping views. Five minutes by car are two good restaurants where the locals eat. Ribérac is six miles: shops, church and superb *marché au gras* on Fridays in winter: to stock up on truffles, duck, delectable foie gras. *B&B also.*

sleeps 2-4.
rooms 2: 1 double, 1 twin; 1 shower room, 1 separate wc.
price €500-€750 per week.

Éric Borgers
tel +33 (0)5 53 91 38 57
email borgers.eric@wanadoo.fr
web www.le-balet-du-val.com

photo corel images

midi - pyrénées

Le Couvent

Lauzès, Lot

This elegant village retreat started life in 1837 as a convent school for girls: today's sunlit rooms were classrooms and dormitories. Rosalie and Malcolm have renovated in abundant style: original wooden floors, Victorian wrought-iron beds, fluttering muslin at shuttered windows, a free-standing bath. There's a dreamy sense of country life: old floral linen cushions on a sofa in one bedroom, sunlight bouncing off colour-washed walls and a chandelier rescued from a barn in the salon. The old well stands in the gorgeous garden which is on three levels leading up to woodland, so you can chase the sun or retreat to the shade. The dining room table is made from a neighbour's oak wine vat and there's a hungry woodburner in the beautifully fitted country kitchen. The medieval village is listed: a beautiful collage of tiled roofs and mellow stone houses, it hunkers down quietly in a lush valley, encircled by the river Vers. Rosalie and Malcolm are happy to organise painting tuition with a local artist for individuals or families and groups – bring your paints. *Meals available in June.*

sleeps	6.
rooms	3: 2 doubles, 1 twin; 2 bathrooms.
price	£450-£600 per week.
closed	November-April.

Rosalie Vicars-Harris
tel +44 (0)20 7483 2140
+33 (0)5 65 31 28 91
email rosalievh@yahoo.co.uk
web www.lecouvent.pwp.blueyonder.co.uk

La Ferme at Domaine la Grèze

Labastide-Murat, Lot

Rise early to catch deer sniffing the air. Come in May and June and the nightingales sing. This farmhouse, with its jolly green shutters and hilltop views over meadows, is designed to soothe stressed souls. Step inside to bowls of garden flowers, pots of herbs and French country warmth: Wendy has a designer's eye for the personal touch. Rooms are light and airy, dotted by French rustic furniture. In the living room, with is stone walls, rugs on wooden floors and soft earthy colours, are a prettily painted armoire and smart sofas inviting you to curl up with a book and a glass of wine... it must be bliss in winter with an open fire. The farmhouse kitchen is attractive, as are the bedrooms; soft restful spaces with simple wooden furniture, neat embroidered bedcovers, muslin at windows. The ground-floor bedroom is ideal for the less mobile. There's a large dining terrace with a pool tucked below and the owners, warmly enthusiastic, live nearby should you need them. You have walking, cycling, local markets – and a state-of-the-art gym, run by Wendy's daughter. *Children over eight welcome.*

sleeps	6.
rooms	3: 1 double, 2 twins; 3 bathrooms.
price	£350-£850 per week.

	Wendy & Roy Sevier
tel	+33 (0)5 65 23 56 84
fax	+33 (0)5 65 23 56 84
email	la.greze@wanadoo.fr
web	www.lagreze.net

Lavaysierre

Senaillac Lauzès, Lot

Get away from it all to this neat, pretty house, with its sage-green shutters and smart picket fence. On the edge of tiny hilltop Artix, its views float for miles over a patchwork of woods and meadows. Wild deer, red squirrels, birds, frogs, wild flowers surround you, yet it's a 10-minute drive to the shops of Labastide-Murat. Inside, a mixture of vintage French and contemporary furnishings gives a country fresh feel. In summer, throw open the glazed doors of the living area to the terrace by the pool to create a big open space. Kilim cushions and rugs add colour to the simple beige and dark red of the sofas and terracotta floor. There's a quirky fireplace – a talking point – which works a treat in cooler months, and an all-white, everything-you-need kitchen that tucks neatly in the corner. Bedrooms – one ground-floor – are French country style, the two upstairs have a balcony and a terrace. Bathrooms are downstairs, one en suite. Explore cliff-top medieval villages, local markets, Cahors and Sarlat. Wendy and Roy, full of warmth and energy, live nearby.

sleeps	6.
rooms	3: 1 double, 2 twins; 2 shower rooms.
price	£350-£850 per week.

Wendy & Roy Sevier
tel +33 (0)5 65 23 56 84
fax +33 (0)5 65 23 56 84
email la.greze@wanadoo.fr
web www.lagreze.net

Lapèze

Catus, Lot

Recline on your sunbed by the pool, lavender scenting the air, and gaze over the undulating landscape of the wooded Lot valley. The views are delectable – as is your house, prettily perched on the edge of medieval Catus. This is a welcoming, homely place – Elizabeth's second home – where friendly little touches make you smile. Upstairs, bedrooms are pleasantly old-fashioned with mis-matched bedspreads, family-favourite curtains, rugs on wooden floors and simple rustic furniture; on the landing, three sofabeds for children. The cool, stone-walled sitting room with open fireplace is also modestly but comfortably furnished. The farmhouse kitchen easily seats 12 and is a joy to inhabit, with its pretty white and blue tiles and views over the garden. You might eat on the first-floor covered terrace – which opens off another sitting area on the landing – with more of those lovely views. It's a short drive down to the village shops and weekly market, there are restaurants aplenty in Cahors and you have Le Lac Vert for watery fun. Or come in winter for quiet country walks.

sleeps	2-11.
rooms	4: 2 doubles, 2 twins, 3 singles on landing; 2 shower rooms, 1 bathroom.
price	£695-£1,995 per week. £550 per week for 2 in low season.

Elizabeth Tyzack
tel +44 (0)1395 232692
fax +44 (0)1395 232692
email lapeze@eclipse.co.uk
web www.eclipse.co.uk/lapeze

Domaine de Roubignol

Luzech, Lot

The high winding road above the vineyards of the Lot valley, an adventure in itself, brings you to this 17th-18th-century winemaster's house. It is breathtaking in its scale, space and architectural peculiarities: ancient stone floors, creaking floorboards, hidden alcoves and a beam to duck; three eating places inside, four terraces out and, cut into the steep side of the valley below, an infinity pool, underwater-lit at night. There's even an old bell to summon people – frolicking in the pool, playing ping-pong in the barn – to lunch. There are five bedrooms in the main house, from the tiny single in the pigeonnier to the vast Romeo and Juliet room with its balcony and canopied bed. The Tower has a further double, the additional luxury of central heating and a sofabed in its sitting room on the top floor. Furniture is a happy mix of French antique and modern and the L-shaped sitting room is big enough to waltz in. You are five minutes from the shops and market at Luzech (25 on foot down the valley path) surrounded by wine-tastings and gastronomic opportunity. The views sweep and soar... A heavenly place.

sleeps	5. Tower 2-4.
rooms	5 + 1: 2 doubles, 2 twins, 1 single; 2 bathrooms, 1 shower room. Tower: 1 double, 1 sofabed in sitting room; 1 bathroom.
price	Main house €650-€1,950. Tower €290-€430 only available July-August with main house. Prices per week.
closed	Main house: November-March.

Roger & Jill Bichard
tel +44 (0)1225 862789
+44 (0)1380 828677 (evenings)
email info@moxhams-antiques.demon.co.uk
web www.moxhams-antiques.demon.co.uk

Maison Castera

Puy l'Évêque, Lot

The setting is magical. You are in one of the prettiest villages in the Lot valley, where every view sweeps down to the river past those grand, gracious, honey-stone houses… and the castle of the Bishops of Cahors at the top. Your little family house, thick-walled and terracotta-roofed, is attached to the Arnetts' and borders their garden, which you share. Enter via the practical, well-equipped kitchen, then up to the living room, sandwiched by bedrooms on either side (a good layout ensuring privacy) and onto the window-boxed terrace, inviting with parasol and plastic table and chairs. The views are marvellous – what a place to eat out in summer! The rooms are light and a good size, the furnishings fairly workaday: a blue sofa with yellow cushions, rugs on a wooden floor, two bookshelves, some old framed photographs of the town. Your hosts are lovely and give you drinks when you arrive; they like to keep gîte and B&B separate and make sure that for much of the day you have the garden and pool to yourselves. There's masses to do on the river, and riding, cycle hire and tennis are close by. *B&B also.*

sleeps	5-7.
rooms	3: 1 double, 1 twin, 1 single, 1 sofabed in sitting room; 1 bathroom, 1 shower room.
price	€690-€1,073 per week.

Bill & Ann Arnett

tel	+33 (0)5 65 36 59 39
fax	+33 (0)5 65 36 59 39
email	williamarnett@hotmail.com
web	www.puyleveque.com

Cubertou

St Martin le Redon, Lot

Both place and setting are completely delightful. Warm, golden stone, shuttered windows, cascades of vines and wisteria… crickets hum, buzzards wheel, there are acres of meadow and woodland to escape to. The farmhouse and barns, round a grassy courtyard, were turned into a summer art school in the 1960s by an eccentric painter and his ballerina wife. Their love of colour is still in evidence, particularly in the striking, peacock-blue salon with its Provençal cushions. Taken as a whole, Cubertou sleeps up to 23 but you can rent the main house alone and still have the place to yourself. The bedrooms are simple and interesting – two are in the pigeon tower – and the bathrooms adequate; views are to the valley. Cooking for large numbers is no problem in the brilliantly designed kitchen, or on the terrace barbecue. The huge open games barn at the far end of the courtyard also makes a marvellous place for candlelit suppers. Generous owners, friendly locals, a housekeeper, cook and babysitter on request, and various lively weekly village markets selling melons, strawberries, goat's cheese, foie gras…

sleeps	21-23.
rooms	13: 1 double, 6 twins, 5 singles, 1 family room; 1 bathroom, 3 shower rooms, 5 separate wcs.
price	€600-€2,160 per week.
closed	November-March except Christmas & New Year.

	Claire & John Norton
tel	+33 (0)5 63 95 82 34
fax	+33 (0)5 63 95 82 42
email	claire@cubertou.com
web	www.cubertou.com

La Grange & Les Places

Serignac, Lot

In bed, table, floor and beam, carpenter-sculptor Stephen has left his mark. The fine old Lot farmhouse and adjoining barn have been converted by he and his partner Tessa into two solidly comfortable holiday homes, with balconies and terraces for wraparound views. It's the smells that hit you first: sun-scorched lavender outside, earthy reclaimed chestnut and oak in. The owners' house (self-catering in summer only) has an ultra-modern walk-in shower and a kitchen flaunting handsome woodwork; the 100-year-old barn, too, has been renovated perfectly. Vaulted ceilings, pillars and posts remain; a generous 1930s-style fridge makes a statement in an attractive kitchen. Bedrooms have traditional furniture and the owners' delightful artwork on the walls. Children may run free in the gardens and splash in the infinity pool, there's canoeing on the Lot, horse riding next door, clay and sculpture classes in the pipeline, and you may join your hosts – the loveliest people – for *table d'hôtes* from September to June. *July-August: rental of main house & barn together. B&B Sept-June.*

sleeps	La Grange 4-5. Les Places 7-10.
rooms	La Grange: 1 double, 1 family room for 3; 1 bathroom. Les Places: 2 doubles, 2 twins, 1 room with bunks; 4 shower rooms.
price	Grange £240-£400. Grange & Places £1,540-£1,820. Prices per week.
closed	Les Places low season only.

Tessa Collier

tel +33 (0)5 65 36 51 10
fax +33 (0)5 65 36 51 10
email In7thheaven@wanadoo.fr
web www.lesplaces.com

Lagardelle

Ste Croix, Montcuq, Lot

Much of Europe was like this half a century ago – few cars, many species of birds and flowers, lots of space. That line from the brochure gives you a taste of what to expect when you arrive at this stunning 17th-century stone barn surrounded by fields of lavender and sunflowers. It gives you an idea, too, of the infectious enthusiasm of its nature-loving, knowledgeable owners, Ben and Susanna, who do B&B next door. If you want to walk, you're in the best hands as Ben runs walking holidays and knows the Quercy Blanc intimately. The couple have converted the barn with religious respect for original materials and structures (resisting the temptation to enlarge the small upstairs windows) and have aimed for a mood of calm and simplicity. There are clean wooden floors, white and stone walls, a welcoming woodburner for cooler evenings. Engravings in the sitting room depict the various ports Ben (ex-Navy) has sailed into. Visit medieval Montcuq to stock up at its vibrant Sunday morning market... then back to cool off in the pool. Simply heaven. *B&B also*

sleeps 5.
rooms 3: 1 double, 1 twin, 1 single; 1 bathroom, 1 separate wc.
price £200-£725 per week.

Ben & Susanna Hawkins
tel +33 (0)5 65 31 96 72
fax +33 (0)5 65 31 81 27
email hawkinsben@aol.com

Domaine Lapèze – Cottage & Atelier

Montcuq, Lot

Once a resting place for pilgrims on their way to Santiago de Compostela, this is a place to linger. Those who come find much to recharge city-drained batteries: pool, vineyards, plum orchards, peace. The starkly beautiful collection of old stone buildings is wrapped in 12 acres of blissful rolling country and you can gaze across to an 11th-century tower in Montcuq (busy with two markets, three bars, four restaurants, shops with all you need). Caroline and Knud have renovated magnificently in both cottage and studio – expect rich, warm colours and oodles of style. Terracotta tiles keep you cool, white walls soak up the sun. In the Cottage, an open-plan living area with yellow sofa and armchairs, big fireplace and beautifully equipped kitchen, a red and orange bedroom, a fresh and summery feel. The kitchen in the Atelier is simpler; the double bed has a pale pink and white quilt. Both gîtes have private patios. There's a gorgeous pool (floodlit at night) which you share with B&B guests, bikes to rent, horses to ride, lakes to swim in, wine to taste and Romanesque churches to visit. *B&B also.*

sleeps	Cottage 4. Atelier 4.
rooms	Cottage: 1 double, 1 twin; 1 bathroom, 1 separate wc. Atelier: 1 double, 1 twin; 2 bathrooms.
price	Cottage €600-€900. Atelier €500-€800. Prices per week.

Caroline & Knud Kristoffersen

tel +33 (0)5 65 24 91 97
fax +33 (0)5 65 24 91 98
email lapeze@libertysurf.fr
web www.domainelapeze.com

Caussé

St Paul d'Espis, Tarn-et-Garonne

Nothing is too much trouble for Sue and Robert, eager that your stay will be perfect. The pretty, studio apartment just below their own 300-year old cottage has been thoughtfully and generously fitted out. Traditionally restored, it has a cool, tiled floor and exposed stone and yellow plaster walls. The beds – a double plus bunks – are very comfortable and the linen excellent. There's a small corner kitchen with some charming crockery and French windows that lead onto a private terrace overlooking the garden – seven gorgeous hectares of it, full of fruit trees and potager (you're welcome to help yourself) and enticing spots, sunny or shady, in which to settle with a drink and a book. This is a great-value place to stay and Robert and Sue are infinitely kind – and flexible about arrangements. They'll provide breakfast at a small extra charge, or a picnic lunch; they'll even, on occasion, babysit or cook dinner. Robert's pâté is excellent, especially if he has been listening to Verdi! (Mozart, apparently, provides a less inspiring background for paté production.) *Minimum stay three nights. B&B also.*

sleeps	2-4.
rooms	Studio with double & bunks; 1 shower room.
price	€50 per night for two. €68 per night for four.
arrival	Flexible.

Sue & Robert Watkins
tel +33 (0)5 63 29 14 22
fax +33 (0)5 63 29 14 22
email willowweave@libertysurf.fr

Las Bourdolles – Le Pigeonnier

Tréjouls, Tarn-et-Garonne

Deep in rural France, a square, creamy-grey stone tower topped by a pointed roof. Its deep-set windows look out over 20 acres of woods and fields belonging to the 17th-century farmhouse owned and run by Erica and Linda. Having restored the main house and established a B&B, they have now turned the little pigeon house into a delightful gîte. Ladder-like stairs link each rough-walled room to the one above. At ground level are a small, newly fitted kitchen, dining area and shower room; on the first floor, a simple, attractive bedroom with painted screens and a handmade oak bed. (A roll-top bath stands in front of the window, so you can gaze at the countryside as you soak.) Up another stair to the comfortable sitting room with a sofabed and a gloriously beamed ceiling. You have your own tiny courtyard, too, but may wander at will in Las Bourdolles' grounds, and use the saltwater pool. There's central heating and an open fire to keep you snug in winter, and if you tire of self-catering you can always dine at the farmhouse: Linda and Erica are fabulous cooks. *B&B also.*

sleeps	2-4.
rooms	1 double, 1 sofabed; 1 bathroom, 1 shower room.
price	€350-€600 per week.
arrival	Saturday, flexible low season.

Linda Hilton & Erica Lewis

tel	+33 (0)5 63 95 80 83
fax	+33 (0)5 63 95 80 83
email	erica.lewis@wanadoo.fr
web	www.frenchbedbreakfast.com

Las Bourdolles – Le Puits

Tréjouls, Tarn-et-Garonne

In the fruit-garden of France, where orchards are laden with peaches and pears, is this ground-floor gîte for two. The old bread oven – all Quercy limestone and ancient timbers – has been simply, dreamily revived, one step and a curtain dividing bedroom from *sejour-cuisine*. Imagine 20 square metres of warm maple, walls of creamy stone, a bed dressed in white linen and a chair of vintage wicker. The living space has a woodburning stove, an L-shaped kitchen in wood, a farmhouse table with church pew and almost every mod con. A sliding glass wall leads to a white stone terrace; take a glass of something sweet and local (Moissac, maybe) to its teak table and relax in the shade of the chestnut tree. You share the owners' saltwater pool, the organic gardens, from which you may pluck the produce, and the valley views – stunning whatever the weather. Book in for a meal and you may feast on seared salmon with fresh sorrel sauce, or asparagus soup with truffle oil toasts. Cazes-Mondenard has a Romanesque church and provisions, Montcuq a Sunday market and 12th-century dungeon. *B&B also.*

sleeps 2.
rooms 1 double; 1 shower room.
price €350-€650 per week.
arrival Flexible.

Linda Hilton & Erica Lewis
tel +33 (0)5 63 95 80 83
fax +33 (0)5 63 95 80 83
email erica.lewis@wanadoo.fr
web www.frenchbedbreakfast.com

La Petite Grange & La Petite Maison

Tréjouls, Tarn-et-Garonne

Two diminutive gîtes in a delicious setting outside the hamlet of Tréjouls. They stand with their backs to the hillside at different levels in the Nortons' seven-acre garden. Thick stone walls keep you cool and the rooms are pleasantly furnished, with splashes of colour from cushion and poster. Petite Grange, reached by a flight of steps, is a multi-stable conversion, its several doors opening onto the lawn: a comfortable, one-storey house with an L-shaped living room/kitchen. Lavender and morning glory edge the patio. The other end of the barn is open-sided, providing shade for hot-weather meals near the pretty, shared pool. Petite Maison is smaller, with an overhanging roof and long, south-facing terrace. Its bedsitting room has an antique bed and spectacular views, but you have to go onto the terrace to reach the shower and wc. John and Claire are a charming couple with two teenage children, and two friendly cats, certain to come and visit. You may prefer the greater comfort of La Petite Grange in winter, with its central heating, dishwasher and own washing-machine.

sleeps	Grange 2. Maison 2.
rooms	Grange: 1 double; 1 bathroom. Maison: 1 double; 1 shower room.
price	Grange €200-€400. Maison €150-€300. Prices per week.

Claire & John Norton

tel	+33 (0)5 63 95 82 34
fax	+33 (0)5 63 95 82 42
email	claire@cubertou.com
web	www.cubertou.com/petite

Catusse-Haut – La Fermette & La Grange

Montalzat, Tarn-et-Garonne

What a place to celebrate a special birthday! Jo delights in cooking for occasions and will make the dinner table look magical; even if it's not a special event, she's happy to cook for you twice a week. She and Robert are a friendly, considerate couple who have taken the best bits from all the places they've stayed in over the years and introduced them to their own barn conversions. The immaculate Fermette is given a smart-rustic makeover thanks to deep sofas, pretty beams, books and watercolours painted by the family – and there's a farmhouse-style kitchen in which to linger over meals. All the bedrooms are pleasing but you need to climb some rather steep stairs to reach the crowning glory – a gorgeous, white, loft suite, with a sitting area at one end and a fabulous shower room. La Grange is smaller but charming and full of light: its big, living/kitchen area is open plan, walls are exposed stone and the décor includes pieces picked up by Jo in Thailand. Both houses have their own private terrace, partly covered for shade, with wide views over rolling farmland. A lovely pool beckons.

sleeps	La Fermette 8. La Grange 4.
rooms	La Fermette: 2 doubles, 2 twins; 2 shower rooms. La Grange: 1 double, 1 twin; 1 shower room.
price	La Fermette €485-€1,325. La Grange €395-€940. Prices per week.

Jo & Robert Everett
tel +33 (0)5 63 03 17 93
email relax@catusse.co.uk
web www.catusse.co.uk

Maison Monclar – Les Vincens

Monclar de Quercy, Tarn-et-Garonne

A fully-catered holiday house! The moment Annie and Barry found their Quercy farmhouse they set about creating a place of restful stress-free living. Rooms are filled with light, peppered with family antiques, dotted with stylish sofas. Annie has imbued each bedroom with its own character: dove-grey furniture and washed aqua walls, toile de Jouy curtains and rattan chairs. Three have their own little terrace. She goes to market each morning, chooses what's freshest and plans the menus accordingly. In winter, expect her French country dishes and good wines to be served in front of a log fire; in summer, there's a dining room with magnificent views – and you can eat outside. Annie encourages a house-party feel but there's no lack of space if you want privacy. Outside, 30 hectares of rambling grounds teeming with wildlife; the land, protected from hunters, is a retreat for both man and beast. And there's a lake, big enough to boat on and fish. To ensure your idleness is complete, Annie will rustle you up a picnic and deliver it to your chosen lakeside spot. *B&B also.*

sleeps	8-11.
rooms	4: 3 doubles, 1 family suite for 5; 4 bathrooms.
price	€2,800 per week. €840 for 8 for a weekend. Length of rental flexible. Fully catered.
arrival	Flexible.

Annie & Barry Proud
tel +33 (0)5 63 67 41 31
fax +33 (0)5 63 67 41 31
email annie@maisonmonclar.com
web www.maisonmonclar.com

Barrau

Esparsac, Tarn-et-Garonne

Terrifically earthy and wonderful for those who long to leave creature comforts behind and lose themselves in the hills. The main house, where Jennifer lives, is 30 yards away. This is ideal for a couple or a solo traveller, secluded on a 15-acre hillside estate with two sitting-out areas, one filled with lavender and figs. And trees, long views and wildlife. Deer and badgers live on the land, 42 species of butterflies have been identified, nightingales sing, the odd salamander scampers by and beehives dot the landscape. Your retreat is a former house for the pigs and hens (it dates to 1890) and has been renovated simply. This is like camping but without the tent. You have a pine-floored, rugged room with a laminate table, a cupboard, a radio/cassette player, two beds and two easy chairs, a tiny creamy-brick shower room, a corridor kitchen. Jennifer has a telescope and will let you borrow it; the night skies are pollution-free. She is also an expert on the churches and brocante fairs in the area. Expect the tree frogs to sing you to sleep. *Extra charge for heating.*

sleeps	2.
rooms	1 twin; 1 shower room.
price	€160-€300 per week.
arrival	Saturday but flexible out of season.

Jennifer Boncey
tel +33 (0)5 63 26 12 72
email boncey@wanadoo.fr
web www.haumont.com

La Guiraude – La Grande Maison

Beauteville, Haute-Garonne

On its own at the end of a country road, the 1843 farmhouse has a stylish Spanish hacienda feel. You have here three homes in one (including your hosts'): a large, light, cool complex of indoor spaces and outdoor terraces, secluded gardens and delicious pool. A huge hall leads to an even huger sitting room with lofty ceilings and the original fireplace. Art decorates cream walls, Chinese rugs soften pale tiles and there's a light-filled gallery brimming with leather sofas, books, music and French and English TV. From the dining room, French windows lead to a big terrace with shade and panoramic views. The kitchen has two electric ovens and a refrigerator of which Americans would be proud, the games room sports table tennis, exercise bike and step machine, bedrooms have big beds and cheerful colours, bathrooms have walk-in showers and are as immaculate as the rest. But, however tempting the kitchen, you don't have to chop and stir; your host, Alistair, is an excellent cook, unfazed at the prospect of catering for 20 when a retreat group or wedding party takes on the whole fabulous place. *B&B also. See opposite.*

sleeps	10.
rooms	5: 3 doubles, 2 twins; 5 bathrooms.
price	€1,700-€3,000 per week.
arrival	Saturday in high season.

Alistair & Janine Smith

tel	+33 (0)5 61 81 42 05
fax	+33 (0)5 61 81 42 05
email	guiraude@wanadoo.fr
web	www.guiraude.com

La Guiraude – La Toscane

Beauteville, Haute-Garonne

The name suggest the colours of Tuscany: ochres, siennas and terracottas prevail. Your friendly hosts, who live next door (see opposite), have poured energy into this new venture: the attention to detail is superb and summer staff keep it tickety-boo. Lovely Toscane, in spite of its size, has an intimate feel. At both ends of the sitting/dining area, French windows lead to terraces, one with a teak table for ten; there are big lamps, good sofas, an open fire for the cooler months. Bedrooms have colourwashed walls and original beams, the furnishings are immaculate and there are towels for bathrooms *and* pool. New appliances in the kitchen, swish crockery and glassware, every bedroom en suite – this is better than home! Each house has its own fragrant walled garden; pathways are illuminated by night and views stretch across landscaped trees to far fields. The shared pool is tucked discreetly to one side with a stylish pool house; there are secret spots, an arbour with a pond and a playground with swings. Cathar trails, châteaux and vineyards beckon – should you plan to leave. *B&B also.*

sleeps	8-10.
rooms	4: 2 doubles, 1 twin, 1 family room for 4; 4 bathrooms.
price	€1,200-€2,200 per week.

Alistair & Janine Smith
tel +33 (0)5 61 81 42 05
fax +33 (0)5 61 81 42 05
email guiraude@wanadoo.fr
web www.guiraude.com

Gîte de Figarol – Lower & Upper Gîtes

Figarol, Haute-Garonne

Jean and Neil lost their hearts to this farmhouse the moment they saw it. Fields and wooded hills roll to the Pyrenees rising in the distance; buzzards and kites swirl above; the garden glows, shady spots invite you to linger. One is irresistibly drawn to the terraces of these two gîtes – the upper and lower floors of a converted barn – to drink in the scenery. Inside, all is simplicity and charm. The living area of the lower gîte is a cottagey mix of beamed ceiling, tiled floors and well-loved furniture; the kitchens of both are sturdy affairs with generous helpings of crockery and pans. In the gîte upstairs, no sitting room – but who cares when a covered terrace stretches the width of the place? You'll do all your living outdoors here, an outside heater ensuring warmth on cooler nights. Bedrooms are simple, modern and colourful. This is outdoors country – walking, birdwatching, fishing; there are markets at spa town Salies du Salat, Pau has its castle and Toulouse is 45 minutes. Too tired to rustle up supper? Jean loves cooking and Neil is an expert on local wines. Unpretentious, friendly hosts, and great value. *B&B also.*

sleeps	Lower gîte 4. Upper gîte 4.
rooms	Lower gîte: 2 doubles; 1 bathroom. Upper gîte 2: 1 double, 1 twin; 1 shower room.
price	Each gite €240-€420 per week.
closed	Upper gîte Nov-March.

Jean & Neil Adamson
tel +33 (0)5 61 98 25 54
fax +33 (0)5 61 98 25 54
email info@figarolgites.com
web www.figarolgites.com

Les Rosiers

Cescau, Ariège

Breathe in the fresh mountain air as you step out of this old farmer's cottage into its wild (but enclosed) garden and drink in the High Pyrenean panorama. Get out the walking boots as the coffee warms on the woodburning stove and you plan your day's pilgrimage – or prepare for a shopping trip to St Girons to stock up the larder. Les Rosiers stands wonderfully secluded on the edge of Cescau, an ancient village embedded in a steep hill facing those breathtaking mountains. Its owners, Teresa and Bernard, are artists with something in common: a love of peace and natural beauty that will inspire the creative flow. And they look after the house beautifully; its décor is simple and spotless, its wooden floors and beams give a nice old country feel. Children will enjoy the amazing wooden spiral stair – tread carefully! – that leads to the bathroom and the twin under the rafters, with skylights for moon gazing, while you will rest easy in your huge bed downstairs after a hearty meal cooked over the old stone barbecue.

sleeps	4.
rooms	2: 1 double, 1 twin + cot; 1 bathroom.
price	€320-€400 per week.

Teresa Richard
tel +33 (0)5 61 96 74 24
email tiziricard@caramail.com
web www.ariege.com/les-rosiers

Madranque

Le Bosc, Ariège

Amazing for walkers, mountain bikers, cross-country skiers, rare fauna-lovers, children, dogs. Woods and more woods, hills and more hills and rarely a house to be seen. In a tiny *hameau* of three dwellings, here is a wonderful example of mountain architecture 200 years ago. Simply and sympathetically restored by its artistic owner, it is on three levels with a 'walk-in' hearth and dining/living room in the middle. On the down-valley side is a large, grassy garden with a hand-hewn table for picnics and a gorgeous view. Low ceilinged, tile-floored bedrooms are a good size, shower rooms are darkly rustic; the walls are open stone or white-plaster and there's no shortage of colombage. In addition to the main room – with well-equipped kitchen in the corner – is a *petit salon* on the first floor with a desk and TV. Birgit has her atelier next door and her tapisseries and weavings add charm. Here in the Pyrenean foothills the views up and down this long, narrow, heavily wooded valley are all-enveloping. Foix is 16km, a good country restaurant is a short drive. *B&B also.*

sleeps	8-11.
rooms	4: 2 doubles, 1 family room for 3, 1 family suite for 4; 4 shower rooms.
price	€795-€1,275 per week.

Birgit Loizance
tel +33 (0)5 61 02 71 29
fax +33 (0)5 61 02 71 29
email birgit.loizance@libertysurf.fr
web www.lavalleeverte.net

Le Poulsieu – Paris & Amsterdam

Serres sur Arget, Ariège

Hairpin bends and a single-track road lead you up to a world of snow-capped peaks and hillside villages. High in the foothills of the Pyrenees, this place has a haunting but beautiful remoteness. The air is clean, the views sharp, the peace tangible. Although Andorra, medieval Mirepoix and the castle at Foix are within driving distance, this is an outdoorsy place; 5,000 kilometres of trails criss-cross the area. Hans, an experienced walker, will advise, even guide, or arrange riding, rafting and fishing. Or you could loll by the pool, shared with B&B guests, and breathe in the views. The two gîtes, in farmhouse outbuildings, are well separated, each with a terrace for al fresco meals. Wooden floors, beams, whitewashed walls and a woodburning stove create a rustic comfort, and furniture is simple – all you need after an exhilarating day outside. 'Amsterdam', with its well-equipped dining kitchen and fun, quadruple-bedded room, suits families. 'Paris' is perfect for a couple, perhaps with one child. Dutch-born but English-speaking, Hans and Mieke are relaxed, fun and offer good-value suppers. *B&B also.*

sleeps Paris 2-4.
Amsterdam 4-6 cot.

rooms Paris: 1 double, sofabed in living-room; 1 bathroom.
Amsterdam: 1 double, 1 quadruple; 1 bathroom, 1 separate wc.

price Paris €295-€525.
Amsterdam €395-€650.
Prices per week.

Mieke Van Eeuwijk & Hans Kiepe
tel +33 (0)5 61 02 77 72
fax +33 (0)5 61 02 77 72
email le.poulsieu@wanadoo.fr
web www.ariege.com/le-poulsieu

La Petite Écurie

Leran, Ariège

Cross the courtyard from the Furnesses' grand 18th-century townhouse and there is La Petite Écurie, '1758' inscribed over its door. John and Lee-anne have done much of this stables conversion themselves – and made a great job of it. The overall effect is assured, pleasing and comfortable. In the bedrooms you have chestnut wood floors and exposed stone walls to show off the tapestries that hang richly behind the beds; the beamed living room is restful and elegant; the kitchen has every appliance you can think of. This is a quiet corner of town and the garden, with its hammock and pool, is pleasant and secluded. John and Lee-anne came to live here in 1999: they're Australians, enthusiastic and very likeable. Lee-anne is an accomplished chef and you can book a meal with them in their fine big house where they do B&B. They love living here and know all about the area and its scattering of Cathar castles. Take a picnic hamper (Lee-anne will provide – very well) and go exploring, or spend the day basking on the sunny shores of Lac Montbel. *B&B also.*

sleeps	4.
rooms	2: 1 double, 1 twin; 1 bathroom, 1 shower room.
price	€340-€600 per week.

John & Lee-anne Furness

tel	+33 (0)5 61 01 50 02
fax	+33 (0)5 61 01 50 02
email	john.furness@wanadoo.fr
web	www.chezroo.com

Larriberau

Mirannes, Gers

Come for the sound of silence – bar your children frolicking in the pool. (It's perfect even for the youngest, being gently stepped at one end.) This is an old Napoleonic farmhouse, built in 1811, with loads of character and a hilltop position: countryside rolls out on every side and on clear days you can see the Pyrenees. There's an easy, relaxed feel: squashy floral sofas in front of a big fire which roars in winter, a large kitchen with beautiful Gascon fireplace, a salon that doubles as a library and TV/video room, and numerous bedrooms, some of which are in the next-door barn – heaven for kids. The bedrooms in the house have a faded French charm: big flowers on old-fashioned wallpaper, a four-poster, a quaint sofa. Fans keep you cool in summer. There's masses of space out as well as in: a big, safe garden bordered by ancient oaks and a cavernous barn with table tennis and a table for 20. You can eat in the house, too, and there's a barbecue for meals under the stars. Couples on their own love it here too, and the area is great for cyclists and walkers.

sleeps	2-12 + cots.
rooms	6: 3 doubles, 1 twin, 1 single, 1 family room for 3, 2 cots; 4 bathrooms, 1 shower room.
price	£450-£1,950 per week.

	Hugh & Nony Buchanan
tel	+44 (0)1367 870497
fax	+44 (0)1367 870497
email	huggymummy@hotmail.com

Castelnau des Fieumarcon

Lagarde Fieumarcon, Gers

Traffic-free, full of secret places, heaven for kids. Leave your car, your laptop, your phone outside the walls, step through the gateway and wrap yourself in history. This fortified village on a rocky spur overlooking the Ouchy valley has been reclaimed with the lightest of touches by owner Frédéric Coustols and his parents. Built in the 13th century by local feudal lords – who for a time during the Hundred Years War pledged allegiance to the English crown – the stronghold had been left to crumble until a couple of decades ago when the Coustols family restored the ramparts, renovated the houses, created gardens for each one and left much of the creeper-clad old stone untouched. There is nothing mock or tricksy here: the golden Gers stone and the old terracotta floors glow, gardens have ancient trees and the pool is outside the walls with valley views. Getting in is almost an initiation. Pass through a large Renaissance portal and spot a music stand and a welcome sign; then ring the gong. If all you hear is a bird calling, you are in the right place. *B&B also.*

sleeps	Up to 64.
rooms	10 houses sleeping 2-8.
price	€690-€2,100 per house per week.
arrival	Flexible.

Yves & Nicole Everaert

tel	+33 (0)5 62 68 99 30
fax	+33 (0)5 62 68 99 48
email	office@lagarde.org
web	www.lagarde.org

Castelnau des Fieumarcon

Lagarde Fieumarcon, Gers

Rooms in even the smallest house feel luminous and generous, with the grandeur that comes from original features – a gracious spiralling stone stair, a great 11th-century beam, a chunk of 13th-century wall. The houses are not 'interior decorated' but simple, with understated touches to add sophistication: framed dried herbs on the painted walls; mosquito-net bed canopies; a massive Louis XV armoire; antique Gascon treasures. Beds are individually designed, some with those canopies, all with white linen and a surplus of pillows; bathrooms are large, comfy and cool with mosaic showers. Kitchens are less high-class – small ovens, half fridges – but fine for holiday cooking; bread is delivered every morning. Castelnau is on high ground so the views from every window are astounding, giving off a timeless hazy glow from the low-lying hills and surrounding fields. Stendhal called it the French Tuscany. He would be at home here: no cars, no TVs, no telephones. Instead, vineyards, fairs, brocante, foie gras and Toulouse a little further. Not cheap but priceless as a rare pearl. *B&B also.*

See opposite entry.

Yves & Nicole Everaert

tel +33 (0)5 62 68 99 30

fax +33 (0)5 62 68 99 48

email office@lagarde.org

web www.lagarde.org

Domaine de Peyloubère – Les Rosiers

Pavie, Gers

Peyloubère is a dreamlike grouping of 300-year-old buildings in acres of gorgeous parkland. There are a river, a lake up the hill, a rose garden and langorous walks across the fields. The owners do B&B in the manoir once inhabited by the Italian 20th-century artist Mario Cavaglieri. Les Rosiers, on the ground floor of the house itself, feels nicely private, and the Martins' sensitive refurbishment makes the most of its one piece of "genuine Cavaglieri": a vibrant, hand-painted ceiling. No longer the dining room of the big house, this room now has an extremely comfortable brass bed. The living room is large and airy with white-painted beams, walls washed with Strassevil chalk and an inglenook fireplace. For inclement days there are books, games, videos, music and central heating. Tall French windows lead into a private shady garden with the original well house – still in working order but safely secured – and children will love the secret summer house in the woods and the magical waterfall. To share: a heated swimming pool, table tennis, badminton and a spa in the former pig shed. *B&B also.*

sleeps	3-4.
rooms	2: 1 double, 1 room with bunks; 1 shower room.
price	€600-€1,200 per week.

Theresa & Ian Martin

tel	+33 (0)5 62 05 74 97
fax	+33 (0)5 62 05 75 39
email	martin@peyloubere.com
web	www.peyloubere.com

Domaine de Peyloubère – Fermier

Pavie, Gers

Look out for hoopoes by the waterfall; it's fed by the river Gers that flows through the estate of the 17th-century manor. With 35 acres of lawns, Italian gardens, woodland and wonderful trees, there's space to roam. You'll scarcely be aware of the guests in the adjoining cottages, or of the delightful English owners. Peyloubère used to be a working farm and Fermier was the farmer's cottage: its original beamed inglenook fireplace still warms the living room. Today it's super-cosy with central heating and furnishings crisp and new: light beech furniture, deep-blue sofas, full-length curtains. The state-of-the-art kitchen is painted grey-green and sunflower-yellow, with a Saint Hubert dresser and steps to a sunny downstairs double bedroom. French doors lead out to the patio and a large heated pool shared with the other gîtes, and the garden beyond. Gaze over the fields, listen to the birds, identify wild flowers, fish in lake and river – and don't forget the armagnac after supper, the dry golden brandy for which the area is famous. *Health spa with sauna for guests. B&B also.*

sleeps	8.
rooms	4: 2 doubles, 2 twins; 1 bathroom, 1 shower room, 2 separate wcs.
price	€800-€1,600 per week.

Theresa & Ian Martin
tel +33 (0)5 62 05 74 97
fax +33 (0)5 62 05 75 39
email martin@peyloubere.com
web www.peyloubere.com

Setzères – Petit Setzères

Marciac, Gers

The house is the converted stables of a fine manor set on soft slopes in this unspoilt part of rural France. Petit Setzères has a big, well-furnished ground-floor living area where you can snuggle down in front of a log fire in winter (there's central heating, too). In summer, take lunch into the lush garden and picnic on the terrace under a high old barn roof; the Pyrenees look down on you with a different face every day. Above the living room are three pretty bedrooms with good beds, functional storage, lots of books, glorious views. One bathroom upstairs, a shower room downstairs and an excellent, fully-fitted kitchen complete the picture. You feel perfectly secluded and have your own garden space beside the lily pond, yet are free to share the pool and main garden with other guests and the attentive, civilised Furneys. It is a quiet and beautiful spot, and there's badminton and tennis (and, in May, French cookery classes) to keep you busy. You could even set off for a day's skiing in the Pyrenees: leave at 8am and you'll be there by 10.
Long winter lets available at £600 per month. B&B also.

sleeps	6-7.
rooms	4: 1 double, 1 twin, 1 room with bunks, 1 tiny single; 1 bathroom, 1 shower room.
price	€518-€1,630 (£360-£1,130) per week.

Christine Furney
tel +33 (0)5 62 08 21 45
fax +33 (0)5 62 08 21 45
email setzeres32@aol.com
web www.setzeres.com

Setzères – Le Grenier

Marciac, Gers

In the same stupendous surroundings of fine old buildings, green garden and stunning views, the smaller of the Setzères cottages is in the old grain loft and a rustic outside staircase leads to its new yet typically gabled front door. The Furneys have done another excellent conversion here. There's a lovely warm feel (enhanced by central heating in winter), with four characterful old armchairs on an oriental carpet, a round table with Windsor chairs and a window like a lens homing in on a slice of green country topped by snowy peaks beyond. This is a roomy, one-storied space for four. The neat sky-lit kitchen, a mix of natural wood and blue tiles, gives onto this end of the room; the bedrooms are off either side. The yellow and pink double is smallish but has its own basin; the pink-tinged twin room is larger; both are well lit, have good storage and share the neat white bathroom. A terrace area and a good patch of garden are yours alone but you can also share the wonderful grounds and pool with other guests. White-water rafting is a two-hour drive. *Long winter lets available at £400 per month. B&B also.*

sleeps	4.
rooms	2: 1 double, 1 twin; 1 bathroom.
price	€375-€895 (£260-£620) per week.

Christine Furney
tel +33 (0)5 62 08 21 45
fax +33 (0)5 62 08 21 45
email setzeres32@aol.com
web www.setzeres.com

Place de l'Église – Two Apartments

Tillac, Gers

A village address in the gently rolling Gers. The village is a jewel, predating even the lovely bastide towns of the region; the Place de l'Église is a medieval colonnade opposite the church and beside the village green. The old *boulangerie* – divided into one apartment for the owners and two for the guests – is at the end of the colonnade. It's a sensitive restoration that reveals the original colombage, the Toulousane brickwork and the lovely *tomettes*. Each home has two floors – downstairs light, lofty and open plan, upstairs cosy. Shower rooms are compact, the twin bedrooms are small but ideal for kids, and furnishings are plainly traditional: white walls, floral curtains, new sofas, brocante finds. At the back is a little courtyard in which you may barbecue a brochette in summer, then take a table into the colonnade and enjoy it. The helpful couple who live opposite welcome you with an aperitif and before you know it you're immersed in village life. Tillac has a bar/restaurant, a friendly shop (try the yeast-free *campaillou*) and a flower festival in spring.

sleeps	2 apartments each for 4.
rooms	Each gîte apartment: 1 double, 1 twin, 1 sofabed + cot; 1 shower room.
price	£230-£350 per week per apartment.
arrival	Saturday preferred.

Ann & Geoff Coombs
tel +44 (0)1275 474451
fax +44 (0)1275 472554
email geoff.coombs@btinternet.com
web www.holidaysintillac.com

Château de Garrevaques

Garrevaques, Tarn

Here you have all the advantages of the hotel (two restaurants, two pools, bar, spa, gardens and the gentle attention of the staff) yet you are wonderfully private. Your two-storey house next to the orangery – once the estate manager's quarters – is quarry tiled, rustically furnished (the odd piece on loan from the château), comfortable, roomy... perfect for families. There's a dishwasher in the kitchen, two rooms with satellite TV (one for the children, one for you), an office for workaholics, a terrace with a barbecue, central heating, an open fire. The grounds, too, are a good place to be, studded with old trees as grand as the château, and big shrubs for hide and seek. There's an easy mood here, in spite of the brand-new pool and spa – it's the sort of place where children leave their bikes lying around and no one will worry. There's a Wendy house, swings, slides and an old tennis court, too. Marie-Christine loves having people around and is unstoppable; she organises cookery courses, itineraries, even flying lessons next door. You are in good hands. *Babysitting available. Hotel also.*

sleeps	11-13.
rooms	6: 2 doubles, 2 twins, 1 single, 1 family room for 2-4; 2 bathrooms, 1 shower room, 2 separate wcs.
price	€1,000-€2,300 per week.

Marie-Christine Combes
tel +33 (0)5 63 75 04 54
fax +33 (0)5 63 70 26 44
email m.c.combes@wanadoo.fr
web www.garrevaques.com

Maison Puech Malou – The Cottage

Teillet, Tarn

In its own little garden, the prettiest gîte. You step straight into a whitewashed, pine-floored, open-plan living room with woodburning stove, cheerful red sofa, books and easy chairs. The galley kitchen has sun-yellow tiles, dishwasher, hob and oven. The bedroom is cosy and cool – white walls, antique pine, bed linen and towels to match, and a shower room en suite. You have your own terrace, with barbecue, to the rear, and, off the lovely courtyard, reached via an outside stair, an extra bedroom you can rent – ideal for grandparents, older children or anyone wanting some independence. Monique is charming, bakes her own bread (which she's happy to sell), keeps her own hens. There's nothing she likes better than to prepare dinner for a big friendly crowd: enjoy *table d'hôtes* in the garden, helped by good local wines. You're high on a sunny hill (Puech means 'hilltop' in the regional dialect, Malou is a type of apple) in a garden lush with lavender, hibiscus and shady corners. Teillet for simple shops is a five-minute drive, Albi and Toulouse are under an hour. *Pool may be available by arrangement. B&B also.*

sleeps	2-4 (12-14 with Farmhouse).
rooms	1 double; 1 shower room. Extra double & shower available with outside entrance.
price	€250-€350; €450-€650 with extra room. Prices per week.

Monique Moors

tel +33 (0)5 63 55 79 04

fax +33 (0)5 63 55 79 88

email info@maisonpuechmalou.com

web www.maisonpuechmalou.com

Maison Puech Malou – The Farmhouse

Teillet, Tarn

A beautiful restoration that is both immaculate and rustic. You arrive via a very pretty back road through wooded country at the creeper-clad 19th-century farmhouse. Inside, a graceful, calming home full of antiques, swimming in crisp light. Walls are exposed stone or white, the floors are terracotta, ceilings are beamed in heavy oak. The master suite has a generous bed and a romantic feel, a couple of bedrooms come with stripped pine boards, another, super-private, is entered by a staircase that rises from the covered courtyard where pots grow colour. The sitting room has two huge open fireplaces, the dining room a big rustic dining table and you eat under beams. The generous kitchen is delightfully designed. Good teak furniture stands on the terrace and the lawn runs down to the pool, there's a vegetable garden you are welcome to plunder and a marked trail that leads from the garden into the hills. Dutch Monique is friendly, hands-on, bakes her bread daily and offers excellent *table d'hôtes*. A gorgeous place. *Cooking holidays available. B&B also.*

sleeps	10 (12-14 with Cottage).
rooms	5: 2 doubles, 3 twins; 3 bathrooms, 1 shower room, 1 separate wc.
price	€1,350-€2,400; €1,800-€3,050 with cottage. Prices per week.

Monique Moors
tel +33 (0)5 63 55 79 04
fax +33 (0)5 63 55 79 88
email info@maisonpuechmalou.com
web www.maisonpuechmalou.com

Les Buis de St Martin

Marssac sur Tarn, Tarn

Madame is a dear and loves having people to stay. The 19th-century manor, in its park on the banks of the Tarn, has been her home for 25 years; the gîte is in its own wing. How relaxing to wander down to the water's edge in this quietly special place. Inside, a charming minimalism prevails. The ground floor is terracotta, the first floor polished wood; muslin blinds hang at deep-set windows, walls are whiter-than-white. Its contemporary look suits the light and lofty space: furniture is wood, wicker or aluminium, there's a clean-cut sofa, a big lemon-yellow bed with matching cushions, a few pictures, a simple rug. The galley-style kitchen and walk-in shower are chic and white; even the bedroom beam has been painted in Madame's favourite colour. Outside, your own garden with plunge pool and teak loungers. Little Marssac is delightful and has the basic shops, and Albi and hilltop Cordes are close by. The area is filled with restaurants serving duck in all its forms, cassoulet, ewe's and goat's cheeses; the wines of Gaillac, less well-known than the Bordeaux, are one of France's best-kept secrets. *B&B also.*

sleeps	2-4.
rooms	1 double, 1 sofabed in living room; 1 shower room, 1 separate wc.
price	€290-€1,000 (£190-£650) per week.

Jacqueline Romanet
tel +33 (0)5 63 55 41 23
fax +33 (0)5 63 53 49 65
email jean.romanet@wanadoo.fr
web perso.wanadoo.fr/les-buis-de-saint-martin/

La Croix de Fer

St Martin Laguepie, Tarn

The 18th-century barn has it all – stone walls, beamed ceilings, rolling views, ancient peace – but it is the way in which Jacqui and Francis have decorated that makes it sparkle. Step into a big, light living and kitchen area, with cream floor tiles, soft green sofa and chairs, a vase of dried flowers. On one side, the palest exposed-stone wall, on the other, white rough plaster; the space spills with light. The twin bedroom is soft lilac and lemon; Jacqui fell in love with the bed throws and linen, then designed the room around them. The double comes in cream and rose, with sofa, beams, a wrought-iron bed and windows on two walls with views of rolling hills. The house stands in ten acres of grass and woodland, the silence broken only by birdsong. There are deckchairs, loungers, shady trees and a delicious terrace by the pool from which to worship the sun. Jacqui has thought of just about everything: fluffy towels in very good bathrooms, a music centre, books and a beautifully equipped, wooden kitchen. You can hire bikes in the local village, go riding nearby or walk your socks off in the Aveyron valley.

sleeps	4.
rooms	2: 1 double, 1 twin; 1 bathroom, 1 shower room.
price	£300-£650 per week.
closed	November-April.

Jacqui & Francis Suckling
tel +33 (0)5 63 56 25 20
fax +33 (0)5 63 56 25 20
email suckling@wanadoo.fr

Château de Fourès

Campes/Cordes, Tarn

Swap stress for bliss at this gem of a cottage in the grounds of a 19th-century château. Come for a beautiful renovation, a tranquil setting in the foothills of Cordes and a secluded tennis court and pool which you have almost entirely to yourselves. The charming and hospitable owners live here – Madeleine from Paris and Swiss husband Peter – but are discreet. The also speak excellent English. Inside the cottage is steeped in charm: furnishings are good quality, furniture is country antique or new pine, there are pictures on open stone walls, vintage lamps suspended from beamed ceilings, cheerful checks and fresh flowers. And an open fire for winter. You eat at a round table in the bright, light corner kitchen that is beautifully equipped, or outside in your own delightful courtyard garden. And the grounds and flowering gardens are yours to share. Relax by the lily ponds, set off for lively Cordes, a mile away, or soak up the peace and the woodland views from your own roof terrace. Unbeatable value and perfect for two or a family with children.

sleeps	2-4.
rooms	1 double + 2 pull-out beds in sitting room; 1 shower room.
price	€600-€900 per week.
closed	November-April.

Madeleine Camenzind-Acory

tel +33 (0)5 63 56 13 55
fax +33 (0)5 63 56 13 55
email camenzind@wanadoo.fr

Puech Blanc – Le Duras & Le Syrah

Fayssac, Tarn

Wholly delightful. Ian and Andrea love it here and want their guests to have a memorable, stress-free holiday. And their welcoming, laid-back attitude is reflected in the way they have tackled the conversion of two old outbuildings next to their farmhouse. Simple, well thought-out and pleasing, the gîtes, named after local grape varieties, are engaging places to stay. Le Duras is in essence one generous living room, with exposed stone walls, a sofabed and French windows opening to a private terrace with views of rolling vines. Above is a prettily-railed mezzanine with a double bed and more views. Le Syrah, reached via an outside staircase to the first floor, has open-plan, studio-style accommodation. This large space has been cleverly planned and the bed prettily screened by muslin curtains. Both gites have well-equipped galley kitchens and good bathrooms. Andrea and Ian will happily provide cots and highchairs as required (they have two youngsters of their own) as well as new-laid eggs from their hens and unsprayed fruit from their trees. Local villages and shops are a ten-minute drive away.

sleeps	Le Duras 2-4. Le Syrah 2.
rooms	Le Duras: 1 double, sofabed downstairs; 1 bathroom. Le Syrah: 1 double; 1 bathroom.
price	£225-£425 per week.

Andrea & Ian Sutherland

tel +33 (0)5 63 57 54 14
fax +33 (0)5 63 57 54 14
email info@puechblanc.com
web www.puechblanc.com

Domaine de Villeneuve

Villeneuve sur Vère, Tarn

A *maison de maître*, a sublime house set in private parkland, has ravishing views across meadows to an ancient church steeple; if you're lucky bells will chime. A place to come and hole up for a week in blissful isolation. The pool is flanked by rampant greenery with a rose pergola to one side, the terrace is sail-shaded with long views across open country. Inside, a sweeping wooden staircase, an enormous stone fireplace, oak and beamed ceilings and a *fleur-de-lys* tiled floor; the whole house swims in light. Mike, a collector, has a good eye. Acquisitions include an antique pram, a restored water trough, church pews and antique baskets. Upstairs, large airy bedrooms have voile curtains and wooden floors. One room has a marble fireplace, another a canopied wooden bed, and the room on the ground floor has floor-to-ceiling windows opening to the garden. Expect unremitting comfort: deep sofas, period furniture and old rugs. French windows lead from the well-equipped kitchen to a terrace that runs along two sides of the house. The medieval towns of Albi and Cordes are close by.

sleeps	12.
rooms	6: 4 doubles, 2 twins; 4 bathrooms.
price	£975-£1,750 per week.
arrival	Sunday.

Mike Simler

tel +33 (0)5 63 56 01 74

email mike.simler@wanadoo.fr

web www.mikesimler.com

Maraval

Cordes sur Ciel, Tarn

There's a feeling of remoteness here, although Cordes is no distance at all; only birdsong and the stream flowing beneath the house tickle the peace. Maraval stands at the end of a long, secret country lane, an ancient farmhouse in 100 magical acres of woodland, cliffs and pasture. Behind, at the head of the valley, trees cluster steeply round the lawned garden and the lovely pool. The house itself is full of original features – massive beams, uneven floors, a creaky, eccentric staircase – and has white-painted walls and stunning views. Books, pictures, corner sofas and rugs make the split-level sitting room particularly inviting. The kitchen, too, is a delight, with a vast open fireplace (and logs for cool evenings), an ancient farmhouse table, blue and white tiles and an armoire stuffed with crocks and glassware. Outside is a wonderful covered dining terrace. The large, pretty bedrooms are carpeted and furnished with rural antiques and comfortable beds; one bedroom suite is on the ground floor with French windows onto the terrace; the other two are upstairs with the second bathroom.

sleeps	6.
rooms	3: 2 doubles, 1 twin; 2 bathrooms.
price	£700-£995 per week.
arrival	Sunday.
closed	November-April.

Mike Simler
tel +33 (0)5 63 56 01 74
email mike.simler@wanadoo.fr
web www.mikesimler.com

La Colombe

Donnazac, Tarn

There's a homely, welcoming feel to this beautifully restored stone house. Built on the edge of a vineyard-wrapped hamlet, it has rooms on three floors (and lots of stairs). The front door takes you straight into a beamed kitchen – a warm, glorious mix of old and new, with a Rayburn, big bleached pine table and comfortable sofa, as well as all mod cons. A small corridor leads to a summer dining room, where French windows open onto the terrace. Up a flight of stairs from the kitchen is the main sitting room, overlooking the walled, secluded garden and new, lavender-fringed pool beyond. It's a charming, low-ceilinged room in cream and green with the palest beams. There are two bedrooms on this floor, each with a bathroom, and two on the floor above. All are big, comfortable, full of light and character; the bathrooms, too, are roomy and cheerful with rugs and rattan chairs. The bustling medieval hilltop town of Cordes, which has a *son-et-lumière* and lots of summer festivals, is a ten-minute drive; Albi is not much further, with its fortified cathedral and Toulouse-Lautrec museum.

sleeps	8.
rooms	4: 2 doubles, 2 twins; 3 bathrooms.
price	£800-£1,450 per week.
arrival	Friday.

Mike Simler
tel +33 (0)5 63 56 01 74
email mike.simler@wanadoo.fr
web www.mikesimler.com

Couxe

Vieux, Tarn

This shimmering white-stone house stands on high ground. You can't miss it as you approach: sunlight bounces off the walls. Inside, a temple to the colour white, be it the walls, the handmade kitchen units, the painted beams or the stone that flanks the glimmering pool. It is unremittingly luxurious and contemporary. The enormous kitchen/dining room is full of the latest top-of-the-range equipment, cabinets are fronted with glass, framed black-and-white photographs hang on the wall. Bedrooms are big, flood with light, have white voile curtains and terracotta floors. Baths and power showers are immaculate... one bathroom is big enough for its own table and chairs (white, of course). Everything has been designed with a cool contemporary crispness. There's discreet up-lighting, sisal matting, modern prints on the walls and central heating for winter. Seek refuge from the sun on the covered terrace, or sunbathe by the pool on teak loungers. You are on the edge of a pretty village with a 14th-century church, and the views are stunning. Shops and restaurants are a ten-minute drive.

sleeps	12.
rooms	6: 3 doubles, 3 twins; 4 bath/shower rooms.
price	£1,100-£2,200 per week.
arrival	Friday.

	Mike Simler
tel	+33 (0)5 63 56 01 74
email	mike.simler@wanadoo.fr
web	www.mikesimler.com

La Bourth

Vieux, Tarn

Gaze from the fountain at the mesmerising views, doze by the pool or take your book and a glass of something to the shady breakfast terrace. So much space, so many rolling views of vineyards – the best wine in the Gaillac area; you could lose the rest of your party and only meet at mealtimes. This handsome, prettily shuttered *maison de maître* is full of light and cool with space. Rooms are uncluttered yet comfortable, antique-shop finds mixing with contemporary lighting and sofas to show off the richness of the original features – wide spiral staircase, beams, wood and terracotta floors. Bedrooms are restful with creamy walls, traditional rugs on polished floors, walk-in dressing rooms, and antique washstands and mirrors in the bathrooms. Children will love the quirkily beamed attic rooms. Visit historic Cordes or St Antonin, go wine tasting or spend the day at home, playing games on the sweeping lawns. Cooking dinner is fun in the big, farmhouse style kitchen. More fun is eating it in the huge, three arched, open barn. Lunches will be long, suppers will drift into dawn.

sleeps	8.
rooms	4: 2 doubles, 2 twins; 3 bathrooms, 1 separate wc.
price	£825-£1,500 per week.
arrival	Friday.

Mike Simler

tel +33 (0)5 63 56 01 74

email mike.simler@wanadoo.fr

web www.mikesimler.com

Pechingorp

Castlenau de Montmiral, Tarn

The large stone farmhouse set in three and a half acres is reached by a small country track and has no close neighbours – peace and quiet are assured. You are surrounded by vines and open farmland, with the bastide village of Castlenau de Montmiral framed on top of the hill; floodlit at night, it's a magical sight. Pull up at a gravelled courtyard where stone steps on one side lead to a wonderful covered terrace – the hub of the place – with a huge table at which to dine, wine, play games, chat. Beyond, a trim lawn surrounds a big pool that gets day-long sun. Inside, good bedrooms, beamed ceilings, stone walls, wooden floors, powerful showers and a ceiling open to the rafters. Beds are comfy, walls are white, most rooms are light and airy, views are superb. It is an ideal property for two families as the house divides seamlessly into two (there are two rooms on one side, two on the other and both have their own sitting room and kitchen), so you won't feel on top of each other for a moment. Gaillac with its wine and market is 20 kilometres away, the village and all you need are up the hill.

sleeps	8.
rooms	4: 2 doubles, 2 twins; 4 bath/shower rooms.
price	£800-£1,450 per week.
closed	November-April.

	Mike Simler
tel	+33 (0)5 63 56 01 74
email	mike.simler@wanadoo.fr
web	www.mikesimler.com

Château de Mayragues

Castelnau de Montmiral, Tarn

Superlatives cannot describe this remarkable cottage in its château grounds. It has everything: history, vineyards, atmosphere. The château is 14th century and, with its overhanging balcony circling the upper storey, is an outstanding example of the region's fortified architecture. Its authentic eight-year restoration won charming Laurence and her husband Alan a national prize. Your home is, improbably, the château's old bakery; it is the prettiest place imaginable and has a south-facing terrace on which to relax with a glass of organic estate wine. It's cosy, light and simply but charmingly furnished – a mix of old and new. There's a living room with a wonderful contemporary kitchen at one end and an open stair to a tiny mezzanine with a single bed. The cool, roomy double has a blue and white theme with pretty checked curtains and new sisal on the floor; the shower room is excellent. Look out onto the 17th-century pigeonnier 'on legs'. Should you tire of being here, there's walking country all around and the medieval hilltop village of Castelnau de Montmiral is well worth a visit. *B&B also.*

sleeps	2-3.
rooms	2: 1 double, 1 mezzanine with single; 1 bathroom.
price	€350-€450 per week.

Alan & Laurence Geddes

tel +33 (0)5 63 33 94 08

fax +33 (0)5 63 33 98 10

email geddes@chateau-de-mayragues.com

web www.chateau-de-mayragues.com

La Croix du Sud – Sucre d'Orge & Pain d'Épices

Castelnau de Montmiral, Tarn

Barely have you arrived than your children will be heading for the boules, ping-pong, swings and slides. You, meanwhile, can lounge round the pool with its views of the Gaillac vineyards and the bastide town of Castelnau de Montmiral. Two next-door gîtes, created from a 15th-century stone barn, and B&Bers across the courtyard, ensure instant friends. Catherine's grandchildren might also join in the fun – but don't worry, there are private terraces for peaceful naps and mealtimes too. Inside, all is light, space and simplicity. Stone walls, creamy plaster, beams, terracotta tiles and wooden floors mix with bright but unfussy modern furniture and lighting. Downstairs is open plan with an exceptionally well-equipped kitchen. Upstairs, bedrooms are cool and uncluttered and bathrooms crisp with walk-in showers. Browse the local markets, visit Albi with its cathedral and Toulouse-Lautrec museum, or just enjoy the pool and grounds. There's bags of space and ex-Air France hostess Catherine (perfect English) creates a great family atmosphere. Meals, too, if you're too lazy to cook. *B&B also.*

sleeps	Sucre d'Orge 6. Pain d'Épices 4.
rooms	Sucre d'Orge: 2 doubles, 1 twin; 2 bathrooms. Pain d'Épices: 1 double, 1 twin; 1 bathroom.
price	Sucre d'Orge €390-€920. Pain d'Épices €300-€790. Prices per week.

Catherine Sordoillet
tel +33 (0)5 63 33 18 46
fax +33 (0)5 63 33 18 46
email catherine@la-croix-du-sud.com
web www.la-croix-du-sud.com

Enrouzié

Salvagnac, Tarn

This really is a home from home: the owners of the old farmhouse divide their time between the nearby bastide town of Salvagnac and here. The character of the rooms reflects Nuala's sunny personality and the overall impression is one of friendly comfort and space. There are beautiful rafters in every room, new terracotta floors downstairs, stripped pine up, and the dreamy farmhouse kitchen is brilliantly equipped, with stacks of cookery books and lovely country crocks; the owner has quite a collection. You may help yourself to provisions, then replace them before you go. Furniture – some old, some modern – is country style, the bed linen is pretty and there are good prints and pictures on the walls. And masses of space outside as well as in: the fenced garden is child-friendly, with even a lock to the pool area. There's also a handy summer kitchen, so you can lunch out here with ease – or just lounge with a cool drink. You have plenty of shops and restaurants close by... and the deep shade of the plum tree for outdoor dining in front of the house.

sleeps	8-10.
rooms	4: 1 double with wc, 1 twin with wc, 2 family rooms for 3; 2 bathrooms, 1 shower room.
price	€1,250-€2,350 (£875-£1,650) per week.
closed	October-April.

Nuala O'Neill
tel +33 (0)5 63 40 50 05
email m.scott@wanadoo.fr

Combenègre

Ste Cécile du Cayrou, Tarn

Anticipation rises as the small, unmade road winds its way through vineyards and gorgeous countryside. At the end: Combenègre, a beautifully proportioned 18th-century farmhouse in five hectares. To one side, in its own garden and of the same rosy stone, is your gîte. Climb the outside stairs to its vast first-floor terrace and take in the splendour of the views... Inside, a light-filled, open-plan room, beautifully designed, elegantly furnished. The uncluttered sitting area has deep, comfortable chairs, watercolours, rugs, books and a cosy woodburner for winter; the kitchen/dining space is generously equipped and charming. Wooden stairs lead to a fresh, airy twin bedroom and bathroom; white walls, stripped wooden floors and soft pastel fabrics create a restful air. The double en suite bedroom is equally lovely. The charm spills over outside – into the lovely garden and the Roman-style courtyard with fountain and heated, saltwater pool. Kirk and Sally have already made Combenègre their own, and their friendliness and enthusiasm are infectious. Your nearest restaurant is a five-minute drive. *B&B also.*

sleeps	4.
rooms	2: 1 double, 1 twin; 1 bathroom, 1 shower room.
price	£235-£655 per week.

Kirk & Sally Ritchie
tel +33 (0)5 63 33 11 89
fax +33 (0)5 63 57 40 48
email contact@verevalley.com
web www.verevalley.com

Rouyre – Braucol & Mauzac

Ste Cécile du Cayrou, Tarn

Golden boulders contrast with the springy turf surrounding this low, 18th-century stone farmhouse and its two attached gîtes. The terracotta roofs are deliciously mottled and there are far-reaching views over vineyards, sunflowers and corn. The houses have been named after a local variety of grape – Braucol and Mauzac – and have been imaginatively converted from an outbuilding. Open-plan interiors, walls of cream-painted plaster or stone, rugs on wooden floors: a light, airy feel. The kitchen areas are lavishly equipped, the living spaces bright and inviting, the sparkling bathrooms have little bottles of goodies. (Brian and Sandra-Anne owned a top hotel in the Cotswolds and know how to spoil.) Braucol has three upstairs bedrooms, one with stunning views, two looking over a wooden balustrade to the living area. Heavy curtains to ensure privacy. Mauzac's double bedroom is on the ground floor; the twin is reached by a solid pine staircase. Each gîte has its own decked terrace with table and chairs, as well as use of the wonderful curved, deep pool. *Children over nine welcome.*

sleeps	Braucol 6. Mauzac 4.
rooms	Braucol: 2 doubles, 1 twin; 1 bathroom, 1 shower room. Mauzac: 1 twin, 1 double; 1 bathroom.
price	Braucol £275-£795. Mauzac £240-£695. Prices per week.

Brian & Sandra-Anne Evans

tel	+33 (0)5 63 40 48 24
email	contact@tarnprofonde.com
web	www.tarnprofonde.com

La Montarnie

Lescure Jaoul, Aveyron

A sleepy hamlet – the entire village is a farm – though a handsome young baker passes through twice a week to peddle his wares. It's postcard-pretty: cattle graze, birds sing, there are orchids in the meadows in spring. Relax on the wooden swing-seat in the shade of the walnut tree in your walled, suntrap garden; spot the wagtails nesting in the barn wall. The stone house, dated 1860, was once a barn and stands engulfed by a sea of greenery and wild flowers. It's a rustic little homestead place in a warm, contemporary style. Bedrooms are light and delightful, cool in summer and with good views onto the garden. Downstairs: wicker dining chairs, a comfortable new cream sofa, CDs, books, an open fire (central heating, too). Baskets hang from beams and you eat at a long pine table with wooden church pews resting against stone walls. Rent bikes in nearby Najac, one of the loveliest old towns in the northern Cathar country. Fish, canoe, swim in the river, or head for historic Rodez and Albi. This is simple, rural France with few tourists, especially in winter.

sleeps	4.
rooms	2: 1 double, 1 twin; 1 bathroom, 1 shower room, 2 separate wcs.
price	€360-€470 per week.
arrival	Sunday but flexible.

Sarah & Charles Drury
tel +44 (0)1981 550235
fax +44 (0)1981 550235
email montarnie@amserve.com
web www.lamontarnie.com

Le Ran

La Salvetat Peyrales, Aveyron

Horses and cattle grazing next door, higgledy-piggledy outbuildings, rolling farmland: it's peaceful, rural, remote. Rescued from neglect by the English owners, the rambling farmhouse is filled with an easy-going mix of country French antiques and Middle Eastern furnishings (they spent years in Oman). The hub of the family-friendly house is, quite rightly, the kitchen – all hand-crafted units, old and friendly sofa, scrubbed table for lingering meals. Kids can spread out in the TV room while you can relax in the lived-in chic lounge with its creamy colours, rugs and wood-burning stove. Bedrooms range over two floors, all large, comfortable and with a relaxed, understated style; country furnishings mix with Malaysian bedheads, Oman prints and oriental rugs. There's a kids' bedroom tucked away off the family room, while stylish bathrooms have great showers and – in one – a claw-foot bath. A fine choice for lively friends or two families with boisterous kids. Enjoy the pool and garden, dine on the terrace. The neighbours will look after you, even cook a meal, and it's a five-minute drive to the local shops.

sleeps	10-13.
rooms	5: 3 doubles, 1 triple, 1 family room; 2 shower rooms, 1 bathroom.
price	£750-£2,000 per week.
arrival	Saturday but flexible out of season.

Yasmina & Aldwin Wight
tel +44 (0)7900 49 3338
fax +44 (0)207 2294477
email yasminawight@aol.com

La Vieille Grange

Salles la Source, Aveyron

Thank heavens there are still villages like this in France: utterly unspoilt. Indeed, it will help if you speak some French as you are unlikely to encounter another Englander. The place is so tiny there isn't a shop or café in sight – but... some excellent mobile shops pass through several times a week and Marcillac, with plenty to offer, is a 10-minute drive. La Vieille Grange is the Woolston family's second home – not just a rental property – and has a delightfully personal feel. Tall, stone-sturdy and slender, it has an endearingly steep roof. Solid steps lead up via a private terrace (ideal for alfresco meals) to the front door; inside is an airy, welcoming living space – an inglenook fireplace, attractive rugs, antique and modern country furniture, books, magazines and an excellent galley kitchen. A lovely staircase curves up to three large, light bedrooms, comfortable with good mattresses and linen. This isn't just a summer house: central heating and a woodburner mean that it's snug all year round. And the Aveyron is an area you'll be reluctant to leave.

sleeps	6.
rooms	3: 2 doubles, 1 twin; 1 shower room, 1 separate wc.
price	£275-£400 per week.

Susan Woolston

tel +44 (0)1608 652664

fax +44 (0)1608 652668

email susanannwoolston@aol.com

web www.lavieillegrange.co.uk

photo corel images

languedoc – roussillon

El Pinyol d'Oliva

Ile sur Têt, Pyrénées-Orientales

In March the valley is a sea of blossom: the little walled town is the peach capital of France. Views sweep from your roof terrace to the streets below and the snowy peaks of the Canigou beyond. The old house sits on a small square, a stone's throw from the church, and its large, luminous rooms glow with good taste. Whitewashed walls rub shoulders with bare Catalan stonework, beams are high, floors terracotta and the entrance has a hand-set pebble floor. Cushions and curtains give bright bursts of colour, there's art on the walls and one of the shower rooms is triangular – the whole house vibrates with light and originality. On the ground floor is a studio that can be let individually; slip out early for croissants from your private door. Up a winding stair to a rustic-chic kitchen and a farmhouse table that seats 12; original walnut doors lead to a bedroom at either end. Then up to a sitting room with sofas and books and a bedroom with sloping rafters. Perpignan is a 15-minute drive, the airport 20, and you are in Spain within half an hour. *Cooking courses & walking tours in the offing. B&B option available.*

sleeps	8-10.
rooms	4: 1 double, 3 twins/doubles; 2 bathrooms, 2 shower rooms.
price	€1,400-€2,100 per week.

Anne Guthrie
tel +33 (0)4 68 84 04 17
email web-enquiry@elpinyoldoliva.com
web www.elpinyoldoliva.com

Domaine de Sicard

Ribouisse, Aude

Heaven for nature lovers: in spring you hear nightingales. The farmhouse stands in 25 acres of woods and pasture, the Pyrenees lie at your door. The Van Vliets abandoned successful careers in Holland to find a stress-free environment in which to bring up their daughter; she's now left home, but they still look after cats and a horse called Stix. Wout devotes much of his time to drawing and painting. The charming and dynamic couple have renovated this ancient farmhouse stone by stone and turned one half of it into a holiday cottage. On summer days you can snooze in the garden among lilac trees, lavender and roses, then have lunch on your private terrace. The house is immaculate and there's an exquisite new wood-beamed ceiling in the living room. Furnishings are modest but comfortable in authentic 1960s style; bedrooms have wonderful views of the gardens and the mountains. The unmissable medieval towns of Mirepoix and Carcassonne are nearby, and there's horse riding, too. Great value.

sleeps	4.
rooms	2: 1 double, 1 twin; 1 shower room.
price	€259-€434 per week.

	Wout Van Vliet
tel	+33 (0)4 68 60 50 66
fax	+33 (0)4 68 60 50 66
email	domainesicard@hotmail.com

La Maison d'Oc

Villemoustaussou, Aude

One visitor called this small, three-storey house of delights "a nest for lovers". The perfectly restored gamekeeper's cottage has a private walled gravel courtyard, attractive with flowers, teak chairs, stone barbecue and a splash pool; relax here with a glass of fruity Minervois after a day exploring medieval Carcassone or the Canal du Midi. Or swim in the pool under the spreading cedar. A stable door leads directly into your kitchen/living room; it may feel on the small side for four but it is very attractively furnished in whites and blues and has a cleverly designed corner kitchen. There's a brilliant cooker with a small dishwasher underneath, a washing machine and a dryer – all sparkling new – and a traditional sink. Upstairs, a pretty mosaic frieze surrounds the gleaming white marble tiles of the generous shower room. The main bedroom on the second floor is indeed a romantic resting place; orange and yellow tones glow warmly next to mahogany, coconut matting and bamboo. You have plenty of storage space, and sweeping vineyard views. Gorgeous. *B&B also.*

sleeps	4.
rooms	2: 1 double, 1 twin; 1 shower room.
price	€650-€1,100 per week.

Christophe & Catherine Pariset

tel +33 (0)4 68 77 00 68

fax +33 (0)4 68 77 01 68

email cpariset@trapel.com

web www.trapel.com

Le Relais Occitan – Lo Barralier

Marseillette, Aude

This fabulous old winery, with its giant oak vats – one now a library! – antique tools and buildings that go back 300 years has been turned into four holiday cottages by Anita and Jean Louis. It's been a labour of love, but labours of love are nothing unusual for this interesting Franco-Italian couple. Both writers and journalists – their passions history and poetry – they are as likely to discuss troubadour verse as 19th-century winemaking techniques over your welcoming aperitif. Surrounded by sunflowers and vines, all the cottages here – once the homes of the families working on the vineyard – have been refurbished with a rustic simplicity. Lo Barralier, once inhabited by the barrel-maker, is the oldest and smallest cottage. Within its simple living room is a tiny kitchen with a Fifties feel; a Catalan staircase leads up to a beamed bedroom for three, a second sitting room and a small roof terrace with shimmering views. A huge covered barbecue area with a wood-burning oven for homemade pizza is yours to share; on Sundays there are pizza and wine parties, hugely popular with guests. *B&B also.*

sleeps	2-4.
rooms	1 family room for 3, 1 double sofabed; 1 shower room.
price	€300-€440 per week.

Jean Louis Cousin & Anita Canonica

tel +33 (0)4 68 79 12 67
fax +33 (0)4 68 79 12 67
email j-l.cousin@wanadoo.fr
web perso.wanadoo.fr/relais.occitan/

Le Relais Occitan – Lo Podaire

Marseillette, Aude

History, wine and culture are what Le Relais Occitan is about. It's a delightful enterprise run by delightful people, with an orchard and vegetable garden you may help yourself to, a circular above-ground pool for the children under the trees and loungers for you. Lo Podaire, the old vine-cutter's house, has a walnut staircase and polished wooden floors, and is decorated with various objects picked up by Anita during her travels to distant lands. Sip a glass of the domaine's extremely drinkable wine and soak up the views from the terrace of your little bedroom on the second floor; lunch and dinner can be enjoyed on the bigger terrace in front. There are bikes to borrow, aromatherapy steam baths in the former wine tank and cruises on the peaceful green waters of the Canal du Midi: Jean Louis' houseboat departs every Wednesday. All these treats are on the house. Further afield are the history-laden Cathar castles and the medieval fairytale city of Carcassonne, perched above the Aude, is a short drive. *B&B also.*

sleeps	2-4.
rooms	1 double (+ sofabed for children); 1 bathroom, 1 separate wc.
price	€365-€560 per week.

Jean Louis Cousin & Anita Canonica

tel +33 (0)4 68 79 12 67

fax +33 (0)4 68 79 12 67

email j-l.cousin@wanadoo.fr

web perso.wanadoo.fr/relais.occitan

Paradix – Apartment One

Nissan lez Ensérune, Hérault

The handsome gateway is 19th century but the interiors are resolutely modern: old and new coexist effortlessly in this collection of four apartments (see next entry). This was once the *maison de maître* of a wine merchant and vines sweep in every direction. The stables and outbuildings have been imaginatively transformed by architect Colin and his Swiss wife, Susanna; they once ran an auberge in Tuscany, now they live here. Apartments have two storeys and a small patio garden; the rest – lawns, shady spots, chlorine-free pool – are to share. Inside: a minimalist look with the occasional cushion or Matisse print in colourful contrast to perfect white walls and pale terracotta floors; there's light, space, clean lines. Apartment One, the biggest, sleeping four, has an immaculate kitchen with every mod con, a large sitting/dining room with space in which to sit and read, and views to the lovely jasmine- and oleander-tumbled gardens that keep each apartment private. A yellow spiral staircase leads to luxurious but stylishly simple bedrooms, with beds dressed in fine white linen. *Shared laundry. See opposite.*

sleeps	4.
rooms	2 doubles; 1 shower room.
price	€850-€1,050 per week.

Susanna, Colin & Yvonne Glennie

tel	+33 (0)4 67 37 63 28
fax	+33 (0)4 67 37 63 72
email	glennieauparadix@wanadoo.fr
web	www.glennieauparadix.com

Paradix – Apartments Two, Three, Four

Nissan lez Ensérune, Hérault

You can tell from the beautiful blue and white kitchens that Colin Glennie was once a professional chef: they're so well equipped that the most reluctant cook will be inspired. All is perfection in these apartments, the interiors a serene symphony of light woods and natural fabrics. Study, read or relax in the large, light sitting/dining rooms; the lighting is excellent and central heating keeps you cosy in winter. In summer, swim in the delicious pool, read under the plane trees, or stroll among the roses and oleander in the communal garden. Or set off for Béziers (don't miss the riotous four-day *feria* in August), the Oppidum d'Ensérune (the nearby site of a 1,600-year-old Gallo-Roman settlement) and the Canal du Midi with its colourful barges. If you want a cheaper option, there's a first-floor studio for two, where striking blues and reds are offset by white walls. Come to Paradix if you're seeking a week of minimalist perfection in discreet and beautiful surroundings and a village you can walk to: Nissan is a lively little place with both market and shops. *Shared laundry.*

sleeps	3 apartments for 2.
rooms	3 apartments with 1 twin/double; 1 shower room each.
price	€580-€850 each per week.

Susanna, Colin & Yvonne Glennie
tel +33 (0)4 67 37 63 28
fax +33 (0)4 67 37 63 72
email glennieauparadix@wanadoo.fr
web www.glennieauparadix.com

Hameau de Cazo – La Vigne

St Chinian, Hérault

Simple and quietly elegant, this little pink village house will delight all who eschew fussiness and clutter. And the dreamy views of vineyards and the red-earthed hills of the Minervois clear the mind. In a small working hamlet, these three storeys have been beautifully restored by Dutch owners Monique and Reinoud, who live in a village nearby. Neat box trees flank the front door; inside, old patterned Languedocian floor tiles are enhanced by clean white walls and simple furniture. Dine round the large farmhouse table or among the almond trees and lavender in the walled, sunny garden. Upstairs to colourful bedspreads and curtains, russet-red hexagonal floor tiles and, in the double, an open fire. It's a charming little house and a well-equipped one: central heating and two open fires, TV and CDs, coffee-maker, dishwasher, washing machine. Walk in the vine-braided hills and the Mont Caroux, swim in peaceful rivers, drink in simple village life – preferably with a glass of St Chinian wine – while you watch sheep and goats lazily graze. *House for four to five next door.*

sleeps	4 + 1 child. (L'Amandier for 4-5 next door.)
rooms	2: 1 double, 1 twin & child's bed; 1 bathroom.
price	€320-€640 per week.

Monique & Reinoud Weggelaar-Degenaar

tel +33 (0)4 67 89 35 68
fax +33 (0)4 67 89 35 68
email monique@midimaison.com
web www.midimaison.com

Maison Hirondelles

Cazedarnes, Hérault

Wine and tennis, a winning combination. Antiques dealer Simon knows about the former, Meg is the local tennis champ and will whirl you around the courts. Fun and interesting, they moved to this wine-making village a few years ago, turning the 19th-century stone house into a two-bedroom B&B with gîte on top. With its own entrance you can be as private or as sociable as you like, share the pool and garden; retreat to your secluded courtyard and relax under the shady chestnut and Japanese maple. High sloping ceilings, plenty of windows and cool white walls give rooms space and light. The open-plan living area, comfortably but unfussily furnished, has French windows to a veranda with views of vineyards and hills. The kitchen is crisp and modern with good quality everything; bedrooms spoil you with antiques, pretty bedcovers, lovely views and spanking new bathrooms. With maps and bikes to borrow you can explore vineyards, hike in the Canal du Midi, browse markets and visit Carcassonne or the coast (only 15 minutes). Good eateries too – from posh to simple – in the local villages. *B&B also.*

sleeps	6.
rooms	3: 1 double, 2 twins/doubles; 3 bathrooms.
price	£300-£900 per week.

Meg & Simon Charles
tel +33 (0)4 67 38 21 68
fax +33 (0)4 67 38 21 68
email info@maison-hirondelles.com
web www.maison-hirondelles.com

Château de Grézan – Les Meneaux

Laurens, Hérault

Enter the battlemented gateway in the 'medieval' castle walls (those turrets are 19th-century follies), cross the cobbled yard and ascend the old stone stairs. Les Meneaux feels big and somehow modern – yards of lovely, wide, original floorboards, high rafters, immaculate white walls and a kitchen that is resolutely 21st-century. The flat is big, light and uncluttered, its paintwork picked out in blue, its sideboard filled with well-chosen china. It has country furnishings, a pretty blue double bedroom, a smaller, spring-flowered twin and a two beds up on the mezzanine beneath the roof window. Outside the castle walls is the swimming pool, beautifully protected by palm trees and bamboo, where you can relax and eat; beyond, a sea of vines shimmers beneath the great Languedoc sky. The garden, a superb mixture of wild and formal, has some fascinating native species and you can buy estate Faugères wine. Delightful Madame does B&B, there's a restaurant within the walls and a gîte in the tower, so others share the pool and the grounds. A lovely relaxed place with masses of space. *B&B also.*

sleeps	4-6.
rooms	3: 2 doubles/twins, 2 singles on mezzanine; 1 bathroom.
price	€515-€1,050 per week.
arrival	Saturday but flexible out of season.

Marie-France Lanson

tel	+33 (0)4 67 90 28 03
fax	+33 (0)4 67 90 05 03
email	chateau-grezan.lanson@wanadoo.fr
web	www.grezan.com

Château de Grézan – La Tour

Laurens, Hérault

La Tour is inside the castle gate, by the lovely pool, and its kitchen and bathroom fit within a circular tower – amazing. The antique-style oval windows and the 'arrow-slits' allow limited light from the outside world but with great beams, old stones and fresh paintwork this is more atmospheric than gloomy, and blessedly cool in high summer. A sofa and a couple of deep chairs still leave space on the tiled ground floor for a good country table and a great armoire full of crockery. To one side is the double bedroom with a soft-curtained bed and window opening onto the vines. The twin room, behind a curtain on the beamed mezzanine, gets air and light from the entrance hall and faces the old-fashioned bathroom in the tower at the other end of the gallery. The kitchen, off the living area below, is diminutive but fine for holiday cooking. A wildly romantic castle setting, a pool beneath the palms, sloping lawns and massive trees, a little restaurant in the ramparts, and holistic massage to tempt you. Madame Lanson, who is charming, has organised a fascinating wine trail for English speakers. *B&B also.*

sleeps	2-4.
rooms	2: 1 double, 1 twin on mezzanine; 1 bathroom.
price	€400-€820 per week.
arrival	Saturday but flexible out of season.

Marie-France Lanson

tel +33 (0)4 67 90 28 03

fax +33 (0)4 67 90 05 03

email chateau-grezan.lanson@wanadoo.fr

web www.grezan.com

Le Château – Le Pêcheur & Le Peintre

Colombières sur Orb, Hérault

There's some serious fishing here: the rivers Orb and Jaur both pass 700 metres from the château (Sébastien, a fishing guide, is on hand to advise) and there are two lakes at Salvetat. Hence the name of the gîte, Le Pêcheur. It is fresh with whitewashed walls and sand-blasted beams, comfortable with CD systems and satellite TV. Le Peintre is so-named because of the painting courses that your hosts organise several times a year. (They are proud of their jazz and blues evenings, too.) This whole area is a national park, and although you can confidently expect very little to happen, there is much to do. The local walking is some of the best in France and you can stride out from the château and follow paths into the hills that rise behind. In autumn there are mushrooms to pick, in spring, wild flowers bring a patchwork of colour and the scent of rosemary hangs in the air. There's riding, cycling, kayaking, wine-tasting... Those who wish to shun such energetic pursuits can always rustle up a picnic in the summer kitchen by the pool, or find a swimming hole in the river. A great find. *See opposite.*

sleeps	Le Pêcheur 5. Le Peintre 5.
rooms	Le Pêcheur: 2 doubles, 1 single; 1 bathroom. Le Peintre: 2 doubles, 1 single; 1 bathroom.
price	Le Pêcheur & Le Peintre €600-€1,100 each per week.

Thérèse Salavin & Chris Elliott
tel +33 (0)4 67 95 63 62
fax +33 (0)4 67 23 25 58
email christopher.elliott@club-internet.fr
web www.gitesdecharme.biz

Le Château – Le Randonneur & Le Musicien

Colombières sur Orb, Hérault

A rural wonderland, lazy Languedoc at its best. Blow with the wind and you will chance upon hilltop villages, mountain streams, ancient vineyards, the Canal du Midi. And where better to stay than in an immaculately turned-out gîte on a château estate that's been in the family for 200 years? You are welcomed in the lovely *salle d'acceuil*, where the olives were once pressed, by Thérèse, who has poured her heart into restoring the old cellars, wine press and outbuildings. Across the courtyard, four dwellings, each with its own private (though not secluded) terrace. Inside: brand new sofas on parquet or terracotta floors, perfectly equipped kitchens, double basins in most bathrooms, fresh bedrooms with cheerful fabrics and the odd antique. Thick walls keep you cool in summer and warm in winter – along with log fires and central heating. The gîtes are named after the activities of the region; one-storey Le Musicien, the most generously beamed, is brilliantly geared up for wheelchairs. Tiny Colombières has an *épicerie* and a summer snack bar in the Gorges.

sleeps	Le Randonneur 6. Le Musicien 4-5.
rooms	Le Randonneur: 1 double, 2 twins; 1 bathroom. Le Musicien: 2 twins; 1 bathroom. Extra bed available for living room.
price	Le Randonneur €550-€1,000. Le Musicien €700-€1,250. Prices per week.

Thérèse Salavin & Chris Elliott

tel	+33 (0)4 67 95 63 62
fax	+33 (0)4 67 23 25 58
email	christopher.elliott@club-internet.fr
web	www.gitesdecharme.biz

Hello

Prieuré Saint Martial – Three Gîtes & Three Studios

Alignan du Vent, Hérault

Two outdoor pools surrounded by vines and century-old oaks and pines, and a third inside under the rafters – bliss. There's a sauna and a fitness bench, ping-pong and bikes; the local village, with tennis and basic shops, is ten minutes by bike. Old timbers and stones have been restored by perfectionist owners to create the very best in open-plan living. La Chapelle, the old chapel, is understandably vaulted, Le Pigeonnier, the dovecote, is a honeymooners' dream. Again, furnishings are contemporary and natural; smooth plaster walls and old terracotta floors are offset by splashes of colour in cushion, rug or painted cupboard. Big-check sofas harmonise with gleaming country antiques, kitchens are perfectly equipped (dishwashers, coffee machines, state-of-the-art ovens), and there's a beautiful painting or two on every wall. A studio is available by the day for extra guests. Outside: a courtyard terrace for everyone, with a barbecue, and a garden that feels like a park, full of secret corners. And not a stick of plastic in sight.
Babysitting available. *See next two pages.*

sleeps	3 gîtes & 3 studios for 2.
rooms	1 double; 1 bathroom each.
price	€500-€1,000 per week each.
arrival	Saturday but flexible October-April.

Véronique de Colombe
tel +33 (0)4 67 24 96 51
fax +33 (0)4 67 24 99 49
email stmartial@aol.com
web www.stmartial.com

Prieuré Saint Martial – Préau & Ramonettage

Alignan du Vent, Hérault

The Prieuré is near-perfect in winter, with open fires, central heating and three gorgeous pools maintained all year. Each of the ten renovated buildings embraces a central courtyard fringed with oleander and bamboo and you have your own piece of terrace – this is a place where you can be as private or as sociable as you like. Ramonettage, with its thick old walls, was part of the old mill and, like all the gîtes, has a delightfully airy feel. All feels light, white and generous – and there's simply masses of space. Le Préau has a vast fireplace – you could hardly be cosier in winter – and two charming bedrooms with white beds, deep-red cushions and modern art in gilded frames. Véronique greets you with fresh flowers on arrival and will bring you bread and croissants if you ask her the night before; in summer, have breakfast on your terrace. The peace is a balm: just the distant hum of the tractor from the neighbouring vineyard and the chirping of birds. Rouse yourself to fish or swim in the Hérault Park – or head off for delicious sandy beaches, a half-hour drive. *Babysitting available.*

sleeps	Préau 4. Ramonettage 4.
rooms	Préau & Ramonettage: each 1 double, 1 twin; 1 bathroom.
price	€670-€1,350 per week each.
arrival	Saturday but flexible October-April.

Véronique de Colombe
tel +33 (0)4 67 24 96 51
fax +33 (0)4 67 24 99 49
email stmartial@aol.com
web www.stmartial.com

Prieuré Saint Martial – Galerie & Terrasse

Alignan du Vent, Hérault

Always a charming detail to catch the eye, always a personal touch. There are ten gîtes on this Languedocian estate, each one different, each a delight. The owners left Parisian lives for their southern slice of paradise and have been renovating and decorating these 18th-century farm buildings ever since. They have done an immaculate job. Hubert forages for paintings and antiques; Véronique takes care of the guests, and is charming. The gîtes for six have the most secluded terraces: that of Galerie catches the sun, north-facing Terrasse's will be deliciously cool. The lush rambling garden and the views belong to everyone. Le Galerie has a big kitchen with a vast fireplace and its own gallery sprinkled with art. Terrasse has an all-white kitchen and bedrooms with fresh-painted French windows; one has an elegant wrought-iron four-poster. Cheerful modern sofas, clean lines and carpeted bedrooms make for comfort without clutter. This is a peace-filled retreat, yet you are hardly in the sticks: Pézenas, with its narrow streets, shops, cafés and market, is a ten minute drive. *Babysitting available.*

sleeps	Galerie 6. Terrasse 5-6.
rooms	Galerie: 1 double, 2 twins; 1 bathroom. Terrasse: 1 double, 1 triple, 1 single; 1 bathroom.
price	€850-€1,700 per week each.
arrival	Saturday but flexible October-April.

Véronique de Colombe

tel	+33 (0)4 67 24 96 51
fax	+33 (0)4 67 24 99 49
email	stmartial@aol.com
web	www.stmartial.com

Domaine du Cayrat – Alicante, Ramonet, Sellerie

Cazouls d'Hérault, Hérault

It must seem like heaven to the de Barys, who retired here after stressful careers in Paris. The domaine has been in the family for generations and Jacques and Monique have energetically and carefully transformed their trio of barns into well-equipped gîtes. Each one is fresh, simple and immaculate, with space, finely thought-out detail and views over the surrounding vineyards. The furniture is a good mix of old and new and Monique has obviously enjoyed searching out the right pieces – a mirror wreathed in vine leaves, the perfect bedside lamp... French windows open from big white living rooms onto private terraces fringed with infant oleanders. Each terrace has its own teak furniture and a barbecue. Beyond is the grassy shade of the courtyard, dominated by a magnificent, century-old fig tree. Beyond again, hidden behind the courtyard wall, is the pool. This is a great place for families – the de Barys' own grandchildren put in an appearance from time to time – there's masses to do in the area, and if you're a Molière fan, his home town Pézenas is nearby. Fancy getting married here? You can. *B&B also.*

sleeps	Alicante 6. Ramonet 6. Sellerie 6.
rooms	Alicante: 1 double, 2 twins; 1 bathroom. Ramonet: 1 double, 2 twins, 1 bathroom. Sellerie: 1 double, 2 twins; 1 bathroom.
price	€650-€1,600 each per week.

	Monique de Bary
tel	+33 (0)4 67 25 15 44
fax	+33 (0)4 67 25 15 44
email	info@lecayrat.com
web	www.lecayrat.com

Domaine de Rives Près

St André de Sangonis, Hérault

Fling open the French windows and scent fills the air: lavender, thyme, rosemary, pine. The ground-floor rooms of this ice-cream-coloured farmhouse – vanilla walls, pistachio shutters – open directly to the garden. Beyond, the Languedoc vineyards roll into the hazy distance. This is an indoors/outdoors place with cool tiled rooms drifting into terraces, balconies, trees for shade and a secluded swimming pool. Inside, all is space, light and white: stone or plaster walls, beams, vast windows, a series of archways linking the downstairs rooms. Furnishings are uncluttered – all white linen sofas, modern paintings, fine bronze sculptures and well-loved family antiques. You get smart bathrooms, fresh bedrooms with glorious views and a smallish but well-equipped kitchen (plus another on the second floor). Toss a coin for the master suite with its balcony and window-ed veranda, or the garden bedroom with terrace, ideal for grandparents. Canoeing and sailing nearby, beaches within an hour, shops, restaurants and weekly market walkable – perfect for large families who love peace, luxury and style.

sleeps	9-10.
rooms	5: 2 doubles, 2 twins, 1 single + 1 folding bed; 4 bathrooms, 1 separate wc.
price	£750-£1,750 per week.

Brenda Kemp

tel	+33 (0)4 67 96 61 25
fax	+33 (0)4 67 96 61 25
email	bookings@rivespres.net
web	www.rivespres.net

La Maison Neuve & La Porche

Bréau et Salagosse, Gard

Interior designers Elizabeth and Paul bought this old farm in the wilds of the Cévennes after upping sticks with their children and selling their British home. The old ruin is now a delectable holiday home and the layout is fascinating, the rooms leading off a central hall and forming internal balconies on the upper floors. Elizabeth and Paul have tamed La Maison Neuve and its metre-thick walls, preserving original materials – floor and roof tiles and glorious timbers – with passionate respect. Creaking nail-studded doors, gnarled roof beams and blackened stone fireplaces are a perfect foil for simple, decorative wrought-iron beds hung with voile, and Elizabeth's fine paint pigments, applied with rags to create an exquisite look. And you want for nothing: kitchen mod cons, CD and radio, towels for the pool, even cot, highchair and buggy. La Porche, on the same site, is centrally heated and equally fine. Laze in the orchards, take a dip in your private pool; each gîte has one. In summer, there are Elizabeth's organic onions and raspberries to buy.

sleeps	La Maison Neuve 12. La Porche 4-5.
rooms	La Maison Neuve: 3 doubles, 3 twins; 1 bathroom, 2 shower rooms. La Porche: 1 double, 1 triple; 1 bathroom, 1 shower room.
price	La Maison Neuve €750-€2,200. La Porche: €500-€1,100. Prices per week.
arrival	Saturday but flexible during low season.

Elizabeth Adam & Paul Wellard
tel +33 (0)4 67 82 49 09
fax +33 (0)4 67 82 49 09
email betjeadam@aol.com
web www.ecoleisure.net

Mas de la Bousquette – Le Grenier

Lussan, Gard

Before you, meadows of silky, waving grass – a place for children to romp with the Forsters' affable dogs. This lovely *mas* was once a sheep and cattle farm: ancient stone buildings cluster round an entrancing courtyard, a cypress tree pushes through a gap in a hotchpotch of slanting roofs, goldfish glitter in a pool. The garden is big and open, with a willow tree beside a pond, a hammock and lazy chairs, plenty of shade. There's an old orchard too – peg out your washing among the rare-breed chickens, a couple of peacocks pecking round your feet. The two gîtes, separated by a long covered veranda, are equally fetching. In the old grain store – two storeys within the south-west tower – you get a lovely big split-level living area: rafters, creamy stone walls, a fresh modern décor. Bedrooms have large and comfortable beds, French windows open to a private terrace and there are ceiling fans for summer. The kitchen is perfectly equipped, there are bikes to borrow, and the gardens have a shared pool and a barbecue spot just for you. *Extra B&B room for two on request.*

sleeps	4-6.
rooms	2: 1 double, 1 twin + sofabed on mezzanine; 2 bathrooms.
price	€520-€1,450 per week.

Tim & Pippa Forster

tel	+33 (0)4 66 72 71 60
fax	+33 (0)4 66 72 71 58
email	mas-bousquette@wanadoo.fr
web	mas-bousquette.com

Rue du Château

Aigremont, Gard

Behind the arched blue door lies a restored 15th-century silk mill, its vaulted cellar rooms intact. It is an Aladdin's cave, an intoxicating mix of French, English, Moroccan and Indian treasures. Escape the blistering heat into this cool, calm space; the village is cooly perched in the foothills of the Cévennes and you are in the middle of it. No garden, but a peaceful gravelled courtyard with chairs for dozing, a barbecue, a fountain and a summer shower. Inside, your gaze drifts to mellow yellow-washed walls, tiles – the best of old and new – and lofty ceilings. The sitting room is cavernous but is cosy in wintertime: a wood-burning stove, William Morris-covered armchairs, comfy sofas, books, an upright piano. Arched doors lead from the well-equipped kitchen into the courtyard where you may eat. Up a floor and those lofty old silk rooms have magically become bedrooms, one with a dreamy Provençal mural behind the bed, another with a patchwork bedspread. History, big open fields and vineyards await – if you can leave your own little piece of heaven. *July-August: house for 6 with pool also available.*

sleeps	6.
rooms	3: 2 doubles, 1 twin; 3 shower rooms.
price	€450-€850 per week.
arrival	Friday but are flexible.

Caroline Nolder

tel +33 (0)4 66 24 44 43

mobile +44 (0)7977 425530

email carolinenolder@familynolder.com

web www.familynolder.com

Les Belles Pierres

Calvisson, Gard

Slip down a quiet, narrow street and seek out an oak door hiding in a handsome stone façade. Once inside, another surprise: a spiral stone staircase leading to an airy first-floor apartment. Perfect for a couple wanting peace, space and privacy. Part of an 11th-century monastery, added to in later years, the rooms have a cool, uncluttered grandeur; dressed stone or pale plaster walls, white tiled floors, huge windows; a vaulted ceiling in the dining room and a graceful archway to the salon. Furniture is elegant and sober. Eat inside amid candles, or outside on the shady terrace that opens off the kitchen. The thick-walled bedroom is a calming space with ancient fireplace and simple furnishings. There's a sofabed too, but the bathroom is not big so three might feel cramped on long stays. The owners, who weekend here from Paris, leave the key with a neighbour. Calvisson is a friendly little town with cafés and a Sunday food market and you are within easy reach of so much: good walking, the coast (40 minutes), the Camargue, the Route des Moulins and the stunning Pont du Gard.

sleeps	2-4.
rooms	1 double, sofabed in living room; 1 shower room.
price	€470-€705 per week.

	Laurent Conseil
tel	+33 (0)1 42 36 35 09
mobile	+33 (0)6 64 50 52 68
email	lconseil@wanadoo.fr
web	popkkorn.free.fr

Mas du Puech Long – Lavandins, Aubades & Cottages

Calvisson, Gard

Miniature ponies to fall in love with, horses to ride, slides, boules and bike trails, a communal pool, a pick-your-own organic garden, a Moroccan-tiled jacuzzi … this place is amazing. Pottery, silk-painting or mosaics are taught by a resident artist and a chef lets you in on the fine art of preparing a truffle or two. Sunday night is barbecue night and everyone is invited. Two gîtes are near the fine stone *mas* where they do B&B, the others are linked by a terrace a short stroll away. The interiors have a bohemian simplicity and an easy charm: a country corner cupboard, a painting or a poster, a good sofa or two. Small bedrooms have pretty white or toile de Jouy bedspreads and perhaps a wicker chair, kitchens are well-equipped, terraces have barbecues and views to the hills. Children find playmates, travel tips are exchanged, friendships are made and there's *table d'hôtes* in the dining area off the main courtyard – dip in and out as you wish. American Liesa is a mine of information on the prettiest villages – Sommières and Calvisson are close by – and the best antique markets, too. *B&B also.*

sleeps	Les Lavandins 4. Les Aubades 2-3. 3 cottages for 8.
price	€600-€1,000 for 2-4. €900-€1,600 for 8. Prices per week.

Mariette Fryns
tel +33 (0)4 66 63 89 44
fax +33 (0)4 66 63 89 44
email liesa@liesablond.com
web www.masdepuechlong.com

Rue du 4 Septembre – Two Apartments

Uzès, Gard

Glorious Uzès, the first Duchy of France, an architectural masterpiece – a town of towers, vaulted stone walkways and narrow streets. The Wars of Religion came but in the 17th century prosperity returned and magnificent houses such as this one were built in the grand style. Step in off the street and travel back a few hundred years. Here are vaulted limestone rooms, flagstone floors, a flurry of antiques, thick rich fabrics and genuine, old tapestries – one belonged to a duchess who fell on hard times. You have the choice of two apartments, rented separately or together. The one on the ground and first floors is the grandest and has a lovely terrace with olive trees, lavender, tables, chairs and barbecue; the second-floor apartment is reached via a private spiral stair. Both have magnificent old fireplaces and sophisticated bathrooms. The upstairs flat, is slightly less grand and has a simpler kitchen; it would be superb for a family. The market is a wonder of the Provençal world and it's on your doorstep – as are concerts, galleries, restaurants and delectable shops. *Secure parking a 5-minute walk.*

sleeps	Apartment 1: 4. Apartment 2: 4 + 1 child.
rooms	Apartment 1: 2 doubles; 1 bathroom, 1 shower, 1 sep. wc. Apartment 2: 1 double, 1 twin with child's bed; 1 bath, 1 shower, 1 sep. wc.
price	Apartment 1 £450-£600. Apartment 2 £320-£400. Prices per week.

Susie & David Nelson

tel +44 (0)20 7592 9388

email davidandsusienelson@btinternet.com

Hello

La Terre des Lauriers

Remoulins, Gard

The setting – six hectares of woodland stretching down to the bird-rich river – is breathtaking. Let the local canoe-hire people ferry you up the river, then float back home again via that marvel of Roman engineering, the Pont du Gard. These delightful owners have just moved here from Paris; Marianick draws, paints and makes sumptuous jams, Gérard has created a botanic trail down to the river. This 18th-century *bergerie* has been restored with minimalist elegance: the large, lofty, open-plan space, attracive with fine new furniture and yellow and white counter kitchen, is linked by a white metal staircase to mezzanine bedrooms upstairs. You share the huge grounds, pool and garden with B&B guests and those staying in another cottage but have your own terrace for dining, and views of the private vineyard. The wild and flowering surroundings are full of buzz and flutter, there's *table d'hôtes* once a week – book in advance and you're in for a treat – and a gym by the pool where you can work off any extra pounds gained in the area's fine restaurants. Magic for families. *B&B also.*

sleeps	4-6.
rooms	2: 1 double, 1 twin, 1 sofabed in living room; 1 bathroom, 1 separate wc.
price	€800-€1,000 per week.

Marianick & Gérard Langlois
tel +33 (0)4 66 37 19 45
fax +33 (0)4 66 37 19 45
email langlois@laterredeslauriers.com
web www.laterredeslauriers.com

Le Rocher Pointu

Aramon, Gard

It's easy to understand why André and Annie – whose ancestors were English – decided to cut their ties with Paris and move to this 150-year-old stone *bergerie*. Although bustling Avignon is just 15 minutes away, it's a haven of tranquillity here, utterly secluded at the end of a windy track through pine scrub. There's a field with a donkey in front and a vast thumb of rock behind, which gives the place its name. This is the furthest of four apartments recently added to the main house where the owners do B&B; you all share the grounds and the lovely decked pool above. Smart, small, delightfully compact, with old beams, Provençal tiles and some good antique furniture, your apartment has a tiny well-equipped kitchen off the dining/sitting room and a split-level bedroom with a single bed on the top level and a double below. Both kitchen and shower room are attractively tiled. Relax on the terrace among the olive trees and lavender, slip into the pool with its distant views of Mont Ventoux, watch the sun slide behind the mountains at night. *Shared laundry. B&B also.*

sleeps	2 + 1 child.
rooms	2: 1 double, 1 single on mezzanine; 1 shower room.
price	€520-€693 per week.

Annie & André Malek
tel +33 (0)4 66 57 41 87
fax +33 (0)4 66 57 03 78
email amk@rocherpointu.com
web www.rocherpointu.com

Les Bambous

Pujaut, Gard

This tiny, very special getaway for two is in the sort of unspoilt Provençal village where women still wash clothes in the village's stone *lavoir*. You are a short walk from the baker's for croissants – yet, unbelievably, 10 minutes from the centre of Avignon and the glorious Palais des Papes. Friendly, delightful Michèle and Joël, who look after B&B guests in their house next door, have done up this snug space beautifully and enhanced its exposed stone walls, beamed ceilings and terracotta floors. There's an old school desk, Joël's watercolours on the walls and Moroccan touches: they are a well-travelled pair. A ceramicist was commissioned to make the buttercup-coloured tiles in the kitchen area and the lovely navy and yellow tiles that decorate the shower room. Relax in your private garden under the shade of the horse chestnut, or set off to explore this fascinating area. And when you don't feel like cooking, book in at the main house and join the Rousseaus and their guests. *B&B also.*

sleeps	2.
rooms	1 double; 1 shower room.
price	€350-€380 per week.
arrival	Flexible.

Joël & Michèle Rousseau

tel	+33 (0)4 90 26 46 47
fax	+33 (0)4 90 26 46 47
email	rousseau.michele@wanadoo.fr
web	lesbambous.monsite.wanadoo.fr

Lou Rassado

Vallabrix, Gard

Lovingly polished floors, a hammock in the shade, a kitchen of creamy country pots; this is a cherished family house. Indeed, when Francis and his wife – a Red Cross worker and an artist – are not working abroad, this village farmhouse is their home. Added to over the years, it's a maze of staircases and different levels. The double-height main salon, with white stone fireplace, creamy sofas and colourful rugs, has a Moroccan feel. Two further salons are dotted with vibrant prints, sculptures and cushions; the dining room glows with ochre walls, mirrors and a long zinc-topped dining table; the Provençal kitchen is a delightful mix of rustic good looks and modern efficiency. Four bedrooms – one on a mezzanine level, two with their own staircases, a studio bedroom in the courtyard – are airy spaces of country furniture, colourful bed linen and pretty antiques. Plenty of big white bathrooms, too. Spend your days at music festivals, markets and vineyards; then return to the large walled garden with shady spots, rose arbour and plunge pool. All this, and a baker's van passing each day.

sleeps 8-10.
rooms 4 doubles; 3 bathrooms.
price €800-€1,500 per week.

Loïs & Francis Amar
tel +33 (0)4 66 03 44 39
email francisamar@lourassado.net
web www.lourassado.net

Haut Village

Vallabrix, Gard

It's not easy to photograph this stunning village house, sandwiched between the others of enchanting Vallabrix – but believe us, it is special. The old honey-coloured stones embrace a private courtyard and pool and there are countless delights: delicious views across the rooftops to distant hills, rural peace, Uzès close by and an interior among the best we've seen. It's been lovingly restored by its English owners, the stylish fabrics enhanced by old pine furniture and African *objets*. The L-shaped three-storey house has one bedroom off the courtyard, beautifully cool with its vaulted stone ceiling. On the first floor a second bedroom and a vast dining, sitting and kitchen area – sandstone walls, long pine table, comfy sofas, books – leading to a geranium-bright terrace. On the top level, two bedrooms with beautiful parquet or tiled floors, elegant white linen curtains, gorgeous bathrooms. Visit glorious Uzès with its Saturday market (and arrive early to catch a parking space); it is a celebration of everything southern, from sausages and snails to red peppers and Provençal prints.

sleeps	8.
rooms	4 twins/doubles; 3 bathrooms, 2 shower rooms, 1 separate wc, 1 poolside shower room & separate wc.
price	€2,393 (£1,500) per week.
closed	October-June.

Chris Hazell
tel +33 (0)4 66 37 45 79
fax +33 (0)4 66 37 14 78
email hazell.chris@wanadoo.fr

Hello

2 chemin de la Carcarie

Montaren, Gard

Arlette is the perfect hostess, friendly, interested and interesting – and cultured: her tortoises have Greek names. You'll meet them in the garden. Her little patch is the wonder of the house, and Arlette will happily walk you round, passing on the names of the plants and giving you the local gen. Views here take in the pretty village, which has a château. You are part of local life, yet close to Uzès, one of the most beautiful medieval towns in France (and where they filmed *Cyrano de Bergerac*). This 17th-century farmhouse is slightly shabby, but that is also its charm; if you want to sample French village life as the French live it, this is a good place to do so. Upstairs, a big bedroom sleeps four (two single beds are on a mezzanine), but the house is best for a couple and if you were going to share, you'd have to know each other well. Dried garden flowers hang from old beams in the dining room, but you eat on the terrace under a Provençal sun. Arlette lives in part of the house. You are private from her, but she is on hand to chat, advise, inform. No dishwasher, so bring your Marigolds.

sleeps	2-4.
rooms	2: 1 double with 1 twin on mezzanine; 1 bathroom.
price	€420-€580 per week.

Arlette Caccamo-Laniel
tel +33 (0)4 66 22 52 14
email alaniel@freesurf.fr

Maison des Cerises

St Marcel de Careiret, Gard

Come in May and pluck cherries from the tree for breakfast; in April, eat under the blossom. This village cottage seduces all. Britta, a German living in France, is a gifted artist with an eye for light, harmony and spotting the potential in bric-a-brac finds. She has restored the house with sympathy and skill – walls are stone or limewashed, floors warm terracotta, beams darkly aged, colours pure and natural. The downstairs bedroom, a creamy space of painted wooden furniture and pretty fabrics, opens to the small garden. Its bathroom is *Country-Living* perfect with a claw-foot bath. Another bedroom, with sparkling shower room, is tucked under the eaves. In between is the light-washed living room – elegantly simple with candlesticks and wine-dark sofa – and the rustic dining room/kitchen with pine dresser and thick, cream china. The living is easy here: step out to the baker's and the grocer's, basket in hand. Take the kids to the water park at Uzès, swim in the river Cèze, hunt for bargains in village markets, then return to your little garden, and feel at peace with the world.

sleeps	4 + cot.
rooms	2: 1 double, 1 twin/double; 1 bathroom, 1 shower room.
price	€450-€850 per week.

	Britta Brand
tel	+33 (0)4 66 63 89 40
fax	+44 (0)8701 205860
email	brittabrand@bigfoot.com
web	www.maison-des-cerises.com

Le Mas de Jasmin

Lussan, Gard

Music or videos to lull you to sleep; luxurious sheets to ensure sweet dreams; in the morning, a monsoon-like shower to prepare you for another day in this blissfully beautiful part of southern France. Julie and John, gentle, open, generous people who will share a four-course dinner with you in the evening should you wish, have spared no expense in making the farmhouse as perfect as possible. The dining/living room and kitchen on the first floor have a fresh, roomy feel, with sand-coloured stone floors and pastel-painted walls hung with prints and gilded mirrors; the west-facing veranda is a great spot for evening drinks. Bedrooms, all but one on the ground floor, all with their own entrance, have exposed stone or cool blue walls and tiled floors heated for winter. The painted furniture was decorated by an artist from Toulouse: dolphins on one of the bedheads, cast-iron baths prettily stencilled. Eat out on your private terrace or by the huge heated pool amid manicured lawns. Views sweep across pastures to the distant Cévennes and the sound of doves mingles with tinkling goats' bells.

sleeps	8.
rooms	4: 3 doubles, 1 twin; 4 bathrooms.
price	€400-€2,600 per week.

John & Julie Milligan
tel +33 (0)4 66 72 91 57
fax +33 (0)4 66 72 91 57
email Mjohn11947@aol.com

Hello

Mas de la Bousquette – Le Mûrier

Lussan, Gard

The ancient, rose-roofed *mas* rests at the foot of Huguenot village Lussan, perched high with a castle on its top. The countryside rolls out before you, the air is pure and the sun is golden – even in winter. In the north-west tower where silkworms were once reared is a charming little gîte, its balcony-terrace tucked beneath a glorious roof. Fresh and clean with inspired touches, it makes a romantic nest for two. Living room and kitchen are beautifully equipped and the bedroom has a delightful simplicity: white walls, *terre cuite* floor, antique iron and brass bed, muslin curtains. Pippa and Tim are warm, generous people and offer you everything: books, games, binoculars, fresh fruit, bowls of lavender, fresh bread outside the door, towels for the pool. Pippa loves cooking, gives you a free dinner on arrival and runs a little shop selling delectable homemade jams and new-laid eggs. This is southern France at its most peaceful, walking distance from an excellent restaurant, near lovely Uzès and not far from Avignon and Nîmes.
Extra B&B room for two on request.

sleeps	2-4.
rooms	1 double + sofabed; 1 bathroom.
price	€500-€1,150 per week.

Tim & Pippa Forster
tel +33 (0)4 66 72 71 60
fax +33 (0)4 66 72 71 58
email mas-bousquette@wanadoo.fr
web mas-bousquette.com

La Maison de Marie

Rochegude, Gard

The village clings to the hillside under the ruins of the château, the house stands just above. You park in the square below, then ascend – it's not far. And you arrive... to music, books and a south-west-facing terrace with views that stretch all the way to the Cévennes. It is a seductive, deeply peaceful place. This is also a house that feels it belongs; Marie comes here to meditate and write when there's no-one else around. Starting from the bottom up: the cellar, housing washing machine and bikes, then the kitchen/dining room with terrace. Up a circular wooden stair to a sitting room filled with sunshine and a shower room to the side; and the bedroom on a mezzanine under white-painted eaves. A country mood fills the kitchen, with its fresh walls, new terracotta floors, pleasant blue paintwork and gaily checked table; the most reluctant cook would happily put a meal together here. Marie teaches yoga, makes jam and leaves lavender soaps, goat's cheeses, organic wine and fresh flowers to welcome you. Perfect for a couple wishing to hike, bike and escape the world – for a short but magical while.

sleeps	2-3.
rooms	1 double, 1 sofabed in office; 1 shower room, 1 separate wc.
price	€480-€650 per week.

Robert & Marie Freslon

tel +33 (0)4 66 72 93 16
fax +33 (0)4 66 72 93 16
email chanu2@wanadoo.fr

Les Trémières

Fons sur Lussan, Gard

This little jewel of a house used to be the village bakery; upstairs, nurtured by the warmth from below, silkworms were bred to make the cloth for which the area was once famous. It sits just off the church square of this delightful village and is blissfully quiet. Relax in the cottage garden overlooking fields, play a tune on the piano and look forward to good swimming and canoeing on the river Cèze. You could also book yourself a yoga lesson with the owners Marie and Robert who live next door. This delightful Parisian couple had known the house for over 30 years – they used to come every summer – before settling for the Good Life. They've decorated gently, giving the gîte a homely rather than a stylish feel; furniture is a mix of antique and modern, there is an intriguing collection of antique irons and coffee grinders in the open-plan living and kitchen area and an original washing plank by the old stone fireplace. The carpeted double bedroom is in the attic and has a sloping pine-clad ceiling. Marie leaves homemade lavender soap, wine, flowers and other treats for your arrival. *B&B also.*

sleeps	4.
rooms	2: 1 double, 1 twin with separate entrance; 1 bathroom.
price	€480-€650 per week. €53 for two per night.

Robert & Marie Freslon

tel +33 (0)4 66 72 93 16

fax +33 (0)4 66 72 93 16

email chanu2@wanadoo.fr

L'Auzonnet

Les Mages, Gard

A magical place. One minute you're in an ordinary village street, the next you enter a cool dark stone tunnel and emerge into a sunlit, secret courtyard. Hydrangeas splash the walls with colour, a stone stairway leads up to the little gîte: enchanting. The kitchen/living area has delightful painted panelling, pine furniture and brightly coloured crockery. Up on the mezzanine is a Wedgwood-blue and white bedroom – light, pretty and open- plan – and a shower room decorated with mosaics. The private terrace overlooks the Auzonnet river but you're also welcome to make the most of the wonderful garden. Cross the courtyard, go through another arch and you find yourself at the top of lovely green terraces dropping down to a small pool and the river. Sit and watch and you may see the hunched form of a heron or glimpse the blue flash of a kingfisher. This is the edge of the Cévennes National Park and is utterly secluded and peaceful. Lucy and Duncan, who have recently bought the house, are completely taken with it all and relish the relaxed pace of life. *Unsuitable for young children or the infirm.*

sleeps	2-3.
rooms	1 double, 1 sofabed downstairs; 1 shower room.
price	€550-€750 (£350-£500) per week.

Lucy & Duncan Marshall
tel +33 (0)4 66 25 39 98
email lucy@auzonnet.com
web www.auzonnet.com

La Rouvière

Bonnevaux, Gard

Not for party animals! This secluded place is reached via a long and winding drive and just when you think you've arrived, there's further to go… but the beauty of the place suffuses your soul. The word 'rouvière' comes from the patois for 'oak' and the hillsides are full of them; chestnut trees too. No hint of civilisation to be seen: just the slate roofs of an old farmhouse in the valley below. Come in May and June for the wild flowers, in autumn for the trees, in summer for buzzing bees, cicadas and birds. This is almost a *hameau*, with the lovely old house, the barns and the terraces on many levels. Dining room, sitting room and kitchen drift into a terrace, there are two sofas, a fireplace that works, a round dining table, a polished old floor; easy to make this one's home. Grey-painted cupboards hide white plates in the well set-up kitchen and bedrooms have pine bedsteads and beams (a secret double room lies beyond the terrace). Outside are a pool with spa jets and a hammock under a fig tree: gaze on vast views and dream. The owners are not here but fine meals may be ordered from a friend.

sleeps	5.
rooms	3: 2 doubles, 1 single; 1 bathroom, 2 separate wcs.
price	€370-€900 per week.
closed	November-March.

Claude & Annette Jost
tel +33 (0)4 66 61 18 17
fax +33 (0)4 66 61 18 17
email claudejost@free.fr
web claudejost.free.fr

photo corel images

rhône valley – alps
provence – alps – riviera

La Ferme du Nant

La Chapelle d'Abondance, Haute-Savoie

In summer, you rent one or both of the floors and self-cater; in winter, you have one beautiful catered chalet. Floor to ceiling windows span the front of the old house pulling in the light; the views are pure Heidi. Downstairs is a cosily restored living area with a wonderful central fireplace, country dining table and big open kitchen. Upstairs, past a collection of ancient wooden sledges, are pine floors, halogen spotlights illuminating white walls, sand-blasted timbers, big blue sofas. Two bedrooms are on the mezzanine – fun for kids – and there's a long, rustic, south-facing balcony to catch the sun. Furniture is a mix of Savoyard and modern with the odd giant pop-art portrait to add a sparkle. Bathrooms are white with mosaics. A trap door leads to a DVD cellar, a sloping garden has been reshaped to take a terrace and heated pool (the old cheese store makes great changing rooms) and the village is a six-minute walk downhill. The owners live on the top floor with their labrador; Susie also owns a horse and the riding is wonderful. *Min. three nights & flexible departure dates in winter. B&B also.*

sleeps	12-16 (or 6-8 + 6-8).
rooms	Ground floor: 3 twins/doubles; 2 bathrooms, 1 shower room. First floor: 3 twins/doubles; 3 shower rooms. Extra beds available.
price	€840-€1,260 per floor (6-8 people) per week.
arrival	Saturday in summer, flexible in winter.

	Susie Ward
tel	+44 (0)1872 553055
	+33 (0)4 50 73 40 87
email	susie@susieward.com
web	www.susieward.com

Châlets de Philippe – Les Clarines & Le Marmotton

Chamonix, Haute-Savoie

Hard these days to find a *mazot* that hasn't been snapped up by a city dweller fulfilling a rural dream. It was 20 years ago that Philippe Courtines snapped up his: in the little village of Lavancher, at the end of a birdsung valley. Persuading the peasant farmer to sell to him – and not the Italian who was planning to ship it all to Italy – he had the old granary dismantled stone by stone, then re-built it. More weathered chalets were discovered and restored, and the rest is history. Philippe has created one of the loveliest little *hameaux* in the Alps, a terraced cluster of chalets that wrap themselves around a cosy mini-cinema, an exquisite steam bath and a woody dining room that seats 14 – you may book in a chef for a treat. In two-storey Les Clarines, reclaimed flagged floors rub shoulders with ancient timbers, rooms burst with personality and gorgeous old beds, and the dining room opens to a large sunny terrace. Two small children – or one granny – will be as snug as winter bunnies in Le Marmotton next door, with its one sweet bedroom, basin and wc. *B&B also.*

sleeps	Clarines 2-3. Marmotton 1.
rooms	Clarines: 1 double, 1 single; 1 shower room. Marmotton: 1 single with basin & wc.
price	Clarines €660-€1,220. Marmotton €400. Prices per week.
arrival	Flexible.

Philippe Courtines
tel +33 (0)6 7 23 17 26
fax +33 (0)4 50 54 08 28
email contact@chamonixlocations.com
web www.chaletsphilippe.com

Châlets de Philippe – Les Barrattes & Les Cantates

Chamonix, Haute-Savoie

At the foot of the most exciting ski mountain in the world is a collection of gingerbread houses: weathered beams, timber balconies and Hansel and Gretel windows. But peep inside and you find multi-jet showers and state of the art technology. It seems a dream but it's a museum of social history – meticulously researched by its owner. Les Barattes, its three storeys leading to a balcony or terrace, oozes Alpine charm. In the kitchen/dining room, a black and copper cooking range, a stove with a gas-fuelled glow, a raft of mod cons and an arched door leading to sleeping quarters upstairs. The main bedroom has a domed blond wood ceiling and a carved wooden basin tucked into a corner – simplicity itself; in the child's room, a stunning old wardrobe and an antique *lit clos*, perfect for keeping winter chills out. More cosiness, luxuriousness and the sweet smell of beeswax in Les Cantates, a two-storey nest for a family of four. There's babysitting for parents who plot an escape, while children will fall in love with the suave leather-chaired cinema equipped with surround sound. *B&B also.* *See next page.*

sleeps	Barattes 4 + 2 children. Cantates 2-3.
rooms	Barattes: 1 double, 1 double with child's bed; 2 shower rooms. Cantates: 1 double, 1 sofabed; 1 shower room.
price	Barattes €1,540-€3,000. Cantates €820-€1,500. Prices per week.
arrival	Flexible.

Philippe Courtines
tel +33 (0)6 07 23 17 26
fax +33 (0)4 50 54 08 28
email contact@chamonixlocations.com
web www.chaletsphilippe.com

Châlets de Philippe – Trolles & Grandes Jorasses

Chamonix, Haute-Savoie

Majestic Mont Blanc towers above this *village de calme* (no wonder the famous stay here) and unpretentious antiques warm the bedrooms of Les Trolles. In the children's bedroom is an enticing 18th-century *lit clos* dressed in fine flannel with cushions… at any minute Father Bear, Mother Bear and Baby Bear might come trotting round the door. This generous chalet has a superb kitchen with a white and chrome range and a rustically flagged floor, a seductive living room in which clubby armchairs gather round a hearth hewn from Mont Blanc, and a suntrap terrace. There are Alpine landscapes on wooded walls, lovingly collected antiques and huge country charm. Les Grandes Jorasses, eventually sleeping up to 17 in luxury on three floors, has a slicker feel: new pine beds, a low-slung living room with an L-shaped open fire, a glass-topped table, recessed ceiling lights, an Alpine garden to spill into. We can't think of a downside – except that you might want to rip your own kitchen out after trying one of these! *B&B also.* *See previous pages.*

sleeps	Trolles 4 + 2 children. Grandes Jorasses 4 + 2 children.
rooms	Trolles: 1 double, 1 double with extra single, 1 children's twin; 1 bathroom, 1 shower room. Grandes Jorasses: 1 double, 1 twin with children's twin attached, 1 separate wc.
price	Trolles €3,300-€4,900. Grandes Jorasses €4,300-€4,600. Prices per week.
arrival	Flexible.

Philippe Courtines

mobile	+33 (0)6 07 23 17 26
fax	+33 (0)4 50 54 08 28
email	contact@chamonixlocations.com
web	www.chaletsphilippe.com

Le Château du Bérouze

Samoëns, Haute-Savoie

Probably the finest manor in Samoëns. It's very old – the main part dates back to 1485 – yet was once on the verge of being demolished. New Zealand journalists Jack and Jane came to the rescue, pouring love and talent into reviving old timbers and stones, then opened the large and extravagantly carved doors to guests. Up the stone steps to an elegantly proportioned first-floor apartment, perfectly restored. You get an ample, open-plan kitchen, a modern living room and bedrooms sharing two bathrooms, one with a claw-foot bath. Lofty ceilings are a criss-cross of white-painted beams, lintels are ancient stone, floors rug-strewn, fireplaces vast, and big old radiators keep you warm. Outside is a garden that is every bit as lovely, with lush lawns, orchards and flowers, terrace and potager. A moat surrounds the house; streams flow in and out, home to ducks and trout. It's a special place in every season: come for skiing and skating in winter, rafting and riding in summer, high hiking in spring. Shops and bars are a five-minute stroll, and your kind hosts will babysit if you ask them.

sleeps	6-8.
rooms	3: 2 twins/doubles, 1 quadruple; 2 bathrooms.
price	£850-£1,500 per week.

Jack & Jane Tresidder
tel +33 (0)4 50 34 95 72
fax +33 (0)4 50 34 95 91
email jane.tresidder@libertysurf.fr
web www.chateauduberouze.com

Le Boën

Praz sur Arly, Haute-Savoie

Sporty families would be in their element – or anyone in love with the mountains. Your young Canadian log cabin looks as if it's been here for ever; the family live above, you live below. In summer come for walks and wildflower pastures, golf, tennis and mountain biking. In winter, snowboard or ski: it's walking distance from the lift that whisks you up to the Megève ski arena. The Bouchages are a skiing family and know every inch of terrain, so you are in the best hands. Inside, an L-shaped kitchen/sitting room, white walls, tiled floors (heated for winter), old-fashioned sofa and armchairs, a table for six. The kitchen is a good size and newly equipped, and there are sliding doors to a plastic-furnished terrace. (And swings and boules in the big garden, yours to share.) The main bedroom, with pastel bedding and extra bunks, has sensational views; the second bedroom is darker due to its high windows. There's a perfect alpine auberge in the village and others in nearby Prazaly, while Megève – the 'St Moritz of France' – has every shop and restaurant you could wish for, and a summer jazz festival.

sleeps	4-6.
rooms	2: 1 triple, 1 family room for 3; 1 bathroom.
price	€511-€951 per week.

Josiane & Christian Bouchage
tel +33 (0)4 50 21 98 14
email bouchagechris@aol.com

Château de Thorens

Thorens Glières, Haute-Savoie

How many holiday apartments are reached via a 13th-century tower? Its steep stone spiral stair brings you into the château itself, inhabited by the de Sales family since 1559. People book in summer to visit its dungeons and guards' rooms, its magnificent kitchens and its elegantly furnished public rooms. Your first-floor apartment, refurbished since gracious *grand-mère* moved into her cottage in the grounds, is a touch more modest. The open-plan living space has cream walls with curtains to match, a small green velvet sofa and three upright chairs, a brand-new white kitchen with a round dining table. Bedrooms have courtyard or garden views; one has rose-coloured furnishings, the other pale yellow. The bathroom is nice and light with an old enamel bath and a huge wash basin. Outside, a strip of grass on the old moat wall, a teak garden swing, chairs, a table and mountain views – a pretty spot for an evening picnic. There are restaurants in Gliers (a stroll away), shopping in Annecy (a short drive) and skiing in the Aravis (35 minutes). *B&B also.*

sleeps	4.
rooms	2: 1 double, 1 twin; 1 bathroom.
price	€490-€1,280 per week.

	Isabelle & Marie Roussy de Sales
tel	+33 (0)4 50 22 42 02
fax	+33 (0)4 50 22 42 02
email	chateaudethorens@free.fr
web	www.chateaustory.com

Souffle de Vent

Barjac, Ardèche

Down a narrow cobbled street, through an arch, up an impressive stone stair. From this light-filled townhouse, views stretch over the rooftops of Barjac to distant, vine-covered slopes. These four apartments on two floors, with a small courtyard on the first, have a fresh, open feel in spite of the 'centre ville' setting. Whitewashed walls, parquet floors, glowing terracotta, a mix of pale modern furniture and antiques – an iron bedstead piled with cushions, a painted wardrobe – create a cool, peaceful feel. Bedrooms are simple but cosy with creamy bed linen, some with muslin drapes; bathrooms are unexpectedly large. The open-plan kitchen and living rooms, one with a wood-burning stove (free logs!), have big windows so you can watch the world go by. This is outdoorsy France; pack a picnic and go hiking, biking and swimming around the three nearby rivers. Or browse Barjac with its shops, ateliers and *pétanque* on the square. The young Dutch owners live nearby and organise cookery and French-language courses. *Parking in town. Apartments also available as B&B, min. 2 nights.*

sleeps	2; 2-3; 2-3; 2-4.
rooms	4 apartments: 2 for 2-3, 1 for 2-4, 1 for 2; each with 1 bathroom.
price	€350-€550 per week.

Jan Willem Schipper

tel	+33 (0)4 75 39 31 09
fax	+33 (0)4 75 39 31 09
email	info@souffledevent.com
web	www.souffledevent.com

La Filature – Orange & Bleu

St André de Cruzières, Ardèche

A vast building, an ambitious project. This young Dutch family have taken on a stunning old silkworm factory built in 1872, and their B&B and gîtes are up and running. An event space is planned for the old workshop: seminars, weddings. Evelyne and Luc speak perfect English (of course), are full of creative energy and enjoy summer cooking twice-weekly for guests: expect a candlelit table under a vine-clad pergola, a market-inspired menu, flowing wine and happy talk. The two apartments, 'Orange' and 'Blue', have their own entrances and terraces, the living is easy, there's masses of space, you are way off any main road and the children can go barefoot or bare-bum. As for the interiors, these are large, light and luminous with white walls and parquet floors, white duvets on big beds, white throws on sofas, beautifully equipped kitchens and fine vineyard views. Lovely for families: a little play area on the mezzanine, a big safe garden, a trampoline, ping-pong, a super shared pool, and the loungers are wicker, not plastic. There's a restaurant you can walk to and many more in Barjac. *B&B also.*

sleeps: Orange 6.
Blue 4. Extra children's beds.

rooms: Orange: 3 twins/doubles;
1 bathroom, separate wc.
Blue: 1 double, 1 twin; 1 bathroom.

price: Orange €550-€950.
Blue €350-€750. Prices per week.

Eveline Evelyne & Luc Matter
tel: +33 (0)4 75 36 44 40
email: info-filature@wanadoo.fr
web: www.la-filature.com

Salivet & La Sousto

Truinas, Drôme

Few places have it all but this must be one of them. Breathtaking mountain views, a lovely artistic owner and a fascinating, secluded old farm. Honey-stoned Salivet stands where the oxen sheds and haylofts used to be; the ruins of the original farmhouse are still visible in the garden. Jane, an English artist who specialises in silk screen printing, lives next door; she and her architect partner have restored and furnished the place simply but beautifully with old beams, terracotta floors, whitewashed walls, stone fireplaces and antique furniture. On summer nights you can sleep on the roof terrace; during the day, sit on the terrace under the wisteria, snooze on the lawn under the weeping willow or cool off in the shared pool. La Sousto is similarly delightful and unspoiled. Jane runs courses on silk decoration to include a 'silk tour', which can be booked in advance. She sells honey, homemade jams and truffles in season, cooks fabulous meals on request (much organic) and will supply walking itineraries, maps and flower guides to this beautiful area.

sleeps	Salivet 7-8 + cot. La Sousto 2 + 2 children.
rooms	Salivet: 1 double, 1 double with cot, 1 single, 1 twin, 1 single (mezzanine); 1 bath, 1 shower, 2 separate wcs. La Sousto: 1 double, 1 children's twin; 1 bathroom, separate wc.
price	Salivet €750-€1,000. La Sousto €400-€550. Prices per week.
closed	Mid-October-Easter.

Jane Worthington

tel +33 (0)4 75 53 49 13

email worthingtonjc@aol.com

L'Atelier du Duire – Les Mûriers

Venterol, Drôme

No fuss, no luxury. Jill is an artist and sculptress; her Danish husband is a raku specialist and runs pottery courses in the summer. Lovely people, they have lived and worked here for 30 years. The grass is unmown to preserve the wild flowers, the trees are full of birds, there are cherries in early June, beehives for honey, herbs in the garden and truffles on the land. And a shared swimming pool, protected by a hedge from the wind. Your gîte was once the farm's bread oven – rebuilt, it has a rose-covered veranda for shade. The main room has big ochre floor tiles, a sofa and two wicker armchairs, a long dining table, a country cupboard. The bedrooms have open hanging space, pretty olive curtains, good sculptures by Jill. In the kitchen: a hob, an oven, a pottery clock. Slip down to the bottom of the garden with a glass of something chilled and watch the sun set over the vineyards and the hills. No sound – bar the neighbour's dog at supper time. You're up high here and it's a magical spot. Come in spring for the hiking, in summer for the music at Orange, all year round for the peace.

sleeps	3-4.
rooms	2: 1 twin/double, 1 single; 1 shower room, 1 wc.
price	€450-€550 per week.

Jill Ratel
tel +33 (0)4 75 26 22 08

L'Amiradou

Mérindol les Oliviers, Drôme

The name means 'high on the hill with long views' – and you'll be moved by them: every window frames a Cézanne. The drive through the herb-scented hills is out of this world, the familiar white flank of Mont Ventoux is ever present. The builder who helped Susan and Andrew renovate this old cottage thought they'd made a mistake: standing above the main house, it has the best views! Many levels give both house and garden huge character (but make it unsuitable for the very young) and the interior is immaculate. An Indian patchwork hangs in one bedroom, a vast baker's table separates kitchen from living room, there are hand-painted tiles round bathroom mirrors, smart sofas and antique pine. You have a log fire and central heating for winter and a well-equipped kitchen. Susan and Andrew love their adopted land, are delighted to advise you about the best places to visit and otherwise leave you quietly to yourselves. You share their pool; the south-facing pool-house and terrace, scented with lavender and honeyuckle, is all yours. Restaurants and markets abound.

sleeps	4.
rooms	2: 1 double, 1 twin; 2 bathrooms.
price	€600-€1,100 per week.

Susan & Andrew Smith

tel	+33 (0)4 75 28 78 69
fax	+33 (0)4 75 28 78 69
email	smitha@club-internet.fr
web	www.lamiradou.com

L'Amiradou – Tréfouli

Mérindol les Oliviers, Drôme

An iron gate in a garden wall: enter a small paradise. Built five years ago, Tréfouli stands in perfect keeping with the land that surrounds it – and that land is ravishing. Set on the same hillside as L'Amiradou, it overlooks valleys of orchards and vines and Cézanne's evocative mountain. Inside, a delightful interior of white walls and terracotta, a baker's table dividing dining room from kitchen, luminous bathrooms with generous showers, a fireplace full of logs. Thanks to high ceilings the rooms feel lovely and spacious. French windows open to a covered veranda with a Moroccan-tiled table and stylish ironwork chairs… then numerous terraces, nooks and crannies. Big flat slabs of stone curve over the honey-coloured gravel and lead to a blissful pool where the water is warm from mid-May to September. On this steeply terraced site – unsuitable for tinies – the land drops away beneath you into wild oak woods full of songbirds and chirruping cicadas. In an area famous for its Roman sites and Côtes du Rhône villages, you are in the heart of the 'golden triangle' of ancient Vaison la Romaine. Bliss.

sleeps	4.
rooms	2 doubles; 1 bathroom, 1 shower room.
price	€700-€1,400 per week.
arrival	Thursday.

Susan & Andrew Smith

tel +33 (0)4 75 28 78 69
fax +33 (0)4 75 28 78 69
email smitha@club-internet.fr
web www.lamiradou.com

Les Estelles & Bode Villa

La Roche sur Le Buis, Drôme

Hard to find a lovelier spot. Apricot orchards, lavender, a stream… Take a drink onto the terrace and watch the sun set behind Mount St Julien. The skies are very clear here and the nights unbelievably starry. You'll forgive the house its modernity because it's so welcoming and superbly equipped. It's divided into two. Upstairs is Casey and Michael's own home, which they let when they go travelling. They're Americans who have fulfilled a long-held dream to live in France. Their salon is full of antiques from all over the world and their kitchen is quite something (Casey is a self-confessed gadget addict). The downstairs apartment has a big living room/kitchen with an entertaining collection of old French cycling posters. The bedrooms are excellent: the Bodes know a thing or two about comfort. A white stone stairway with black wrought-iron railings connects the two levels and is closed off – unless the apartments are being rented together. All around are wonderful bike rides and walks; follow the stream down the valley and in 15 minutes you reach a captivating little market town.

sleeps	Les Estelles 6-8. Bode Villa 8-10.
rooms	Les Estelles: 3 doubles; 3 shower rooms. Bode Villa: 4 doubles; 1 bathroom, 4 shower rooms, 3 wcs.
price	Les Estelles €1,000. Bode Villa €2,000. Prices per week.

Casey & Michael Bode

tel +33 (0)4 75 27 50 42

fax +33 (0)4 75 27 77 59

email caseyairstew@mac.com

Les Granges de Saint Pierre

Simiane la Rotonde, Alpes-de-Haute-Provence

Everything in this remarkably converted 14th-century grange – once attached to the priory – is stylish and caring. Lavender-infused air, simple iron furniture, modern art, a fine use of colour, an inner terrace where lemons grow – it has a sense of peace and space. Arched doorways with new doors and ancient locks lead to big, light bedrooms with tiled floors and colourwashed walls. Bathrooms are sophisticated in rust-red and white. You have a sunny, lofty, white-beamed living room with cream drapes, canvas directors' chairs and big sofas in front of an even bigger fire. The kitchen is in the corner: terracotta-painted units, old country furniture, stripped floor. Rooms gather round a central terrace filled with geraniums, there's fruit in the orchards and chickens in the pen. Josiane, kind and intelligent, lives with her husband in the château next door where the magical pool half hides in a walled garden. Simiane la Rotonde, once the regional capital of lavender, is a gem: a hilltop village with a 16th-century market place, surrounded by vast purple fields. A heavenly place. *B&B also.*

sleeps	6.
rooms	3: 2 doubles, 1 twin; 3 shower rooms.
price	€670-€980 per week.

Josiane Tamburini
tel +33 (0)4 92 75 93 81
fax +33 (0)4 92 75 93 81
web communities.msn.co.uk/lesgrangesdesaintpierre/home.htm

St Jean et Bel Air

Sainte Croix à Lauze, Alpes-de-Haute-Provence

Luxury in the woods with huge views over the Luberon. This brilliantly restored 17th-century farmhouse is for those seeking wilderness; strike out from the door on intrepid walks. Or simply gaze over fields and oaks to distant hills from the terrace by the gorgeous pool – floodlit for midnight swims. Jean-Patrick fell in love with a pile of old stones, put them back together, *et voilà*, paradise! You have three doubles in the main house, another bed on the mezzanine of the studio that adjoins. The feel is contemporary: the whitest walls, the palest tiled floors, a warm yellow throw on a sofa, a red leather armchair, paperbacks on white shelves, the odd rug. There's a modern open fireplace in the sitting room, a charming little dining room and a small kitchen with all you need. One bathroom has lovely handmade tiles and a view from the tub. Bedrooms are strikingly simple and the master suite opens onto a terrace, so pull the bed out and sleep under the stars. Restaurants are 10km away in Cereste, the shops are nearer. *At the end of long dirt track; arrange to meet owners on turn-off to Viens.*

sleeps	6-10.
rooms	3 + 1: 3 doubles; 2 bathrooms; 1 studio for 4 with separate entrance, 1 double on mezzanine, 2 singles on ground floor; 1 shower room.
price	€495-€1,905.

Isabelle & Jean-Patrick Chesne

mobile	+33 (0)6 08 88 71 91
fax	+33 (0)4 92 79 08 42
email	ijp.chesne@wanadoo.fr
web	www.gite-luberon.fluo.net

…ntry 316

Le Vieil Aiglun

Aiglun, Alpes-de-Haute-Provence

Getting here is half the fun – up a steep, windy but well-tarred road. And your arrival at this ancient hilltop village is rewarded with an unforgettable panorama – most of Haute Provence spreads out before you. An energetic, creative and very lovely Belgian family opened Le Vieil Aiglun's rustic doors in 2003: five B&B bedrooms in a huge barn; a dining room in a vaulted byre; a pool, a play area and a gîte. Privately separate, your apartment has two bedrooms, one up, one down, a well-planned kitchen/dining room with a sofabed, a bathroom with two pretty white basins and an enclosed garden in the walls of an old ruin. Plus views of a Romanesque church on a hill, romantically floodlit at night. It's perfectly gorgeous inside: fresh white walls and rafters, plain linen curtains, red and orange bedspreads, Moroccan lights. After a hard day's sunbathing by the fenced pool (open June-September) book in for twice-weekly *table d'hôtes*. The long glamorous candelabra-lit table – with special low table for tinies – is stunning, and a huge open fire turns bad weather days into the cosiest nights. *B&B also.*

sleeps	4-6.
rooms	2 twins, 1 sofabed; 1 bathroom.
price	€560-€810 per week.

Charles & Annick Speth
tel +33 (0)4 92 34 67 00
fax +33 (0)4 92 34 74 92
email info@vieil-aiglun.com
web www.vieil-aiglun.com

Domaine la Condamine

Crillon le Brave, Vaucluse

Seven generations of wine-growers have breathed their first in this pretty 17th-century domaine and Madame, an energetic businesswoman, organises tastings of her own delicious Coteaux du Ventoux. The apartment, at the far end of the farm, has its own entrance and a courtyard where you can dine on sultry evenings. Colours in the lovely, large, colourwashed living area are soft and southern and there's a genuine old *mas* feel. Bedrooms upstairs have simple hand-painted furniture, decorative wall borders and views across the vineyards to Mont Ventoux – wonderful. The pool is decked with loungers, fringed with grass and oleander, busy on a hot day; Madame runs a large B&B and you may join the guests for dinner (held on the terrace in summer). Visit the lively Monday market in Bédoin or the larger one in Vaison la Romaine, stock up on wine at the local *caves*, then return to your big authentic family kitchen. There's lacework at Montmirail, Roman splendour at Orange, vineyards, lavender and all the beauty of Provence. A lovely, simple, genuine old place for a family stay. *B&B also.*

sleeps	6.
rooms	3: 1 double, 2 twins; 1 shower room, 1 separate wc.
price	€400-€750 per week.

Marie-José Eydoux

tel +33 (0)4 90 62 47 28

fax +33 (0)4 90 62 47 28

email domlacondamine@hotmail.com

web www.lacondamine.info

La Lauzière

Puyméras, Vaucluse

This delightful 18th-century Provençal farmhouse has views on one side over Côtes du Rhône vineyards. Wander around the garden and you will discover an orchard of cherry trees: you may indulge in season. For 300 days a year sunshine bathes on this staggeringly beautiful land: the setting is spectacular. The farmhouse has a pretty covered terrace and a gorgeous pool. It is a long, low stone-walled building with sea-green shutters on the walls and wrought-iron on the terrace. The interior is done in a contemporary Provençal style: white walls, colourful fabrics, terracotta floors and iron beds. Bedrooms have views of either pool or courtyard, while downstairs there is a choice of sitting rooms. Matisse prints hang on the walls, there's an open fireplace in the yellow-walled kitchen and central heating for winter. The typically Provençal village of Puyméras is a five-minute stroll – it has tennis courts, two bistro-cafés and a restaurant. Close by is medieval Vaison la Romaine with its Roman ruins and popular market. As for the walking – mountain, valley and gorge await you.

sleeps	7.
rooms	4: 2 doubles, 1 twin, 1 single; 2 bathrooms, 1 separate wc.
price	€1,225-€2,450 per week.

Ralf Maurer
tel +33 (0)1 53 01 09 14
fax +33 (0)1 53 01 09 14
email mail@provenceliving.com
web www.provenceliving.com

Les Convenents

Uchaux, Vaucluse

Pure Provence: the views from your green-shuttered, traditional stone *mas* are of vines, sunflowers and distant pines. Sarah and Ian, who do B&B in the house next door, stock the kitchen of the small gîte with basics – fruit, wine, olive oil – and often invite guests next door for a drink. They are also happy for you to share their pretty pool, but if you prefer the privacy of your own sitting-out area (with barbecue) that's fine too. Inside, the feel is contemporary, light and bright; there's a dear little living/kitchen area with pale tiled floors, sandy walls, cheery blue and yellow curtains with matching cushions and throws, attractive cane armchairs, pale beams. The kitchen in the corner is cleverly designed to include oven, fridge and freezer. (If you need bigger pots and pans, you can borrow them.) Upstairs are two small but adequate bedrooms whose yellow and blue bedspreads, cushions and curtains echo the furnishings downstairs. There's ping-pong, boules and bikes to borrow, and Vaison la Romaine, with restaurants and Tuesday market, is happily nearby. *Cot and high chair provided. B&B also.*

sleeps	4 + cot.
rooms	2: 1 double, 1 twin; 1 shower room.
price	€500-€750 per week.
arrival	Friday.

Sarah Banner

tel	+33 (0)4 90 40 65 64
fax	+33 (0)4 90 40 65 64
email	sarahbanner@wanadoo.fr
web	www.lesconvenents.com

La Maison aux Volets Rouges

Uchaux, Vaucluse

Step off the street into the red-shuttered house to be wrapped in a warm embrace. Family photographs line the hall and stair; this is a much-loved home, and its sprawling lay out – two staircases to separate parts of the house – makes it ideal for three-generation parties. Rooms are big with tiled floors (rugs in winter), beams, family antiques. The salon, with working fire, opens to the garden while the dining room opens off a farmhouse kitchen, equipped so that cooks may hone their skills. High-beamed bedrooms have good storage and individual touches – a brass bed, an arched window, a baby bed with a teddy bear. Three minutes and you're by the pool – a peaceful distance from the children's frolics. The pool house, surrounded by lawns and shady trees, is almost a second home: kitchen, barbecue, veranda and shower. Borrow a bike, play tennis at the local club (no charge), and be sure to visit glorious Avignon and Aix. Restaurants are a mere stroll. Brigitte, who lived in England for 30 years, is chatty, enthusiastic, wants guests to enjoy her family home and lives in the same village.

sleeps	9 + cots.
rooms	5: 3 doubles, 1 twin, 1 single + 2 cots; 3 shower rooms, 1 bathroom.
price	€1,800-€2,400 per week.
arrival	Saturday but flexible low season.

Brigitte Woodward
tel +33 (0)4 90 40 64 56
fax +33 (0)4 90 40 64 56
email richer.bruno@wanadoo.fr

Mas du Clos de l'Escarrat – Studios & Apartments

Jonquières, Vaucluse

If ever more sumptuous décor and glitzy bathrooms have started to pall, try a return to simplicity. This 17th-century stone farmhouse (a complete ruin when the Barails took it on ten years ago) is pleasingly quiet and unassuming. Ignore the approach road winding past an industrial area and lorry park: you'll soon be away from it all among the vines, gazing on distant mountains. The gîtes – two apartments and two small studios – are basic but very pleasant, decorated in soft yellow tones. Provençal fabrics and some unexpected features – a marble table, a beautiful pottery bowl – add arresting touches. Kitchens and bathrooms are small but perfectly adequate. In the shared garden a host of trees jostle for space – linden, fig, oleander, bamboo – and the swing in the plane tree will be irresistible to small visitors. The swimming pool is Monsieur's pride and joy – and when he is not tending it, he will take you on a wine tour, followed by a gastronomic dinner at the mas. He and Madame are retired – a warm, friendly couple who have travelled extensively in Latin America. *WiFi connection. B&B also.*

sleeps	2; 2; 2-3; 2-4.
rooms	2 studios for 2, 1 apartment for 2-3, 1 apartment for 2-4.
price	Studio for 2 €400. Apartment for 2-3 €530-€660. Apartment for 2-4 €530-€790. All prices per week. September-June ask for prices per night.

Charles & Andrée Barail
tel +33 (0)4 90 70 39 19
fax +33 (0)4 90 70 39 19
email visitenprovence@free.fr
web www.visite-en-provence.com

Les Cerisiers – Les Tilleuls, Les Oliviers & Les Cyprès

Carpentras, Vaucluse

Almost too good to be true! An old stone farmhouse with sweeping views, Provençal décor and *tommette* floors, fine linen, helpful hosts, a gorgeous pool. You have it all, in a hamlet, surrounded by vineyards and cherry orchards. Two-storey Les Tilleuls has its own terrace and barbecue with lime trees for shade, adjoining the lush shared landscaped gardens. Downstairs is open plan, contemporary and cool: pale sofa and ironwork chairs, a corner kitchen, an open fire. Bedrooms are up: good big beds, white walls, beams. Bath and shower rooms sparkle. Up independent outside stairs are two chic little apartments with a roomy, sunny, open-plan feel: yellows and greens in Les Oliviers, dramatic dark blues and yellows in Les Cyprès. Relax on their terrace and sip Côtes de Ventoux as the sun goes down. Tory and Carol have not stinted on a thing, be it air conditioning, central heating, crockery or towels for the pool. Go to Carpentras for its Friday market, Avignon for art and architecture. A sunny, civilised place to stay.
Dishwasher in Tilleuls. Shared laundry. Cook available.

sleeps	Tilleuls 6-7. Oliviers 2-4. Cyprès 2-3.
rooms	Tilleuls: 3 doubles (+ 1 extra bed); 1 bath, 1 shower. Oliviers: 1 twin/double, 1 sofabed; 1 shower. Cyprès: 1 twin/double, 1 sofabed; 1 shower.
price	Tilleuls €700-€1,800. Oliviers €400-€775. Cyprès €375-€725: 20% supp. p.p. for sofabed. All prices per week.
arrival	Oliviers: Thursday.

Carol Chaplin & Tory Johnston
tel +33 (0)4 90 67 76 10
fax +33 (0)4 90 67 76 11
email info@les-cerisiers.com
web www.les-cerisiers.com

Le Mas de Miejour

Le Thor, Vaucluse

You get the oldest part of this pretty Provençal farmhouse, with your own entrance and garden with barbecue. Frédéric and Emmanuelle came here to bring up their children (Frédéric turns potter in the winter months) and they share their home with both gîte and B&B guests. The atmosphere is utterly restful – white walls, wooden beams and ceilings, old honeycomb tiles on the floor. The kitchen – well-equipped yet nicely old-fashioned and homely with its low ceiling, little windows and ancient tiles – is dominated by an ancient bread oven, perhaps originally pillaged from the 12th-century château nearby. Up steepish steps are the salon, with comfy sofa and leather armchairs, and the bedrooms. The double bed is huge and the white-tiled bathroom is small but fine. Views are over the garden or fields; Mont Ventoux lies beyond. The land here is flat with a high water table so the garden, sheltered by trees and the surrounding tall maize and sunflowers in summer, is always fresh and green. There's a lovely, fenced pool you are most welcome to share. *B&B also.*

sleeps	5.
rooms	3: 1 double, 1 twin, 1 single; 1 bathroom.
price	€450-€900 per week.
closed	November-February.

Frédéric Westercamp
& Emmanuelle Diemont

tel	+33 (0)4 90 02 13 79
fax	+33 (0)6 68 25 25 06
email	frederic.westercamp@wanadoo.fr
web	www.masdemiejour.com

La Gardiole

Bonnieux, Vaucluse

The oldest of Bonnieux' two churches, crowning this perfect hilltop village, is surrounded by ancient cedars so huge they can be spotted for miles. Here, on the lower flanks of the hill, is an unexpectedly simple and inexpensive place to stay. Owned by the good people who run the town's small, lofty *hôtel de charme*, La Gardiole, this is perfect for two. Your rooms are in the lower half of a newish stone building, the top floor occupied but quite separate. Décor is neither stylish nor contemporary but simple and clean with a certain old-fashioned charm. You get a white-walled double room with flowery curtains and comfy beds, a small blue-tiled bathroom, a round dining table, a new sofa, and a small kitchen with shining pans and two rings. Views open wide to the Luberon and your garden, with a cherry tree for shade, has a delightful private pool. Bonnieux is one of the less touristy *villages perchés*, its steep, winding streets numerous enough to get lost in, its restaurants fashionable, its Friday market carnival-like in summer.

Two further houses for four & six in nearby village.

sleeps 2-4.
rooms 1 twin/double, 1 sofabed in living room; 1 bathroom.
price €350-€600 per week.

M & Mme Pierre Maurin
tel +33 (0)4 90 75 88 48
fax +33 (0)4 90 75 88 57
email le-clos-du-buis@wanadoo.fr
web www.leclosdubuis.com

Hello

Jas des Eydins

Bonnieux, Vaucluse

Among vineyards and cherry orchards, with views to the Luberon hills, a blissful retreat at the end of a private lane. Recline on teak loungers by the heavenly pool, enveloped in the scent of roses and lavender. These 18th-century stone buildings, once a sheepfold and part of a Provençal farm, were restored by their architect owner and his elegant art historian wife. There's a charming simplicity, a soothing, serene mix of country antiques and modern bits and pieces. You have a large, beautifully equipped kitchen and open-plan sitting room and three peaceful bedrooms (one in an adjoining building) shaded by a trellis of Banksaii roses. On hot summer days relax in the big garden and revel in views of Mont Ventoux; in the evenings, dine on the covered terrace to the chirrup of the cicadas. There's a fabulous outdoor kitchen with chimney and built-in barbecue. Shirley and Jan live next door and are on hand if you need them but also leave you to relax in peace. Escape the summer beaches to explore the enchanting hillside villages inland. *Additional twin bedroom in main house, with own entrance, at extra charge.*

sleeps	6.
rooms	3: 2 twins/doubles, 1 twin; 2 bathrooms, 1 shower room.
price	€1,300-€1,950 per week.
closed	November-mid-March.

Shirley & Jan Kozlowski
tel +33 (0)4 90 75 84 99
fax +33 (0)4 90 75 96 71
email jasdeseydins@wanadoo.fr
web www.jasdeseydins.com

Château de la Loubière – La Grange, Les Plantanes & Sebastian's

Pertuis, Vaucluse

Space, peace and much to explore. Ten acres of parkland surround these three stone-built gîtes, outbuildings of the 16th-century château. While the kids run riot in the grounds, you can slip into the pool or gaze on the Provençal countryside. In a mad moment, you might even play tennis; a court lies hidden among the trees. Nicely separated, each gîte has been renovated by the McDougalls, who live in the château, to keep its Provençal charm intact. Rooms have exposed stonework, terracotta floors and fresh white walls, furnishings are bright and uncluttered and quirky features have been retained – one bathroom has an iron hayrack, another an old eating trough. The open-plan living areas, some with fireplaces or beams, have sunny terraces for alfresco eating. Kitchens are modern and well-equipped, bedrooms light and breezy with pretty bedcovers and soft lamps. Toss a coin in La Grange for the bedroom with the terrace. There's walking, riding, the Luberon National Park, festivals in Aix, restaurants in Pertuis. The McDougalls can provide meals and a babysitter.

sleeps	La Grange 10. Les Plantanes 4. Sebastian's 6.
rooms	La Grange: 2 doubles, 1 twin, 2 twins/doubles; 3 baths, 3 sep. wcs. Les Plantanes: 1 double, 1 twin/double; 1 bath. Sebastian's: 2 doubles, 1 twin; 1 bath.
price	La Grange €1,700-€2,500. Les Plantanes €600-€1,300. Sebastian's €500-€1,200. Prices per week.

Deb & Alec McDougall

tel +33 (0)4 90 09 53 96

email info@laloubiere.com

web www.laloubiere.com

Mas des Genêts

Saignon, Vaucluse

Set among vineyards and lavender fields just below the charming village of Saignon, perched like a fort on turrets of white rock, this one-up-one-down stone cottage is a sweet retreat in the popular Luberon. Reached by a private drive, the pale-stoned extension (once a tractor shed) is part of an old farmhouse that has been skilfully converted by American-born Stephen and his English wife Meg. They live in the main part of the house and there's a twin-bedded ground-floor apartment for two next door. Each property has its own private terrace and lawn from which to take your fill of birdsong and big mountain views. Inside, original beams, new terracotta tiles, modern pine tables and chairs, books, puzzles and games... even underfloor heating for winter stays. There's a functional kitchenette in one corner and a sunny upstairs bedroom with a big brass bed, sloping beamed ceilings and blue and green floral blinds. Take the footpath to Saignon 25 minutes, or walk in the Luberon hills: you can hike straight from the door. And don't miss the superb Saturday market in Apt.

sleeps	2.
rooms	1 double; 1 shower room.
price	€380–€580 per week.

Meg & Stephen Parker

tel +33 (0)4 90 04 65 33

fax +33 (0)4 90 74 56 85

email masdegenet@aol.com

Villa Agapanthe

St Saturnin lès Apt, Vaucluse

Henrietta is a bit of a star, goes the extra mile and welcomes you with wine and flowers. Her 1975 one-storey villa is not the most striking of houses but its spoiling interior and its beautiful garden make up for any plain-ness. Inside, light, airy rooms hold the odd hidden treasure. There's a pink Art-Deco-style bathroom, a wrought-iron day bed in the sun room, a couple of cavernous white sofas in the sitting room. Big shuttered windows flood each room with light and bedrooms are screened to keep bugs at bay. Beds are dressed in fine linen, blue and green voile curtains billow in the breeze and sofas and armchairs are coloured by pink scatter cushions. Delicate floral friezes run along pale cream walls and bedroom have views of the garden, the village, its famous windmill, a ruined castle and the distant hills. Outside, the garden bursts with life. There are pretty flowerbeds, Provençal herbs, lavender bushes, an olive grove and fig and cherry trees. You are bang in the centre of the village. Brilliant. *Children over eight welcome.*

sleeps	6.
rooms	3: 2 doubles, 1 twin; 1 bathroom, 1 shower room, 1 separate wc.
price	€700–€1,700 per week.

Henrietta Taylor
tel +33 (0)4 90 75 49 64
email henrietta@henriettataylor.com
web www.henriettataylor.com

Rose Cottage

Saignon, Vaucluse

Luberon without the crowds. The centre of Saignon, perched precariously along a vast saddle of rock, is a minute's walk but here you look onto a sleepy little square where cats roam and geraniums bloom. Henrietta lives in the next village but will pop by should you need her. She has created a refreshing mood of light and space through a blend of white walls and honey-coloured stone. Even the kitchen work surfaces are made of the soothing stone; no expense has been spared in bringing original features back to life. Old doors and ancient stone stairs have been superbly restored; terracotta floors are washed with lavender-scented water; a vaulted *cave* serves as a stunning utility room. Furniture is minimalist, much of it ironwork, and Henrietta has added charming touches like twigwork animals and handcrafted curtain rods. Bedrooms, with deliciously luxurious linen, are light and white; showers have Salernes tiles for the odd splash of colour. The flagged kitchen is a happy place to chop and stir or you can dine out on the terrace of the restaurant next door.

sleeps	4.
rooms	2: 1 double, 1 twin; 2 shower rooms.
price	€615-€920 per week.

Henrietta Taylor
tel +33 (0)4 90 75 49 64
email henrietta@henriettataylor.com
web www.henriettataylor.com

Place de la Fontaine

Saignon, Vaucluse

Nod off to the tinkling of the village fountain and the soothing murmur of the outdoor restaurant goers from your crisply dressed bed. This is an ancient house in the central square of a lovely, lesser-known Luberon village, and a heavenly place to stay. Henrietta, its Australian owner, has decorated the three immaculately limewashed storeys with artistic flair and respect for the building's history. Soothing and sophisticated ochres and creams in the kitchen and living room are enhanced by delightful *objets* that Henrietta has picked up from craftsmen and brocantes. Kitchen floors and work surfaces have old wooden borders; immaculate crockery and modern gadgets are stored on free-standing ironwork shelves. Up a narrow, spiral stair to light, minimalist bedrooms with original wooden doors and beams, basketwork tables and simple concrete floors. The airy double on the third floor has a tiny flower-decked terrace that gives onto the beauty of Provence. In summer, relax with a glass of local wine; in winter, snuggle up on a sofa before the open fire.

sleeps	6.
rooms	3: 2 doubles, 1 twin; 1 bathroom, 1 shower room.
price	€715-€1,000 per week.

Henrietta Taylor
tel +33 (0)4 90 75 49 64
email henrietta@henriettataylor.com
web www.henriettataylor.com

La Grande Bastide – La Maison des Rosiers & de L'Auvent, L'Appartement Colorado

Rustrel, Vaucluse

Through the brown iron gates and down the drive fringed with ancient oaks to the grand bastide. The setting is stunning – the hills to the east, the valley to the west – and hikers will be in heaven. You walk, or cycle, out of the house into the multi-coloured landscape of the Colorado range, famous for its ochre pigments (once mined). These three gîtes, neat as new pins, separated by thick walls, stand apart from the owners' living quarters in a wing of the old house – and share a huge pool and a walled courtyard garden full of roses with mulberry trees for shade. All is spotless and spacious; there are beams and new terracotta tiles, pale sofas, light-wood tables and chairs, perfect beds and linen and a big farmhouse table in each sparkling kitchen. It's a top restoration job that feels new outside and in; the character will follow and the landscaping has begun. You are north of Sault, famous for its lavender and nougat, and south of Apt, whose all-day Saturday market is legendary. Peaceful Rustrel, walkable from here, holds a bakery, a store and a sprinkling of restaurants and bars.

sleeps	Rosiers 6. L'Auvent 3. Colorado 3.
rooms	Rosier: 2 doubles, 1 twin; 2 bathrooms. L'Auvent: 1 double, 1 single; 1 bathroom. Colorado: 1 double, 1 single; 1 bathroom.
price	Rosiers €1,200-€1,600. L'Auvent €700-€1,100. Colorado €600-€1,000. Prices per week.

André & Yangbin Marini

tel	+33 (0)1 47 20 98 11 +33 (0)1 53 76 81 89
fax	+33 (0)1 47 20 64 58
email	bin.yang@wanadoo.fr

Mas des Tourterelles

St Rémy de Provence, Bouches-du-Rhône

Climb the steps to your veranda and let the views wash over you. All around, peace, greenery, your little pool tucked into the garden – and the bustling centre of St Rémy mere minutes away. The Aherns have thrown themselves into their new life in the Alpilles; Richard restoring the farmhouse with its honey-coloured stone, beams and tiles, Carrie adding the light and deceptively simple touches – pale walls, linen curtains, sisal carpets, splashes of colour. Bedrooms – you can 'add on' extra from the adjoining B&B – are restful spaces of white and grey with pretty bedcovers and striking photographs on the walls. Bathrooms are neat, well-planned oases of shiny white. Relax in the elegantly simple sitting room, dine on your veranda. There's also a smart dining table in the cool, *Country-Living* kitchen – big range, white sink, pots and pans hanging from the rafters. On some nights you might join Carrie and Richard for supper or wander into town. There's bags to do – the Van Gogh Museum, the Camargue, hiking in the Alpilles. Then return to your perfectly simple retreat. *B&B also.*

sleeps 2-6.
rooms 1 double; 1 bathroom; 2 additional doubles with bathrooms can be combined with first-floor apartment.
price €600-€1,720 per week.

Richard & Carrie Ahern
tel +33 (0)4 32 60 19 93
fax +33 (0)4 32 60 19 93
email richard.ahern@wanadoo.fr
web www.masdestourterelles.com

Hello

Le Clos des Oliviers

St Cannat, Bouches-du-Rhône

Out in the countryside, five minutes from the charming little town of St Cannat, the house sits quietly on its own. Vineyards, olive groves, open grassland, majestic pines and a hammock between the trees – a special spot. The one-storey gite was added to the house 12 years ago and a garden and terrace swiftly followed. Your main room is refreshingly uncluttered: sunny, light and simple with white walls, bamboo furniture, yellow curtains, sofabed, good Indian dresser, maps, magazines and a practical kitchen separated by a tiled bar. It is spotless and very French. The bed is not huge but there's good cupboard space, a super big shower and pretty Provençal curtains. This is Nicole's project, she loves having guests and is helpful in every way. Book in to join her *table d'hôtes*; she has a teenage daughter who will babysit should you bring a child. There's walking from the door, golf at Port Royal, a Wednesday market in the village and the glories of Aix a 15-minute drive. Marvellous to be so near its architecture, life and culture, then to to return to a peaceful place at the end of a winding country lane. *B&B also.*

sleeps	2-4.
rooms	1 double, 1 sofabed in living room; 1 shower room.
price	€460-€590 per week.

Nicole Auriol
tel +33 (0)4 42 57 37 64
email nicole.auriol@worldonline.fr

Mimosa & Magnolia

Éguilles, Bouches-du-Rhône

Wonderful to be so near Aix, yet in such a serene spot. From the pretty, one-acre hillside garden, full of big trees and flowering shrubs, there are views to the enchanting hilltop village of Éguilles. Down a few steps and hidden among the lush greenery is a super big pool enveloped by terrace and lawn. The friendly, relaxed owners and their children live quite separately on the upper floor of the 50-year-old, ivy-swathed house, which also has a round tower room rented out for B&B. The self-catering apartments are on the ground floor, simply furnished, freshly painted and spotlessly clean. Bedrooms are cool and dark, bathrooms functional and there's central heating. Magnolia has a big sitting/dining room and a little galley kitchen; Mimosa's beamed and whitewashed living/kitchen area opens onto a shady terrace with a barbecue. Both kitchens are really well equipped – but it would be a pity to eat in every night. Take advantage of the restaurant in the thriving village – or in fashionable, irresistible Aix. *B&B also.*

sleeps	Mimosa 4-6. Magnolia 4-6.
rooms	Mimosa: 2 twins/doubles, 1 sofabed; 1 bathroom, 1 sep. wc. Magnolia: 2: 1 twin/double, 1 family room for 4, 1 sofabed; 1 bathroom.
price	Mimosa €500-€1,200. Magnolia €500-€1,200. Prices per week.

Chris & Aban McAndrew

tel	+33 (0)4 42 92 49 57
fax	+33 (0)4 42 92 49 57
email	info@chemindesbaoux.com
web	www.chemindesbaoux.com

Hello

Appartement Quatre

Aix en Provence, Bouches-du-Rhône

A stylish bolt hole in the centre of one of France's loveliest towns – all fountains and leafy squares. The building dates from 1900 and was designed for the Carmelite nuns whose chapel stands next door. Step off a narrow pedestrian shopping street to ascend a wide and gracious stairwell, then up to a smart apartment. An immaculate façade, a cool Provençal interior: linen curtains billow in the breeze, the scent of lavender fills the air. There are tiled floors, shuttered windows and air conditioning, wicker furniture in the bedroom, a wild pink ceiling in the bathroom and a jacuzzi bath. The kitchen comes in green and blue and is well-equipped so it's the market in the morning, then a feast at night. In the sitting room you'll find a huge white L-shaped linen sofa and a round antique dining table. The feel is very much that of a home, albeit a rather smart one, with the latest glossy magazines lying about. Gabriele, a designer, is delightful. She will advise on just about anything, from where to get the best croissants to what's on at the opera. Perfect peace – even by day. *German spoken.*

sleeps	2-3.
rooms	1 double, 1 single on a mezzanine; 1 bathroom.
price	€600-€2,800 per week.

Gabriele Skelton
tel +33 (0)4 90 75 98 98
fax +33 (0)4 90 75 98 99
email gabriele.skelton@wanadoo.fr

Le Bastidon

Fuveau, Bouches-du-Rhône

This is a dinky little house for two. Standing in Monique and Michel's peaceful garden in the shade of the ancient oaks, it is quite delightful, absolutely tiny and deeply restful. The lovely owners are there when you need them; Michel is a graphic designer and the interiors reflect his eye for fresh colour and clean lines. Make no mistake, the gîte is minute! There's a bedroom with mirror, walls and rafters in cool white, a large bed with blue and white duvet and curtains to match, garden views and Michel's watercolours on the wall. The shower room sparkles with sea-green tiles and towels; the kitchenette is stylish, with small table and chairs. There's no sitting room, but outdoor furniture for warm days. There's also *pétanque*, table tennis and a superb pool with teak loungers and views off to Montagne Sainte Victoire. Beyond, but hidden from view, is a golf course – you are a short put from the sixth hole, and a round or two can easily be arranged. Atmospheric Aix is close by, Cassis and its *calanques* not much further, and you can dine out every day if you choose at the auberge down the road.

sleeps	2.
rooms	1 double; 1 shower room, 1 separate wc.
price	€300 per week.
closed	July-August.

Monique & Michel Cassagne

tel +33 (0)4 42 53 34 38

fax +33 (0)4 42 53 39 93

email m-cassagne@wanadoo.fr

web www.provencelocationaix.com

La Galéjade

Rousset, Bouches-du-Rhône

The views from the terrace to Mont Sainte Victoire will have you reaching for your boots. There are walking trails from the doorstep – and bikes to borrow – through Cézanne's Provence. Or you could settle for badminton and boules in the garden, a lovely pine-scented area full of sunny and shady corners. Afterwards, cool off in the pool. This is a simple, quiet spot with your gîte tucked round the back of the main house. Unpretentious from the outside, inside it's full of warmth, colour and easy living. The open-plan downstairs has a spanking new kitchen at one end, a big red sofa and Moroccan themed dining area at the other. Bedrooms have a similarly exotic feel – the loo is pink – with jewel-coloured fabrics, simple furniture and views over sunflowers and vines. Adi, a lively and easy-going Australian, and her Dutch husband Frits, are new to the area but know everyone already. They will point you towards restaurants in Rousset, village markets and the best local baker. And you're welcome to pick vegetables and fruit from their garden.

sleeps	4-6.
rooms	2: 1 double, 1 family room for 3, 1 sofabed; 1 bathroom, 1 separate wc.
price	€500-€1,000 per week.

Adi Bukman

tel +33 (0)4 42 93 27 90

email adi@lagalejade.com

web www.lagalejade.com

Les Bréguières

Rousset, Bouches-du-Rhône

This is a real 'find', a place beyond the designer's grasp: authentic, simple, refreshing. Madame, who lives in the nearby house, is warmly human yet assures your privacy, Monsieur spends his free time in the olive grove, and you may occasionally bump into the grandchildren by the pool. Inside the old *cabanon* are simple wood and warm colours. All is homely and delightful – an L-shaped banquette, books, lovely old pine; there are terracotta tiles on the floor, pictures on the walls and French windows to fling open. The kitchen/living area is filled with morning sun; above is the bedroom on the mezzanine (with beams to be ducked). A giant cherry tree bows with fruit in a little piece of garden, vines and hills surround you, there are mountains in the distance, and the backdrop is dominated by Cengle de Sainte Victoire, a vast wall of white rock that rises mightily into the sky. The pool, all mosaic and terracotta, is reason enough to come here. Ping-pong and boules on the spot, riding and golf close by, and Aix for all things Provençal. Come and forget the world.

sleeps	2-4.
rooms	2: 1 double on mezzanine, 1 twin; 1 bathroom.
price	€487-€760 per week.

Jean-Pierre & Sophie Babey
tel +33 (0)4 42 29 01 16
fax +33 (0)4 42 29 01 16
email jp.babey@club-internet.fr

Villa Chapelet

Puyloubier, Bouches-du-Rhône

Tall pines high against the sky offer shade from the sun, vineyards and olive groves roll away before you, Montagne Sainte Victoire rises behind. The house is gracious but not grand, ample and much-loved; indeed, it's the Coutrots' home when they're not travelling. Pale olive floor tiles sweep through the downstairs rooms, walls are washed ochre and beams painted white. Rooms glow with southern light. Furnishings are uncluttered, immaculate; rugs on parquet floors, a few carefully chosen country pieces, cream sofas, pine cupboards in a new kitchen. Joséphine's colourful patchwork is displayed in a glass-fronted cabinet in the salon, breezy colours give bedrooms a relaxed air and four bathrooms mean no queues. Joséphine is a passionate walker – there's no shortage of maps and guides – and with trails starting from the garden it couldn't be easier. Lovely, bustling Aix is no distance at all, the coast is nearby and there's a handy bus stop so teenagers can mooch off on their own. You may prefer to stay put, dreaming or reading on the shady pool terrace.

sleeps	10.
rooms	5: 4 doubles, 1 twin; 1 bathroom, 3 shower rooms.
price	€1,890-€2,590 per week.

Joséphine Coutrot

tel	+33 (0)4 42 66 34 78
fax	+33 (0)4 42 66 34 78
email	villa.chapelet@wanadoo.fr
web	villachapelet.monsite.wanadoo.fr

La Maison du Faïencier

Varages, Var

Step in from the village square and be catapulted into the early 17th century. Built in 1609, this captivating house was home to three master potters; there are ateliers still in the village. The living area is a cool sweep of the palest terracotta, the kitchen has the French equivalent of an Aga, the welcome pack is the best we've seen. Beneath a vaulted ceiling, a majestic stair transports you to huge dreamy bedrooms where whiteness and softness bring instant seduction: sisal floors, pale timbers, delicate ironwork, generous wicker... Some have sloping skylight windows, others overlook the garden. Stonework has been left exposed where possible, old walls stand at jaunty angles, hand basins have been crafted to fit into uneven walls, showers have 'sunflower' heads. Warmly humorous Fiona and Ron have kept the soul of the place, then added a touch of their magic. Stone martins nest in the courtyard, the garden is sweet with lilacs, apricots and figs, the pool resembles a Roman bath and the village offers two markets a week and bikes to hire. Head for the Verdon Gorges and watery adventure!

sleeps	10-12.
rooms	4 twins/doubles, 1 family room for 4; 1 bathroom, 4 shower rooms.
price	€1,500-€3,000 per week.

Ron & Fiona Alldridge
tel +33 (0)4 94 77 81 01
email info@lamaisondufaiencier.com
web www.lamaisondufaiencier.com

Pimaquet – La Magnanerie

Entrecasteaux, Var

Two old stone houses – one Mimi's – hunker down on the hill, separated by an office and studio; once a university lecturer, Mimi is now a painter. La Magnanerie – the rock on which it was built still visible as one goes upstairs – did indeed house silkworms at the time when the industry flourished. It climbs the hillside in four half storeys, each level with a terrace under the shade of a majestic oak. The bedrooms have valley views and a homely mix of old furniture, the bathrooms are bright and beautiful with handmade tiles, the kitchen is charming and nicely equipped. In winter, a wood fire adds a cosy glow. Behind the house is a remarkable feature, a Roman irrigation canal, fast-flowing and pristine; Mimi pays £12 a year for the privilege of using it. This is a dreamy place to laze on languid summer days, in gardens shady with mulberry trees, lush with oleander, dotted with butterflies. Then down to the cooling trout stream across the field, to swim, paddle or sit and read. Find shops, markets and restaurants in the twisting streets of medieval Carcès and Entrecasteaux.

sleeps	6 + cot.
rooms	2 doubles, 1 twin; 3 bathrooms.
price	£100-£500 per week.

Mrs June Watkins
tel +44 (0)20 8891 2656
email junewatkins@lineone.net

La Canal

Lorgues, Var

Slip through the arched entrance in one of Lorgues' quiet streets and time seems to stand still. This comfortable old manor house, with its hexagonal tiled floors and fleets of marble fireplaces, exudes calm; clearly, a much-loved home. Nicola, mainly London-based and a veteran Sawday B&B host, adores children; there are cots, highchairs and a TV den plus swing and climbing frame in the garden. Grown-ups have their spaces, too: an elegant salon, shady spots and a hammock in the walled garden, and teak loungers surrounding the Roman-style pool. Bedrooms are furnished in traditional but uncluttered style with nice individual touches: a pair of antique wooden beds, a bright kilim, a headboard fashioned from a wooden door. The cosy, well-stocked country-style kitchen entices you to make jams and bake cakes. A dining table seats 14 but you'll mainly eat on the terrace beneath the ancient mulberry trees, where views reach to the Var hills. This is an outdoorsy place: riding, walking, canoeing in the Verdon canyon, watersports on the Var lakes. And music festivals galore. *B&B when not let.*

sleeps	12.
rooms	6: 2 doubles, 4 twins; 1 bathroom, 3 shower rooms, 1 separate wc.
price	€1,950-€3,250 per week.

Nicola D'Annunzio
tel +33 (0)4 94 67 68 32
fax +33 (0)4 94 67 68 69
email lacanallorgues@aol.com
web www.lacanal-lorgues.com

Bastide des Hautes Moures – Gîte Anis

Le Thoronet, Var

A track deep in the Var forest leads to this exquisite 1780 *bergerie*. Attached to the main house it stands in a hollow amid 14 acres of gnarled scrub oak, surrounded by cypresses, roses and lavender. Birds sing, butterflies shimmer. The cottage has been brought back to life in spectacular fashion, a monument to Catherine's flamboyant style and her love of colour; she is also an assiduous seeker of antique and *brocante* finds. You have a vast, lofty, open-plan kitchen/dining/sitting room decorated in aniseed green – hence the name – and an enchantingly pretty bedroom with floral canopied bed and yellow Provençal quilt. The bathroom is charming, the kitchen superb. Antoine was a restaurateur so if you don't want to cook, he will: stuffed vegetables, bass, foie gras, fine breads and jams. You can breakfast with the B&B guests if you prefer, for a small extra charge. Outside is your own little stone terrace with white wrought-iron tables and chairs, but it's an easy drive to Aix from here and there's masses to do – once you've raised yourself from the teak loungers that flank the shared pool. *B&B also.*

sleeps	2.
rooms	1 double; 1 bathroom.
price	€380-€950 per week.

Catherine Jobert & Antoine Debray

tel	+33 (0)4 94 60 13 36
fax	+33 (0)4 94 73 81 23
email	jobertcatherine@aol.com
web	www.bastide-des-moures.com

Bastide des Hautes Moures – Gîte de la Piscine

Le Thoronet, Var

The old pool house has been spectacularly converted into a discreet, single-storey refuge for two. From a concealed terrace, your views are to the pool, a piece of beautifully landscaped garden, and the wooded hills. Step into the stone-flagged living area and you will be instantly seduced; the owners have brought back fine things from their travels and there's a restful, 'out of Africa' feel. Sofas, a low table and a wrought-iron screen divide the cosy dining corner from the kitchen, which, with its stone sink set into a white lava worktop and its wide stone-arched window drawing the eye to the distant hills, is one of most delectable we've come across. Muslin curtains round the four-poster bed float softly in the breeze, the linen is crisp, the bed wide and firm, the shower room has an antique console embracing its basin. Catherine, young and soignée, looks after B&B and gîte guests with imagination and warmth, chef Antoine knows about the eateries in the area and the whole place could scarcely be more peaceful. All this, and the wondrous Abbey of Le Thoronet almost next door. *B&B also.*

sleeps	2.
rooms	1 double; 1 bathroom.
price	€500-€910 per week.

Catherine Jobert & Antoine Debray

tel	+33 (0)4 94 60 13 36
fax	+33 (0)4 94 73 81 23
email	jobertcatherine@aol.com
web	www.bastide-des-moures.com

Bastidon Saint Benoît

Flassans sur Issole, Var

Pine, rosemary, thyme and lavender fill the air in this corner of the Var Vert. With the olive trees, oaks and broom that range around this sunny one-storey house, they bring welcome relief from hot summers. The fresh, light interiors sing with Provençal colour; there are cool terracotta floors, large picture windows and Anne Marie's joyous stencil work – sprinkled on walls, bedhead and lampshades – to add to the breezy feel. Kitchen and bathroom are roomy and modern while the large sitting/dining room – log fire for cooler months – opens to the terrace; shaded by a pine tree and roll-down awning, this is a lovely spot for dining and lounging. It sits above a neat garden that manages to squeeze in a lawn, an exotic palm and a children's swing. There are also shared boules, ping-pong and pool, but please avoid using the pool at meal times; the owners, former Sawday B&B hosts, are a warm, welcoming couple. Perfectly pitched, half-way between the Verdon Canyon and the Iles du Levant, close to the beaches and water sports of Lac de Sainte-Croix, you are brilliantly placed.

sleeps	2-4.
rooms	1 double, 1 sofabed in sitting room; 1 shower room.
price	€450-€600 per week.

Jean & Anne Marie Pinel Peschardière

tel	+33 (0)4 94 04 01 04
fax	+33 (0)4 94 04 01 04
email	bastidonsaintbenoit@wanadoo.fr
web	www.giterural-provence.com

Les Pêchers

Ile de Porquerolles, Var

Wonderful Porquerolles! An off-season island retreat for a select few – and for many more in high summer. The pretty harbour is the hub of island life, and it's an easy walk to the village whose rooftops can be glimpsed in the distance. Built in the 1960s on the road to the lighthouse, Les Pêchers stands in a huge, nostalgically crumbly garden: paradise for children. Life is mostly lived under the bamboo awning of the large patio-terrace – you'll feel private and relaxed. The whole place has been recently redone: outdoors soft pink and lavender, indoors, a medley of colours and fabrics, and tiles and beds all new. Breezes blow in from the sea so bedrooms feel cool, and the kitchen has a comfortably family feel. A small two-bedroomed flat with sparkling bathroom and charming kitchen feeds off the salon but also has its own entrance and terrace. (The two gîtes can be rented separately.) Cars are banned so hire your bikes to explore the pure white sandy beaches and cliffs, the vineyards and pheasant-thronged woods. A super place for a family holiday, and beaches abound. *Linen for hire locally.*

sleeps 8-10. Annexe sleeps 4-6.

rooms 3 + 2: 2 doubles, 1 family room for 2-4, 1 sofabed in sitting room; 1 bathroom, 1 separate wc. Annexe: 1 double, 1 twin in sitting room; 1 bathroom, 1 shower room,1 separate wc.

price €800-€2,920. Annexe €450-€1,050. Prices per week.

Christine Richet
tel +33 (0)1 39 50 88 14
fax +33 (0)1 39 50 88 14
email info@lespechers.com
web www.lespechers.com

Robin's Nest

La Garde Freinet, Var

The carved wooden door, with its elaborate lock, hints that this is no ordinary place. Slip inside and be greeted by good wine, cheeses, meats and fresh flowers; someone wants to spoil you. Louise and Robin, the South African/British owners who live on the ground floor, have restored the 17th-century village house – originally three dwellings – with an élan bordering on the lavish. Set against the wooden beams and parquet flooring is an exotic mix of Provençal antique furnishings and smart-modern. The first-floor, open-plan living area – oriental carpets, sofa, handsome refectory table – overlooks the bustle of La Garde Freinet's medieval streets. The kitchen corner, swish with black granite and Italian marble, wants for nothing. Up to the bedroom, a restful space of rich reds and creams, cushions, a piece of salon, and views over rooftops and forests to the Alps. Two bathrooms, one with spa bath, glisten with marble and luxurious unguents. Set off for the coast (beach towels provided), Aix, the Verdon Gorges; stroll around the village cafés and ateliers. Then back to your love nest in the sky. *B&B also.*

sleeps	2.
rooms	1 double; 1 bathroom.
price	€685-€980 per week.
closed	Mid January-mid March.

Louise & Robin Swart

tel	+44 (0)118 9582511
fax	+44 (0)118 9582511
email	louiseswart@hotmail.com
web	www.escape2provence.com

Hameau l'Autourière

La Garde Freinet, Var

The tortuous drive along the track to this 300-year-old hamlet is worth the bumps. Up eight stone steps to your single-floor studio, you enter a haven of rustic cosiness. Warm rusts, creams and yellows enhance the sense of comfort; ethnic artefacts brought back from Africa add interest. Beyond the cosy and peaceful sleeping and sitting areas are a simple kitchenette and an intimate dining 'room'. Old terracotta floors, tiny windows and low beamed ceilings convey the great age of this *magnanerie* – where silkworms used to be reared – and keep you cool in the hottest weather. Charming Mrs Woodall lives in the farmhouse next door with Clio, her golden retriever and often hosts a stream of friends and relations. You may meet them by the magnificent pool among the trees or over a barbecue under the sprawling mulberry, but if you want privacy there are three hectares of meadows, lawns and borders, skilfully tended by Mrs Woodall's green fingers. Visit medieval and fashionable La Garde Freinet; walk the heavenly Route des Crêtes through the Massif des Maures. *No children but babes-in-arms.*

sleeps	2.
rooms	1 studio with double; 1 bathroom.
price	€420-€630 (£300-£450) per week.
arrival	Flexible.

Mrs Philippa Woodall
tel +33 (0)4 94 43 63 47
fax +33 (0)4 94 43 63 47

Villa Les Oliviers

Bargemon, Var

Given wings, you could launch yourself from the terraced garden and drift over the rooftops of Bargemon. The villa hangs above the village with views to forested hills and, on a good day, the sparkle of the Med. Its terraces of vines, fruit trees and lavender are interspersed with shady corners, eating areas and a balustraded pool with pool house. Behind, a steep path climbs to a studio – perfect for writing, or an extra guest. The house – with more steepish steps outside – has been furnished with taste yet has an intimate feel. When not travelling, it's the owners' home; he's a diplomat and writer, she's an art dealer. The living area, with its fireplace and creamy sofas, has a dining table overlooking those stunning views; the lovely Provençal kitchen opens onto a terrace furnished with a Raj tent. Antique beds and modern art fill the bedrooms (the single very small); there are books and art everywhere. The owners are not always there but leave a generous welcome pack. Ideal for coast or mountains, exploring hilltop villages or medieval Bargemon's galleries and restaurants.

sleeps	7-8.
rooms	4: 3 doubles, 1 single; 1 bathroom, 3 shower rooms, 2 separate wcs.
price	€1,900-€3,800 per week.

Frédérique Neuville

tel	+44 (0)20 7823 4704
email	provencemagique@msn.com
web	www.provencemagique.com

La Maison Blanche

Bargemon, Var

You're hard by one of the prettiest, most fashionable villages of east Provence but here you see no-one. Cradled by pine-clad mountains, this old farmhouse is surrounded by lawns, flower-filled meadows and orchards. In spring you'll hear nightingales and smell wild narcissi; in summer the fruit trees yield apricots, cherries and figs, all of which you're free to gather. The house has been deeply renovated by the English owners, although they have kept old beams and some lovely honeycomb floor tiles. Furniture is mostly antique French and English, with some unusual items such as an ancient workbench-turned-sideboard in the dining room and wooden doughboards at the heads of two of the beds. The charming end bedroom, once the hayloft, has a vine-clad balcony from which you can pluck grapes in the autumn. As bedrooms are reached by two staircases, the house is ideal for two families holidaying together. The village, with a weekly hiking party *and* a market, is a short walk up the hill. Then back for lunch on the huge terrace under the shade of the limes and a dip in the heavenly pool.

sleeps	10.
rooms	5: 1 double, 4 twins; 3 bathrooms, 1 shower room.
price	£470-£2,050 per week.
arrival	Thursday.

Janet Hill
tel +44 (0)1628 482579
fax +44 (0)1628 482579
email dsimons@onetel.com

30 rue Pierre Porre

Mons, Var

Come for the hilltop village, perched above the forest like an eagle's nest. It's an echo of a France long lost, a medieval wonder beautifully preserved – and not recommended for the less than sprightly! Your house is very old in parts with 17th- and 19th-century additions and a serenity borne of age. Bedrooms, up very steep stairs, have a cultivated simplicity: a brass bed, fresh walls, a writing desk, a rooftop view, a watercolour by a friend; those under the eaves are much the nicest. The kitchen is tiny yet well-equipped. In the garden some intriguing bits of carved stone are scattered around – some of them probably Roman. As for the views… the village is the second highest in the Var and the vistas extend for miles across wide stretches of forest and hill before falling off into a distant sea. There's no pool but you won't give a fig. Don't miss the village square (you park here out of season) and its fountain; there's almost a feel of the Italian riviera. *Not suitable for young children due to steep stairs. Tricky parking. B&B also.*

sleeps	6.
rooms	4: 2 doubles, 2 singles; 2 shower rooms, 2 separate wc.
price	€350-€600 per week.
arrival	Saturday in

Ursula Mouton

tel	+33 (0)2 38 80 65 68
email	ulimout@yahoo.fr
web	www.geocities.com/ulimouton/

La Ferme de Guillandonne

Tourrettes, Var

This enchanting 200-year-old farmhouse is the height of country-hideaway chic. Earthy, stylish, magical, it stands under the sprawling embrace of an ancient oak (one of many) and is bordered on one side by a stream. You are wrapped in 10 acres of countryside. Rows of lavender run along one side of the pool while on the other a tunnel of wisteria leads down to a sun-trapping terrace. The interior is equally satisfying. Walls are washed in traditional colours – cool yellows, cosy reds, pale greens. There are old beams and a big arched window gives onto the terrace. One of the bedrooms has a magnificent high ceiling and a window that looks out onto a Chinese mulberry tree, another an original open fireplace and views over the pool. Marie-Joëlle, a former English teacher, and her husband, an architect, have renovated with a happy respect for the spirit of the place, for its history and the landscape that envelops it. You are in one of the loveliest parts of the Var and villages here have musical events running throughout the summer. This is a *bona fide* classic, a very special place. Don't miss it. *B&B also.*

sleeps 6-7 + cot.

rooms 3: 2 doubles, 1 twin, extra bed available; 2 bathrooms, 1 shower room, 1 shower room with separate entrance.

price €1,000-€2,300 per week.

Marie-Joëlle Salaün

tel +33 (0)4 94 76 04 71

fax +33 (0)4 94 76 04 71

Apartment

Mandelieu, Alpes-Maritimes

From first-floor windows, an expanse of sky. Below, green fairways, trees and distant hills. The communal pool is out of sight, the motorway a distant hum, the golf course beckons... there is peacefulness, light and space. Your three-bedroom apartment in this gated, pink and white 'village' is probably one of the largest and surely the most immaculate. Slip a CD into the state-of-the-art music centre, slide open the glass doors to the (almost) wraparound balcony, roll down the electric shade, unfurl on a white-cushioned lounger. The owners have employed the most talented artisans and have decorated to their own design – the result: a spare, sweeping, luxurious décor with a red and cream theme and oriental touches. Everything is crisply, perfectly new: the pale quarry tiles, the creamy drapes, the Turkish carpet, the de Dietrich oven, the huge TV (plus videos for kids). And when you've tired of the fine linens and the silk cushions, there's the sea two miles away, and Nice, Mougins, St Tropez. Not forgetting three tennis clubs and innumerable golf courses... the nearest laps at your feet.

sleeps	6.
rooms	3 twins/doubles; 2 bathrooms, 1 shower room, 1 separate wc.
price	€1,500-€2,100 (£1,000-£1,400) per week.

Ennis & Barry Bartman

tel +44 (0)1582 769728

mobile +44 (0)783 1636644

email mandelieuappt@aol.com

web www.rivieragolf.info

La Chansonnière

Cannes, Alpes-Maritimes

The immaculate 1930s house hides down a back street five minutes from sea air and La Croisette. Of course, it's perfect for film festival folk in May (catering included) but big family groups would love it too. The white-walled, marble-floored, palm-dotted main space is divided into two stylish sitting areas, one with cream leather sofas, media deck and vast TV; the dining area seats up to 16, the techie corner has all the works. The kitchen is as super as you would expect and French windows lead to a little sun deck with teak loungers and 'three-stroke' pool, prettily lit at night. The wide, white-metal stair with stained-glass windows is pure Thirties, sweeping you up to bedrooms on two floors – all a good size, the master room with its own terrace. New windows, white walls, electric rolling shutters, cream beds, bathrobes, slippers, shower caps, even a rubber duck. Character comes in the shape of stitched quilts, a 'distressed' Provençal armoire, a draped curtain on a corner window. It is all perfectly fabulous, and in the very heart of Cannes. *Housekeeper optional.*

sleeps	18.
rooms	9: 6 doubles, 3 singles, 1 suite for 3; 10 bathrooms.
price	£4,000–£5,000 per week.
arrival	Saturday but flexible.

Michael Callis

tel +44 (0)20 7224 2990
fax +44 (0)20 7224 1990
email mc@22yorkstreet.co.uk
web www.cannesvillas.co.uk

Villa Gardiole

Biot, Alpes-Maritimes

'Twixt Cannes and Nice: a protected, gated hideaway. This two-hectare, hillside paradise – built in the 1950s – includes the owners' house, your charming villa and one other… and all rooms lead to the garden, it seems. Wisely: this is a glorious expanse of grass, trees, landscaped bushes and potager (yours to poach), a discreet lake-like pool, a wooden pergola, a serene all-glass weights room (that opens up in warm weather), swings, slides, treehouse, hammocks and bamboo forest. And your dining courtyard. Inside, rustic terracotta floors, a polished country dresser, a copper *batterie de cuisine*, a touch of trompe l'oeil – the feel is immaculate Provençal. Downstairs, a pale green-check sofa, a working chimney and an open country kitchen; upstairs, a gaily canopied bed and an en suite terrace. Madame Severgnini can arrange a maid, a cook, a yoga teacher, a personal trainer, a gardening course with an expert, Italian cookery with her. The Brague National Park starts from the back door and there are so many cultural and sporty ways in which you may fill your hours. Fabulous!

sleeps	7.
rooms	3: 2 doubles, 1 twin, 1 single; 4 bathrooms.
price	€2,000–€3,500 per week.
arrival	Flexible.

Ignazia Severgnini

tel	+33 (0)4 93 65 55 08
fax	+33 (0)4 93 65 50 44
email	severgnin@aol.com
web	www.villagardiole.com

Les Coquelicots

Le Rouret, Alpes-Maritimes

Annick, a well-travelled, restful and kind person, has turned the living space under her little house into a sweet retreat – perfect for a couple with young child. A former riding instructress, she is now more likely to be helping people into hammocks than onto horses: the peaceful garden, its awesomely ancient olive trees dotted about terraces and among lush grasses, is ideal for a siesta and bliss for children – big, overgrown and full of secret corners in which to hide. Over this looks your light-filled, quarry-tiled garden suite, with its own entrance, a kitchenette tucked into a corner, a small sofabed and a shower. Annick also has a smaller room normally set aside for B&B, which you may use if you are more than three; a charming room with its own entrance, it has blue walls, a vast antique wardrobe and fine linen on an old wooden bed. If it's not too hot for the delightful, all-glass, orchid- and bamboo-filled veranda, breakfast (an optional extra) is served in the saffron-yellow living room upstairs. Alternatively, Annick delivers fresh bread every morning. *B&B also.*

sleeps	2-3.
rooms	1 double, 1 sofabed; 1 shower room.
price	€490 per week. Extra B&B room €55.

Annick Le Guay

tel +33 (0)4 93 77 40 04

fax +33 (0)4 93 77 40 04

email annick.coquelicot@tiscali.fr

La Bergerie

Le Bar sur Loup, Alpes-Maritimes

The soft stone walls of the sweet *bergerie* – the shepherd's hut – keep you cool in the hottest weather. Enjoy your morning coffee at the old manger – now a breakfast bar – or out on the terrace, and watch the sun come up over the hilltop village of Le Bar sur Loup, a 20-minute walk away. Surrounded by grass, oaks, olives, pines and rocky-peaked mountains, this is a blissfully peaceful place. Sylvie, an actress, and Pascal, have restored and decorated the cottage in a stylish but informal way. Floors are bleached wood, wooden ceilings are painted, there are simple, charming touches and the bedroom has fabulous views. This sporty young couple – they met hang-gliding – and their three children make you feel warmly at home yet leave you to your own devices. Come for cherries in May, fireflies in June: a spring and summer paradise. It's a short hop to the coast if you fancy the razzmatazz of the Riviera; gentler forays might include visits to the stunning 'perched villages' of the area. There is another slightly more up-to-date cottage 50 metres away, which sleeps two plus child.

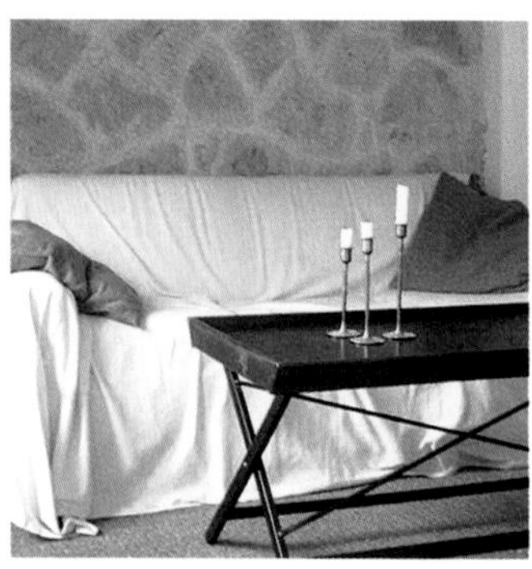

sleeps	2-3.
rooms	1 double, sofabed in dining room; 1 shower room.
price	€350-€620 per week.

Sylvie & Pascal Delaunay
tel +33 (0)4 93 42 50 08
email chemindelachenaie@hotmail.com
web www.chemindelachenaie.com

La Maison

Vence, Alpes-Maritimes

One of the loveliest places in this book. Not the smartest or the most beautiful, just utterly authentic and sure of itself. It is a place to chance upon, as if the house were too modest to seduce you in advance. Those lucky enough to wash up on its shores find an old Provençal stone farmhouse that stands beneath the protective gaze of Le Baou, a sugar-loaf mountain. Your immediate surroundings are wilderness; beyond are the suburbs of Vence and distant traffic hum. Your apartment is on the top floor, reached via open stone steps and a (shared) terrace shaded by an ancient olive. Laurence, warm cultured and full of life, lives on the ground floor with her children, another family are on the second. Bedrooms are simple and cosy, beds dressed in fine linen. One has whitewashed walls and a beautiful 18th-century 'built-in' cupboard, the other an antique desk and views through trees. There's a long refectory dining table in the kitchen and rush-seated chairs, and a tiny but adorable sitting room. Stroll down to the waterfalls and swimming holes of the Cagne river. *Parking on road.*

sleeps	4 + 1 child.
rooms	2: 1 double, 1 twin, child's bed available; 1 bathroom.
price	€300-€500 per week.

Laurence Thiébaut

tel	+33 (0)4 93 58 13 95
fax	+33 (0)4 93 58 13 95
email	lamaisondelaurence@hotmail.com
web	www.lamaisondelaurence.com

National and Regional Parks

General De Gaulle signed the initial legislation for the creation of its National and Regional Parks in 1967. Forty national and regional nature parks in France now represent 11% of its landmass. Most are off the beaten track and are often missed by the foreign visitor. The motorway network is such that one swishes by huge patches of beautiful countryside without even realising it.

The National and Regional Parks charter promotes:

- Protection and management of natural and cultural heritage
- Participation in town and country planning and implementation of economic and social development
- Welcoming and informing the public, raising environmental awareness

There is a ban on hunting, camping, building and road construction in the six national parks: Cévennes, Ecrins, Mercantour, Port-Cros, Pyrénées and Vanoise. Access can be difficult but the rewards are considerable.

There are regional parks to be found in the mountains of Queyras (Hautes Alpes), the plains of Vexin (Ile de France), along the coast of Camargue (Provence), in the woodlands in the Northern Vosges (Alsace-Lorraine), in the wetlands of Brière (Western Loire) and off-shore in Port-Cros (Côte d'Azur).

All are ideal for rambles. Serious walkers can choose from the sentiers de Grandes Randonnées (GRs for short) which range through the parks and all park offices can provide maps of local walks.

There are grottos and museums to visit along with animal parks roaming with bison, yak, greater kudu and a pack of wolves. Activities include: horseriding, cycling and bike rentals, canoeing and kayaking, canal boating, sailing, fishing, spa treatments, wine tours, bathing, rock climbing, handgliding, ballooning. There are packhorses in Livredois-Forez (Auverge) and donkeys for hire in Haut-Languedoc (Languedoc).
A range of activities make them ideal for children and a multitude of crafts are to be observed: clog-making, silk weaving, glass working, stone working in the Morvan (Burgundy), cheesemaking and pipe-making in the Haut Jura (Franche Comté).

www.parcs-naturales-regionaux.tm.fr

This central web site links to all the other parks. All have English language versions.

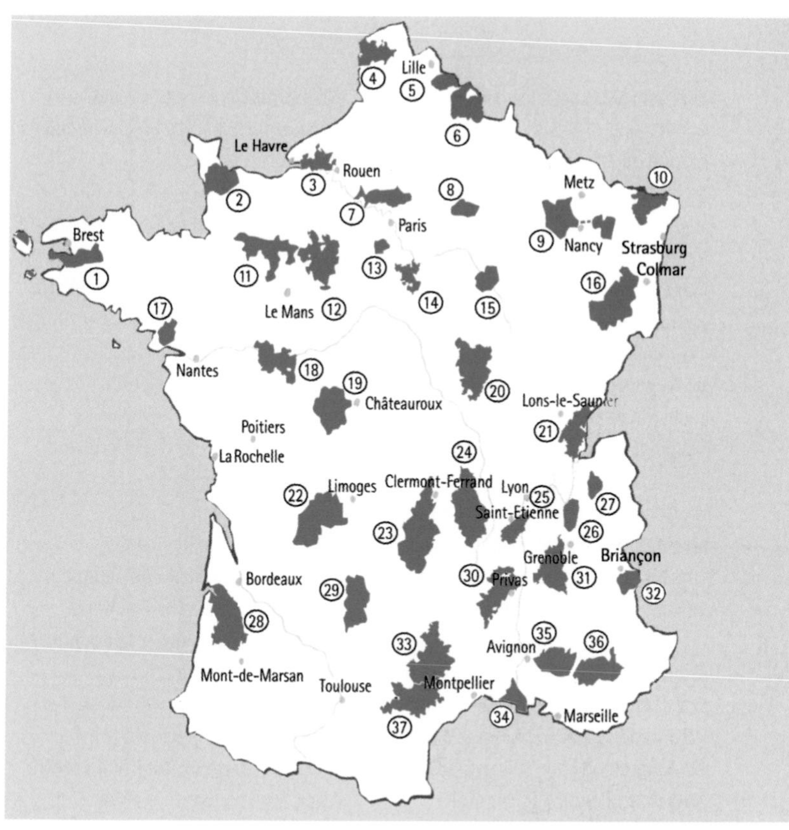

1. Armorique
2. Marais du Cotentin et du Bessin
3. Boucles de la Seine Normande
4. Caps et Marais d'Opale
5. Scarpe-Escaut
6. Avesnois
7. Vexin français
8. Montagne de Reims
9. Lorraine
10. Vosges du Nord
11. Normandie-Maine
12. Perche
13. Haute-Vallée de Chevreuse
14. Gâtinais français
15. Forêt d'Orient
16. Ballons des Vosges
17. Brière
18. Loire-Anjou-Touraine
19. Brenne
20. Morvan
21. Haut-Jura
22. Périgord Limousin
23. Volcans d'Auvergne
24. Livradois-Forez
25. Pilat
26. Chartreuse
27. Massif des Bauges
28. Landes de Gascogne
29. Causses du Quercy
30. Monts d'Ardèche
31. Chartreuse
32. Queyras
33. Grands Causses
34. Camargue
35. Luberon
36. Verdon
37. Haut-Languedoc

Walking in France

With over 60,000km of clearly marked long distance footpaths, or sentiers de Grandes Randonnées (GRs for short), and a fantastic variety of landscapes and terrains, France is a superb country in which to walk. Hike in the snow-topped glaciers of the Northern Alps, walk through the lush and rugged volcanic 'moonscapes' of the Auvergne, or amble through the vineyards of Burgundy, Alsace or Provence.

Stroll for an afternoon, or make an odyssey over several months. Some long-distance walks have become classics, like the famous GR65, the pilgrim road to Santiago de Compostela, the Tour du Mont Blanc, or the 450km long GR3 Sentier de la Loire, which runs from the Ardèche to the Atlantic. Wild or tamed, hot or temperate, populated or totally empty: France has it all.

Wherever you are staying, there will almost certainly be a GR near you. You can walk a stretch of it, then use other paths to turn it into a circular walk. As well as the network of GRs, marked with red and white parallel paint markings, there's a network of Petites Randonnées (PRs), usually signalled by single yellow or green paint stripes. In addition, there are sentiers de Grandes Randonnées de Pays (GRPs), marked by a red and yellow stripe, and any number of variants of the original GR route which eventually become paths in their own right. Paths are evolving all the time.

The paths are lovingly waymarked and maintained by the Fédération Française de la Randonnée Pédestre (FFRP), which was founded in 1947 under another name. The federation is also responsible for producing the topo-guides, books for walkers containing walking directions and maps (see under Books).

The great reward for walkers is that you'll penetrate the soul of rural France in a way you never could from a car. You'll see quaint ruined châteaux, meet country characters whom you'll never forget and you'll encounter a dazzling variety of flora and fauna if you look for it. France has a remarkably rich natural heritage, including 266 species of nesting birds, 131 species of mammal, and nearly 5,000 species of flowering plants. Look out for golden eagles, griffon vultures and marmots in the Alps and Pyrénées, red kites and lizard orchids in the Dordogne, and fulmars and puffins off the rocky Brittany coast. There's no room for complacency, however, as hundreds of species are threatened with extinction: 400 species of flora are classed as threatened and about 20 species of mammals and birds are vulnerable or in danger of extinction.

When to go

The best months for walking are May, June, September and October. In high mountain areas, summers are briefer and paths may be free of snow only between July and early September. In the northern half of France July and August are also good months; southern France is ideal for a winter break, when days are often crisp and clear.

The Code du Randonneur

- Love and respect nature
- Avoid unnecessary noise
- Destroy nothing
- Do not leave litter
- Do not pick flowers or plants
- Do not disturb wildlife
- Re-close all gates
- Protect and preserve the habitat
- No smoking or fires in the forests
- Stay on the footpath
- Respect and understand the country way of life and the country people
- Think of others as you think of yourself

Maps

The two big names for maps are IGN (Institut Géographique National) and Michelin. IGN maps are likely to be of most use for walkers. A useful map for planning walks is the IGN's France: Grande Randonnée sheet No. 903 which shows all the country's long distance footpaths. For walking, the best large-scale maps are the IGN's 1:25,000 Serie Bleue and Top 25 series. Also look out for IGN's 1:50,000 Plein Air series which includes GRs and PRs, plus hotels and campsites. Unfortunately they cover only limited areas.

Books

The FFRP produces more than 180 topo-guides – guidebooks for walkers which include walking instructions and IGN maps (usually 1:50,000). Most of these are now translated into English so it's worth buying one before you leave.

Clothing and equipment

This obviously depends on the terrain, the length of the walk and the time of year, but here's a suggested checklist:

Boots, sunhat, suncream and lip salve, mosquito repellent, sunglasses, sweater, cagoule, stick, water bottle, gaiters, change of clothing, phrase book, maps, compass, field guides to flora and fauna, waterproof daypack, camera and spare film, Swiss Army knife, whistle (for emergencies), spare socks, binoculars, waterproof jacket and trousers, emergency food, first-aid kit, torch.

Cycling in France

Two and a half times the size of the UK, France offers rich rewards to the cyclist: plenty of space, a superb network of minor roads with little traffic, and a huge diversity of landscapes, smells and terrains. You can chose the leafy forests and gently undulating plains of the north, or the jagged glacier-topped mountains of the Alps. Pedal through wafts of fermenting grapes in Champagne, resinous pines in the Midi, or spring flowers in the Pyrénées. Amble slowly, stopping in remote villages for delicious meals or a café au lait, or pit yourself against the toughest terrains and cycle furiously.

You will also be joining in a national sport: bikes are an important part of French culture and thousands don their lycra and take to their bikes on summer weekends. The country comes to a virtual standstill during the three-week Tour de France cycling race in July and the media is dominated by talk of who is the latest *maillot jaune* (literally 'yellow jersey' – the fellow in the lead). Cycling stars become national heroes and heroines with quasi-divine status.

Mountain bikes are becoming increasingly popular. They are known as VTTs (*vélos tout terrain*) and there is an extensive network of VTT trails, usually marked in purple.

When to go

Avoid July and August, if possible, as it's hot and the roads are at their busiest. The south is good from mid-March, except on high ground which may be snow-clad until the end of June. The north, which has a similar climate to Britain's, can be lovely from May onwards. Most other areas are suitable from April until October.

Getting bikes to and through France

If you are using public transport, you can get your bicycle to France by air, by ferry or via the Channel Tunnel. Ferries carry bikes for nothing or for a small fee. British Airways and Air France take bikes free if you don't exceed their weight allowance. If you are travelling by Eurostar, you should be able to store your bike in one of the guards' vans which have cycle-carrying hooks, with a potential capacity of up to eight bikes per train. To do this you need to reserve and pay extra.

Some mainline and most regional trains accept bikes, sometimes free of charge, most for a fee. Some have dedicated bike spaces, others make room in the guard's van. Information is contradictory on timetables and ticket agents may not have up-to-date information. Trains indicated by a small bike symbol in the timetable may no longer accept bikes, some without the symbol do. To be sure, check out the train at the station the day before you depart. Insist on a ticket *avec réservation d'un emplacement vélo.* If you are two or more make sure the réservation is multiple. In the Paris area, you can take bikes on most trains except during rush hours and at certain central RER stations.

Maps

The two big names are Michelin and the Institut Géographique National (IGN). For route-planning, IGN publishes a map of the whole of France showing mountain-biking and cycle tourism (No. 906). The best on-the-road reference maps are Michelin's Yellow 1:200,000 Series. IGN publishes a Green Series at a scale of 1:100,000. For larger scale maps, go for IGN's excellent 1:25,000 Top 25 and Blue Series (which you will also use for walking).

A new map of Paris showing bike routes, one-way streets, bus sharing lanes, rental facilities, weekend pedestrian and bike only streets is available at some bookstores. Order it online: www.media-cartes.fr

Repairs and spare parts

Bike shops are at least as numerous as in Britain and you should be able to get hold of spare parts, provided you don't try between noon and 2pm.

Some useful contacts

- Fédération Française de la Randonnée Pédestre (FFRP) www.ffrp.asso.fr Leading organisation for walkers and ramblers. Many of their guide books have been translated into English.
- Fédération Française de Cyclotourisme www.ffct.org
For cyclists and mountain bikers.
- SNCF (French Railways)
www.voyages-sncf.com

Bike rental

- Maison Roue Libre
Affiliated to Paris's public transport system RATP
www.rouelibre.fr (0)1 44 76 86 43
- Mike's Bike Tours-Pars
www.mikesbiketoursparis.com
(0)1 56 58 10 54
Bike tours designed with the English-speaking tourist in mind; day and night tours of Paris; day trips to Versailles and Monet's Garden at Giverny. Also organise Segway (self-balancing motorized scooter) tours of Paris and Nice.
- Mieux se Déplacer à Bicyclette
www.mdb-idf.org (0)1 43 20 26 02
Advocate group for bicycles and their use in Paris. Members can join free weekend trips outside of Paris, longer ones in the summer all over France.
- Paris Tourist Office:
www.parisinfo.com
Click on 'roller' for details of roller-blading tours (Fridays and Sundays).

French words & expressions

armoire cupboard, wardrobe
bastide it can be a stronghold, a small fortified village or, in Provence, another word for mas
bergerie sheepfold, sheep shed
brocante secondhand furniture, objects, fabric, hats, knick-knacks
cabanon cabin, chalet, or, in Provence, cottage
chambre d'hôtes B&B
château a mansion or stately home built for aristocrats between the 16th and 19th centuries. A castle, with fortifications, is a château fort
châtelain/e lord/lady of the manor
dépendance outbuilding of château, farm etc
domaine viticole wine producing estate
fauteuil armchair
gardien warden
gîte d'étape overnight dormitory-style huts/houses, often run by the local village or municipality, for cyclists or walkers (often with optional meals)
lavoir washing place or wash house
longère a long, low farmhouse made of Breton granite
magnanerie silkworm farm

maison bourgeoise/ maison de maître big, comfortable houses standing in quite large grounds, built for members of the liberal professions, captains of industry, trade etc
maison paysanne country cottage
mas a Provençal country house, usually long and low with old stone walls, pan-tiled roof and painted shutters
maison vigneronne can be a tiny vine-worker's cottage or a comfortable house owned by the estate manager or proprietor
mazot another word for mas, used in the Rhône Valley-Alps
mairie town hall
marché au gras market where you can buy foie gras and other delights
moulin mill
œil de boeuf literally bull's eye window, ie. small circular or oval window
pineau an alcoholic aperitif from the Charantes region made from wine and cognac
pigeonnier pigeon-house or dovecote
pommeau alcoholic drink made from apples
potage/potager vegetable soup/vegetable garden
puys Auvergnat dialect for 'peak'
salle d'accueil reception room
salle d'eau shower room
salle de séjour living room
table d'hôtes dinner with the owners of the house
tommette hexagonal terracotta floor tile

ALASTAIR SAWDAY'S
SPECIAL ESCAPES

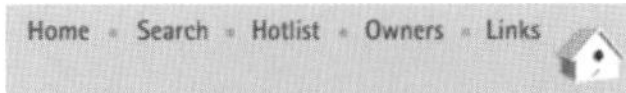

Shutters on the Harbour, St Ives

Cornwall, England

You'd never guess that this 1875 former fisherman's cottage in the belly of the old town is the lap of modern luxury inside. Georgie and Janin have cleverly renovated this tiny dwelling into a funky palace with lots of surprising touches. Originally pilchards were pressed in the old lounge and shipped to Tuscany – now the only remaining sign is the wooden grooves in the stone walls. From the neutral stone-floored lounge with sheepskin rugs on the rattan chairs, scamper into the shower/washing room to wash off the sand – perfect for surfers. Up to a suspended floor with the kitchen with round table, built-in benches and all mod cons and a second chill-out space – both look down to the lounge. A spiral stair leads up to the bedrooms. Here Janin's furniture-design skills were brought in to create wacky bedside tables using driftwood and stylistic shapes. There are painted wooden floors, funky light sculptures, neutral colours and portholes leading to the bathroom - separated by a vibrant sari curtain. It has a beach-house style with a modern homespun element and they have carefully made the most of the limited space; it can be tight in some corners but somehow that adds to the fun. An ideal spot from which to make the most of St Ives.

Owner's Notice Board

BEAUTIFUL ST IVES

Last week of September and all of October still available. STUNNING CONVERSION OF FISHERMAN'S COTTAGE IN HEART OF ST IVES

Note: This information has been provided by the owner or management of Shutters on the Harbour and is not verified or endorsed by ASP.

Details for Shutters on the Harbour

Contact Georgina Lenain

tel: +44(0)7770 431558

fax: +44(0)20 8877 0700

Send E-mail Enquiry

sleeps:

rooms: 2 doubles with shower; shower room.

price: £550.00 – £960.00. In winter short breaks negotiated

closed: Never.

changeover: Saturday- negotiable.

? Details Explanation

Currency Converter

? Symbol Explanations

Why Come Here?

Checklist

Dishwasher

Points Of Interest

Eden Project 1-hour drive.

'Shutters on the harbour' Bethesda Hill

Bedroom 1

Sitting room with winter rugs

Views on Porthminster Beach

Now what?

A whole week self-catering in Britain with your friends or family is precious, and you dare not get it wrong. To whom do you turn for advice and who on earth do you trust when the web is awash with advice from strangers? We launched Special Escapes to satisfy an obvious need for impartial and trustworthy help – and that is what it provides. The criteria for inclusion are the same as for our books: we have to like the place and the owners. It has, quite simply, to be 'special'. The site, our first online-only publication, is featured on www.thegoodwebguide.com and is growing fast.

www.specialescapes.co.uk

Fragile Earth series

The Little Earth Book

Edition 4, £6.99

By James Bruges

A little book that has proved both hugely popular – and provocative. This new edition has chapters on Islam, Climate Change and The Tyranny of Corporations.

The Little Food Book

Edition 1, £6.99

By Craig Sams, Chairman of the Soil Association

An explosive account of the food we eat today. Never have we been at such risk - from our food. This book will help clarify what's at stake.

The Little Money Book

Edition 1, £6.99

By David Boyle, an associate of the New Economics Foundation

This pithy, wry little guide will tell you where money comes from, what it means, what it's doing to the planet and what we might be able to do about it.

www.fragile-earth.com

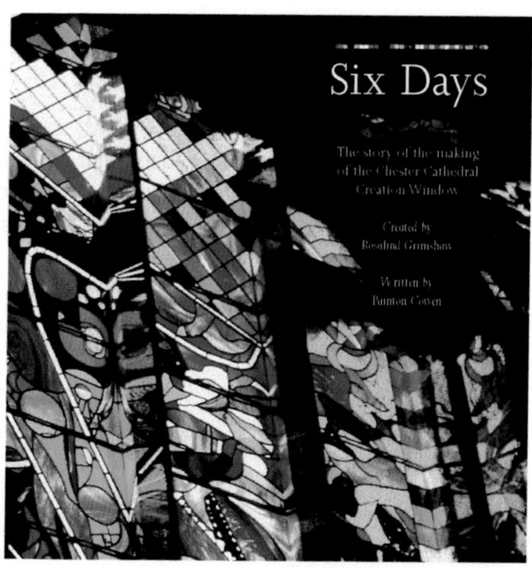

Celebrating the triumph of creativity over adversity.

An inspiring and heart-rending story of the making of the stained glass 'Creation' window at Chester Cathedral by a woman battling with debilitating Parkinson's disease.

"Within a few seconds, the tears were running down my cheeks. The window was one of the most beautiful things I had ever seen. It is a tour-de-force, playing with light like no other window ..."
Anthropologist Hugh Brody

In 1983, Ros Grimshaw, a distinguished designer, artist and creator of stained glass windows, was diagnosed with Parkinson's disease. Refusing to allow her illness to prevent her from working, Ros became even more adept at her craft, and in 2000 won the commission to design and make the 'Creation' Stained Glass Window for Chester Cathedral.

Six Days traces the evolution of the window from the first sketches to its final, glorious completion as a rare and wonderful tribute to Life itself: for each of the six 'days' of Creation recounted in Genesis, there is a scene below that is relevant to the world of today and tomorrow.

Heart-rending extracts from Ros's diary capture the personal struggle involved. Superb photography captures the luminescence of the stunning stained glass, while the story weaves together essays, poems, and moving contributions from Ros's partner, Patrick Costeloe.

Available from Alastair Sawday Publishing £12.99

Order Form

All these books are available in major bookshops or you may order them direct. Post and packaging are FREE within the UK.

British Hotels, Inns & Other Places	£13.99
Bed & Breakfast for Garden Lovers	£14.99
British Bed & Breakfast	£14.99
Pubs & Inns of England & Wales	£13.99
London	£9.99
French Bed & Breakfast	£15.99
French Hotels, Châteaux & Other Places	£14.99
French Holiday Homes	£11.99
Paris Hotels	£9.99
Ireland	£12.99
Spain	£14.99
Portugal	£10.99
Italy	£12.99
Mountains of Europe	£9.99
India	£10.99
Morocco	£10.99
Turkey	£11.99
The Little Earth Book	£6.99
The Little Food Book	£6.99
The Little Money Book	£6.99
Six Days	£12.99

Please make cheques payable to Alastair Sawday Publishing. Total £

Please send cheques to: Alastair Sawday Publishing, Yanley Lane, Long Ashton, Bristol, BS41 9LR. For credit card orders call 01275 464891 or order directly from our web site **www.specialplacestostay.com**

Title First name Surname

Address

Postcode Tel

FSC3

If you do not wish to receive mail from other like-minded companies, please tick here ☐
If you would prefer not to receive information about special offers on our books, please tick here ☐

Report Form

If you have any comments on entries in this guide, please let us have them. If you have a favourite house, hotel, inn or other new discovery, please let us know about it. You can email info@sawdays.co.uk, too.

Existing entry:

Book title: ______________________________

Entry no: ______________ Edition no: ______________

Report:

____

____

____

____

____

____

____

Country: New recommendation:

Property name: ______________________________

Address: ______________________________

____

____

____

Tel: ______________________________

____

Your name: ______________________________

Address: ______________________________

____

____

Tel: ______________________________

email: ______________________________

Please send completed form to ASP, Yanley Lane, Long Ashton, Bristol BS41 9LR or go to www.specialplacestostay.com and click on 'contact'. Thank you.

Quick reference indices

Limited mobility

Need a ground floor bedroom and bathroom? Try these:

The North 1
Burgundy 15 • 26 • 27
Normandy 32 • 41 • 67 • 68 • 71 • 74
Brittany 86 • 89
Western Loire 91• 93 • 98 • 99
Loire Valley 108 • 110 • 111 • 112 • 122 • 123 •125 • 127
Poitou – Charentes 132 • 135 • 137 • 142 • 147
Limousin 151 • 155
Auvergne 156 • 160 • 162
Aquitaine 164 • 165 • 167 • 172 • 173 • 174 • 180 • 183 • 184 • 187 • 188 • 189 • 192 • 193 • 194 • 195 • 196 • 197 • 200 • 201
Midi – Pyrénées 213 • 214 • 216 • 221 • 227 • 232 • 236 • 237 • 238 • 239 • 255 • 261
Languedoc – Rousillon 265 • 273 • 282 • 287 • 293
Rhône Valley – Alps 305 • 311 • 312
Provence – Alps – Riviera 316 • 318 • 324 • 327 • 328 • 329 • 335 • 336 • 347 • 348 • 351 • 352 • 356 • 357

Wheelchair-accessible

These places have fully approved wheelchair facilities.

The North 4
Burgundy 24
Normandy 72
Brittany 88
Loire Valley 118 • 119
Limousin 152
Aquitaine 169 • 170 • 198 • 209
Languedoc – Rousillon 276 • 277 • 281
Provence – Alps – Riviera 326

Gîtes for two guests

The North 2
Burgundy 14 • 17 • 18
Paris – Ile de France 29
Normandy 38 • 45 • 47 • 48 • 52 • 55 • 56 • 57 • 69 • 74
Brittany 82 • 85
Western Loire 97 • 99
Loire Valley 112 • 122 • 124 • 126 • 127
Poitou – Charentes 130 • 148
Limousin 155
Aquitaine 184 • 205 • 211

Midi – Pyrénées 215 • 222 • 223 • 224 • 228 • 236 • 245 • 247 • 249 • 257
Languedoc – Rousillon 268 • 269 • 275 • 286 • 290 • 291 • 294 • 297 • 298 • 300
Rhône Valley – Alps 309
Provence – Alps – Riviera 323 • 326 • 329 • 334 • 335 • 337 • 338 • 340 • 345 • 346 • 347 • 349 • 350 • 358 • 359

Gîtes for large groups

These places are for ten or more people, and include properties where you can rent more than one place on the same site.

Franche Comté 13
Burgundy 22 • 23 • 24 • 25 • 27
Paris – Ile de France 29
Normandy 32 • 34 • 43 • 44 • 45 • 46 • 47 • 48 • 49 • 50 • 59 • 60 • 65 • 66 • 69 • 70 • 72 • 73
Brittany 80
Western Loire 92 • 98 • 99 • 100 • 101
Loire Valley 110 • 111 • 119
Poitou – Charentes 135 • 136 • 141 • 142 • 144 • 150
Limousin 151 • 152 • 153 • 154
Auvergne 159
Aquitaine 164 • 165 • 172 • 173 • 174 • 182 • 188 • 189 • 190 • 191 • 192 • 195 • 200 • 201 • 203 • 204 • 205 • 207 • 208 • 210
Midi – Pyrénées 229 • 230 • 239 • 240 • 241 • 242 • 244 • 245 • 246 • 251 • 255 • 263
Languedoc – Rousillon 274 • 275 • 276 • 277 • 278 • 279 • 280 • 284 • 287 • 297
Rhône Valley – Alps 302 • 303 • 304 • 305 • 311
Provence – Alps – Riviera 328 • 341 • 342 • 344 • 352 • 356

Linen

Sheets are not provided or are provided at an extra charge.

The North 1 • 2 • 3 • 4
Picardy 5 • 6 • 7 • 9
Burgundy 20 • 21 • 26
Normandy 36 • 38 • 39 • 40 • 43 • 45 • 54 • 55 • 56 • 57 • 61 • 65 • 66 • 67 • 71 • 74

Quick reference indices

In the mountains

Public transport

No car? You don't need one to get to these places

Waterside places to stay

Not more than 500m from the sea, a lake or a river.

These places are available for weddings and receptions

Index by town

Index by town

Index by town

1 Loire Valley

The Cottage & The Farmhouse Loft

Le Grand Pressigny, Indre-et-Loire 2

Civray is a tiny hamlet hidden away in the countryside: it would be hard to find 3
anywhere more tranquil. And if you tire of walking, cycling, fishing – or swimming in the silky waters of the river – there are vineyards to visit, *fermes auberges* to discover and all the attractions of the Loire châteaux. Lovely Jill is half Australian, passionate about rural France and has restored this little cluster of ancient stone buildings with the lightest of hands. The Cottage is compact but has all you need: a living area with little pine kitchen, woodburning stove, sofabed, play equipment in the garden. Upstairs, under magnificent curving beams, a large double bedroom, simply and attractively furnished. It has its own rustic balcony overlooking farmland – not another building in sight. Wooden stairs wind down to the gardens, which have a haphazard charm; fresh home-grown vegetables and home-laid eggs are often available. Jill has also converted the Farmhouse Loft, a heavily timbered and imaginative space with three bedrooms and a big, jolly
kitchen/living area, easy for families. *Bring own linen.* 4

sleeps Cottage 2-3 + cot. 5
Farmhouse Loft 5 + cot.
Can be booked together. 6
rooms Cottage: 1 double, 1 single sofabed; 7
1 shower room, 1 bathroom.
Farmhouse Loft: 2 doubles, 1 single;
1 bathroom. 8
price Cottage £150-£250.
Farmhouse Loft £170-£305. 9
Prices per week.
closed Winter.

Jill Christie
tel +33 (0)2 47 94 92 02
fax +33 (0)2 47 94 92 02

11 Map 9 Entry 118

10

Explanation

❶ region

❷ abbreviated addresss
Not to be used for correspondence.

❸ write up
Written by us after inspection.

❹ italics
Mention other relevant details e.g. B&B also, children over 8 welcome.

❺ sleeps
The lower number indicates how many adults can comfortably sleep here. The higher is the maximum number of people that can be accommodated.

❻ rooms
We give total numbers of each type of bedroom e.g. double, triple, and total numbers of bathrooms. We give **wc** details only when they are separate from bathrooms.

❼ price
The price shown is per week and the range covers low season to high season; remember high season can be winter in some areas. Some owners don't include 'extra' costs, such as heating or cleaning in this price so please check before booking.

❽ arrival
This is only given when it is not Saturday.

❾ closed
If we give no details the gîte is rarely closed. When given in months, this means for the whole of the named months and the time in between.

❿ symbols
see the last page of the book for a fuller explanation:

wheelchair facilities
easily accessible bedrooms
all children welcome
no smoking anywhere
Hello some English spoken

guests' pets welcome
working farm or vineyard
at least one room with AC
pool
bikes on the premises
 tennis on the premises

⓫ map & entry numbers
Map page number; entry number.

Where on the web?

The World Wide Web is big - very big. So big, in fact, that it can be a fruitless place to search if you don't know where to find reliable, trustworthy, up-to-date information about fantastic places to stay in Europe, India, Morocco and beyond...

Fortunately, there's **www.specialplacestostay.com**, where you can dip into all of our guides, find special offers from owners, catch up on news about the series and tell us about the special places you've been to.

WWW.SPECIALPLACESTOSTAY.COM